Research Methodology in Second-Language Acquisition

D1739360

SECOND LANGUAGE ACQUISITION RESEARCH:
THEORETICAL AND METHODOLOGICAL ISSUES

Susan M. Gass/Jacquelyn Schacter
Series Editors

Tarone/Gass/Cohen: Research Methodology in
Second-Language Acquisition

Research Methodology in Second-Language Acquisition

Edited by

Elaine E. Tarone
University of Minnesota

Susan M. Gass
Michigan State University

Andrew D. Cohen
University of Minnesota

LEA LAWRENCE ERLBAUM ASSOCIATES, PUBLISHERS
1994   Hillsdale, New Jersey   Hove, UK

Lawrence Erlbaum Associates, Inc., Publishers
365 Broadway
Hillsdale, New Jersey 07642

Cover design by Kate Dusza

Library of Congress Cataloging-in-Publication Data

Research methodology in second-language acquisition / edited by Elaine
   E. Tarone, Susan M. Gass, Andrew D. Cohen.
      p.   cm.
   Includes bibliographical references and index.
   ISBN 0-8058-1423-X. — ISBN 0-8058-1424-8 (pbk.)
   1. Second language acquisition—Research—Methodology.
I. Tarone, Elaine, 1945–   . II. Gass, Susan M. II. Cohen, Andrew
D.
P118.2.R47 1994
418′.0072—dc20   93-34858
                                                        CIP

Books published by Lawrence Erlbaum Associates are printed on acid-free
paper, and their bindings are chosen for strength and durability.

Printed in the United States of America
10 9 8 7 6 5 4 3 2 1

To Grant, Rachel, David, Prairie, Motchka, Leah, and Tone
Elaine E. Tarone

To Josh, Aaron, Seth, Ethan, Champagne, and Burgundy
Susan M. Gass

To my mom, Rena Cohen, who taught me and
still teaches me how to be articulate
Andrew D. Cohen

CONTENTS

PREFACE

Many of the chapters in this volume were originally presented at a conference on Theory Construction and Research Methodology in Second-Language Acquisition held on the campus of Michigan State University in October 1991. We are grateful to Alan Beretta for his participation in the organization of the original conference. Other chapters were solicited because of their particular relevance to the issues debated in this book.

During the spring of 1992, the editors met on the campus of the University of Minnesota. At that time it became apparent that our interests were overlapping and complementary (if not complimentary) and that joining efforts in a venture such as this one would take us in an enjoyable and fruitful direction. We were not disappointed. In determining the order of names for this volume, we decided to put the names in reverse alphabetical order, for no reason other than to be different. Thus, the ordering does not imply lesser or greater contributions by any of the editors.

Judith Amsel of Lawrence Erlbaum Associates deserves our thanks for seeing us through with this project. The anonymous reviewers of our original proposal were helpful in showing us how a slightly different direction and organization of the book would greatly enhance the finished project. We followed their suggestions and are convinced that they were right. We are grateful to all of the authors for their promptness and good-naturedness in responding to our queries. It was indeed a pleasure to work with each and every one of them. We also wish to thank India Plough of Michigan State

University who read, critiqued, and edited most of the chapters. Her insight-fulness and assistance have made this a better volume. Finally, we each express gratitude to the others. We worked well as a "team" and always resolved differences with good humor and good sense.

—Elaine E. Tarone
—Susan M. Gass
—Andrew D. Cohen

INTRODUCTION

Susan M. Gass
Michigan State University

Andrew D. Cohen
University of Minnesota

Elaine E. Tarone
University of Minnesota

The validity of any discipline is predicated on the assumption that the research methods used to gather data are sufficiently understood and agreed upon. This book explores issues related to research methodology as it pertains to second-language acquisition (SLA).

The possibilities for inclusion of topics in a book of this sort are broad. We have by necessity limited the range of topics to include those that we consider to have theoretical import. The book is intended to uncover, problematize, and debate underlying theoretical issues in research methodology. It covers research issues that relate to the theoretical debate on such basic questions as competence versus performance as well as to issues of data type (e.g., quantitative vs. qualitative, individual vs. grouped data, single subjects vs. multiple subjects). For complementary works that provide comprehensive discussions of such aspects of research as subject selection and reporting, types of methodology (e.g., cross-sectional vs. longitudinal), and statistical analyses, the reader is referred to works such as Brown (1988), Gass and Selinker (1994), Johnson (1992), Larsen-Freeman and Long (1991), Nunan (1992), and Seliger and Shohamy (1989).

Second-language acquisition is a field that draws on many other disciplines (e.g., linguistics, sociolinguistics, child language). But perhaps more than in its source fields, second-language acquisition researchers have debated and continue to debate issues of research methodology. This is not to say that related fields are not concerned with questions of reliability and validity, but rather that these issues have not received the depth of attention in those fields that they have in second-language research. A case in point comes from discussions of grammaticality judgments and their relationship to metalinguistic knowledge and competence. As Foster-Cohen argued:

> First language researchers are making some important strides in developing cunning means of uncovering children's tacit understanding of the L1 (Crain & McKee, 1985; McDaniel & Cairns, 1990). However, these researchers have suggested that we may be seriously underestimating the *metalinguistic* capabilities of young children because our assumptions about their inabilities in this area prevent us from developing the sophisticated techniques of elicitation that would be needed in such an investigation. One type of elicitation for metalinguistic knowledge is the soliciting of grammaticality judgments combined with requests that the speakers "correct" or "improve on" utterances they find unacceptable. SLA researchers, unlike first language researchers, have used grammaticality judgments extensively. (1993, p. 142)

It is clear, as Foster-Cohen noted later, that this particular research methodology needs to be examined in depth. However, it is also clear that the issues of metalinguistic awareness and grammaticality judgments have indeed received considerable attention in the second-language literature (cf. Birdsong, 1989; Chaudron, 1983).

The purpose of this book is to elucidate issues of research methodology and to contextualize them within the current field of SLA. As one reads through the chapters in this book, it will become clear that there are two major splits in the SLA field: (a) research that investigates contextualized data, and (b) research that examines second-language sentence-level production regardless of the context in which the sentences/utterances occur. Throughout the discussion, what is important to keep in mind is that research methods are not applied in a vacuum. Rather, they are intimately related to the theoretical questions being addressed. For example, a main tenet within the Universal Grammar (UG) paradigm is the determination of an underlying competence as a primary research goal. Competence is an abstraction and as such is context-independent. To elicit data from a variety of contexts is irrelevant to those operating within this paradigm. On the other hand, those who conduct research within a variationist paradigm are ultimately concerned with how language changes as a function of the context in which language is being used, with context being broadly defined to include situational, social, and task context. In order to examine these issues, it is imperative that samples of data be gathered in the context that is being investigated.

Issues such as numbers of subjects are also dependent on research questions and overlap with issues of contextualized and noncontextualized data. Within a competence-based paradigm, a typical methodology is the gathering of data based on grammatical intuitions of large groups of subjects. However, as Eckman (chapter 11) notes, if universal principles (whether UG or typological) are available to second-language learners, they should be available to all learners. Assuming the correctness of this position, the examination of appropriate data from one learner should be sufficient, barring a performance slip, to test and/or generate hypotheses (cf. Kumpf, 1984, for an example).

Those working within a variationist paradigm are more likely to require more than one subject in their quest for reliable and valid generalizations, because the perception of a particular social or situational context varies from individual to individual. There is no theoretical claim of uniformity across individuals. However, as with a competence-based model, one can also examine data from a few individuals or even a single individual, by gathering data across tasks or across social or situational contexts.

Yet another methodological decision that depends on the research question has to do with the use of production versus "forced" elicitation data. A competence-based theory attempts to determine which sentences are allowed by learner-grammars and which sentences are not allowed. Production data are less frequently used within this paradigm for two main reasons, one practical and the other theoretical. The practical reason has to do with the probability of eliciting a sufficient number of tokens of a given sentence type. Given that UG parameters are often tested through complex syntax, it is unlikely that the appropriate sentences will be used spontaneously with any frequency. For example, consider a sentence such as the following:

(1) Elaine persuaded Susan to give Andrea a picture of herself.

If one is interested in determining the appropriate anaphoric reference of *herself*, it is nearly impossible through spontaneous production to elicit sentences like (1). Further, even if a sentence such as (1) were uttered, it would not always be possible to determine through the context what *herself* referred to, which, after all, is the primary theoretical concern. The theoretical reason for the inadequacy of production data (but see Lakshmanan, 1991, for the successful use of production data within a UG paradigm) relates to the determination of disallowable sentences. The production of a given sentence provides little or no information about whether or not alternatives are possible. To return to sentence (1), if, through context, we could determine that for a given second-language speaker *herself* referred to *Andrea*, we would not know whether it disallowed reference to one or both of the other NPs (*Elaine* or *Susan*).

Thus, in understanding and critiquing different research methods, it is essential to understand how each relates to the theoretical paradigm being investigated. It is only at that point that we can begin to question the fundamental questions of reliability and validity.

This book is divided into three sections: Part I, Evaluating Competing

Frameworks; Part II, Methodologies for Eliciting and Analyzing Language in Context; and Part III, Methodologies for Eliciting and Analyzing Sentence-Level Data. In Part I, the thrust is on argumentation for or against different paradigms. The first chapter, by Eckman, sets the tone of the book by dealing with a central issue in second-language acquisition—that of a theory's domain. Should a theory of second-language acquisition be a theory of competence? If so, what sort of competence? Where does variation fit in? Eckman makes the argument that the current debate as to whether second-language acquisition theory should be concerned with variation data is not productive, framed as it is in terms of a priori assumptions. The question is, rather, an empirical one and should be determined on the basis of relevant evidence. In Eckman's view, the crucial question is: What sort of evidence is needed to resolve the debate? The position Eckman takes is that it is incumbent upon variationists to conduct studies designed specifically to elicit data that occur in the process of second-language acquisition and that can be accounted for only in variationist terms. Eckman provides specific suggestions with regard to the kind of evidence that variationists must produce in order to resolve the issue.

Berent's chapter (chapter 2) is framed within a Principles and Parameters approach to SLA and considers the question of argumentation in the determination of theoretical constructs. His main point is that the Subset Principle applies to both first- and second-language acquisition. Berent reviews a number of studies that provide arguments against the Subset Principle in second-language acquisition as it pertains to: (a) the Adjacency Parameter, (b) the Configurationality Parameter, and (c) the Governing Category Parameter. For each of these arguments Berent proposes an alternative analysis to show that those studies do not in fact provide evidence against the Subset Principle in second-language acquisition. He also presents a parameter not discussed within the SLA-UG literature (the Relative Clause Parameter) and argues that the Subset Principle does apply to second-language acquisition with respect to this parameter as well.

Bardovi-Harlig (chapter 3) also focuses on the issue of evidence, considering the type of data that would be necessary for distinguishing between competing hypotheses. She presents a case study of hypothesis formation and testing in a small but active area of investigation in SLA: the acquisition of tense and aspect by adult second-language learners. Bardovi-Harlig outlines two rival hypotheses: (a) interlanguage verbal systems are primarily aspectual in nature, and (b) interlanguage verbal systems are primarily determined by discourse structure. The central question considered is: What type of data would constitute evidence for either of these two positions? After reviewing existing studies for their findings and for their research design and methodology, Bardovi-Harlig concludes that current evidence is still at the level of anecdote, and that no systematic database yet exists that can be considered incontrovertible evidence for either of the two conflicting hypotheses.

Hagen (chapter 4), like Berent, begins with a Principles and Parameters approach to SLA, making the important suggestion that other linguistic theories that have generally been ignored in SLA have a bearing on SLA research issues. Hagen identifies three problematic aspects of an SLA-based Principles and Parameters approach:

1. Such models have heretofore taken for granted that the constructs being studied are correctly laid out in Government-Binding theory and have ignored counterclaims from other theories that have a direct bearing on issues raised in SLA research.
2. Research methodology in this area needs to be sharpened. (Specific suggestions are made with regard to measurement validation and hypothesis testing.)
3. If evidence bears out the notion that UG principles are not available to adults despite their being available to children, it will become necessary to develop an explanation of why L2s differ from L1s in this respect.

In the final chapter in this section, Markee (chapter 5), by showing how researchers from two traditions use data, focuses on the ways in which quantitative and qualitative research complement each other. Markee critiques the current nomothetic orthodoxy in second-language studies on the grounds that it is premature for such a young field to be concerned with questions of paradigmatic stability. He discusses the nature of an ethnomethodological respecification of second-language studies and develops a conversation-analytic account of the availability of turn-taking and repair as mechanisms that are entailed in successful language learning within English as Second Language (ESL) classrooms. By means of a conversation-analytic approach, Markee demonstrates the theoretical and practical implications of ethnomethodology for theory construction in second-language studies.

Part II deals explicitly with methodology for gathering contextualized language data. In the first chapter in this section, Douglas and Selinker (chapter 6) focus on combined research methodology, showing how the methodology they suggest, namely, that grounded in a UG framework, complements data from other research domains. This chapter describes issues of research methodology associated with the analysis of data from oral and written tests of English for specific purposes. They start by justifying the need for subject-specialist informants to distinguish ambiguous language that is a result of interlanguage semantics and rhetorical structure from ambiguous language that is particular to the semantics and rhetorical structure of a particular discipline. They describe initial efforts to conduct research on interlanguage in context within the framework of language testing. In particular, the chapter reports on differences between the interlanguage discourse of math and chemistry majors and that of nonmajors on field-specific versions of the oral test under investigation.

Shohamy (chapter 7) brings the field of language testing into the discussion of theory construction and research methodology and deals explicitly with the question raised by Hagen, that of validation. This emphasis is important in light of recent efforts to bring these two fields together. Her chapter focuses on the role of language testing in SLA research and contrasts this role to that of standardized tests in making decisions about individuals and programs. Shohamy delineates three ways in which language testing contributes to SLA theories: (a) defining and identifying means of measuring language ability (the dependent variable in SLA research), (b) improving the quality of the data collection instruments used in SLA research, and (c) identifying and testing SLA hypotheses. She also considers three ways in which SLA research and theory can contribute to language testing: (a) identifying areas and subareas to be tested and suggesting approaches to the analysis of the language samples, (b) proposing a variety of testing and nontesting tasks that are useful in the collection of language data, and (c) alerting language testers to the need for task selection that accommodates individual differences.

Cohen and Olshtain (chapter 8) continue the discussion of language in context, outlining the range of data collection possibilities in speech act research and arguing for the triangulation of methods. Their focus is on theoretical and applied issues regarding the researching of speech acts. In their arguments, they consider the demands put on the linguistic repertoire of the speaker in the successful realization of a speech act, along with the need to select one or more speech act strategies that are appropriate for the given context. They emphasize the range of data collection techniques for studying speech act behavior, and they draw on their recent research on speech act production as a basis for discussing issues of research design. In reporting on data obtained through the use of role-play interviews coupled with verbal report, they exemplify the search, retrieval, and selection of language forms for use in apologies, complaints, and requests by nonnative speakers of English.

Bayley (chapter 9), recognizing the importance of variation in a theory of SLA, argues that work on variation has been unnecessarily limited to a few research methods. Despite widespread recognition of the importance of variation, few researchers have explored the implications of the Labovian quantitative paradigm for theories of SLA or used techniques of variable rule analysis developed by sociolinguistics to model variation in native languages. Bayley's chapter applies the theoretical assumptions and methodological procedures of quantitative sociolinguistics to the study of a highly variable interlanguage structure, past tense marking. Multivariate analysis of nearly 5,000 past-reference verbs extracted from sociolinguistic interviews with Chinese learners of English indicates that past tense marking in Chinese–English interlanguage is systematic and is conditioned by multiple independent linguistic, social, and developmental factors. The results for the two main linguistic factor groups, the phonetic form of the past tense and grammatical aspect, show that the ordering of factors within groups remains constant as acquisition proceeds. Both low- and high-proficiency speakers are more likely to mark more salient past tense forms and aspectual perfectives and less likely to mark less salient forms and aspectual imperfectives. Results for grammatical aspect are particularly robust and strongly support a variable rule model of SLA. The effect of perfective and imperfective aspect on the likelihood of past tense marking remains stable for individual speakers of all levels of English proficiency examined in this study. Importantly, Bayley shows how research in SLA can avail itself of the many techniques used by sociolinguists and explores the implications of research on variation (with particular emphasis on the quantitative paradigm) for the development of a theory of SLA.

The third section deals with sentence-level research with a strong focus on elicited imitation and judgment data. The use of judgment data has been controversial from the beginnings of its use in second-language research. In fact, as far back as 1972, Selinker argued that researchers should "focus . . . analytical attention upon the *only observable data to which we can relate theoretical predictions*: the utterances which are produced when the learner attempts to say sentences of a TL" (pp. 213–214). This effectively eliminates the use of judgment and intuitional data from the second-language research paradigm. Whatever one's belief's about the use of grammaticality judgments, if they are to be used in second-language research, there must be a means of establishing their reliability and validity. However, little experimental work has been directed to this end. This section fills this gap. In addition, the section emphasizes the comparison of judgment data and elicited-imitation data, both of which involve methodologies that "force" data, a necessary aspect of certain research paradigms, as we discussed earlier.

The first chapter in this section, by Lakshmanan and Teranishi (chapter 10), relates to differences in using preferences versus actual judgments of grammaticality. The chapter treats a theoretical area dealt with in Part I (Berent), that of the Subset Principle. Lakshmanan and Teranishi provide evidence that previous findings on the role of the Governing Category Parameter in SLA stem from a methodological bias. In particular, they note that there is a semantic bias in most test sentences used in earlier research and that there is a bias associated with the format of interpretation tasks. In a reanalysis of previous research, they show that so-called grammaticality judgment tasks provide us with information about subjects' preferences but not with their grammaticality judgments. This chapter presents an alternative methodology that overcomes previous difficulties. Importantly, it also presents an analysis of individual data, not just grouped data.

Eckman's chapter (11) in this section is similar to the Lakshmanan and Teranishi chapter in that he, too, deals with the Governing Category Parameter and the Proper Antecedent Parameter. He argues that one cannot look only at grouped data, because grouped data often obscure what is going on within an individual. We are ultimately concerned, he argues, with individual learners. Eckman, through data from second-language learners of English and Japanese, finds that some learner-languages fall outside of the constraints of UG. He discusses these results in relation to SLA theory and to linguistic theory. The theoretical question that is addressed is: What is the force of learner-language data that do not conform to principles of UG? Do they bear on SLA theory (i.e., on the question of access to UG)? Or do they bear on linguistic theory (i.e., the linguistic theory needs to be evaluated and perhaps modified, as discussed by Gass, 1993)?

Munnich, Flynn, and Martohardjono (chapter 12) compare elicited imitation data with grammaticality judgment data. The main focus of this chapter is to specify (a) what aspects of linguistic competence each of these research methodologies taps and (b) in what way these tasks relate to one another. Data are presented from two production tasks (an oral and a taped elicited imitation test) and two comprehension tasks (an oral and a taped grammaticality judgment task). The results indicate that the tasks measure distinct but overlapping areas of linguistic competence. These results are important in terms of our understanding of differences that emerge among studies using distinct methodologies and in terms of the future experimental development of the field.

Bley-Vroman and Chaudron (chapter 13) deal exclusively with one of the methodologies discussed in the previous chapter, that of elicited imitation. They analyze the elicited imitation process in light of its use in experimental studies. Not only do they provide an account of the elicited imitation process itself, but they also take a critical look at claims made on the basis of results from experiments that have used elicited imitation. Their concern is that findings of elicited imitation experiments, especially those involving second-language learners, must be interpreted with caution. This is because the instrument itself is a delicate one, with strong floor and ceiling effects and with a narrow band of extreme sensitivity to interacting factors.

The chapter by Goss, Zhang, and Lantolf (chapter 14) problematizes the issue of grammaticality judgments by arguing that learners of different proficiencies approach the task of judging the grammaticality of sentences differently. The authors argue that a major problem with the use of L2 grammaticality judgments is that they are often drawn from individuals who have yet to stabilize their linguistic competence in the L2. They question how learners can render a valid assessment of sentences designed to exhibit linguistic principles as abstract as those proposed for UG. Through the use of a joint problem-solving procedure, Goss, Zhang, and Lantolf demonstrate that learners do not always do what reseachers think they are doing when responding to grammaticality judgment tasks. It is also shown that the strategies learners deploy in making judgments evolve over time, becoming more similar to those used by native speakers. Because so-called beginning and intermediate learners have not yet developed a stable linguistic competence, they may be inappropriate sources of data when testing for UG effects. Thus, when asked to respond to grammaticality judgment tasks, these learners are forced to press into service various coping strategies, including translation, memory of pedagogical rules, and on-line ad hoc strategies, whose sole function is to facilitate compliance with the stated goal of the experiment.

The final two chapters (Cowan & Hatasa, chapter 15, and Gass, chapter 16) take a more positive view on the issue of grammaticality judgments. Cowan and Hatasa deal with the issue of reliability, showing how issues of complexity enter into the debate and how actual judgments are related to on-line measures of complexity. This chapter considers the controversy surrounding the use of grammaticality judgments by comparing judgments of L2 complexity by both native speakers and L2 learners with an active, on-line measure of complexity and comprehension. Cowan and Hatasa note that past studies involving both L1 and L2 subjects found different orders of complexity on judgment tasks involving four types of English and Japanese relative clauses. In this chapter they investigate the extent to which this was due to the fact that the Japanese stimuli employed by each investigator contained different postposition subject/theme markers. The results of their own study of Japanese native speakers and English learners of Japanese indicated that the active measures were identical for both groups of subjects. The L2 learners were found to be sensitive to surface structure detail important for processing, a fact that explains the disparate rating orders obtained in other studies. A comparison of the active measure with the ratings assigned by the L2 speakers reveals that their judgments were highly accurate and consistent with regard to the ends of a continuum of complexity. However, only an active on-line measure provides a stable index of intermediate values. In this chapter the authors sharpen issues such as that of the development of learners' intuitions about L2 phenomena, and they make specific recommendations regarding the use of judgmental data in L2 research.

Gass argues that the conclusions drawn from previous studies designed to show the unreliability of grammaticality judgments are without justification. She calls for a program of research that examines factors that jeopardize the reliability of grammaticality judgments. It is recognized that there are many factors that influence reliability. One such factor is indeterminacy (a learner's potentially incomplete knowledge or lack of knowledge of parts of the second-language grammar). She presents the results of an empirical study conducted on two occasions, consisting of grammaticality judgments of relative clauses by ESL learners. By means of options on judgment tasks coupled with retrospective interviews, it is established what is determinate and what is indeterminate knowledge. This information permits more accurate appraisal of reliability, since only determinate knowledge is relevant in the determination of the structure of a learner's grammar. Her data provide evidence for the view that judgment data are reliable. They further provide support for the view that individuals behave in a consistent manner. On the other hand, there is evidence to suggest that low reliability occurs in just those areas where greater indeterminacy is predicted—in more peripheral areas of the grammar. In general, Gass finds that grammaticality judgments are reflective of patterns of second-language use.

In the conclusion, Tarone (chapter 17) pulls together many of the strands presented in this book. She points out various ways in which research paradigms and hence methodologies can be classified (e.g., nomothetic vs. hermeneutic, profligate vs. conservative) and places the chapters along those continua. As stated here, Tarone makes the important point that research methods must be related to research paradigms. One cannot understand the importance, for example, of contextualized data if one does not understand the theory behind the use of noncontextualized data. Tarone's discussion of UG approaches to SLA touches on a number of central issues, among them that of the interpretation of evidence. Linguistic argumentation is at the basis of this thread of research, but the questions addressed become even thornier when compounded by the fact that we are dealing not with natural languages for which there is at least some agreement as to what the basic facts are, but rather with languages produced by learners with indeterminate systems. Tarone further discusses the issue of research methodologies within the UG paradigm, unifying the chapters by acknowledging a common thread in the need for multiple and complementary elicitation measures. Through her examination of the chapters in this book, she concludes that a quest for a single unifying theory for the field of second-language acquisition will not carry forward research in our field. Rather, she emphasizes the multifaceted and complex nature of this aspect of human behavior, and she therefore rejects the notion that a single theoretical (and therefore methodological) approach will serve the development of knowledge in the field of SLA.

REFERENCES

Birdsong, D. (1989). *Metalinguistic performance and interlinguistic competence*. Berlin: Springer-Verlag.

Brown, J. D. (1988). *Understanding research in second language learning*. Cambridge: Cambridge University Press.

Chaudron, C. (1983). Research on metalinguistic judgments: A review of theory, methods, and results. *Language Learning, 33*, 343–377.

Crain, S., & McKee, C. (1985). Acquisition of structural anaphora. In S. Berman, J. W. Choe, & J. McDonough (Eds.), *Proceedings of the 16th Northeastern Linguistic Society Meeting*. Amherst, MA: Graduate Linguistics Student Association.

Foster-Cohen, S. (1993). Directions of influence in first and second language acquisition research. *Second Language Research, 9*(2), 140–152.

Gass, S. (1993). Second language acquisition: Past, present and future. *Second Language Research,* *9*(2), 99–117.

Gass, S., & Selinker, L. (1994). *Second language acquisition: An introductory course.* Hillsdale, NJ: Lawrence Erlbaum Associates.

Johnson, D. (1992). *Approaches to research in second language learning.* New York: Longman.

Kumpf, L. (1984). Temporal systems and universality in interlanguage: A case study. In F. Eckman, L. Bell, & D. Nelson (Eds.), *Universals of second language acquisition* (pp. 132–143). Rowley, MA: Newbury House.

Lakshmanan, U. (1991). Morphological uniformity and null subjects in child second language acquisition. In L. Eubank (Ed.), *Point counterpoint* (pp. 389–410). Amsterdam: John Benjamins.

Larsen-Freeman, D., & Long, M. (1991). *An introduction to second language research.* London: Longman.

McDaniel, D., & Cairns, H. S. (1990). The child as informant: Eliciting linguistic intuitions from young children. *Journal of Psycholinguistic Research, 19,* 331–344.

Nunan, D. (1992). *Research methods in language learning.* Cambridge: Cambridge University Press.

Seliger, H., & Shohamy, E. (1989). *Second language research methods.* Oxford: Oxford University Press.

Selinker, L. (1972). Interlanguage. *International Review of Applied Linguistics, 10,* 209–231.

EVALUATING COMPETING FRAMEWORKS

1

THE COMPETENCE–PERFORMANCE ISSUE IN SECOND-LANGUAGE ACQUISITION THEORY: A DEBATE

Fred R. Eckman
University of Wisconsin—Milwaukee

One of the ways in which a discipline advances is through scholarly debate. When the proponents of different sides of an issue can confront each other with proposals, critiques, and counterproposals, it is possible to highlight the distinctions among the positions and to focus on the facts and argumentation that would decide the issue one way or the other. And out of such debate distills progress.

However, not all scholarly debates are worthwhile. Occasionally, issues that should be decided on empirical grounds are debated on a priori considerations that have no bearing on the matter. Such debates, rather than advancing the field, have the opposite effect: Time and energy that should be applied to data gathering and analysis are expended instead in advancing and parrying arguments.

This chapter argues that there is such a debate currently going on in the field of second-language acquisition (SLA) theory, and that the two sides involved in this discussion should cease immediately and get on with the job of theorizing about SLA. I attempt to show that the issue in question is an empirical one, that it is not being addressed on empirical grounds, and that it cannot be decided on the basis of the arguments that are currently being advanced.

The debate in question centers around whether the proper domain for a theory of SLA should be the abstract linguistic competence of the L2 learner, or alternatively, whether the domain should incorporate within-speaker variation. On one side of the issue, Gregg (1989, 1990) argued that the linguistic competence of the L2 learner constitutes the only viable subject of study for any SLA theory. Central to this position is Gregg's claim that real progress in SLA can be made only by achieving the level of abstraction entailed in studying an idealized construct, namely, the linguistic competence of the L2 learner. According to Gregg, linguistic competence must be abstracted away from the within-speaker variation that exists in virtually all L2 data. Gregg's position is that such variation is part of performance and can be safely ignored or discounted by the investigator.

Opposing this view are Ellis (1990) and Tarone (1990), who argued that variability is one of the hallmarks of interlanguages, and that theories that fail to recognize and explain this variability will necessarily be uninsightful.

In this chapter I make the following two points:

1. Gregg's contention that SLA theory must confine itself to the linguistic competence of the L2 learner is misguided and cannot, in principle, be demonstrated.
2. The proponents of a variationist model have not advanced the most convincing type of evidence that IL variability must be taken into account.

What both sides in this debate have apparently missed is that the issue is an empirical one and therefore must be decided on empirical grounds.

The organization of this chapter is as follows. First, I attempt to characterize the two positions in the debate, presenting Gregg's criticisms of the variationists' model, followed by the response of Ellis and Tarone. I argue that the major area of contention revolves around what the domain of a theory of SLA should be, specifically, whether or not this domain should include data on variability. I then attempt to shed light on the matter by putting the issue into a larger context, in which I consider the types of arguments that have force in debates about domains of scientific theories, in general, and of linguistic theories, in particular.

THE POSITIONS

Gregg's Criticisms

As just suggested, the debate between Gregg and the proponents of the variationist model centers around what the subject matter of a theory of SLA should be. Gregg claimed that the domain for such a theory is the linguistic competence of the L2 learner: "It is this knowledge, acquired or innate, that I believe should be viewed as the domain of SLA theory" (Gregg, 1989, p. 18).

For Gregg, the study of linguistic competence excludes data on variability, which, presumably, would be included under linguistic performance: "But if we are careful to establish the domain of a theory of second language acquisition so that it is confined to the acquisition of linguistic competence, then we will not be compelled to account for those data on variability as far as that theory is concerned" (Gregg, 1989, p. 22).

Gregg maintained that the variationist model fails to make the distinction between linguistic competence and linguistic performance: "The trouble with this concept of language is that it fails to distinguish between competence and performance"[1] (Gregg, 1989, p. 18). Failure to make this distinction, according to Gregg, excludes the variationist model as a viable theory of SLA: "I am taking it for granted that if the variable competence model cannot . . . lead to an explanation of the acquisition of competence it cannot be the basis for a successful SLA theory" (Gregg, 1990, p. 365). He argued further:

> The distinction between performance and competence has been with us for over twenty years now, and although not without problems or controversy, it has pretty much established itself in linguistic theory and (to a lesser extent perhaps) in acquisition research. . . . Making this distinction is simply a fundamental prerequisite to progress in the scientific study of language acquisition. (Gregg, 1990, p. 370)

Gregg's position in this debate can be summarized as in (1); and although there are other points that he makes in his critique of the variationist model, the following constitutes a fair representation of his position.

(1) a. The domain of a theory of SLA must be the linguistic competence of the learner.
   b. The study of linguistic competence necessarily excludes the type of within-speaker variability that is important to variationist models.
   c. Theories of SLA that attempt to account for this variability blur the competence/performance distinction, which, in turn, prevents such models from forming the basis for a successful theory of SLA.

The Responses

The responses that Ellis and Tarone made to Gregg's criticisms were similar, although not identical.

Ellis' counterargument to Gregg's contention that his model obscures the competence/performance distinction was the claim that variability is part

---

[1]K. Gregg (personal communication, November 1, 1991) stated that "this concept of language" refers to Searle's (1969) concept of language as part of a theory of action. However, Gregg included Tarone (1979) as part of this discussion.

of the L2 competence of the learner. That is to say, for Ellis (1990) the domain of study for a theory of SLA includes variability data: "My position, therefore, is that the learner's competence is variable" (p. 387).

Tarone's (1990) approach was to suggest that the competence/performance distinction is unnecessary: "If we view knowledge itself as containing variability, the competence/performance distinction may become unnecessary" (p. 394). Both Ellis and Tarone attempted to defend their models by arguing that variability is part and parcel of the subject matter of SLA theory. Let us now attempt to evaluate the two sides of this debate.

CONSIDERATION OF THE DEBATE

In this section, I argue that Gregg's criticisms of the variationist model are not compelling, because they are based on assumptions about linguistic competence that are not defensible. More specifically, Gregg's arguments assume that data on within-speaker variability are necessarily excluded from any SLA theory dealing with the linguistic competence of the L2 learner. This position is not defensible because there is no permanent boundary between competence and performance. That is to say, Gregg's argument assumes two things: (a) that linguists know ahead of time what must be included under the study of competence and what is included under performance, and (b) that the study of competence excludes data on variability. As I show here, this position cannot be defended. The boundary between linguistic competence and performance is not fixed but instead is adjusted as the field advances. This being the case, criticisms of the variationist model on the grounds that such a theory does not distinguish linguistic competence from performance are beside the point.

I then conclude this section by evaluating the counterargument of the proponents of the variationist model.

Gregg's Arguments

I begin with Gregg's argument that within-speaker variability is necessarily excluded from the study of linguistic competence. This position is evidenced in the following quotation, which is repeated for convenience: "But if we are careful to establish the domain of a theory of second language acquisition so that it is confined to the acquisition of linguistic competence, then we will not be compelled to account for those data on variability as far as that theory is concerned" (Gregg, 1989, p. 22).

The point that Gregg is trying to make here is that variationist models of SLA run into difficulty because they do not confine themselves to the study of the L2 learner's linguistic competence. The way one knows that the variationists are not dealing with competence is that they include data on variability as part of their domain.

Gregg's claim here does not go through for two reasons: First, the domain of any theory is itself a hypothesis, and second, what is included within the domain of linguistic competence is not fixed but instead changes with advancements in the field. We consider each of these points in turn.

Let us grant, for the sake of argument, Gregg's assumption that a theory of SLA should explain an L2 learner's linguistic competence. The question to be considered is exactly what this competence includes. As Gregg correctly points out, this issue pertains to what the domain of SLA theory is.

The domain of any theory is the body of information that, at a given stage of investigation, is considered to be the subject of study. The basis for this consideration is the belief that some set of facts is related, and that it is therefore possible to give a unified account of these facts. Because the belief that a set of facts is related is dependent on the state of knowledge of the field at that time, the domain of a theory is itself a hypothesis (Shapere, 1977). In this context, Gregg's statement that we must be careful to "establish the domain of a theory of second language acquisition," so that the domain excludes data on variability, has no force: One does not "establish" the domain of a theory any more than one "establishes" any hypothesis. Rather, the domain of a theory entails a claim that has to be defended, and that may change over time as more is learned about the subject matter.

In the early stages of a theory's development, it may be believed that certain facts are not related and are therefore to be explained differently. It may turn out, upon further investigation, that these differences are superficial, that there exists a deeper relationship between the facts in question, and that this relationship permits a unified account. In other words, in the early stages of a theory, it may be believed that certain facts are not part of the domain of that theory, but, upon further investigation, it may turn out that those facts are to be included within the theory's domain.

Let's look at a concrete example. In the early 19th century, electricity and magnetism were thought to be distinct subjects of investigation for which different explanations were to be given. This belief was based on the observation that there existed a number of differences between electricity and magnetism. Whereas a magnet required no stimulation or friction to attract objects, static electricity did require friction; whereas a magnet attracted only magnetizable substances, electricity attracted all substances; and whereas the attraction by a magnet was not affected by interposing a screen, electric attraction was destroyed by a screen. These differences formed the basis for the belief that electricity and magnetism were fundamentally different. However, in 1833 Faraday succeeded in showing that every known effect of magnetism and surface electricity could be obtained either by friction or from a voltaic cell, thereby supporting the unity of the two (Gilbert, 1958, cited in Shapere, 1977). Thus, by the middle of the 19th century, it had been shown that these fields were subsumable within the same theory and therefore did not constitute different domains of inquiry.

The point of the example just given with regard to the competence/performance distinction is this: What is to be included as part of competence and what is to be considered performance is a matter of hypothesis. Two linguists could be in total agreement that the subject matter of SLA theory is the competence of the L2 learner, and yet these same linguists might disagree as to what that competence entails. Therefore, it simply carries no force for Gregg to assert that the variationist model is not a viable theory of SLA because it blurs the competence/performance distinction.

An example from linguistic theory may help illustrate the second point: that the boundary between competence and performance is not permanent but instead moves as progress is made in the field.

Chomsky (1965) argued that the explanation of certain facts about sentences with center-embedded clauses, such as those in (2), lay outside the domain of linguistic competence and therefore fell within the domain of performance.

(2) a. ??Did that John showed up please you?
    b. ??That that John showed up pleased her was obvious.

Chomsky pointed out that not all sentences with center-embedded clauses were deviant, but that there appeared to be a limit on the number of center-embedded clauses that a sentence could contain; exceeding this limit made the sentence unacceptable/ungrammatical. He argued that incorporation of principles to account for this fact would unnecessarily complicate the grammar. Consequently, a grammar of English did not have to explain this aspect of center-embedded clauses; rather, the explanation of this fact was excluded from the domain of inquiry. Sentences with unlimited center-embedded clauses were generated by the grammar, and their ungrammaticality/unacceptability, along with the deviance of the sentences in (2), was considered to be an artifact of performance.

However, Kuno (1973) showed (a) that certain sentences containing center-embeddings, for example, those in (3), were not deviant; and (b) that it was possible to formulate general principles that would explain the grammaticality or ungrammaticality of certain center-embeddings without undue complication of the grammar.

(3) a. That what used to cost a dollar now costs a lot more is very annoying.

    b. The cheese (which) the rat that was chased by the cat ate was spoiled.

In so doing, Kuno provided an argument for including some sentences with center-embeddings under a theory of competence. Thus, some data that were excluded from the domain of competence in 1965 were argued to be part of this domain in 1973, showing that the boundary between competence and performance is not permanent.

Consequently, Gregg's argument that variability data do not belong to the domain of competence is not at all compelling. It depends crucially on the assumption that no one can demonstrate that variability data do belong to the realm of competence. This, however, is an empirical question and can be settled only on empirical grounds.

In making the counterargument to Gregg's critique, I granted for the sake of argument that the domain of SLA theory is the competence of the L2 learner. I then argued that a linguist establishes empirically, not a priori, what is included under that competence. I now take a different approach and consider Gregg's criticisms from the point of view of a theory that does not make a competence/performance distinction. That is to say, I now consider Gregg's claim that any viable theory of SLA must restrict itself to the linguistic competence of the L2 learner, a position represented in one of the preceding quotations and repeated for convenience:

> The distinction between performance and competence has been with us for over twenty years now, and although not without problems or controversy, it has pretty much established itself in linguistic theory and (to a lesser extent perhaps) in acquisition research. . . . Making this distinction is simply a fundamental prerequisite to progress in the scientific study of language acquisition. (Gregg, 1990, p. 370)

Gregg's position in this case is tenuous because he is again arguing on a priori grounds rather than on empirical grounds. It is not possible for someone to demonstrate that a theory of SLA, or any other theory, must confine itself to the investigation of some idealized construct, such as linguistic competence. Making a distinction between linguistic competence and linguistic performance might be a sound way to proceed in constructing a theory of SLA. As is well known, similar arguments have been made for linguistic theory (Chomsky, 1965, 1981, 1986). However, the question to be considered is whether it is necessary, as Gregg contends, for a theory of SLA to make such a distinction.

In considering this question, we need to be clear about the theoretical status of the concept of linguistic competence. This notion is introduced in order to simplify the investigator's task. Linguistic competence is an idealized construct, similar to abstractions like frictionless planes and ideal gases, which enables the investigator to ignore certain data that might otherwise compli-cate the investigation.[2] But it is important to realize that, despite Gregg's claims that such a distinction is a prerequisite to progress, there is nothing necessary about such idealizations. A linguist would be as justified in not mak-ing a competence/performance distinction as is a physicist who takes fric-tion or inelastic collisions into account.

In fact, it is doubtful whether Gregg or anyone else could give a compel-ling argument that a given theory must restrict itself to the study of some idealized construct. A linguist such as Gregg, for example, may believe or assert that SLA theory can best proceed by restricting itself to the study of a learner's linguistic competence. But this is different from arguing that a theory that went beyond the study of competence and included, for exam-ple, variability data would not be an insightful theory. Yet Gregg appears to be advancing just this position. His claim that the subject matter of SLA theory is the linguistic competence of the L2 learner, and that no progress would be made if the theory took real-world factors, such as variability, into account is tantamount to a physicist's claim that one could not construct an insightful theory by investigating inclined planes that have friction, or real gases where particle collisions are not perfectly elastic.

It is important to note that the argument that Gregg is advancing in the works under discussion is different from the arguments justifying the restric-tion of linguistic theory to the investigation of an ideal native speaker's com-petence. These arguments claim that it is legitimate to make the abstraction and to restrict linguistic theory to the study of competence on the grounds that the investigation of human languages can better proceed if linguistic theory is so restricted (Chomsky, 1965, 1966). It is not claimed, however, that a theory of language is not viable unless that theory limits the investigation to this competence. In this context, Gregg's argument represents somewhat of an anomaly in its emphasis on idealizations. Whereas such arguments have gener-ally been advanced to claim that it is reasonable to postulate an idealized construct and to limit the investigation to this idealization, Gregg is arguing that a theory of SLA is not viable unless it is restricted to such an idealization.

The foregoing should not be interpreted as an argument that the distinc-tion between competence and performance is unreasonable. As stated previ-ously, the arguments for idealized constructs in general, and for the competence/performance distinction in particular, are long-standing. The point is simply that theories that do not distinguish competence and perform-ance cannot be dismissed out of hand simply because they do not make this distinction. Rather, such theories must be evaluated on the same grounds as theories that do distinguish these notions, namely, on the basis of the

[2]I am hopeful that my analogy can go through without my being accused of "physics envy" (Tarone, 1990).

explanations that the theories provide, and not on the basis of a priori considerations.

To summarize up to this point, I have argued that Gregg's claims are not compelling because he cannot show that (a) SLA theory must be confined to the study of the ideal learner's linguistic competence, and (b) variability data could not be part of that competence.

The Variationist Argument

This brings me to the final topic of this section: an evaluation of the counter-arguments advanced by the variationist position.

As stated before, the issue at hand revolves around what the natural domain of a theory of SLA should be.[3] This being the case, it is not sufficient for proponents of the variationist position to claim that their model of SLA is superior because it incorporates more data, or because it accounts for variability. Because Gregg states explicitly that he does not consider variability to be under the purview of his theory of SLA, it is pointless for a proponent of the variationist model to criticize him for not accounting for variability. Such arguments are beside the point because the question before us is not whether a theory of SLA can account for variability. Rather, the question is which of the two domains under discussion, the one that excludes variability data or the one that includes variability data, constitutes a natural domain. In other words, the question is which theory leads to the most insightful explanation.

Proponents of the variationist model must argue that it is necessary for a theory of SLA to take variability into account, lest that theory risk being uninsightful. There are at least two ways in which such an argument could be made. First, if one could show that variability data could be readily accounted for without unduly complicating SLA theory (i.e., a theory of the linguistic competence of the L2 learner), then such data should be included

---

[3]In general terms, the domain of a theory is "natural" to the extent that adjusting the theory to account for additional types of facts causes a complication in the theory. The domain of a theory is "unnatural" to the extent that additional types of facts can be included under the theory without causing the theory to become more complex, that is, without necessitating additional constructs or other theoretical apparatus.

In the context of the present discussion, this is an important point. Insofar as theories are concerned, "bigger is not necessarily better." To put it more technically, it is not always appropriate to include additional types of facts under the purview of a theory, especially if such inclusion complicates the theory.

A good analogy is the phonological concept of *natural class*. The segments [p, t, k, b, d, g] constitute the natural class of English obstruent stops, which can be specified by the features [-sonorant, -continuant]. Notice that adding an additional segment, say [f], to the class destroys its naturalness; the set of segments [p, t, k, b, d, g, f] can no longer be specified by the features [-sonorant, -continuant], or, for that matter, by any other features.

as part of the theory's domain. In this case, there would be no good reason to exclude the data, because the theory in question could be naturally extended to explain them. The second way to present such an argument would be to demonstrate that, by taking variability data into account, one could explain some previously unexplained fact, F. If one could do this, then one would be compelled to include such data within the domain, because to exclude them would mean that the theory would fail to explain Fact F.

This second type of argument was, of course, put forth by Labov (1965) and by Weinreich, Labov, and Herzog (1968) for linguistic theory. In these works it was argued that the mechanism of language change can be explained only by a theory of language that recognized inherent variability. This type of argument is outlined also in Tarone (1990).

Specifically, Tarone assumed that language change in linguistic theory correlates in SLA theory with a change in a learner's interlanguage (i.e., acquisition of the target language). This idea is suggested independently in the work of Bialystok and Sharwood Smith (1985). Drawing on the work of other proponents of a variationist model, including Ellis (1985), Tarone (1990) outlined a possible mechanism by which new forms are acquired. She suggested that these forms emerge spontaneously and are incorporated into a system that assigns them to different linguistic contexts or to distinct meanings. Tarone contended that under this view, variability is crucial in explaining how a form is acquired. It is clear, as Tarone admitted in her discussion, that much more has to be done in this area, and that details have to be worked out. Nevertheless, if this type of argument could be empirically supported, it would constitute a convincing case that variability must be incorporated into the theory of SLA. However, until this demonstration is forthcoming, the issue in question must remain open.

To summarize, I have contended that the issue under debate is an empirical one and therefore must be settled on empirical grounds. The burden of proof seems to fall on the proponents of the variationist model of SLA, just as it fell on Labov in the case of linguistic theory, to show that variability must be included within the domain of SLA theory.

I turn now to some possible implications for theories of SLA.

IMPLICATIONS FOR SLA

In all scholarly debates, it is hoped that, through rational discussion, the issues will become focused, the respective positions will be clarified, and the supporting arguments will be closely scrutinized. The ultimate goal is that, out of the heat of the debate, the field will make progress. It is not clear that this is what is happening in the present debate.

As argued earlier, the directionality of the criticism in this debate seems to be a bit strange. The variationist model, because it is proposing an expansion of the domain of inquiry to include additional data, seems to have the burden of proof. In this context, it would be natural for proponents of the variationist model to criticize the shortcomings of the idealized competence model, arguing that such shortcomings can be rectified by the inclusion of variability data. In fact, one sees some of this type of argumentation in Tarone (1984). In general, however, the position of the variationists seems to be that expressed by Ellis, namely, that the two camps must coexist in order to pursue different goals. In the present debate, the criticism is coming from the other direction, from the competence model, with Gregg arguing that the variationist model cannot be a viable theory of SLA.

If we are correct that it is an empirical question whether or not variability is to be considered part of linguistic competence, then it is unclear whether criticisms such as Gregg's can have a positive effect. Because the burden of proof already seems to rest on the variationists, the most that Gregg's critique can accomplish on the positive side is to spur the variationists on to provide such proof. On the negative side, there is always the possibility that researchers will become needlessly sidetracked.

Finally, there is the question of the particular discipline in which the debate is taking place. SLA theory is a relatively young discipline in which there are many issues and relatively little that is agreed on as "conventional wisdom." As a result, it may be premature to advance some types of arguments. Specifically, one of Gregg's positions in the controversy is that the competence/performance distinction has played a major role in linguistic theory, which deals with primary languages; therefore it is reasonable, Gregg suggested, to expect that this distinction will play a similar role in the study of secondary languages. Although the reasoning is not specious, it might be wise to be more conservative here until we know more about the nature of secondary languages. That is, it is not implausible that the competence/performance distinction could play a major role in the study of primary languages, but a diminished role in the study of secondary languages.

We have seen distinctions between these two language types in other areas. Thus, for example, although linguists will readily consider data from groups of speakers in the study of a primary language, the same is not done in the case of secondary languages. It is generally assumed that L2 learners, even those from the same native language background, are to be treated individually, simply because it has not been shown that such learners will develop exactly the same interlanguage. Until this is shown, the safest position is to keep the data separate.

It is not absurd to believe that the same could be true with respect to the competence/performance distinction: In the study of primary languages, we may safely ignore some data as due to performance factors; in the case of secondary languages, the facts may not be as clear, and we should be reluctant to ignore any data. In any event, until the status of the data is more certain, it might be wise to take the safer position.

CONCLUSION

In this chapter, I have considered the current debate on whether SLA theory should be concerned with variability data. I have argued that neither side in the debate has presented compelling arguments in its favor. Proponents of the competence model (Gregg, 1989, 1990) cannot in principle demonstrate that no important insights would be forthcoming by including data from variability. On the other hand, proponents of the variationist model have not as yet presented the kind of data that would be most convincing for their position. The question is an empirical one, and its resolution must await the presentation of such data.

ACKNOWLEDGMENTS

Preliminary versions of this chapter were presented at the Michigan State University conference on theory construction in second-language acquisition, East Lansing, October 4, 1991, and at the UWM Linguistics Colloquium, Milwaukee, October 30, 1991. I thank the members of the audience at both of these presentations for useful comments and discussion. I would like to single out the following for taking the time to read and comment on an earlier version of this chapter: Dan Dinnsen, Kevin Gregg, Greg Iverson, Michael Liston, Edith Moravcsik, India Plough, Bill Rutherford, and the editors of this volume. As usual, all of those just mentioned are responsible to some extent for causing me to clarify my thinking on this topic, and none is responsible for any remaining unclarities, oversights, misinterpretations, or errors of fact.

REFERENCES

Bialystok, E., & Sharwood Smith, M. (1985). Interlanguage is not a state of mind. *Applied Linguistics, 6*, 101–117.
Chomsky, N. (1965). *Aspects of the theory of syntax*. Cambridge, MA: MIT Press.
Chomsky, N. (1966). *Topics in the theory of generative grammar*. The Hague: Mouton.
Chomsky, N. (1981). *Lectures on government and binding*. Dordrecht: Foris Publications.
Chomsky, N. (1986). *Knowledge of language*. New York: Praeger.
Ellis, R. (1985). Sources of variability in interlanguage. *Applied Linguistics, 11*, 384–391.
Ellis, R. (1990). A response to Gregg. *Applied Linguistics, 6*, 118–131.
Gregg, K. (1989). Second language acquisition theory: The case for a generative perspective. In S. Gass & J. Schachter (Eds.), *Linguistic perspectives on second language acquisition* (pp. 15–40). Cambridge: Cambridge University Press.

Gregg, K. (1990). The variable competence model of second language acquisition, and why it isn't. *Applied Linguistics, 11*, 365–383.

Kuno, S. (1973). Constraints on internal clauses and sentential subjects. *Linguistic Inquiry, 4*, 363–385.

Labov, W. (1965). On the mechanism of linguistic change. *Georgetown University Monographs on Languages and Linguistics, 18*, 91–114.

Searle, J. (1969). *Speech acts*. Cambridge, England: Cambridge University Press.

Shapere, D. (1977). Scientific theories and their domains. In F. Suppe (Ed.), *The structure of scientific theories* (pp. 518–565). Champaign-Urbana: University of Illinois Press.

Tarone, E. (1979). Interlanguage as chameleon. *Language Learning, 29*, 181–191.

Tarone, E. (1984). On the variability of interlanguage systems. In F. Eckman, L. Bell, & D. Nelson (Eds.), *Universals of second language acquisition* (pp. 3–23). Rowley, MA: Newbury House.

Tarone, E. (1990). On variation in interlanguage: A response to Gregg. *Applied Linguistics, 11*, 392–399.

Weinreich, U., Labov, W., & Herzog, M. (1968). Empirical foundations for a theory of language change. In W. Lehmann & Y. Malkiel (Eds.), *Directions for historical linguistics* (pp. 98–195). Austin: University of Texas Press.

2

THE SUBSET PRINCIPLE IN SECOND-LANGUAGE ACQUISITION

Gerald P. Berent

National Technical Institute for the Deaf at
Rochester Institute of Technology

Research on second-language acquisition (SLA) often evaluates the extent to which second-language (L2) data support the constructs and predictions of linguistic theories. For example, in recent years considerable attention has been devoted to exploring SLA in the context of Chomsky's (1981, 1986b) Principles and Parameters Theory (see especially White, 1989b). Whenever the goal of an acquisitional study is to examine the compatibility between a linguistic theory and acquisitional data, the study should be submitted to at least two tests. First, it must be established that the learner data actually do reflect knowledge of the phenomena under investigation; and, second, it must be established that the linguistic constructs under investigation are theoretically sound and defensible, given the current state of a theory's development. If the study fails either one of these tests, its results cannot be considered a valid contribution to SLA theory construction.

In this chapter I apply these two tests in evaluating SLA studies that have explored a possible role for the *Subset Principle* (SP) in SLA. Although the SP has been offered as a general learning constraint on first-language acquisition (Berwick, 1985; Wexler & Manzini, 1987), the few SLA studies that have examined the SP have generally concluded that the SP does not apply in SLA. Using the two tests of a study's validity, I demonstrate that the arguments offered to date against application of the SP in SLA cannot be considered valid. I show that, in some instances, the SLA studies have design problems and that, therefore, the L2 data offered as evidence do not accurately represent knowledge of the phenomenon under investigation. In other instances I argue that current developments within linguistic theory motivate a reanalysis of the constructs under investigation and that, consequently, the studies' conclusions have no relevance to the SP.

Establishing that existing arguments against application of the SP in SLA are not tenable does not, of course, demonstrate that the SP applies in SLA. In this regard, I offer an analysis of relative clause formation along with arguments that the SP in fact applies to relative clause acquisition. On the basis of existing L2 relative clause data, I then provide evidence that the SP does apply in SLA. The approach to research methodology taken in this chapter incorporates the assumption that successful theory construction in SLA requires careful scrutiny of both the appropriateness of task design and the soundness of theoretical proposals.

THE SUBSET PRINCIPLE

Berwick (1985) promoted the SP within a computational approach to language acquisition as a general learning constraint guiding much of language acquisition. Referring to a broad range of acquisitional phenomena, Berwick demonstrated how the SP guarantees that, where one hypothesized language is properly contained within another, the acquisition procedure will always guess the smallest language compatible with the positive evidence so far encountered. Because it is generally assumed that language learners have no access to negative evidence, the SP protects a learner from hypothesizing a language larger than the target language, given that there would be no way to retreat subsequently to the correct smaller language without negative evidence.

Wexler and Manzini (1987) and Manzini and Wexler (1987) interpreted the SP more narrowly within a parametric theory of language acquisition (Chomsky, 1981). They viewed the SP as an independent learning principle that interacts with principles of Universal Grammar (UG) during acquisition to guide the setting of UG parameters. They formulated the SP as in (1) (Wexler & Manzini, p. 61) and illustrated its application to their *Governing Category Parameter* (GCP) in (2) (p. 53), a parameter of binding theory determining the interpretation of anaphors and pronominals.

(1) The learning function maps the input data to that value of a parameter which generates a language:
   a. compatible with the input data; and
   b. smallest among the languages compatible with the input data.

(2) γ is a governing category for α iff γ is the minimal category which contains α and
   a. has a subject, or

     b. has an Infl, or
     c. has a TNS, or
     d. has an indicative TNS, or
     e. has a root TNS

The GCP was formulated on the basis of the actual domains within which anaphors and pronominals in various languages are interpreted. English happens to have GCP value (2a) for both anaphors (e.g., *himself*) and pronominals (e.g., *him*).

Crucially, in order for the SP to determine every value of the learning function, that is, to guide the acquisition of parameter values, Wexler and Manzini (1987) argued that the languages generated by the various values of a parameter of UG must lie in a strict subset relation to one another. This restriction, their *Subset Condition* (p. 60), is given in (3).

(3) For every parameter p and every two values i, j of p, the languages generated under the two values of the parameter are one a subset of the other, that is, $L_{(p(i))} \subset L_{(p(j))}$ or $L_{(p(j))} \subset L_{(p(i))}$.

In those instances where a parameter's values yield languages that do not lie in subset relations to one another, the SP does not apply.

Wexler and Manzini demonstrated that the languages generated by the five values of the GCP do in fact lie in a subset relation to one another. Each of the five values in (2) defines a successively larger syntactic domain within which an anaphor requires a c-commanding antecedent and within which a pronominal disallows a c-commanding antecedent, in accordance with Chomsky's (1981) binding principles. In accordance with Binding Principle A, an anaphor is bound in its governing category, and in accordance with Binding Principle B, a pronominal is free in its governing category.[1]

In the English sentences represented in (4), the labeled bracketing corresponds to those values of the GCP in (2) that are relevant to English.

(4) a. [e John knows that [c Bill wants [b Tom to discuss [a Mike's criticism of *himself*]]]]
     b. [e John knows that [c Bill wants [b Tom to discuss [a Mike's criticism of *him*]]]]

Because English has GCP value (2a) for anaphors, *Mike* in (4a) binds *himself* as the only possible c-commanding antecedent within the governing category

---

[1]A node α *c-commands* a node β if neither node dominates the other and the first branching node that dominates α also dominates β. An NP is *bound* if it is c-commanded by an NP with which it is coindexed; an NP is *free* if it is not bound.

labeled *a*. Because English also has value (2a) for pronominals, *Mike* in (4b) is the only noun phrase (NP) that cannot serve as the antecedent for *him*, because *him* must be free in its governing category. In this case, any of the NPs *Tom, Bill, John*, or some sentence-external NP referent could serve as the antecedent of *him*, because all are outside of the governing category labeled *a*. Thus, (4b) actually represents four sentences of English, one for each interpretation of *him*, whereas (4a), with its one interpretation of *himself*, represents only one sentence of English.

Where the Subset Condition holds and the SP applies, Wexler and Manzini (1987) defined *markedness hierarchies* on the basis of the subset relations among the languages generated by a parameter's values. The parameter value that yields the smallest language is the unmarked value, and each successive value yielding a larger language is more marked than the preceding value. As Wexler and Manzini illustrated, the markedness hierarchy for anaphors is the opposite of the markedness hierarchy for pronominals. For anaphors, GCP value (2a) is unmarked because it defines the smallest language, and values (2b), (2c), (2d), and (2e), in that order, are progressively more marked. On the other hand, for pronominals, GCP value (2e) is unmarked because it defines the smallest language, and values (2d), (2c), (2b), and (2a), in that order, are progressively more marked.

From the learnability standpoint, a child learning English will require minimal positive evidence to set the GCP at the unmarked value (2a) for anaphors, because that value defines the smallest possible language. In setting the GCP for pronominals, however, a child learning English will require considerably more positive evidence to arrive at value (2a), because (2a) is the most marked value with respect to pronominals, the one defining the largest language.

THE PSYCHOLOGICAL REALITY
OF THE SUBSET PRINCIPLE

Berent and Samar (1990) provided independent psycholinguistic evidence in support of the learnability predictions of Wexler and Manzini's (1987) SP. A 56-item pencil-and-paper test in which half of the items were sentences containing the English anaphor *himself* and half were parallel sentences containing the English pronominal *him* was administered to 35 prelingually deaf college students and to a control group of 19 hearing college students. The sentences, which exhibited a variety of syntactic structures similar to those in (4), were constructed to determine the subjects' GCP values for English anaphors and pronominals.

Each test sentence was followed by a series of *yes/no* questions that probed subjects' interpretations of possible antecedents for the anaphor or pronominal contained in that sentence, including the possible selection of an external antecedent. In answering the questions about possible antecedents, subjects were instructed to consider a variety of interpretations for any given sentence. A sample test item is shown in (5).

(5) Jack learned that Don voted for himself.
    a. Can himself = Jack?   YES NO
    b. Can himself = Don?   YES NO
    c. Can himself = another person?   YES NO

Subjects' responses to the composite of the structures used in the 56-item test would reveal which of the GCP values in (2) had been set independently for anaphors and pronominals.

The deaf subjects comprised two separate groups that did not differ significantly in age, degree of hearing loss, age of onset of deafness, hearing status of parents, or sign language proficiency. They did differ, however, in their overall English language proficiency as measured by the *Michigan Test of English Language Proficiency* (1977). The High Proficiency group had a mean score of 77.3 (SD = 1.2), and the Low Proficiency group had a mean score of 51.3 (SD = 1.4). Previous studies of prelingually deaf students' English language knowledge have revealed that deaf students often have greater knowledge of the unmarked properties of English but lesser knowledge of the marked properties of the language (see Berent, 1983, 1988, in press; Quigley & King, 1980; Swisher, 1989).

Therefore, Berent and Samar (1990) hypothesized that the subjects who tend to exhibit a more restricted knowledge of the marked properties of English might also have restricted knowledge of the marked values of UG parameters, in this case, the GCP. Specifically, it was predicted that both the Low Proficiency group and the High Proficiency group would show evidence of having set the GCP for anaphors at the correct unmarked value (2a), which defines the smallest language and which, from the standpoint of learnability, requires the least evidence to set. However, it was further predicted that, in view of their more restricted knowledge of the marked properties of English, the Low Proficiency group would also exhibit evidence of the unmarked, but incorrect, GCP value (2e) for pronominals because it, too, defines the smallest language and requires the least evidence to set. In contrast, the High Proficiency group, with its greater knowledge of the marked properties of English, was expected to approximate the correct marked value (2a) for pronominals.

These were precisely the results obtained. The High Proficiency group, along with the hearing control group, showed evidence of the unmarked value (2a) for anaphors and the most marked value (2a) for pronominals. The Low Proficiency group also showed evidence of the correct value (2a) for anaphors but indeed approximated the unmarked, but incorrect, root TNS value (2e) for pronominals. These parameter values were verified in a separate analysis of spontaneous writing samples from the two deaf groups. Thus, in the acquisition of a first language under conditions involving a severe restriction of positive (auditory) language evidence, individuals with lower general English proficiency appear to select grammars characterized by parameter values that generate a smaller set of sentences.

The results of Berent and Samar (1990) provided independent psycholinguistic evidence in support of Wexler and Manzini's (1987) parametric theory of learnability. In verifying the markedness predictions of the SP, these results supported the SP as a determinant of the learning function for parameters of UG whose values conform to the Subset Condition.

SECOND LANGUAGE ACQUISITION

Although the SP has been offered as a learning constraint on language acquisition from positive evidence, it was motivated by the learnability considerations of first-language acquisition. In the context of SLA, empirical support for the SP has not been readily forthcoming. In fact, most investigations of a possible role for the SP in SLA have offered evidence against it (see the discussions in Rutherford, 1989, and White, 1989b).

In the context of SLA, White (1989b) summarized three presumed parameters of UG—the *Adjacency Parameter*, the *Configurationality Parameter*, and the *Governing Category Parameter*—and reviewed arguments against the role of the SP in SLA in the (re)setting of these parameters by L2 learners. In what follows, I address the arguments against the SP in SLA, and for each parameter I suggest an alternative analysis or cite problems with task design on the basis of which these arguments might be refuted. Finally, I review an analysis developed in Berent (1990) that supports the role of the SP in SLA.

The Adjacency Parameter

Stowell (1981) proposed the *adjacency condition* on the assignment of (abstract) Case to NPs, which requires an object NP, for example, to be adjacent to a governing verb, as in (6a) or (6b).

(6) a.   Paul quickly opened the door.
    b.   Paul opened the door quickly.
    c.   *Paul opened quickly the door.

Stowell (p. 113) noted that the adjacency condition varies among languages. Whereas (6c) is ungrammatical in English because *the door* is not adjacent to *opened*, the equivalent French or Italian sentence is grammatical despite the intervening adverb. Stowell concluded, therefore, that the adjacency condition in its strict form applies in English: Even an intervening adverb is sufficient to block Case assignment.

In Berwick's (1985) computational approach to the SP, strict adjacency was interpreted as the most restrictive assumption, therefore the unmarked case (p. 284). Because adjacency violations like (6c) will never be encountered in English, the assumption of strict adjacency will never be dropped. However, when positive examples equivalent to (6c) in a language like French or Italian are encountered, indicating that adjacency is violated, then the most restrictive assumption is loosened.

Drawing on this interpretation, White (1989a) explored the Adjacency Parameter in the context of SLA, using as subjects French speakers learning English as a second language (ESL) and English speakers learning French as a second language (FSL). Because English has the unmarked value [+ strict adjacency] of the Adjacency Parameter whereas French, admitting sentences analogous to (6c), has the marked value [− strict adjacency], it is possible to determine whether the SP guides ESL learners' acquisition of English relative to adjacency.

White (1989a) considered two hypotheses, the *subset hypothesis* and the *transfer hypothesis*. According to the subset hypothesis, the French-speaking ESL learners should assume the unmarked value [+ strict adjacency] for English despite the fact that their first language has the marked value [− strict adjacency]. Therefore, they should not accept or produce adjacency violations as in (6c). According to the transfer hypothesis, the ESL learners should allow adjacency violations as in (6c), transferring the marked value from French. This result would provide evidence that the SP is not operative in SLA.

With respect to the English-speaking FSL learners, the subset hypothesis predicts that they will reject adjacency violations in French, that is, reject grammatical French sentences analogous to (6c). However, the transfer hypothesis predicts the same result because, in this case, the FSL learners would be transferring the unmarked English value onto French. Therefore, evidence for or against the SP in SLA hinges on the performance of the ESL learners.

The subjects completed two types of grammaticality judgment task and one sentence preference task in the target language. The results revealed that the FSL learners rejected many of the (grammatical) adjacency violations, applying strict adjacency to French. Because both hypotheses predict that the unmarked value [+ strict adjacency] should be assumed initially, the FSL learners' performance supports neither hypothesis. The ESL learners' performance, on the other hand, revealed that many of them accepted (un-grammatical) adjacency violations, assuming that English, like French, has the marked [− strict adjacency] value. This result supports the transfer hypothesis over the subset hypothesis. White (1989a) concluded, therefore, that the SP fails to apply in SLA.

Actually, a more recent proposal in linguistic theory provides a new per-spective on the distribution of adverbs in English and French and suggests a reinterpretation of adjacency phenomena that renders the preceding argu-ments against the SP vacuous. Pollock (1989) attributed a broad range of word order differences between English and French with respect to adverbs, sen-tence negation, questions, and quantifiers to a parameter of UG affecting *thematic role* (Θ-role) assignment.

The sentences pertinent to the current discussion are given in (7) (Pollock, p. 367).[2]

(7) a. *John kisses often Mary.
    b. Jean embrasse souvent Marie.
    c. John often kisses Mary.
    d. *Jean souvent embrasse Marie.

Pollock proposed that the differences within minimal pairs (7a, b) and (7c, d) stem from a difference between English and French in verb-raising. With-in the *barriers* framework of Chomsky (1986a), the relevant structures are as in (8) (based on Pollock's (77), p. 397).[3]

(8) a. $[_{CP} [_{IP} [_{NP}$ John$] [_{I'}$ INFL $[_{AgrP}$ AGR $[_{VP} [_{ADV}$ often$]$
       $[_{V'} [_{V}$ kisses$]$ Mary$]]]]]]$
    b. $[_{CP} [_{IP} [_{NP}$ Jean$] [_{I'}$ embrasse $[_{AgrP} t_i [_{VP} [_{ADV}$ souvent$]$
       $[_{V'} [_{V} t_i]$ Mary$]]]]]]$

UG requires that verbs assign both Case and Θ-roles to their NP arguments. In the barriers framework, when V raises to INFL (= I), it transmits its Θ-roles to its NP arguments from its raised position. Pollock maintained that the differences in (7) derive from the fact that verb movement to I is obliga-tory in French but is blocked in English. In French, V (*embrasse*) in (8b) must

---

[2]In discussing White (1989a), White (1989b) acknowledged without comment the ungram-maticality in French of sentences like (7d) and Pollock's (1989) alternative analysis of the differ-ences under discussion between English and French. White (1991) dealt with Pollock's verb-raising analysis as an independent proposal without reference to the Adjacency Parameter analysis of White (1989a).

[3]CP = complementizer phrase, C = complementizer, IP = inflectional phrase, I = INFL or inflection, AgrP = agreement phrase, AGR = agreement, VP = verb phrase, ADV = adverb.

move out of VP first to AGR, leaving a *trace*, t_i, in its original position, and then to INFL, leaving another trace in the AGR position. The resulting structure leaves the adverb (*souvent*) between the verb and the object NP, as in (7b). In English, V (*kisses*) in (8a) remains within the VP between the adverb and the object NP, as in (7c).[4]

Pollock's explanation was that French AGR is *transparent* to Θ-role assignment because it is morphologically "rich" but that English AGR is *opaque* to Θ-role assignment because it is not rich enough morphologically to transmit a verb's Θ-roles. Accordingly, all lexical verbs in French raise to I, whereas lexical verbs in English cannot raise to I. The only verbs in English that raise to I are those that do not assign Θ-roles, namely, *be* and *have*. This is evident from the position of *always* in *John is always happy* and in *John has always been happy*.

Assuming Pollock's (1989) analysis, strict adjacency is simply a consequence of the opacity of AGR in English.[5] Given this Opaque/Transparent AGR Parameter, if it were the case that French, relative to English (or vice versa), had a wider distribution of adverb positions—for example, if both (7b) and (7d) were grammatical options in French but only (7c) were grammatical in English—then it would appear that the opaque value was marked, because it would generate a larger language than the transparent value relative to potential adverb positions. However, this is not the case; the relevant pairs in (7) are in complementary distribution. Accordingly, the two values of the AGR parameter do not define languages that satisfy the Subset Condition (3), and so the SP does not apply to determine the learning of this parameter.

---

[4]Iatridou (1990) offered a counterproposal to Pollock (1989), arguing against the constituent AgrP. In most of the instances where Pollock proposed that verbs move to INFL in both English and French, Iatridou also assumed movement to INFL, though not through any AgrP. White (1991) was in fact incorrect in stating: "Iatridou (1990) argued that adverb-placement differences between English and French are not, in fact, a consequence of differences in verb-raising possibilities" (p. 358). Despite Iatridou's counterproposal, it is still verb-movement that contributes to the different distribution of adverbs in English and French. Therefore, even if correct, her analysis does not affect the arguments in this chapter against strict adjacency.

[5]Given the preceding arguments, there is no longer any motivation for an Adjacency Parameter per se. This is not to say, however, that there is no Case adjacency principle determining the order of complements. As Chomsky (1986b) noted: "Where Case is not morphologically realized, a Case-marked element must be adjacent to its Case-assigner . . . if a verb takes an NP and a PP complement, the former will be closer to the verb ('put [the book] [on the table],' *'put [on the table] [the book]')" (p. 82).

The Adjacency Parameter discussed earlier pertains not to the phenomenon of Case adjacency determined by UG but to adjacency violations where an adverb intervenes between a verb and its object NP. White (1989a) did not distinguish between the two phenomena in her task stimuli. Accordingly, there was great variability in her subjects' responses among certain sentences that supposedly reflected the same phenomenon (but in fact did not).

Under these circumstances, the argument offered in White (1989a) against the SP in SLA is untenable.[6]

The Configurationality Parameter

Zobl (1988) explored the possible role of the SP in guiding SLA in the context of Hale's (1983) Configurationality Parameter. With respect to this parameter, [+ configurational] languages like English have argument positions that are structurally governed by a verb, whereas [− configurational] languages like Walpiri have argument positions that are not structurally governed but are instead associated with a verb via coindexing. Structural government in configurational languages results in relatively strict word order, whereas the lack of structural government in nonconfigurational languages results in relatively free word order.

Zobl (1988) considered the [+ configurational] value the unmarked value of the Configurationality Parameter. From the computational perspective, Berwick (1985) claimed that the narrowest language is one in which thematic and syntactic units are strictly aligned, for example, where agent-action-patient parallels subject-verb-object. If a language also allows the order patient-action-agent (as in passive sentences), it constitutes a larger language. Berwick therefore argued that, in accordance with the SP, the learner's first hypothesis will be strict thematic-syntactic alignment. Then nonconfigurational languages, which do not maintain a strict thematic-syntactic alignment, would reflect the marked value [− configurational] of the configurationality parameter.

Some linguists (e.g., Hale, 1983) have described Japanese as a nonconfigurational language, although others have not (see the following discussion). Zobl (1988) assumed that it is. As a test of the SP's applicability to SLA, Zobl conducted a study using as subjects adult Japanese speakers learning ESL. These subjects were given an "adjacency judgment" task consisting of eight sentences, including those in (9):

(9) a. I washed the glasses (carefully).
   b. The girl cut her birthday cake (with a knife).
   c. She asked me what I was doing (in a loud voice).

---

[6]White (1991) explored differences between English and French in the distribution of adverbs, not with reference to the Adjacency Parameter but with specific reference to Pollock's (1989) Verb-Movement Parameter. In an instructional experiment involving French-speaking ESL learners, White found that knowledge of English question formation did not facilitate knowledge of English adverb placement. Because both phenomena are associated with verb raising, White concluded that positive evidence of one set of properties relating to a parameter does not result in the successful L2 acquisition of another set of properties relating to the same parameter. However, Schwartz and Gubala-Ryzak (1992) reinterpreted White's data and concluded that her results do not pertain to parameter (re)setting but can instead be explained as the employment of a pattern-matching strategy by L2 learners.

Subjects were required to mark the best location in each sentence for the portion given in parentheses. Zobl hypothesized that if the subjects committed certain adjacency violations, for example, if they inserted *with a knife* directly after *cut* in (9b), this would indicate that they were treating English as [− configurational] like Japanese by allowing constituents within the VP to appear in any order. This result would provide evidence against the SP because these L2 learners would not be assuming the unmarked [+ configurational] value of the Configurationality Parameter as their initial hypothesis.

Zobl's results revealed that, with increasing English proficiency (as measured by an in-house placement measure), his subjects made fewer adjacency violations in their judgments. Zobl concluded that the adjacency violations admitted by the subjects with lower English proficiency indicate that their hypothesized grammars do not exhibit structural government within the VP and that they therefore are viewing English as a nonconfigurational language. In contrast, the lower frequency of adjacency violations of the more advanced subjects implies structural government within the VP, characterizing a configurational language. This situation indicates an initial assumption of the marked value [− configurational] for English and the subsequent resetting to the unmarked value [+ configurational], in contradiction to the learnability predictions of the SP.

However, Zobl also reported production data from the same subjects that contradict the results of the adjacency judgment task. In journal entries and English compositions, the subjects committed very few adjacency violations, and there were essentially no differences in adjacency violations according to English proficiency level. These results imply an initial assumption of the unmarked value [+ configurational], in full accordance with the SP.

White (1989b) pointed out certain design problems with the study reported in Zobl (1988), for example, the lack of a native English-speaking control group and the fact that the stimulus materials consisted of one token each of only eight sentences. I add to these criticisms, arguing that the SP does not pertain to the phenomena investigated.

More recent developments in Japanese linguistics (e.g., Saito, 1985; Kuroda, 1988) indicate that Japanese is in fact a configurational language, that NP arguments are governed within the VP, and that the relatively free word order of Japanese results from NP-movement under certain conditions. Given these developments, if there were a Configurationality Parameter, English and Japanese would reflect the same unmarked value [+ configurational].

With regard to the free word order among Japanese argument NPs, subject, object, and oblique NPs may generally appear in any order before the verb. The sentences in (10) illustrate three of the six possible word orders for the same Case-marked NPs.[7]

---

[7]I thank Susan Fischer for providing me with these examples.

(10) a. John ga   hon   o   Bill kara nusunda.
        John NOM book OBJ Bill OBL stole
        'John stole a book from Bill.'
     b. Hon o Bill kara John ga nusunda.
     c. Bill kara John ga hon o nusunda.

In each sentence, *ga* unambiguously reflects nominative Case (NOM), *o* unambiguously reflects objective Case (OBJ), and *kara* unambiguously reflects oblique (OBL) Case. Now if there were a Configurationality Parameter and if the Japanese speakers in Zobl's (1988) study initially assumed the marked [− configurational] value for English, as claimed, then, in addition to the kinds of adjacency violations targeted in Zobl's study, the subjects at the lower proficiency levels should be expected to accept and to produce in English, as in Japanese, any of the constituent orders in (11), as well as three other possible orders.

(11) a. John stole a book from Bill.
     b. A book stole from Bill John.
     c. From Bill stole John a book.

The marked value of the Configurationality Parameter would generate a language including all of these sentences.

   However, in describing his subjects, Zobl characterized those at the lower proficiency levels as exhibiting SVO word order and a phrase-initial head position in their English interlanguage, properties of a [+ configurational] language and, specifically, properties of English. Therefore, it is theoretically impossible that these subjects would accept or produce sentences like (11b) or (11c), treating English as [− configurational].

   There are other grounds on which the word order differences between Japanese and English are not comparable in any way relevant to the SP. The two languages differ fundamentally in their Case-marking devices (see Kuroda, 1988). Case in Japanese is reflected essentially through morphology; Case in English is reflected essentially through word order. With respect to this difference, there is no one-to-one correspondence between the Japanese and the English sentence in each of the pairs (10a)–(11a), (10b)–(11b), and (10c)–(11c). In other words, sentence (11a) could be considered a subset of the three sentences in (10) only if English not only associated NOM Case with the preverbal subject position but also marked NOM Case morphologically. The fact that English does not mark Case morphologically is precisely why sentences (11b) and (11c) are ruled out independently by the Case filter of Chomsky (1981). Thus, the sentences of (10) and the sentences of (11) comprise two disjoint data sets.

   From the standpoint of thematic-syntactic alignment, the two sets are also disjoint. As noted earlier, Berwick's (1985) assumption was that the learner's first hypothesis will be strict thematic-syntactic alignment, as reflected in canonical SVO word order in English, for example. This implies that Japanese, with its free word order, is not characterized by a strict thematic-syntactic alignment. But if the alignment entails, as Berwick maintained, that agent = subject and patient = object, then Japanese also instantiates this alignment, but in a typologically different manner. In Japanese, the alignment is a strict thematic-morphological alignment. If the learner's first hypothesis is in accord with the SP, then a strict thematic-syntactic alignment and a strict thematic-morphological alignment are equally restrictive assumptions. They are merely two typological dimensions of the same phenomenon.

Given the foregoing discussion, there appears to be no basis for the existence of a Configurationality Parameter with respect to which English carries the unmarked value and Japanese carries the marked value. Furthermore, as noted, there were problems with task design in Zobl (1988) and contradictions between the judgment and production data. Therefore, the results of Zobl (1988) cannot be viewed as offering any evidence against the role of the SP in SLA.

The Governing Category Parameter

The GCP of Wexler and Manzini (1987), defined in (2), remains the only UG parameter under discussion whose values have been shown to generate languages that satisfy the Subset Condition and to which the SP therefore must apply. It is also the only parameter for which the SP's learnability predictions have been verified in an independent learnability experiment for first-language acquisition under crucial test conditions of restricted input (Berent & Samar, 1990). However, research on the GCP in SLA appears to provide some of the strongest legitimate evidence against the SP in that context.

White (1989b) provided a summary of much of the SLA research on the GCP (pp. 157–163). She discussed the results of Finer and Broselow (1986), Finer (1989), Hirakawa (1989), and Thomas (1989). All of these studies, and more recently, Thomas (1991) and Lakshmanan and Teranishi (this volume, chapter 10) have investigated, through picture-identification or multiple-choice tasks, L2 learners' acquisition of the English anaphor *himself/herself*. The structures that these studies focus on include sentences like those in (12) (from Finer & Broselow, p. 160).

(12) a. Mr. Fat thinks that Mr. Thin will paint himself.
      b. Mr Fat asks Mr. Thin to paint himself.

In accordance with Binding Principle A, and under the English value (2a) of the GCP, *himself* must be bound within the *that*-clause in (12a), namely, by

Mr. Thin, because the *that*-clause is the minimal category that contains the anaphor and has a subject. Similarly, in (12b), *Mr. Thin* binds *himself* because here the minimal category containing the anaphor and a subject is the infinitival clause (see (15b)).

Collectively, the SLA studies examine interpretations of English sentences containing anaphors by speakers of Spanish, Korean, Japanese, and Chinese. Although English and Spanish share value (2a) of the GCP, the other three languages have governing categories larger than that defined by (2a), specifically, value (2e). Therefore, these studies could reveal whether L2 learners assume the unmarked value of the GCP, transfer to English the more marked GCP value of their first language, or adopt some other GCP value for English.

Generally, the results of these studies suggest that L2 learners do not initially assume the unmarked GCP value (2a) for anaphors. This finding militates, of course, against the role of the SP in SLA. In particular, Finer and Broselow (1986) and Finer (1989) found that local antecedents are favored in sentences with an embedded finite clause (i.e., *Mr. Thin* in (12a)), but that the assignment of nonlocal antecedents is quite frequent in sentences with an embedded infinitive clause (i.e., *Mr. Fat* in (12b)). This pattern of results suggests value (2c) of the GCP, which is intermediate between English value (2a) and value (2e) of the Korean- and Japanese-speaking subjects who participated in those studies.

However, Hirakawa (1989), Thomas (1989, 1991), and Lakshmanan and Teranishi (this volume, chapter 10) reported somewhat higher incidences of nonlocal antecedents chosen in sentences like (12a) (though local antecedents are still preferred). This result is consistent with value (2e), the value associated with Korean, Japanese, and Chinese, rather than with a "compromise" value (2c). It would be reasonable to assume that subjects were transferring the GCP value of their first languages to the L2 if it were not for the fact that Thomas' Spanish-speaking subjects also showed evidence of adopting value (2e) for English. This rules out the transfer hypothesis, because Spanish has value (2a).

Overshadowing this entire theoretical discussion is the fact that all of the studies exploring the GCP in SLA suffer from methodological problems concerning task design (cf. the discussion in Lakshmanan & Teranishi). The study of binding theory and associated parameters is by nature more complicated than, say, the study of word order and associated parameters. Word order is a more salient feature of language than is the invisible association of two or more nominal expressions through coreference. Given the formidable task of developing reliable measures for assessing coreference in emerging grammars, the results of many child language studies that address binding theory have been held suspect (see the discussion in Grimshaw & Rosen, 1990, and in Berent & Samar, 1990).

Studies of the application of binding principles and the acquisition of GCP settings in SLA are susceptible to many of the same methodological problems to which child language studies are susceptible. Thomas (1991) argued that L2 coreference judgments may reflect subjects' preferences rather than actual grammars. She noted that Finer and Broselow's (1986) speculation that Korean-speaking subjects assume GCP value (2c) in their grammars cannot be confirmed unless the subjects actually disallow nonlocal antecedents for sentence type (12a), rather than just show what may be a preference for local antecedents.

Clearly, intricacies of task design can influence subjects' responses. For example, in explaining her task procedures, Thomas (1989) provided three sample task items, including (13) (p. 286).

(13) David could see that Bill was looking at himself in the mirror. Who did Bill see in the mirror?
   a. Bill
   b. David
   c. Either Bill or David

In this multiple-choice task, subjects are required to read the sentence and the following question and to circle one of the three possible choices of antecedent for the anaphor. Thomas explained that choices for the local antecedent, in this example, (a), and the nonlocal antecedent, (b), are listed in random order throughout the task, but that choice (c) always appears last.

There are problems with this design. First, one cannot take for granted that subjects at all proficiency levels will appropriately process the *wh*-question to which choices (a), (b), and (c) pertain. Processing this particular question, in which *who* is the object of *see*, presumes the acquisition of English *wh*-movement and *do*-support. In this example, moreover, the same verb, *see*, occurs both in the matrix clause of the target sentence and in the question as a substitute for *looking at* in the embedded clause of the target sentence. Second, having thought through choices (a) and (b) as possible antecedents of the anaphor, subjects must rethink the associations for choice (c) after they have, most likely, decided between (a) and (b). Therefore, (c) choices should be artificially low, if only because they are always last. Furthermore, the disjunction *either . . . or* is acquired late in first-language acquisition, and this may also be the case in SLA, so that choice (c) may not be fully understood. These disjunctions, moreover, are actually ambiguous, having an inclusive meaning (either *p* or *q*, or both) and an exclusive meaning (either *p* or *q*, but not both). Combined, these factors severely weaken the reliability of a subject's responses.

Similar task design problems occurred in Lakshmanan and Teranishi. The sample item they provided from their English interpretation test is given in

(14), where subjects were to read the sentence and think about each of the following statements separately when indicating whether they agreed or disagreed.

(14) John said that Bill saw himself in the mirror.
    1. 'Himself' cannot be John.   agree   disagree
    2. 'Himself' cannot be Bill.   agree   disagree

Although this design solved problems by avoiding *wh*-questions and by not requiring subjects to rethink options after making choices, it introduced other problems. Specifically, the negative statements employing *cannot* followed by positive and negative agreement options place a heavy cognitive load on subjects (e.g., agreeing requires a negative response to a negative statement). Assuming that this cognitive load in the L2 is alleviated somewhat as English proficiency level increases, it is not surprising that, as Lakshmanan and Teranishi noted, their subjects at the lower proficiency levels gave the highest percentage of incorrect responses.[8]

The task design employed in Berent and Samar (1990) to establish the GCP settings of prelingually deaf adults avoided the problems noted in the previous discussion. As illustrated in (5), there are no *wh*-questions for subjects to process, only simple *yes/no* questions in equation form, presented randomly. Furthermore, subjects were instructed to consider a different possible interpretation for a given sentence for each *yes/no* question. Finally, a procedure was employed that identified responses motivated by pragmatic bias and eliminated them from the statistical analysis. (This design is currently being employed with L2 learners of English in a study in progress.)

Methodological problems notwithstanding, suppose that the results of all of the SLA studies pertaining to the GCP were accurate characterizations of English interlanguage grammars. How could they be explained, and what would be their implications for the SP in SLA?

In Berent (1992), I provided an explanation for the results of existing SLA studies of the GCP that suggested that those results, even if accurate, do not constitute evidence against the application of the SP to SLA. Although Wexler and Manzini (1987) defined the GCP as in (2), Manzini and Wexler (1987) elaborated a more detailed definition of the GCP that incorporates Chomsky's (1981) notion of *accessible subject*. Under this definition a governing category for an anaphor must contain an accessible subject, which includes the subject

---

[8]There are other design problems with Lakshmanan and Teranishi (this volume, chapter 10). One problem involves the fact that there are only 10 test items. Of these, one contains a picture NP, which should not have been included because picture NPs do not abide by the usual GCP constraints. Also, as the authors discussed, responses to some of the test items are susceptible to pragmatic bias. Therefore, the theoretical conclusions that the authors drew are based on subjects' responses to one token each of fewer than nine acceptable sentences.

2. THE SUBSET PRINCIPLE IN SLA

of an NP, infinitive, or small clause, but not the subject NP of a finite clause. In the case of a finite clause, the subject is the agreement element AGR, which is coindexed with the lexical NP and is responsible for subject-verb agreement and the assignment of nominative Case to the lexical subject.

Because of the significant role of AGR in the Principles and Parameters Theory and, in particular, its role as an accessible subject, reasonable questions from the acquisitional perspective are: How and when is AGR acquired in SLA and how does its acquisition influence the setting of GCP values? Errors in phenomena like tense, agreement, and question formation persist for very long periods in SLA. All of these phenomena depend on AGR, either in its role in verb-raising or in its capacity to transmit Θ-roles and agreement features and to assign Case (Chomsky, 1989; Pollock, 1989). Therefore, the lack of AGR in an interlanguage grammar, or its incomplete development, might have far-reaching consequences.

If, in fact, the full instantiation of AGR occurs very late in SLA, then accessible subjects in finite clauses will also be a late development. Under this supposition, the results of the SLA studies of the acquisition of GCP values have a logical explanation irrespective of the SP. Where L2 learners bind anaphors in the root sentence, they do so by virtue of the absence of an accessible subject. Indeed, Aoun (1985) has demonstrated with respect to binding theory that a root sentence is the governing category for a governed element that lacks an accessible subject.

Consider now the sentences in (12) from Finer and Broselow (1986), repeated in (15) with structural detail added.

(15) a. Mr. Fat AGR thinks that [Mr. Thin will AGR paint himself]
     b. Mr. Fat AGR asks Mr. Thin [PRO to paint himself]

If AGR in the embedded clause in (15a) is available to the L2 learner, then this AGR is an accessible subject for the anaphor and defines the embedded clause as the governing category under GCP value (2a). Therefore, *himself* should be bound by *Mr. Thin* in accordance with the SP. But if neither AGR in the embedded clause nor AGR in the matrix clause is available to the learner, then there is no accessible subject for the anaphor and the root sentence serves as the governing category. Accordingly, *himself* may be bound by either *Mr. Fat* or *Mr. Thin*. Pragmatic or semantic considerations should guide the selection of an antecedent, especially in forced-choice tasks requiring judgments on sentences out of context.

In (15b), the presence of the PRO subject of the infinitival clause introduces other acquisitional factors. As noted earlier, the subject of an infinitive is an accessible subject. Therefore, the embedded clause in (15b) is the governing category for *himself* and *himself* is bound by PRO (= *Mr. Thin*), which receives its reference in accordance with both binding and control theory (Chomsky,

1981, 1986b). If L2 learners at certain stages have not acquired the nonlexical category PRO, then there will not be an accessible subject within the infinitival clause in (15b) and the governing category will again be the root sentence as in (15a). Equating the acquisition of AGR with the acquisition of PRO is a reasonable approach inasmuch as Chomsky (1981, p. 52) considered PRO and AGR to be identical: They are both nominal elements that carry person, number, and gender features.

With respect to the acquisition of the English GCP value in SLA, I noted earlier that the results of Finer and Broselow (1986), Finer (1989), Hirakawa (1989), Thomas (1989, 1991), and Lakshmanan and Teranishi (this volume, chapter 10) purportedly provide evidence against a role for the SP in SLA. However, the absence of AGR and PRO as accessible subjects in SLA (Berent, 1992) permits a principled alternative analysis of the results obtained so far in SLA studies of the GCP. The SP would not be expected to apply to the setting of GCP values in SLA until AGR and PRO are acquired. Given this analysis, the results of these studies cannot be taken as evidence against the SP in SLA.

EVIDENCE FOR THE SUBSET PRINCIPLE IN SECOND LANGUAGE ACQUISITION

In the preceding discussions of the Adjacency Parameter, the Configurationality Parameter, and the GCP, I have provided arguments to refute claims in the literature that the SP is inapplicable to SLA.[9] In what follows, I provide evidence in support of the SP's applicability to SLA.

In Berent (1990), I reinterpreted Keenan and Comrie's (1977) *noun phrase accessibility hierarchy* (NPAH) as a parameter of UG associated with the UG principle pertaining to *operator-variable binding*. This principle states that an operator is licensed by binding a variable (Chomsky, 1986b). Within the barriers framework (Chomsky, 1986a), in the sentences of (16), the *wh*-operator *who* moves to the specifier position of the complementizer phrase (CP), leaving behind a coindexed trace, t_i, which is a variable.

(16) a. We saw the girl$_i$ [$_{CP}$ who$_i$ [$_{IP}$ t$_i$ [$_{VP}$ bought the book]]]
    b. We saw the girl$_i$ [$_{CP}$ who$_i$ [$_{IP}$ the boy [$_{VP}$ knows t$_i$]]]
    c. We saw the girl$_i$ [$_{CP}$ who$_i$ [$_{IP}$ the boy [$_{VP}$ took the book [$_{PP}$ from t$_i$]]]]

---

[9]MacLaughlin (1993) also explored the relevance of the SP to various UG parameters, concluding that the putative values of the Adjacency Parameter, the Null Subject Parameter, and, most likely, the Bounding Node Parameter do not satisfy the Subset Condition. She also explored Manzini and Wexler's (1987) GCP and their Proper Antecedent Parameter in some detail, noting potential problems of interaction between these two parameters as well as other problems with binding theory. MacLaughlin (1992) explored some of the same issues discussed in this chapter and arrived at conclusions similar to some of those reached here.

Since *who* c-commands and is coindexed with *t* in each sentence, it binds a variable as required by the principle of operator-variable binding. Also relevant to the binding requirements of relative clause formation is Safir's (1986) *R-binding*, which is binding by the head NP of a relative clause. In (16), *the girl* R-binds the *wh*-operator *who* (as well as the variable *t*). These binding relationships must hold in order for relative clause sentences to be interpreted.

The NPAH reflects the fact that, in a given language, certain NP positions participate in relative clause formation whereas others do not and that patterns of relativizable NPs define an implicational hierarchy, wherein relativization of a given position on the hierarchy implies relativization of all higher positions on the hierarchy. For example, the positions of the traces in (16a)–(16c) indicate relativization of an NP subject (SU), direct object (DO), and object of preposition or oblique NP (OBL), respectively. In accordance with the NPAH, if a language relativizes OBL it will also relativize DO and SU, and if it relativizes DO it will also relativize SU, but the reverse implications do not hold.

In associating these options with operator-variable binding in Berent (1990), I reinterpreted the NPAH as a Relative Clause Parameter (RCP) with values based on the number of maximal projections an R-bound *wh*-operator crosses in order to bind a variable.[10] In (16a) the operator crosses one maximal projection, IP; in (16b) the operator crosses two maximal projections, VP and IP; and in (16c) the operator crosses three maximal projections, PP, VP, and IP. I demonstrated that the values of the RCP define languages that satisfy the Subset Condition (3), and that therefore the SP will apply to determine the acquisition of these parameter values. A language with only SU relatives has the unmarked RCP value defining the smallest language; this value is predicted to be the easiest to learn. A language with SU and DO relatives has a more marked RCP value defining a larger language; this value is predicted to be harder to learn. Finally, a language with SU, DO, and OBL relatives has the most marked RCP value defining the largest language; this value is predicted to be hardest to learn (with respect to the structures in (16) under discussion). English exhibits the most marked value of the RCP.

The learnability predictions of the SP for the RCP were tested in Berent (1990) in an experiment involving prelingually deaf college students as subjects. As in Berent and Samar (1990) with respect to the GCP, I hypothesized

---

[10]To account for differences in the extraction of *wh*-phrases across languages, O'Grady (1987) proposed a *phrase type hierarchy*, which characterizes extraction in terms of types of discontinuity permitted within phrases. Quintero (1992) reinterpreted the phrase-type hierarchy in terms of levels of embeddedness and movement across phrase types in a manner similar to the approach in Berent (1990). However, Quintero did not relate *wh*-movement to a specific UG principle and an associated parameter. Instead, she related L2 learners' development of English relative clauses and *wh*-questions to the application of three learning principles: *cumulative development*, *continuity*, and *conservatism*.

that language acquisition under conditions of restricted auditory input associated with prelingual deafness should suppress the positive evidence required to set the marked English value of the RCP successfully. This hypothesis was confirmed. Subjects with lower general English proficiency showed knowledge of the unmarked SU value of the RCP but little knowledge of the more marked values. Overall, subjects' performance supported the learnability predictions of the SP for the RCP by correlating with the NPAH.

With regard to SLA, if L2 learners' acquisition of English relative clauses also correlated with the NPAH (reinterpreted as the RCP), this would provide evidence that the SP did in fact apply to SLA to determine the learning of RCP values. Indeed, the SLA literature includes several studies that demonstrate that L2 learners acquire English relative clauses in an order that correlates with the NPAH. For example, Gass (1979), Gass and Ard (1984), and Fuller (1983) reported results that reveal that L2 learners, despite language background, produce, judge, and avoid English relative clauses in a manner consistent with the accessibility predictions of the NPAH. Furthermore, in instructional experiments, Gass (1982) and Eckman, Bell, and Nelson (1988) provided results showing that, when L2 learners are taught relative clause formation on the more marked NPAH positions, they generalize this knowledge to the less marked positions, even without instruction on the less marked positions.

Given the reinterpretation of Keenan and Comrie's (1977) NPAH in terms of the RCP in Berent (1990) as a parameter of UG associated with operator-variable binding, the results of these L2 studies of English relative clause acquisition provide support for the application of the SP in SLA. Despite language background, L2 learners of English generally exhibit mastery of the unmarked SU value of the RCP but relatively less knowledge of each of the more marked values. Consistent with Wexler and Manzini's (1987) parametric theory of learnability, where the values of a parameter define languages that lie in a strict subset relation to one another in accordance with the Subset Condition, the SP appears to predict the learning of English RCP values in SLA.

CONCLUSION

The goal of this chapter has been to review and evaluate studies that address the applicability of the SP to SLA. In carrying out this goal, I have employed a methodology that involves two tests of a study's validity—one that assesses the appropriateness of task design and one that assesses the soundness of theoretical linguistic proposals. I hope to have shown that attention to both concerns is essential for successful SLA theory construction.

Although the case is by no means closed on the extent to which the SP might apply in SLA, the methodology employed here reveals that arguments levied to date against the SP's application to SLA cannot be accepted as valid and that, furthermore, arguments in support of the SP's application to SLA can be developed on the basis of existing theoretical constructs and existing L2 data. Much further research is required both to identify other UG parameters to which the SP might apply and to determine whether the SP guides the setting of these parameters in SLA.

ACKNOWLEDGMENTS

This study was conducted at the National Technical Institute for the Deaf, a college of Rochester Institute of Technology, in the course of an agreement with the U.S. Department of Education. I would like to thank Vince Samar for offering valuable comments on this chapter. An earlier version of the chapter was presented at the Michigan State University Conference on Applied Linguistics (Theory Construction and Methodology in Second Language Acquisition Research), October 4–6, 1991.

REFERENCES

Aoun, J. (1985). *A grammar of anaphora*. Cambridge, MA: MIT Press.

Berent, G. P. (1983). Control judgments by deaf adults and by second language learners. *Language Learning, 33*, 37–53.

Berent, G. P. (1988). An assessment of syntactic capabilities. In M. Strong (Ed.), *Language learning and deafness* (pp. 133–161). Cambridge: Cambridge University Press.

Berent, G. P. (1990, March). *Relative clause learnability: Second language and deaf learner data*. Paper presented at the 24th annual convention of Teachers of English to Speakers of Other Languages, San Francisco, CA.

Berent, G. P. (1992, April). *Accessible subjects and the governing category parameter in second language acquisition*. Paper presented at the 12th Second Language Research Forum, East Lansing, MI.

Berent, G. P. (in press). The acquisition of English syntax by deaf learners. In W. C. Ritchie & T. J. Bhatia (Eds.), *Handbook of language acquisition*. San Diego, CA: Academic Press.

Berent, G. P., & Samar, V. J. (1990). The psychological reality of the subset principle: Evidence from the governing categories of prelingually deaf adults. *Language, 66*, 714–741.

Berwick, R. C. (1985). *The acquisition of syntactic knowledge*. Cambridge, MA: MIT Press.

Chomsky, N. (1981). *Lectures on government and binding*. Dordrecht: Foris.

Chomsky, N. (1986a). *Barriers*. Cambridge, MA: MIT Press.

Chomsky, N. (1986b). *Knowledge of language: Its nature, origin, and use*. New York: Praeger.

Chomsky, N. (1989). Some notes on economy of derivation and representation. *MIT Working Papers in Linguistics, 10*, 43–74.

Eckman, F., Bell, L., & Nelson, D. (1988). On the generalization of relative clause instruction in the acquisition of English as a second language. *Applied Linguistics, 9*, 1–20.

Finer, D. (1989, February). *Binding parameters in second language acquisition*. Paper presented at the Second Language Research Forum, Los Angeles, CA.

Finer, D., & Broselow, E. (1986). Second language acquisition of reflexive binding. *Proceedings of the North Eastern Linguistic Society, 16*, 154–168.

Fuller, J. W. (1983, March). *Relative clause comprehension and the noun phrase accessibility hierarchy.* Paper presented at the annual convention of Teachers of English to Speakers of Other Languages, Toronto.

Gass, S. (1979). Language transfer and universal grammatical relations. *Language Learning, 29*, 327–344.

Gass, S. (1982). From theory to practice. In M. Hines & W. Rutherford (Eds.), *On TESOL '81.* Washington, DC: Teachers of English to Speakers of Other Languages.

Gass, S., & Ard, J. (1984). Second language acquisition and the ontology of language universals. In W. E. Rutherford (Ed.), *Language universals and second language acquisition.* Amsterdam: John Benjamins.

Grimshaw, J., & Rosen, S. T. (1990). Knowledge and obedience: The developmental status of the binding theory. *Linguistic Inquiry, 21*, 187–222.

Hale, K. (1983). Walpiri and the grammar of non-configurational languages. *Natural Language and Linguistic Theory, 1*, 5–47.

Hirakawa, M. (1989, April). *L2 acquisition of English reflexives by speakers of Japanese.* Paper presented at the Conference on the Interaction of Linguistics, Second Language Acquisition, and Speech Pathology, University of Wisconsin, Milwaukee, WI.

Iatridou, S. (1990). About Agr(P). *Linguistic Inquiry, 21*, 551–577.

Keenan, E., & Comrie, B. (1977). Noun phrase accessibility and universal grammar. *Linguistic Inquiry, 8*, 63–99.

Kuroda, S.-Y. (1988). Whether we agree or not: The comparative grammar of English and Japanese. *Linguisticae Investigationes, 12*, 1–44.

MacLaughlin, D. (1993). *Language acquisition and the subset principle.* Manuscript submitted for publication.

MacLaughlin, D. (1992, October). *Second language acquisition and the subset principle.* Paper presented at the 17th Boston University Conference on Language Development, Boston, MA.

Manzini, M. R., & Wexler, K. (1987). Parameters, binding theory, and learnability. *Linguistic Inquiry, 18*, 413–444.

Michigan Test of English Language Proficiency (1977). Ann Arbor, MI: English Language Institute, University of Michigan.

O'Grady, W. (1987). *Principles of grammar and learning.* Chicago: University of Chicago Press.

Pollock, J.-I. (1989). Verb movement, universal grammar, and the structure of IP. *Linguistic Inquiry, 20*, 365–424.

Quigley, S. P., & King, C. M. (1980). Syntactic performance of hearing impaired and normal hearing individuals. *Applied Psycholinguistics, 1*, 329–356.

Quintero, K. W. (1992). Learnability and the acquisition of extraction in relative clauses and *wh*-questions. *Studies in Second Language Acquisition, 14*, 39–70.

Rutherford, W. (1989). Preemption and the learning of L2 grammars. *Studies in Second Language Acquisition, 11*, 441–457.

Safir, K. (1986). Relative clauses in a theory of binding and levels. *Linguistic Inquiry, 17*, 663–689.

Saito, M. (1985). *Some asymmetries in Japanese and their theoretical implications.* Doctoral dissertation, MIT.

Schwartz, B. D., & Gubala-Ryzak, M. (1992). Learnability and grammar reorganization in L2A: Against negative evidence causing the unlearning of verb movement. *Second Language Research, 8*, 1–93.

Stowell, T. (1981). *The origins of phrase structure.* Doctoral dissertation, MIT.

Swisher, M. V. (1989). The language-learning situation of deaf students. *TESOL Quarterly, 23*, 239–257.

Thomas, M. (1989). The interpretation of English reflexive pronouns by nonnative speakers. *Studies in Second Language Acquisition, 11*, 281–301.

Thomas, M. (1991). Universal Grammar and the interpretation of reflexives in a second language. *Language, 67* , 211–239.

Wexler, K., & Manzini, M. R. (1987). Parameters and learnability in binding theory. In T. Roeper & E. Williams (Eds.), *Parameter setting* (pp. 41–76). Dordrecht: Reidel.

White, L. (1989a). The adjacency condition on case assignment: Do L2 learners observe the Subset Principle? In S. M. Gass & J. Schachter (Eds.), *Linguistic perspectives on second language acquisition* (pp. 134–158). Cambridge: Cambridge University Press.

White, L. (1989b). *Universal grammar and second language acquisition*. Amsterdam: John Benjamins.

White, L. (1991). The verb-movement parameter in second language acquisition. *Language Acquisition, 1*, 337–360.

Zobl, H. (1988). Configurationality and the subset principle: The acquisition of V^1 by Japanese learners of English. In J. Pankhurst, M. Sharwood Smith, & P. Van Buren (Eds.), *Learnability and second languages* (pp. 116–131). Dordrecht: Foris.

3

ANECDOTE OR EVIDENCE? EVALUATING SUPPORT FOR HYPOTHESES CONCERNING THE DEVELOPMENT OF TENSE AND ASPECT

Kathleen Bardovi-Harlig
Indiana University

This chapter addresses the question of what constitutes evidence for hypotheses concerning the acquisition of tense and aspect by adult second-language learners. The hypotheses under investigation are the two that have emerged as the leading competitors in current American and European research on the development of interlanguage temporal semantics. These hypotheses concern the meaning and function of tense and aspect markers in interlanguage, independent of the target language. The aspect hypothesis claims that interlanguage verbal systems are primarily aspectual in nature, and the discourse hypothesis, that they are determined by discourse structure.[1]

To a certain degree, what constitutes evidence for these hypotheses is much the same as what constitutes evidence for any hypothesis in second-language acquisition (SLA) research. In contrast to the chapters in this volume that examine research methodology and the testing of hypotheses in SLA as a field, this chapter presents a case study of hypothesis testing and research methodology in a small but active area of investigation in SLA. The chapter begins with a brief review of the generally accepted stages in the development of temporal systems. The next sections examine the aspect and discourse

---

[1]This chapter will not review traditional or contemporary studies of morpheme acquisition order. For an informative study on the acquisition order of simple past and past progressive, see Bailey (1989). For a discussion of variability in planned and unplanned oral and written narratives, see Ellis (1987).

hypotheses individually. The final sections evaluate the evidence that has been used to support the hypotheses, laying out areas of agreement and conflict, and they suggest modifications in research design for further hypothesis testing.

OVERVIEW

Recent work on the development of temporality in interlanguage examines the meaning and function of emerging verb morphology and may be characterized as belonging to the subfields of semantics and discourse analysis, areas known to European linguists as functional semantics. The investigations have focused on the expression of past time and, as a result, on the acquisition of past tense morphology in a variety of target languages. This chapter reviews 12 recent studies that explore the meaning and function of interlanguage verbal morphology.

Both the discourse and the aspect hypotheses are concerned with accounting for the distribution of tense markers and base forms (i.e., forms with no tense markers). In his study of the acquisition of German as a second language by adult learners, Meisel (1987) found that in the earliest stage of development learners tend to use invariant forms. For the most part, invariant forms are base forms—that is, morphologically unmarked forms—but they may also be morphologically marked forms, such as the English past form *went* or progressive form *going*, not used in alternation with other forms. During this stage, when verb morphology either is not used or is not used systematically, learners rely on other means to convey temporal reference, namely, adverbials, calendric reference, and sequential ordering, as Schumann's (1987) study of adult learners of English showed.[2] It is the point at which verb morphology begins to be used systematically that is of particular interest in the studies reviewed here.

CURRENT RESEARCH

The Aspect Hypothesis

Two aspect hypotheses have been formulated in interlanguage research, the defective tense hypothesis (Andersen, 1986, 1991) and the primacy of aspect hypothesis (Robison, 1990). The defective tense hypothesis states: "In beginning stages of language acquisition only *inherent aspectual* [emphasis original]

---

[2]See Meisel (1987) and Bardovi-Harlig (1992d) for a discussion of the use of adverbials and sequential ordering by more advanced learners.

distinctions are encoded by verbal morphology, not tense or grammatical aspect" (Andersen, 1991, p. 307). Andersen showed that children learning Spanish as a second language use the imperfect and preterite inflections, which encode grammatical aspect in Spanish, to redundantly mark lexical aspect. Robison (1990) proposed an equivalent hypothesis that he called the primacy of aspect hypothesis, explaining that "aspect is primary in the sense not that morphemes that denote aspect in the target language are acquired first, but that target language verbal morphemes, independent of their function in the target language are first used by the learner to mark aspect" (p. 316). He showed that an adult learner of English generally used the regular or irregular past marker to mark punctual verbs and used *-ing* to mark durative verbs in the portion of the language sample that showed use of verbal morphology. Kaplan (1987) showed that college students learning French as a foreign language distinguished perfective from nonperfective aspect in past-time contexts by using the passé composé (functionally a preterite) to mark perfective events and the present to mark nonevents or imperfective aspect. These and other studies are outlined in Table 3.1.

The tendency to mark aspect has also been observed in creoles by Bickerton (1975, 1981) and Givón (1982), and in child language by Antinucci and Miller (1976) and Bronckart and Sinclair (1973), among others. When aspect is expressed at the expense of tense, tense is said to be defective. This led Weist, Wysocka, Witkowska-Stadnik, Buczowska, and Konieczna (1984) to propose the defective tense hypothesis for child language acquisition, which has, as we have seen, been reformulated by Andersen (1986, 1991) for interlanguage.

The Discourse Hypothesis

The discourse hypothesis for interlanguage development states that learners use emerging verbal morphology to distinguish foreground from background in narratives. The interlanguage discourse hypothesis is derived from Hopper's cross-linguistic work on aspectual markers in narrative discourse. Hopper (1979) claimed that aspect could not be understood without reference to discourse organization, specifically the classification of narrative events as either foreground or background. The foreground relates events belonging to the skeletal structure of the discourse (Hopper, 1979) and consists of clauses that move time forward (Dry, 1983). The background does not itself narrate main events, but provides supportive material that elaborates on or evaluates the events in the foreground (Hopper, 1979). Hopper argued that it is a "universal of narrative discourse that in any extended text an overt distinction is made between the language of the actual story line [the foreground] and the language of the supportive material [the background]" (p. 213).

TABLE 3.1
Summary of Research

Study	Subjects	L1/Level	Procedure	Findings/Conclusions
Aspect Studies				
Schumann (1987) (English)	5 adult subjects, contact learners	1 Chinese, 1 Japanese, 3 Spanish speakers/ basilang	Conversational interviews	Only 20% accuracy on past. Verbal morphology (VM) not used to make tense or aspect distinction. Adverbials, chronological order, context used to express temporality.
Andersen (1986, 1991) (Spanish)	2 children, longitudinal, F 8, 10 M 12, 14	English	Interviews	Defective tense hypothesis (DTH): In the beginning stages of language acquisition only inherent aspectual distinctions are encoded by verbal morphology, not tense or grammatical aspect. Preterite→punctual, telic events, activities, states. Imperfect→states, activities, telic events, punctual events.
Robison (1990) (English)	1 adult, 2 years high school, 3 semesters in adult education courses	Spanish/Lower mesolang	60-minute interview, 553 tokens, 171 verbs	Primacy of aspect hypothesis (see DTH): *-ing* tends to mark durative verbs; PAST/*en* tends to mark punctual verbs. Prediction supported is that, although the exact pattern will vary depending on L1, L2, and individual differences between learners, VM correlates with lexical aspect at least during some stage in the development of interlanguage.
Kaplan (1987) (French, FL)	16 college students	English/ Beginning & intermediate	Interviews; FL learners responded to questions	Passé composé is acquired before the imperfect. Passé composé marks perfective events; nonevents (imperfective) are marked first by present tense and imperfect, then by the imperfect alone. Aspectual organization over time marking may be a universal feature of language acquisition.

Study	Subjects	Data	Findings
Trévise (1987) (French)	2 adults, mid-40s, little or no formal education. Subj 1, 3.5 years; Subj 2, 6 months in France	Spanish/level not specified; instruction: Subj 1, < 3 months; Subj 2, 3 months	Narratives from conversational interviews	Learners use little or no verbal morphology. Subj 1 made past/present distinction with a few verbs. Conjunctions, chronological order, and adverbs used. "Aspectual values are complex and should not be reduced to the simplistic active/stative distinction" (p. 241). Trévise concluded that the complexity of the aspectual and temporal relations expressed exceeds the complexity of the verbal morphology used.
Meisel (1987) (German)	45 learners, 15–65 yrs., little formal education; 6 longitudinal subjects	Italian, Portuguese, Spanish/low level	Conversational interviews, some formal tasks and oral proficiency tests	Aspect may be marginal, not systematic in adult L2 acquisition. Child language (L1) and creoles differ from adult interlanguage with respect to functions expressed and formal devices.
Bardovi-Harlig (1992b) (English)	135 ESL classroom learners	Various L1s/6 levels: beginning to advanced	Cross-sectional cloze passage, essays from intermediates	(Lexical) Aspectual categories may influence use of verbal morphology. Highest appropriate use of simple past found for punctual verbs. Highest rate of use of past progressive found on duratives. Essays also showed duratives with past progressive in first occurrence; other innovative use of tense marking: past perfect as a scene-setter in introductions.

Discourse Studies

Study	Subjects	Data	Findings
Véronique (1987) (French)	7 adult immigrants, illiterate in L1 & L2, 30s, 5–25 years in France	5 Arabic, 2 Berber/ 2 low, 3 intermediate, 2 advanced based on oral interaction	Past-time passages from interviews, 3 narratives each where possible	All learners showed V-stem/ (aux)+V+e (past participle) contrast. Learners differ in the way V-stem and past participle forms are distributed between background & foreground. Low level: V-stem appears in foreground, V+e forms in the background. Intermediate and Advanced: V+e forms in foreground, V-stem in background with variation within and across subjects. Use of VM is not determined by backgrounding & foregrounding.

(Continued)

TABLE 3.1
(Continued)

Study	Subjects	L1/Level	Procedure	Findings/Conclusions
Discourse Studies (cont.)				
Kumpf (1984) (English)	1 adult, 28 years residence in U.S., has stopped acquiring	Japanese, rudimentary level, 48% of verbs show tense morphology	Conversational interview (172 verbs)	1. Completed action in the foreground is expressed in the base form. No tensing. 2. Background is the domain of tense. Most verbs are marked for tense, especially statives. Statives are tensed, active Vs are marked for habitual (USETA or IN) and continucus (V + IN) aspect and irregularly for tense.
Flashner (1989) (English)	3 adults, limited instruction in English, in US >2 years, 59+ years old	Russian, 1 beginner, 1 intermed, 1 advanced	Narrative passages from conversational interviews (mean sample 415 clauses)	All 3 speakers had tense system for copula; tense in lexical verbs randomly marked. Aspectual rather than tense distinctions. Past forms indicated perfective actions in foreground, nonpast forms showed imperfective functions that correlated with background. Concluded aspectual system transfers from Russian. That learners mark binary aspectual distinctions in delineating foreground from background is more important than which marking is more prototypical for 2LLs.
Bardovi-Harlig (1992c) (English)	16 ESL classroom learners	Mixed/Intermediate	Oral and written story-retells	Differential influence of discourse on tense use. 9 learners showed discourse-sensitive use of tense; 7 learners showed discourse-neutral use. Foreground characterized by use of past, background by base and present.
Phonetic Studies				
Wolfram (1985, 1989) (English)	32 adult immigrants, 1 adult for discourse analysis	Vietnamese, length of residence 1–3 and 4–7 years	Interviews	Could not replicate Kumpf (1984). Claimed that an unrealistic view of the nature of variation presently represents some attempts to account for shifting tense forms. Marking dependent on the phonetic form of the past tense ending (irregular, /Id/, /d/, /t/).

Analyses of the structure of learner narratives suggest that interlanguage also has such markers (Kumpf, 1984; Flashner, 1989; Bardovi-Harlig, 1992c). The findings from these studies are contradictory, however. Although these studies found the distribution of tense markers to be influenced by discourse organization, conflicting marking has been reported. Kumpf (1984) found that in the English narratives of one adult native speaker of Japanese, punctual verbs in the foreground were unmarked base forms, whereas the background showed morphological marking. This is in keeping with what Givón (1982) described for creole. In contrast, Flashner (1989) and Bardovi-Harlig (1992c) found that foreground verbs typically carry past tense marking, whereas background verbs carry nonpast marking (unmarked base forms and present forms). Véronique (1987) found some learners with one or the other of the two systems and one learner who used both systems, one in each of two narratives and neither in a third narrative. These studies are also outlined in Table 3.1.[3]

Summary

In the closing of his article Robison (1990) observed that "while the exact pattern [of development] will vary depending on L1, L2, and individual differences between learners, verbal morphology correlates with lexical aspect at least during some stage in the development of interlanguage" (p. 330). Although the tentativeness of this claim accurately reflects the state of our combined knowledge, this is a much weaker claim than that made in his original formulation of the primacy of aspect hypothesis. At this stage in the field, neither of the hypotheses seems to be dominant. In spite of this, some investigators apparently assume one hypothesis or the other. Hatch, Shirai, and Fantuzzi (1990) presupposed a discourse hypothesis when introducing the data in their appendix: "We expect the simple tense (past or present) will be used for the main story line . . . Tense cannot be described without reference to narrative structure and the goal of the storyteller" (p. 715).

RESEARCH METHODOLOGY: FROM ANECDOTE TO EVIDENCE

As two promising hypotheses compete in studies of the development of tense and aspect systems in interlanguage, it is appropriate to consider what types of data are necessary to test and evaluate them in order to move from anec-

---

[3]Godfrey (1980) offered a discourse analysis of tense use in the monologues of adult ESL learners, based on tense continuity. Although Godfrey's work was among the earliest to examine discourse-level constraints on tense use, the analysis did not have the influence on the field that Kumpf's study has had and is consequently not reviewed.

dote to evidence. The findings of previous investigations of the use of tense and aspect marking by second-language learners are influenced by a number of factors: level of proficiency, individual variation, number and mode of language samples, subject selection, and first language. These are factors that all interlanguage inquiries must take into account. In addition, in order to test the specific hypotheses discussed here, the choice of task and the type of analysis are central. In the sections that follow, each of the factors is discussed. The first two factors, level of proficiency and individual variation, are crucial to the interpretation of current and future studies. They have been the subject of speculation in the literature but have not been investigated directly.

Proficiency Level

Proficiency level influences the use of verbal morphology, whether we look at this relationship from the point of view of the aspect hypothesis or the discourse hypothesis. Although the studies that have been reported to date are not entirely comparable, development may be schematized as in Fig. 3.1. Schumann's (1987) characterization of very low proficiency learners as showing no systematic use of verbal morphology is taken as describing the initial stage in the development of temporality, regardless of framework. Within the framework of the aspect hypotheses, represented by the path labeled "Aspectual Analyses" in Fig. 3.1, development proceeds as follows: In the initial stages, learners show no systematic use of verbal morphology (Schumann, 1987). As tense morphology emerges, its earliest use is to mark lexical aspect (Andersen, 1986, 1991; Robison, 1990). Intermediate classroom learners show influence of aspectual class with respect to use of verbal morphology, but they also show other innovative uses of verbal morphology (such as using past perfect for scene-setting regardless of temporal reference). This suggests that the not-entirely-targetlike association of verbal morphology and lexical aspect may be merely one of a group of innovative associations made by intermediate learners of English (Bardovi-Harlig, 1992b). Ultimately, the use of tense/aspect marking is generalized beyond its early association with lexical aspect to resemble the target system (Andersen, 1991; Bardovi-Harlig, 1992b).

Within the framework of the discourse hypothesis, the data suggest a similar process of generalization. The earliest use of verbal morphology by low-level learners is unsystematic (Schumann, 1987). The majority of the discourse studies suggest that as tense morphology emerges and begins to be used systematically, it is used to distinguish background from foreground (Flashner, 1989; Kumpf, 1984). This development is represented by the higher path through the discourse-sensitive use of verb morphology in Fig. 3.1 in the

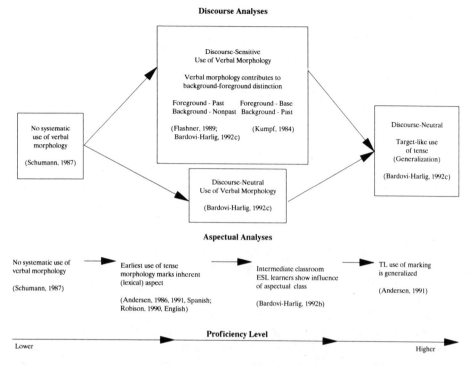

Discourse Analyses

Discourse-Sensitive
Use of Verbal Morphology

Verbal morphology contributes to
background-foreground distinction

Foreground - Past   Foreground - Base
Background - Nonpast Background - Past

(Flashner, 1989;   (Kumpf, 1984)
Bardovi-Harlig, 1992c)

No systematic
use of verbal
morphology

(Schumann, 1987)

Discourse-Neutral

Target-like use
of tense
(Generalization)

(Bardovi-Harlig, 1992c)

Discourse-Neutral
Use of Verbal Morphology

(Bardovi-Harlig, 1992c)

Aspectual Analyses

No systematic use of
verbal morphology

(Schumann, 1987)

Earliest use of tense
morphology marks inherent
(lexical) aspect

(Andersen, 1986, 1991, Spanish;
Robison, 1990, English)

Intermediate classroom
ESL learners show influence
of aspectual class

(Bardovi-Harlig, 1992b)

TL use of marking
is generalized

(Andersen, 1991)

Proficiency Level

Lower   Higher

FIG. 3.1.   Hypothesized routes of development.

section labeled "Discourse Analyses." (We will consider the lower path in the next section.) Targetlike use of past tense morphology in past-time narrative contexts will involve generalization of past tense from a marker of foreground (or background) to a genuine tense marker used throughout the narrative (Bardovi-Harlig, 1992c).

The hypothesized patterns (which are based on unrelated studies) can be tested only through cross-sectional and/or longitudinal investigations. Although cross-sectional studies are very useful in revealing general patterns, only longitudinal studies can potentially answer the question of individual variation: Is it the case that some learners never show aspectual or discourse-sensitive use of target temporal morphology?

Individual Variation

Most of the studies in this area have used a small number of learners, but small populations cannot provide the evidence necessary to test either hypothesis, especially because preliminary evidence suggests that not all learners make the same hypotheses regarding aspect or discourse. In this section

I draw evidence from two studies that I have conducted as part of a larger ongoing investigation of the development of temporality.

In a study that analyzed narratives told by 16 intermediate learners in a story-retell task, I found that nine learners showed discourse-sensitive use of tense and seven did not (Bardovi-Harlig, 1992c). Results in three cases of the seven seem to be related to level of proficiency. Two learners used so little past tense morphology (23% and 15% in past-time contexts) that no pattern can be inferred from its distribution. The third learner was so targetlike that 91% of the verbs were appropriately marked for past. The remaining four learners, however, were at the same accuracy level with respect to the overall use of past tense morphology as their discourse-sensitive counterparts but showed discourse-neutral use of tense morphology. (The discourse-neutral group showed rates of appropriate use ranging from 34% to 52% and the discourse-sensitive group, rates ranging from 31% to 64%.) The differences in learner hypotheses are summarized in the upper portion of Fig. 3.1, labeled "Discourse Analyses." The upper route, marked "Discourse-Sensitive Use," represents the route taken by the learners reported on in Kumpf and Flashner and by nine of the learners in my study. The lower route might be the one taken by the four learners in the study who show discourse-neutral use of verbal morphology at the same relative level of proficiency as that of the other learners who show discourse-sensitive tense use.

In a cross-sectional study of learners at six levels of proficiency, I found that one-third of the intermediate learners (15 learners out of 45) used verbal morphology to redundantly mark lexical aspect (Bardovi-Harlig, 1992b). They used past progressive to mark lexical durativity as in *were living* and *was working* and simple past to mark punctual verbs such as *died*. The other two-thirds showed largely appropriate use of simple past. What cross-sectional data do not show, however, is whether the learners whose interlanguages do not show the hypothesized distribution of verbal morphology ever do produce that distribution. From cross-sectional studies there is no way to tell whether the distribution is due to proficiency level (the learners were too advanced and had just passed through that stage, or they were not advanced enough and had not yet entered that stage) or individual variation (those learners never had entertained or never would entertain that hypothesis). The cross-sectional results are consistent with both Robison's and Meisel's interpretation of the data, even though these interpretations are contradictory. If level is taken to be the relevant variable, then the findings are consistent with Robison's (1990) prediction that "verbal morphology correlates with lexical aspect *at least during some stage* [italics added] in the development of IL" (p. 330). If, however, individual variation is understood as the relevant variable, then Meisel's (1987) claim that the use of aspectual notions may be a learner-specific characteristic is supported.

To address the question of individual variation, studies must be expanded to include more learners. Only the larger studies have revealed noticeable variation (Meisel, 1987; Bardovi-Harlig, 1992b, 1992c). As shown earlier, proficiency level and individual variation are variables that must be teased apart. Longitudinal studies are also crucial in determining the extent to which individuals vary. Although the questions of proficiency level and individual variation must be addressed in order to evaluate the hypotheses, there are other important issues as well.

Language Samples

In addition to collecting language samples from a number of learners, we also need to collect more than one narrative from each learner. Véronique's (1987) findings suggest that learners' use of verbal morphology may vary with topic, as does Selinker and Douglas's work on discourse domains (1985, this volume, chapter 6). Elicited narratives may also differ from personal narratives. Kumpf (1984) observed, for example, that in the 250 clauses from personal narratives, there were twice as many background clauses as foreground clauses. In a story retell task, I found the opposite ratio: There were more than twice as many foreground clauses as background clauses (Bardovi-Harlig, 1992c).

Related to the need to collect more than one narrative from a learner is the necessity of collecting data in different modalities. Although most of the data have been collected orally, the collection of written narratives from classroom second- and foreign-language learners may offer several advantages.[4] In cases like French, where the aspectual forms are separated by only a slight phonetic distinction, learners may show greater differentiation of forms in writing. Moreover, learners may be able to sustain longer narratives in writing than in conversation at early stages of acquisition. A study that examined daily journal entries written by learners and oral interviews during the learners' first six months in an intensive English program found that learners who relied heavily on scaffolding and phrasal responses in conversational interviews were able to produce connected narratives in their journals (Bardovi-Harlig, 1992d). Thus, written data may allow us to test learners at earlier stages.

Written narratives may also prove informative in cases where pronunciation difficulty is hypothesized as the cause of lack of regular past tense marking, as in the case of English (Wolfram, 1985, 1989; Godfrey, 1980). Learners

---

[4]Ellis (1987) tested the influence of modality and planning in narrative discourse on the accuracy rates of three morphemes (regular past, irregular past, and the past copula), examining planned speech, writing, and unplanned speech. There has been no published study that I know of that examines these variables in relation to either the aspect or discourse hypothesis.

may have acquired an orthographic representation for morphemes that they cannot pronounce in particular environments.

Subjects

The research in this area so far has largely focused on untutored second-language learners, although one study has included classroom foreign-language learners (Kaplan, 1987), and two studies, classroom second-language learners (Bardovi-Harlig, 1992c, 1992b). (See Table 3.1 for a summary of the population investigated by each study reviewed here.) A recent study compared the use of tense/aspect morphology by classroom learners of English as a second language and French as a foreign language in narratives elicited by means of a film-retell task (Bardovi-Harlig & Bergström, 1993). The examination of the interlanguage of a variety of populations is necessary to test the proposed universality of the hypotheses.

We must also ask whether all learners are equally likely to establish aspectual or discourse systems. More specifically, we should ask whether untutored learners or untutored fossilized learners are more likely to establish or elaborate nontargetlike systems than are classroom learners or instructed-contact learners (i.e., classroom learners in a host environment). Moreover, from the examination of the published data, contact learners and instructed-contact learners appear to differ in eventual attainment with respect to both accuracy and appropriate use of verbal morphology. The investigation of instructed second-language learners may offer the best opportunity to study the later stages of tense/aspect development.

Subjects should be randomly selected and data from all subjects should be analyzed. This is a well-known principle, but it bears repeating in an area of inquiry that is so dependent on long connected texts for data, and that has been investigated largely by means of case studies. We cannot afford to select only those subjects who are particularly good storytellers or accomplished conversationalists. These learners may conceivably employ different linguistic devices or employ them more skillfully than less accomplished storytellers. Sampling the oral (and written) styles of different types of learners may be necessary for an unbiased view of learner narrative and conversation construction.

First Language

Also related to the issue of subject selection is first language. Although it is not clear what role first language plays in the development of tense and aspect systems, this is an area that has not been adequately investigated. The studies of learners with heterogeneous language backgrounds have shown no apparent difference across first language. Likewise, the case studies offer no evidence of first-language influence. It should also be noted, however, that none of these studies was designed to test transfer phenomena. Only Flashner (1989) concluded that transfer is a factor in determining interlanguage tense and aspect systems. She interpreted the marking of foreground events by past and background events or situations by nonpast as the transfer of aspectual categories from Russian.

A second area of potential first-language influence is in the pronunciation of past tense forms, or what Wolfram has called low-level phonetic constraints. The pronunciation of word-final consonants or consonant clusters would seem to be particularly susceptible to first-language influence. To date, the phonetic-distribution hypothesis has been tested only in a study of Vietnamese learners of English (Wolfram, 1985, 1989) and Chinese learners of English (Bayley, this volume, chapter 9) whose native languages do not allow word-final consonant clusters. Repetition of these studies with speakers of mixed language backgrounds is warranted.

Task Selection

This chapter has discussed some of the modifications in collection procedures that are needed to establish evidence for either hypothesis. To bring this area of investigation to a point where we can determine which hypothesis best captures development in second-language acquisition, we also need to evaluate different hypotheses using the same data. In this case, the selection of the task is constrained by the discourse hypothesis. Because the discourse hypothesis is necessarily concerned with the distribution of verbal morphology with respect to narrative structure, all language samples must be narrative in form. This does not narrowly limit the type of interaction, however, as narratives may be found in conversations as well as stories and may be oral or written.

Elicitation tasks that have been used to supplement narratives in the investigation of the aspect hypothesis alone (e.g., cloze passages and short scenarios modeled on Dahl's 1985 cross-linguistic work; see also Bardovi-Harlig, 1992a, 1992b) are probably not appropriate in studies that test both the aspect and the discourse hypotheses. Although such elicitation tasks have the advantage of balancing production across learners and ensuring equal production of tokens from various aspectual classes, they do not provide learners an opportunity to construct text, an activity that is central to testing the discourse hypothesis. To test the discourse hypothesis, more data must be collected, because of the creative nature of text construction. Learners do not use the same verbs, nor do they provide comparable samples in all aspectual categories and across background and foreground. This makes multiple samples from individuals and larger populations even more necessary.

A second consideration is the choice between personal narratives or elicited narratives. Noyau (1990) argued that the personal narrative that occurs in free conversation gives the "richest picture of [interlanguage] temporality" (p. 147). Labov and Waletzky (1967) demonstrated the advantage of personal narratives, especially the danger-of-death scenario, in narrative research. In these cases, however, it is not possible to manipulate features of the narrative, a technique that might be highly desirable in testing the hypotheses, as discussed later.

In contrast, much work has employed elicited narratives through retelling of silent films (e.g., the well-known Pear Stories, Chafe, 1980; the European Science Foundation investigation, Bhardwaj, Dietrich, & Noyau, 1988), performed stories (Bardovi-Harlig, 1992c), and picture stories (Bamberg, 1987; Bamberg & Marchman, 1990). The advantages of the retell tasks are that the sequence of events is known to the researcher independently of the narrative itself and that such narratives can be compared across learners. Moreover, the content of the story in the case of story- or picture-prompted narratives may be manipulated to test specific rules of distribution. Similarly, films may be chosen on the basis of content. Materials with rich background are important in encouraging learners to include background information, particularly because Tomlin (1984) found that under the communicative pressure of on-line narratives, background information is lost: "This reduction is governed by a foregrounding strategy of producing pivotal or foregrounded information at the expense of background information" (p. 137). It is possible that oral narrative presentations may increase the production of background by providing a model.[5]

The basic considerations having been outlined, we must ask how the tasks could be designed to reveal which hypothesis best accounts for interlanguage tense/aspect use. There is a certain amount of overlap between the two hypotheses insofar as the classification of verbs by aspectual class and grounding is concerned. We assume here that the relevant distinction in aspectual class is between telic verbs and atelic verbs. Telic verbs have inherent endpoints or goals and include achievements (e.g., *die, find, realize*) and accomplishments (e.g., *build a house, paint a picture, walk a mile*). (See Vendler, 1967; Dowty, 1979; and Mourelatos, 1981, for a discussion of aspectual classes.) Atelic verbs have no inherent endpoint or goal and include activities (e.g., *walk, sleep, run*) and states (e.g., *have, own, like*). Telic verbs may populate the foreground and atelic verbs, the background. The aspect hypothesis predicts that telic verbs will carry simple past morphology, and the discourse

---

[5]The oral presentation of narratives for the purpose of retell tasks introduces the additional variable of comprehension, which may make this type of task more difficult for at least some learners (see Bardovi-Harlig, 1992c). In addition, all retell tasks introduce the variable of memory. (See Bley-Vroman and Chaudron, this volume, chapter 13, for a discussion of these and other variables.)

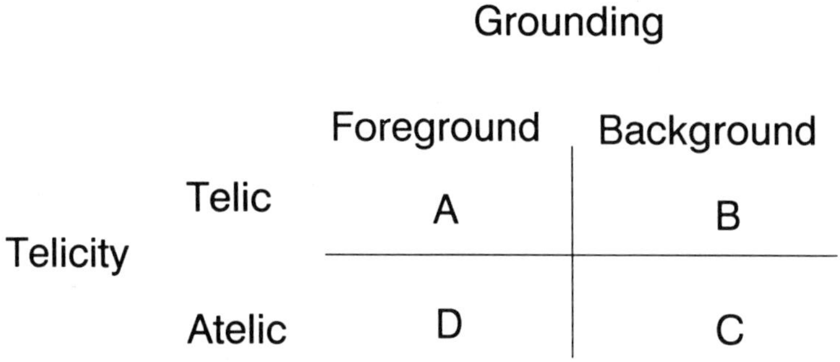

FIG. 3.2. Classification of verbs in the aspect and discourse hypotheses.

hypothesis predicts that the foreground will carry simple past morphology.[6] Thus, when telic verbs occur in the foreground (Cell A in Fig. 3.2), the two hypotheses cannot be distinguished. Similarly, when atelic verbs occur in the background (Cell C in Fig. 3.2), their lack of past tense marking can be interpreted as support for either the aspect or the discourse hypothesis. In other words, when telic verbs are in the foreground and atelic verbs are in the background of a narrative, the aspect and discourse hypotheses cannot be distinguished.

However, the two types of classification do not always coincide. Any event that is reported in sequence can be part of the foreground.[7] Thus, activities can appear in the foreground. In fact, Dry (1981, 1983) argues persuasively that even states can occur in the foreground. Similarly, any event that is reported out of sequence, for example, to provide historical information regarding a foregrounded event, to make a prediction, or to provide an evaluation, belongs to the background regardless of aspectual class. Thus, telic verbs may also be found in the background.

The test cases, then, become those in which telicity and foreground, on the one hand, and atelicity and background, on the other, are not coincident. The revealing cases would be those in which telic verbs occur in the background (Cell B) and atelic verbs occur in the foreground (Cell D). If foreground verbs, regardless of aspectual class, were marked in the simple past tense, and background verbs occurred as base forms in early and/or intermediate interlanguage narratives, then this would constitute evidence for the discourse hypothesis.[8] (I assume here the patterns of morphological dis-

[6]This is stated in terms of English. For Spanish, the preterite would be expected in telic verbs and/or the foreground; in French the *passé composé* (functionally a preterite) would be expected.

[7]*Event* is used here in its nontechnical sense and is not to be understood as indicating a class of verbs that includes achievements and accomplishments, as is the case in Mourelatos (1981) and other works.

[8]Exactly which morphological marking learners assign to background verbs or activities and states depends on the target language. In a cross-linguistic comparison, Bardovi-Harlig and

tribution found by Bardovi-Harlig, 1992c, and Flashner, 1989, rather than those found by Kumpf, 1984.) If, in contrast, telic verbs exhibited simple past tense regardless of grounding, and atelic verbs did not, this would be evidence for the aspect hypothesis. The challenge for the researcher would be to manipulate a film, story, or picture sequence to elicit the desired cases.

The Need for Quantification

There have been arguments against both the aspect hypothesis (Meisel, 1987) and the discourse hypothesis (Wolfram, 1985). Refutation of the hypotheses rests, just as does support, on empirical evidence. Meisel addressed the need for quantification in the study of interlanguage tense/aspect systems. Meisel offered an alternative interpretation of the apparent relationship between the use of tense markers and aspectual categories. In a large study for this area (45 learners in a cross-sectional study and 12 learners in a longitudinal study), Meisel found that although learners make some aspectual distinctions, they do not use aspect systematically with respect to the distribution of verbal morphology. He suggested that an aspectual system in interlanguage "may well be . . . a very marginal phenomenon, occurring only occasionally, which has received too much attention by researchers who based their expectations on findings in L1 studies or on creole studies" and that it may be a learner-specific characteristic. He concluded: "Citing isolated examples will not suffice; quantification is indispensable in this case" (1987, p. 220). I hasten to add that studies testing the discourse hypotheses are open to the same criticism.

The strongest criticism of the discourse hypothesis comes from Wolfram (1985, 1989) and Wolfram and Hatfield (1986), who characterized discourse-level analysis as a "somewhat faddish concern" (Wolfram, 1985, p. 251). Wolfram attempted to replicate Kumpf's (1984) findings with a single adult speaker of Vietnamese learning English, but he found that the pattern of tense marking did not resemble the distribution described by Kumpf.[9] Wolfram proposed as an alternative analysis a phonetic explanation for the distribution of marked and unmarked forms. He stated (1985): "The empirical facts suggest that the direction of these [discourse-level] studies is premature, and that a number of surface-level constraints must be considered before isolating these higher-level constraints" (p. 230). (Wolfram's objections apply equally to the

---

Bergström (1993) found that learners of English use base forms ($\emptyset$ marking as in *go* and *talk*) as the unmarked form, but that French learners seem to use the present in the same way.

[9]As noted earlier, two studies following Kumpf's have reported the past tense marking in the foreground. In fact, the narrative Wolfram described seems to use past primarily in the foreground and base forms primarily in the background (cf. Flashner, 1989, and Bardovi-Harlig, 1992c).

aspect hypotheses, which he does not consider explicitly.) Wolfram's proposal merits serious consideration, but it should be noted that a phonetic explanation of the distribution of tense marking leaves unanswered the question of the form-meaning and form-function associations made by the learners, which constitute the main focus of both the discourse and the aspect hypotheses.

Fully half of the studies reviewed here presented, both in support and in refutation of the hypotheses, data that were not quantified. Lack of quantification makes comparison between the findings from two studies quite difficult. Such a general absence of quantification may be a consequence of the predominance of case studies in the area. Nevertheless, provided that researchers use caution in applying quantitative analyses to small samples, such quantification is necessary to supplement qualitative analyses if the hypotheses are to be tested rigorously. Schumann (1987) provided an example in which samples of individual production were quantified to test competing descriptions.

Looking Forward

Some inquiries have begun to test multiple hypotheses on the same data base. A model for this type of comparison can be found in the study done by Schumann (1987). In that paper Schumann tested (and rejected) an aspect hypothesis, briefly considered (and rejected) a discourse hypothesis, and argued that tense use was unsystematic in the interlanguage of basilang speakers. He introduced and argued for a third hypothesis that basilang speakers use adverbials, serialization, calendric reference, and implicit reference to express temporality. There needs to be more comparative analysis of this type. Only then can we understand the development of tense and aspect systems in interlanguage and then evaluate the strengths of the relevant hypotheses.

Bayley (this volume, chapter 9) has also performed multiple analyses on the same data. Working with 30 hours of conversation from sociolinguistic interviews with 20 ESL learners who are native speakers of Chinese, Bayley showed that both phonetic saliency (Wolfram, 1985, 1989) and aspectual class are relevant in the distribution of interlanguage tense marking. Bayley's study also provides a model for future work on other counts as well: the size of the subject population, the size of the language sample collected from each speaker, the inclusion of two levels of proficiency,[10] and the quantification that was called for by Meisel (1987).

---

[10]Although the two levels are somewhat broadly defined (lower proficiency learners had TOEFL scores of 510 and below, and high-proficiency learners had TOEFL scores of 550 and above), Bayley's study is the first to show that the pattern of morphologically marked perfectives and unmarked imperfectives is maintained across proficiency levels: High-proficiency learners marked a greater percentage of verbs than did low-proficiency learners, but both groups showed approximately the same ratio of marked perfectives to unmarked imperfectives.

CONCLUSION

What is known about the development of tense and aspect systems? There seems to be some agreement that, as Robison said, verbal morphology correlates with lexical aspect during at least some stage in the development of interlanguage. Other studies have found that some learners are sensitive to discourse organization with respect to the distribution of verbal morphology. More evidence is clearly needed to determine whether all learners exhibit aspect-based or discourse-based distribution of verbal morphology at some proficiency level.

In spite of the work that has been done so far, we are still at the early stages in the investigation of this area of second-language acquisition. We have a series of anecdotal studies that, when taken together, suggest patterns of development, some of which are compatible and some of which are conflicting. Although the studies that have been conducted so far are suggestive, we do not yet have the evidence necessary to support either hypothesis with confidence. As outlined earlier, particular attention to level of proficiency, individual variation, number and mode of language samples, and subject selection will lead to a more reliable data base. The quantification of the data as a supplement to qualitative descriptions will facilitate comparison across studies and across languages, a step that is necessary, given the proposed universality of the hypotheses in question. Our understanding of the development of tense and aspect is dependent on our addressing these issues in research methodology. Only then can we move from anecdote to evidence.

ACKNOWLEDGMENTS

This study was supported by Grant BNS-8919616 from the National Science Foundation. I thank Beverly Hartford, Sarah Jourdain, Dudley Reynolds, and Shona Whyte for comments on an earlier version of this chapter. I also thank Andrew Cohen for his editorial direction.

REFERENCES

Andersen, R. (1986). El desarollo de la morfología verbal en el Español como segundo idioma [The development of verbal morphology in Spanish as a second language]. In J. M. Meisel (Ed.), *Adquisición de languaje/Aquisicao da linguagem* (pp. 115–138). Frankfurt: Vervuert.

Andersen, R. (1991). Developmental sequences: The emergence of aspect marking in second language acquisition. In C. A. Ferguson & T. Huebner (Eds.), *Second language acquisition and linguistic theories* (pp. 305–324). Amsterdam: John Benjamins.

Antinucci, F., & Miller, R. (1976). How children talk about what happened. *Journal of Child Language, 3*, 167–189.

Bailey, N. (1989). Discourse conditioned tense variation. In M. R. Eisenstein (Ed.), *The dynamic interlanguage: Empirical studies in second language variation* (pp. 279–296). New York: Plenum.

Bamberg, M. (1987). *The acquisition of narratives.* Berlin: Mouton de Gruyter.

Bamberg, M., & Marchman, V. (1990). What holds a narrative together? The linguistic encoding of episode boundaries. *Papers in Pragmatics, 4,* 58–121.

Bardovi-Harlig, K. (1992a). Adverbs, aspect, and tense. In N. Bird & J. Harris (Eds.), *Selected Proceedings for the Seventh ILE [Institute for Language in Education] Conference: QUILT and QUILL [Quality in Language Teaching and Quality in Language Learning]* (pp. 184–200). Hong Kong: Institute of Language in Education, Education Department.

Bardovi-Harlig, K. (1992b). The relationship of form and meaning: A cross-sectional study of tense and aspect in the interlanguage of learners of English as a second language. *Applied Psycholinguistics, 13,* 253–278.

Bardovi-Harlig, K. (1992c). The telling of a tale: Discourse structure and tense use in learner's narratives. In L. Bouton & Y. Kachru (Eds.), *Pragmatics and language learning* (Vol.3, pp. 144–161). Urbana-Champaign, IL: DEIL.

Bardovi-Harlig, K. (1992d). The use of adverbials and natural order in the development of temporal expression. *IRAL, 30,* 199–220.

Bardovi-Harlig, K., & Bergström, A. (1993, February). *Tense and aspect in SLA and FLL: Learner narratives in English (SL) and French (FL).* Paper presented to SLA-FLL III, West Lafayette, IN.

Bhardwaj, M., Dietrich, R., & Noyau, C. (Eds.). (1988). *Temporality.* (Final Report to the European Science Foundation, Volume 5). (Available from the Max-Planck Institute)

Bickerton, D. (1975). *Dynamics of a creole system.* Cambridge: Cambridge University Press.

Bickerton, D. (1981). *Roots of language.* Ann Arbor: Karoma.

Bronckart, J.-P., & Sinclair, H. (1973). Time, tense and aspect. *Cognition, 2,* 107–130.

Chafe, W. (Ed.). (1980). *The pear stories.* Norwood, NJ: Ablex.

Dahl, Ö. (1985). *Tense and aspect systems.* Oxford: Basil Blackwell.

Dowty, D. (1979). *Word meaning and Montague grammar.* Dordrecht: Reidel.

Dry, H. (1981). Sentence aspect and the movement of narrative time. *Text, 1,* 233–240.

Dry, H. (1983). The movement of narrative time. *Journal of Literary Semantics, 12,* 19–53.

Ellis, R. (1987). Interlanguage variability in narrative discourse: Style shifting in the use of past tense. *Studies in Second Language Acquisition, 9,* 1–20.

Flashner, V. E. (1989). Transfer of aspect in the English oral narratives of native Russian speakers. In H. Dechert & M. Raupach (Eds.), *Transfer in language production* (pp. 71–97). Norwood, NJ: Ablex.

Givón, T. (1982). Tense-aspect modality: The creole prototype and beyond. In P. Hopper (Ed.), *Tense-aspect: Between semantics and pragmatics* (pp. 115–163). Amsterdam: John Benjamins.

Godfrey, D. L. (1980). A discourse analysis of tense in adult ESL monologues. In D. Larsen-Freeman (Ed.), *Discourse analysis in second language research* (pp. 92–110). Rowley, MA: Newbury House.

Hatch, E., Shirai, Y., & Fantuzzi, C. (1990). The need for an integrated theory: Connecting modules. *TESOL Quarterly, 24,* 697–716.

Hopper, P. (1979). Aspect and foregrounding in discourse. In T. Givón (Ed.), *Syntax and semantics: Discourse and syntax.* New York: Academic Press.

Kaplan, M. A. (1987). Developmental patterns of past tense acquisition among foreign language learners of French. In B. VanPatten, T. R. Dvorak, & J. F. Lee (Eds.), *Foreign language learning: A research perspective* (pp. 52–60). Cambridge, MA: Newbury House.

Kumpf, L. (1984). Temporal systems and universality in interlanguage: A case study. In F. Eckman, L. Bell, & D. Nelson (Eds.), *Universals of second language acquisition* (pp. 132–143). Rowley, MA: Newbury House.

Labov, W., & Waletzky, J. (1967). Narrative analysis: Oral versions of personal experience. In J. Helm (Ed.), *Essays on the verbal and visual arts* (pp. 12–44). Seattle: University of Washington Press.

Meisel, J. M. (1987). Reference to past events and actions in the development of natural language acquisition. In C. W. Pfaff (Ed.), *First and second language acquisition processes* (pp. 206–224). Cambridge, MA: Newbury House.

Mourelatos, A. (1981). Events, processes, states. In P. Tedeschi & A. Zaenen (Eds.), *Syntax and Semantics: Vol. 14. Tense and aspect* (pp. 191–212). New York: Academic Press.

Noyau, C. (1990). The development of means for temporality in the unguided acquisition of L2: Cross-linguistic perspectives. In H. W. Dechert (Ed.), *Current trends in European second language acquisition research* (pp. 134–170). Clevedon, UK: Multilingual Matters.

Robison, R. (1990). The primacy of aspect: Aspectual marking in English interlanguage. *Studies in Second Language Acquisition, 12*, 315–330.

Schumann, J. (1987). The expression of temporality in basilang speech. *Studies in Second Language Acquisition, 9*, 21–41.

Selinker, L., & Douglas, D. (1985). Wrestling with 'context' in interlanguage theory. *Applied Linguistics, 6*, 190–204.

Tomlin, R. S. (1984). The treatment of foreground–background information in the on-line descriptive discourse of second language learners. *Studies in Second Language Acquisition, 6*, 115–142.

Trévise, A. (1987). Toward an analysis of the (inter)language activity of referring to time in narratives. In C. W. Pfaff (Ed.), *First and second language acquisition processes* (pp. 225–251). Cambridge, MA: Newbury House.

Vendler, Z. (1967). Verbs and times. In Z. Vendler (Ed.), *Linguistics and philosophy* (pp. 97–121) Ithaca, NY: Cornell University Press. (Reprinted from *Philosophical Review*, 1957, *66*, 143–160)

Véronique, D. (1987). Reference to past events and actions in narratives in L2: Insights from North African learners' French. In C. W. Pfaff (Ed.), *First and second language acquisition processes* (pp. 252–272). Cambridge, MA: Newbury House.

Weist, R. M., Wysocka, H., Witkowska-Stadnik, K., Buczowska, E., & Konieczna, E. (1984). The defective tense hypothesis: On the emergence of tense and aspect in child Polish. *Journal of Child Language, 11*, 347–374.

Wolfram, W. (1985). Variability in tense marking: A case for the obvious. *Language Learning, 35*, 229–253.

Wolfram, W. (1989). Systematic variability in second-language tense marking. In M. R. Eisenstein (Ed.), *The dynamic interlanguage: Empirical studies in second language variation* (pp. 187–197). New York: Plenum.

Wolfram, W., & Hatfield, D. (1986). Interlanguage fads and linguistics reality: The case of tense marking. In D. Tannen & J. Alatis (Eds.), *GURT '85 languages and linguistics: The interdependence of theory, data, and application* (pp. 17–34). Washington, DC: Georgetown University Press.

4

CONSTRUCTS AND MEASUREMENT IN PARAMETER MODELS OF SECOND-LANGUAGE ACQUISITION

L. Kirk Hagen
University of Houston—Downtown

This chapter has to do with universal grammar (UG), its role in second-language acquisition (SLA) research, and the measurement of UG principles as constructs in SLA research. Specifically, I discuss parameter-based approaches to SLA-theory construction that rely on principles from Government and Binding (GB) theory. Because my chapter deals with theory construction rather than theory evaluation—and so assumes that SLA does not yet have any full-fledged theories—I want to call attention to a few troublesome theoretical, methodological, and empirical problems that parameter models will have to work out.

The first of these has to do with syntactic theory itself. I point to some problems raised by non-GB theories like Generalized Phrase-Structure Grammar (GPSG, cf. Gazdar, Klein, Pullam, & Sag, 1985; Pollard & Sag, 1983; Sells, 1985) or Head-Driven Phrase-Structure Grammar (HPSG, cf. Pollard & Sag, 1987), theories that have not received the attention they deserve in SLA research. Parameter models have so far taken the GB framework for granted, even though alternative accounts of some of the phenomena handled by parameter models have been developed in these other theories.

Second, I discuss measurement procedures in parameter models. Generative-based research in SLA sees itself as a branch of psychology, yet it differs from other branches in that it has virtually no coherent program of measurement research of its own (cf. Shohamy, this volume, chapter 7). This has left it vulnerable on a number of fronts, two of which I deal with directly in this chapter. The first is a problem that Eckman (this volume, chapter 11) characterizes as "endemic in all of the research reported thus far on L2 binding and much of the research attempting to test UG principles in SLA"; that is, "research in this area has reported aggregate results rather than results for individuals," and "principles of UG have been interpreted directly with respect to data instead of with respect to IL grammars." The second problem is that, the generative tradition recognizes a distinction between *implicit* knowledge of grammar (what Krashen, 1982, calls "acquired" knowledge and what Chomsky, 1980, might have called "cognized" knowledge; cf. as well Gregg, 1989, for a discussion) and *explicit* or formal knowledge ("learned" knowledge in Krashen, 1982, 1985), yet no such distinction is taken into account in the methods that have been used in SLA research to date. Because implicit knowledge alone is the object of inquiry in parameter models, any systematic effects of explicit knowledge on measurement can contaminate the data.

In the latter part of my chapter, therefore, I describe methods of data analysis that (a) allow for generalizations across IL grammars without confounding differences between individuals, and (b) gauge the effects of explicit knowledge on grammaticality judgment tasks. I discuss three principles in order to illustrate how these methods can be put to use. The first is reflexive binding (*r-binding*), a proposed universal, by which a regular relationship between subjects and reflexive pronouns (*r-pronouns*) holds in all natural languages. The second has to do with parametric variation or has at least been treated as such in some generative-based SLA work (cf. Liceras, 1985). Some pronouns are proclitic in French but either enclitic or proclitic in Spanish. The third involves a language-specific characteristic of English that falls beyond the scope of parameter theory: The morphologies of English reflexive pronouns are distinct from the morphologies of their nonreflexive counterparts.[1] In the study I describe, data on grammaticality judgments and response times from English- and Spanish-speaking learners of French were gathered via a computer-driven program and then analyzed using a factor procedure and a repeated-measures ANOVA. After discussing some of the advantages of the methods used, I argue that the results suggest that neither parametric variation nor r-binding accounts for the observed differential responses on grammaticality judgment tasks.

SLA AND LINGUISTIC THEORY

Let us begin with a general definition of a parameter model, one that I hope is not too distorted. (More thorough descriptions can be found elsewhere, e.g., Cohen Sherman & Lust, 1986; Cook, 1985; Felix, 1988; Flynn, 1983,

---

[1]See Finer (1982), Bès (1986, 1988), and Verheijen and Beukema (1988) for discussions of the syntactic concerns raised here.

1984, 1987a, 1987b, 1988; Liceras, 1988; Lust, 1988; Lust, Solan, Flynn, Cross, & Schuetz, 1986; Ritchie, 1983a, 1983b; Roeper, 1986; van Riemsdijk, 1986.)

A parameter model is supposed to explain why certain structures in certain nonnative grammars (NNGs) are acceptable but others are not. Models of this sort should allow for three kinds of rules or principles that explain NNGs. First, there are "nonviolable universal principles of a quite abstract sort that account to a large extent for the similarities across all languages" (Schachter, 1989, p. 74). These principles are part of what the learner "brings to the language learning task" (Wexler & Chien, 1985, p. 140). The Specified Subject Constraint, which requires that r-pronouns be bound by specified antecedents, is an example of such a principle. Second, "associated with some of these principles are sets of parameters that define possible variations across languages, the setting of each parameter being determined on the basis of experience with the input" (Schachter, 1989, p. 74). In addition to the pro/enclitic parameter, a head-initial/head final parameter (Flynn, 1987a, 1987b), a topicalization parameter (Hulk, 1991), and an adjacency parameter (Berent, this volume, chapter 2) have all been cited as examples of parameters in SLA research. Third, particular languages may have purely parochial or incidental properties that fall beyond the scope of parametric variation. For instance, both Spanish and French have morphologically distinct masculine and feminine definite articles in the singular (*el/la* and *le/la*, respectively), but only in Spanish does the distinction hold in the plural (*los/las*, compared to *les/les* in French). Although this may very well have a bearing on French as an L2 for Spanish speakers, it is doubtful that anyone would choose to construe this difference as a consequence of parametric variation.

Parameter models are parsimonious insofar as they account for what Chomsky (1986) characterized as the "chasm" between the complexity of a language and the limited amount of relevant linguistic data to which the learner has access. Parameter models need to postulate considerably less acquisition in language competence, which seems to be consistent with observations of first languages even if it seems somewhat less so as far as adult second languages are concerned. In any event, if learning the L1 is a matter of setting parameters, then learning an L2 is a matter of resetting parameters (Flynn, 1987a).

It should be emphasized that this line of SLA research has its origins in one of many theories (GB) and has in fact come to be dependent on that theory to the exclusion of all others. For instance, in the third section of Berent (this volume, chapter 2) there is a review of a GB-internal debate regarding the parameter that is responsible for adverb placement in French and English. GB theory itself and its various tenets, however, are taken for granted throughout. In one sense this may be beneficial, inasmuch as GB has become a reasonably homogeneous theory, and its broad dissemination means that a growing number of SLA linguists are familiar with its scope, its terminology, and its methodology. But there will inevitably be some collateral risks to such a restricted view of syntactic theory.

Because we examine r-pronouns and binding later in this chapter, let us look at one relevant study involving first-language acquisition of anaphors and pronouns in order to illustrate some potential difficulties. Wexler and Chien (1985) tested children's sensitivity to two well-known principles of Chomsky's (1981) Binding Theory:

(1) (A) An anaphor is bound in its governing category.
    (B) A pronominal is free in its governing category.

They reported that: (a) children older than 5 years, 6 months know that antecedents must c-command reflexives, (b) children in the same age range do not know that a pronoun cannot have a local c-commanding antecedent, and (c) children's performance on tasks involving the c-command property of reflexives increases continuously from chance level at age 2 years, 6 months to almost perfect performance at 6 years, 6 months.

It is implicit here, as in all SLA research on parameters, that SLA hypotheses can be construed to test the psychological reality of particular formulations of UG principles. Non-GB formulations, however, have so far been roundly ignored. For example, Pollard and Sag (1983) gave an account of r-binding that differs considerably from the one assumed in Wexler and Chien. Pollard and Sag's account relied on an array of metarules and feature-passing principles that have no homologues in GB theory. They claimed that their analysis explains "facts involving reflexive pronouns in dislocated constituents (e.g. in cleft, pseudo cleft and topicalization constructions) which stand as blatant counterexamples to current, widely-accepted treatments within Chomsky's 'binding theory' " (p. 189).[2] As far as I can tell, none of the stimuli in Wexler and Chien present any special problems for either GB or GPSG. The only obvious advantage in couching experimental research in the language of GB, in this case, is in the familiarity of the terminology. But if terminology rather than anything of substance is at issue, then clearly this line of research loses much of its interest. Unless one is prepared to test one theory against another, the jargon of traditional pedagogical grammars would serve equally well and might even reach a wider audience.

Moreover, it may be that GB or GPSG will have to be altered or perhaps even rejected entirely, perhaps for reasons that touch only marginally on whatever syntactic phenomenon one is researching. If one is interested in r-binding in second languages, for example, it is important to keep in mind that, were it shown that GPSG's assumptions about monostratal grammars

---

[2]They cite *What Kim loves most of all is herself* as a counterexample to "commonly held" binding theory assumptions.

could not account for certain types of dependencies or multiple extractions in some languages, then its account of r-pronouns in clefts and dislocations would have to be reworked entirely, because that account depends crucially on the distribution of the SLASH feature.[3]

Of course, the same fate could befall GB. For instance, one hallmark of GPS/HPS grammars is the extraction of linear precedence from immediate dominance. Pollard and Sag (1987) argued, "It is a well-known fact (though little acknowledged in most recent syntactic theorization) that the linear order of sister constituents in a given language is not an idiosyncratic property of particular classes of phrases but rather is determined by general constraints which have force across the whole language" (p. 14). Without going into too much detail, let us recall that GPS/HPS grammars make use of immediate dominance (ID) rules of the form A → B, C. A comma indicates linearly unordered constituents, so that a rule of this sort is compatible with the following structures:

(2) a. A
       B
       C
  b. A
       C
       B

Traditional phrase structure rules like A → B C, on the other hand, are compatible with (2a) only. The linear order of nodes in a local tree is determined by independent principles. This permits generalizations about constituent order across the entire grammar of a language (e.g., that verbs in English are phrase-initial, that determiners and complementizers are phrase-initial even though they are not heads, that English has prepositions rather than postpositions, cf. Gazdar et al., 1985). These generalizations are in fact missing from GB.

This immediate dominance/linear precedence (ID/LP) format, however, is possible only for grammars that have the Exhaustive Constant Partial Order-

---

[3]In Gazdar et al. (1985), both SLASH and REFL are members of the set of FOOT features, which are governed by the Foot Feature Principle (FFP):

(i) *Foot Feature Principle (FFP):*

$$\phi(C_0) \mid \text{FOOT} \sim C_0 = \cup\ \phi(C_i) \mid \text{FOOT} \sim C_i$$
$$1 \le i \le n$$

"The FOOT feature specifications that are instantiated on a mother category in a tree must be identical to the unification of the instantiated FOOT features specifications in all of its daughter categories" (Gazdar et al., 1985, p. 82). The FFP applies across an arbitrarily long series of mother/daughter nodes to record syntactically relevant information (e.g., the relationship between extract and antecedent or r-pronoun and subject).

ing property (ECPO). If a grammar possesses this property, "the set of expansions of any one category observes a partial ordering that is also observed by the expansion of all other categories" (Gazdar et al., 1985, p. 49). Gazdar et al. pointed out that many hypothetical but plausible-looking phrase-structure grammars cannot be put into ID/LP format. Thus, simply to incorporate the ID/LP format into a theoretical framework is to claim that ECPO holds universally for natural languages. If it does, then GB will have to be reworked, because it fails to capture the generalizations expressed by the ID/LP format. It is not difficult to foresee adverse consequences for some work already done in SLA. For example, Flynn's (1987a, 1987b) and Hulk's (1991) research on head initial/head final parameters, as well as Berent's (this volume, chapter 2) account of adverb order in French, would be rendered vacuous because they would presuppose an inadequate theory.

The standard position in the GPSG/HPSG camp has been to ignore the whole question of parameters because it is not yet clear what sort of evidence counts as proof for or against the claims being made. In fact, Gazdar et al. (1985) rather bluntly dismissed "reference to questions of psychology, particularly in association with language acquisition" as "packaging and public relations" (p. 5). Chomsky (1986) also made some interesting remarks:

> Suppose that we have . . . two theories of the states of knowledge attained by a particular person . . . and suppose further that these theories are "extensionally equivalent" in the sense that they determine the same E[xternalized]-language in whatever sense we give to this derivative notion. It could in principle turn out that one of these grammars incorporates properties and principles that are readily explained in terms of brain mechanisms whereas the other does not. . . . Although results of this sort are remote in the current state of understanding, they are possible. (pp. 39–40)

Here we are jumping ahead to matters that concern the neurolinguist, but Chomsky's comments carry over to SLA research. It is possible in principle to develop two distinct generative theories that are descriptively equivalent in that they allow the same class of possible natural languages and disallow the same class of impossible natural languages. Under such conditions, SLA research could perhaps demonstrate by its methods that one of the two grammars incorporates principles that can be conveniently explained by certain psychological postulates in a way the other does not. A perusal of existing research on parameter models will clearly show that SLA is not so well developed at the present.

In fact, the preceding discussion itself begs important questions, because it is not at all certain that adult second languages abide by the sort of principles governing first languages. There is, moreover, neither widespread agreement nor adequate research on the methods of data analysis appropriate for

SLA research. In this section I hope to make a little progress on both fronts by focusing on r-binding in second languages. As a convenient point of departure, let us begin with a familiar version of the general concept of interest (the Specified Subject Constraint), without committing to any particular theory:

(3) *Specified Subject Constraint*: A pronoun must be free in the domain of its nearest subject, and . . . an anaphor such as *each other* must be bound in this domain. (Chomsky, 1986, p. 107)

As far as first languages are concerned, any theory of syntax will allow for some variation among speakers of a language, but not so much variation that this relationship between subject and r-pronoun holds for some speakers but not for others. In fact, because it evidently holds for all speakers of all languages, it is "presumably . . . a principle of UG, or a consequence derived from principles of UG, perhaps with parameters set" (Chomsky, 1986, p. 106), insofar as it cannot be explained in terms of learning or experience alone (following the familiar arguments regarding poverty of stimulus, lack of corrective feedback, and so on). As far as SLA is concerned, research is at a considerable disadvantage because it has to live with far more inter- and intraspeaker variation, variation due to factors like first language, age at onset of acquisition, and type of exposure to the L2.

Still, uncovering any generalizations that may hold for all speakers is methodologically desirable in both first-language and second-language research. In theoretical syntax, for example, GB, GPSG, and HPSG all rely on one general principle to do the bulk of the work involved in r-binding: the Foot Feature Principle in GPSG, c-command in GB, and o-command (oblique command) in HPSG (Pollard & Sag, 1987).[4] Moreover, it is taken for granted in generative grammar that, given two accounts of some phenomenon in a language, the one that generalizes across a wider range of data is the better, other things being equal. Suppose some theory A proposes one principle to explain the relationship between an r-pronoun and its antecedent in local binding examples like (4):

(4) Do you$_i$ know yourself$_i$/*himself$_i$?

A second principle explains the relationship in long-distance binding examples like (5):

(5) He$_i$ is going to make up his mind one of these days to try to control himself$_i$/*herself$_i$.

---

[4]In each grammar, naturally, the general principle interacts with other principles in ways that are not relevant to the present discussion.

A different theory B, on the other hand, proposes a single principle to take care of both cases. The latter would win out, other things being equal. Then again, suppose the single principle in theory B turned out to be too broad in scope—for instance, if examples like (6) were well formed in some language

(6) *Voting for each other is not something Al and Bob are likely to tell Carl to do.

((6) is interpreted as meaning, "Al is not likely to tell Carl to vote for Bob, and Bob is not likely to tell Carl to vote for Al.") then theory A would be vindicated, other things being equal.

This same methodological criterion regarding the scope of principles should apply to SLA research as well. But if one is to come up with a satisfactory account of r-binding as an SLA construct, one needs first to uncover all of the relevant facts about the relationship between subject and r-pronouns in the NNGs under investigation. Any number of questions come to mind: Does the relationship hold in extractions and topicalizations as it does in L1s? Does it hold in embedded VP complements like (5)? And what about adjunct VPs like the following?

(7) Do you have a cup of coffee before washing yourself?

Does it hold at all stages and at all levels of L2 acquisition? In short, how general can one be about binding in L2s, given such a degree of interspeaker variation?

Suppose we set out to measure a construct like r-binding in French as an L2 by comparing grammaticality judgments from English and Spanish speakers for sentences like those in (8):

(8) a. Elle se   lave.
    She herself bathes.
    'She's bathing.'

b. Je me   lave.
    I myself bathe.
    'I'm bathing.'

c. Elle me lave.
    She me bathes.
    'She bathes me.'

d. *Je se   lave.
    I oneself bathe.

In the first place, it would not do to point to one or two speakers who incorrectly judge (8d) to be grammatical, as a counterexample to a supposedly universal trait. There are many plausible explanations. Perhaps the reflexive *se* is unfamiliar to certain speakers/learners, who thus assume some nonreflexive interpretation of the sentence. Perhaps English morphology plays a role; English speakers may reject examples like (8b) because *me* is perceived to be an inherently nonreflexive morpheme like its orthographically identical English counterpart. Thus for some, *se* may be lexically an idiosyncratic, highly underspecified reflexive pronoun meaning nothing more than "self."[5] I raise the issue now because, as has been reported elsewhere (Hagen, 1990), apparent r-binding violations like (8d) from nonnative learners of French are not that uncommon.[6] Interestingly enough, such violations seem to be somewhat more frequent in long-distance examples like (5) and (7) than in local examples like (8b).

But I am reporting anecdotes; let us pursue the matter more rigorously, starting with a few more observations about the English, French, and Spanish pronominal systems. We have already noted that in English, every reflexive pronoun has a morphologically distinct nonreflexive counterpart (e.g., *me/myself, you/yourself*). This is not the case for French and Spanish, however: *me/myself* are *me/me* in both languages. It is reasonable to suppose that this will be a source of error for English speakers. In fact, let us propose this as a first hypothesis:

(9) H1: The morphological identity of reflexive and nonreflexive pronouns in French is a source of error for English-speaking learners of French (but not for Spanish-speaking learners).

Next, recall that Spanish has a pro/enclitic parameter that does not hold in French:

(10) a. ¿Te   lavo? antes de tomar una taza de café.
         Yourself wash before having a cup of coffee
         'Do you bathe before having a cup of coffee?'
     b. ¿Tomas   una taza de café? antes de   lavarte.
         You-have a cup of coffee   before of to wash-yourself
         'Do you have a cup of coffee before washing yourself?'
     c. Tu prends une tasse de café avant de te laver.
     d. *Tu prends une tasse de café avant de laverte.

---

[5]By way of analogy, in the style of newspaper headlines, *Man shoots self* is an acceptable ellipsis of *Man shoots himself*, but *Man$_i$ shoots him$_i$* is not. Sells (1985) included a discussion of a similar phenomenon in Norwegian.

[6]These are precisely the sort of problems that make case studies of second languages so undependable.

Thus let us also propose the following:

> (11) H2: The pro/enclitic parameter in Spanish is a source of error for Spanish-speaking learners of French (but not for English-speaking learners).

Here we do not suggest that English speakers will never err when giving grammaticality judgments for French infinitival phrases with pronouns. Rather, we are claiming that they are neither more nor less likely to err in, say, adjunct-infinitival VPs than in base VPs. Thus those who reject preverbal clitics in (10c) should also reject them in examples like (12):

> (12) Tu te laves avant de prendre une tasse de café.
> 'You wash yourself before having a cup of coffee.'

In fact, if we knew reliably that English speakers did not give the same judgments for reflexive pronouns in, say, base VPs and adjunct VPs, then we would conclude that r-binding is not a monadic or unitary construct as it is in theoretical syntax because it does not hold for the same broad set of grammatical structures. This would be an unexpected outcome, given the assumptions of UG, because notions like base-VP binding, as opposed to adjunct-VP binding, play no coherent role in any generative theory. Although it is unexpected, it is not to be ruled out a priori. Thus consider (13):

> (13) H3: For all second-language speakers, r-pronouns in NNGs are bound in base VPs as they are in adjunct VPs, by virtue of a nonviolable principle.

Now we have to decide how to test such hypotheses. For purposes of exposition, let us focus on the first hypothesis. Imagine a test in which three English-speaking learners of French (call them A, B, and C) were asked to complete VPs like those in (14) with forms like *me, se, moi,* or *moi-même.*

> (14) a. Je _____ lave.
>   b. Tu _____ laves.

Eckman (this volume, chapter 11) made an astute observation regarding data gleaned from tests of this sort: "One cannot determine whether UG constraints have been violated simply by examining the errors. This is true because the principles and parameters of UG do not directly make claims about utterances, but instead make claims about grammars." Thus in the case of (14), notice for example that H1 does not say whether some particular speaker will reject the use of *me* in (14a) or in (14b). We have already pointed out the obvious similarity between the French *me* and the English *me*, which suggests that (14a) is more likely to be accepted. But the opposite scenario is possible as well. Certain common and useful expressions like *je m'appelle* 'my name is', *je me lève* 'I get out of bed' are usually presented early on in adult foreign language courses, well before any general presentation of cliticization. This suggests that reflexives like *me* in (14a) will be acquired at some stage s_i, so that nonreflexives like *me* in (14b) become unacceptable at a subsequent stage s_{i+n}.[7]

Whatever the case, if subjects tend to accept one morpheme as a first-person singular reflexive and another as a first-person singular nonreflexive, there will be three possible outcomes, illustrated in (15) (1 indicates a correct response, 0, an incorrect response):

(15)	F2 speaker	Stimulus/Response	REFL+	REFL−
	A	Je me lave.	1	0
		*Tu laves moi.		
	B	*Je lave moi-même.	0	1
		Tu me laves.		
	C	*Je lave moi-même.	0	0
		*Tu laves moi.		

On the other hand, if language learners tend to accept a single pronoun as both a reflexive and a nonreflexive, as we might expect of Spanish speakers, then they will either get both (14a) and (14b) right or get both wrong:

(16)	F2 speaker	Stimulus/Response	REFL+	REFL−
	D	Je me lave.	1	1
		Tu me laves.		
	E	*Je lave moi.	0	0
		*Tu laves moi.		
	F	*Je lave me.	0	0
		*Tu laves me.		

Even a cursory review of these data will show quite distinct patterns of responses between the group in (15) and the group in (16). Yet, as Eckman (this volume, chapter 11) pointed out:

> If a study reports that [an L2 group] gave local responses on English reflexives in 80% of the cases . . . this result does not tell us whether the principles of

---

[7]Thus in Hagen (1990), some English speakers who rejected sentences like *Je me réveille* said in a follow-up interview that *me* "means 'me'." Others who rejected sentences like *Il me réveille* were convinced that *me* meant "myself."

UG are being obeyed unless we know how those responses are distributed across subjects. Clearly, the case for UG can be made if all of the subjects scored 80%. If, on the other hand, the 80% group result is a composite of subjects compiling many different scores, some of which indicate systematic adherence to UG principles and others which either are unsystematic or indicate non-adherence to UG, then the case for UG governing SLA is not at all clear.

Thus, were we to calculate means for the groups in (15) and (16), we would get an uninformative 33% in each case, and the relevant distinctions would be lost, just as Eckman predicts.

On the other hand, were we to calculate phi-coefficients for these data, we would get magnitudes of 0.50 for (15) and 1.0 for (16). In other words, differential responses on variables where a single morpheme is required tend to suppress correlation coefficients of measures of grammaticality judgments. This in turn may show up in the form of distinct latent variables when the data are factor-analyzed. Such a method would have two additional advantages over the method Eckman used in his study. First, it would not require some arbitrary threshold of systematicity (two out of three, three out of four, or whatever) as did Eckman's study. Any lack of systematicity would merely deflate correlation coefficients and therefore lower factor loadings. Adherence or nonadherence to whatever principle one is investigating would conversely increase factor loadings. Second, it would permit tests of statistical differences. (Eckman did not report such tests in his study.) Typically, in factor-analytic studies, eigenvalues of 1 or greater are taken as indicators of reliable factors.

To give the reader some idea of what sort of results might come from a larger data set, Table 4.1 shows part of a factor matrix from Hagen (1990). In that study, 178 adult English-speaking learners of French gave grammaticality judgments on French pronouns in a wide array of contexts. A factor analysis of the results yielded what was essentially a taxonomy of French pronouns closely aligned with the English pronominal system, with only a few rough edges. Table 4.1 shows one factor for judgments on French *me* and *te* in reflexive VPs and a distinct factor for *me* and *te* in nonreflexive VPs. Incidentally, Table 4.1 also shows that contexts in which *me* and *te* are used with feminine referents do not load on a factor distinct from contexts in which they are used with masculine referents. This makes sense intuitively, since neither French nor English has morphologically distinct pronouns meaning 'my-feminine-self' or 'your-masculine-self'. By the same token, we should not expect distinct loadings for locally bound as opposed to distantly bound reflexives because r-binding, as a universal, holds across arbitrarily long distances in French and in English. In other terms, a factor procedure should not be able to divide r-binding into local binding and long-distance binding because r-binding is not supposed to be a divisible construct. Indeed, no such factors show up in Table 4.1.

TABLE 4.1
Factor Matrix of Grammaticality Judgments of French Reflexives
and Nonreflexives

Label	Referent	PRO-type	Local?	Case	Factor[a] 1	2
ME1	FEM	REFL	NO	DAT	**.75**	.22
ME2	FEM	REFL	NO	ACC	**.79**	.19
ME3	FEM	REFL	YES	ACC	**.76**	.29
ME4	FEM	pro	YES	ACC	.37	**.64**
ME5	MASC	pro	YES	ACC	.18	**.72**
TE1	FEM	REFL	NO	DAT	**.81**	.12
TE2	FEM	REFL	NO	ACC	**.84**	.11
TE3	FEM	REFL	YES	ACC	**.80**	.16
TE4	FEM	pro	YES	ACC	.43	**.63**
TE5	MASC	pro	YES	ACC	.19	**.75**

Note. Excerpt from Hagen (1990).
[a]High loadings are shown in boldface.

The primary goal of the study I discuss in the next section was to sharpen and expand the measurement procedures used in Hagen (1990). One way of doing so was to introduce Spanish-speaking learners of French into the design in order to uncover, if possible, the sort of differential responses between base and infinitival examples that did not turn up in Hagen's study, and to see if they could be attributed statistically to first-language parameter differences. At the same time, one other concern needs to be dealt with. Recall that we have left open the possibility that two distinct mental faculties—explicit and implicit knowledge—come into play when one gives grammaticality judgments. For example, a trained linguist who neither speaks nor understands a word of French could perhaps plod through a test with items like (14) and get a respectable score. Were we to follow suggestions in Gregg (1989) and "establish the domain of a theory of second-language acquisition so that it is confined to the acquisition of linguistic competence" (p. 22), then we would necessarily want to exclude all data having to do with explicit grammatical knowledge. On the other hand, if we were to follow the advice in Eckman (this volume, chapter 11) and "be reluctant to ignore any data" such as these, then it might prove worthwhile to incorporate explicit knowledge into some more comprehensive view of second-language behavior. Any number of plausible theories can be imagined. For example, it may turn out that UG is not available to certain types of adult learners of second languages but that information not supplied by UG is nonetheless available via explicit knowledge or monitoring.

In any case, it would not be worthwhile simply to study data from second-language speakers casually and declare a particular utterance to be an example of implicit or explicit knowledge. Eckman has wisely reminded us that issues like these are empirical and need to be settled on empirical grounds rather than on a priori considerations. Thus let us take a few tentative steps toward the resolution of this particular problem by assuming, as Krashen (1982) does, that "it takes a real discrete-point grammar-type test to meet [the] conditions for Monitor use and encourage significant use of the conscious grammar" (p. 18), and that "in order to think about and use conscious rules effectively, a second language performer needs to have sufficient time" (p. 16). This suggests that resorting to explicit knowledge may have an effect on response times during grammaticality judgment tests. To be precise, it may be the case that (a) explicit knowledge is functional but not effective, (b) explicit knowledge is functional and effective, or (c) explicit knowledge is not functional. In the case of (a), problematic items will result in longer response times and a corresponding decrease in the likelihood of a correct response. Put simply, the subjects spend more time mulling over difficult items but still get them wrong because neither explicit nor implicit knowledge is adequate to meet the challenge. We would then predict some negative correlation between response times and the number of correct answers. In the case of (b), longer response times would be positively related to correct responses because the subjects would access conscious grammar whenever their implicit knowledge was insufficient to solve a problem posed by a test item, and their conscious grammar would then supply the missing information. Finally, under (c), more difficult items will neither speed up nor slow down response times because the subjects do not resort to formal knowledge, so that there is no correlation between response times and number of correct answers.

Let us conclude this section by noting that (a) is essentially the position taken by Krashen over the years, and that only (b) casts any doubt on the viability of using grammaticality judgment tasks in parameter research, because (b) alone allows for the possibility of confounding implicit and explicit knowledge.

METHOD

Let us summarize before going further. We intended to measure three phenomena: (a) the possible effects of English reflexive morphology on the grammaticality judgments of English-speaking learners of French, (b) the possible effects of the Spanish pro/encliticization parameter on the grammaticality judgments of Spanish-speaking learners of French, (c) the effects of r-binding, which is said to be a universal property of natural languages and so presumably not a source of error for any L2 speakers. At the same time, we intended to track response times in order to look for evidence that L2 subjects access explicit grammatical knowledge in the course of completing grammaticality judgment tasks, because such monitoring of grammatical forms would introduce a systematic nuisance variable that precludes generalizations about linguistic competence based on data gleaned from grammaticality judgment tasks.

We start with four sentence types, each of which is treated as a variable:

(17) a. V1: *Reflexive pronouns in base VPs*, for example:
   Avant de prendre une tasse de caf$_5$e le matin est-ce que tu *te laves?*
   Antes de tomar una taza de café ¿*te lavas?*
   Before having a cup of coffee in the morning do you *bathe yourself?*

b. V2: *Reflexive pronouns in adjunct VPs*, for example:
   Est-ce que tu prends une tasse de café le matin avant de *te laver?*
   ¿Tomas una taza de café? antes de *lavarte.*
   Do you have a cup of coffee before *bathing yourself?*

c. V3: *Nonreflexive pronouns in base VPs*, for example:
   Avant de prendre une tasse de café le matin est-ce que je *te lave?*
   Antes de tomar una taza de café ¿*te lavo?*
   Before having a cup of coffee in the morning do I *bathe you?*

d. V4: *Nonreflexive pronouns in adjunct VPs*, for example:
   Est-ce que je prends une tasse de café le matin avant de *te laver?*
   ¿Tomo una taza de café? antes de *lavarte.*
   Do I have a cup of coffee in the morning before *bathing you?*

In every case words have been neither added nor subtracted; they have merely been rearranged to create the desired distinction between reflexive and nonreflexive VPs and between base and adjunct VPs. We obtained grammaticality judgments on four items of each sentence type. Having taken the additional methodological step of recording response times on all items, we had a total of eight variables, shown schematically in (18):

(18)

Label	PRO-type	VP-type	Method
V1$_{gj}$	REFL	BASE	G-judgment
V2$_{gj}$	REFL	ADVP	G-judgment
V3$_{gj}$	~REFL	BASE	G-judgment
V4$_{gj}$	~REFL	ADVP	G-judgment
V1$_{rt}$	REFL	BASE	R-time
V2$_{rt}$	REFL	ADVP	R-time
V3$_{rt}$	~REFL	BASE	R-time
V4$_{rt}$	~REFL	ADVP	R-time

The subscript in the first column is just a convenient way of indicating the method used to gather data. For instance, $V1_{gj}$ indicates grammaticality judgments gathered on items of the first sentence type shown in (17), and $V1_{rt}$ indicates the corresponding response times.

A total of 101 first- and second-year university students of French were tested. Of these, 47 declared English to be their first language, 29 named Spanish, and 25 named another language. This last group was excluded from the study, leaving a population that was 62% English speaking and 38% Spanish speaking.[8] In addition to declaring "the language first learned as a child," all subjects were asked to indicate, on a scale of 0 to 6, how often they spoke Spanish at home (0 = never, 6 = always). A point biserial correlation between this variable and first language yielded $r = .92$; hence there was good evidence that Spanish was both a native language and a dominant language for the Spanish-speaking group.

All were tested on a computer-generated battery that included four items from each sentence type shown in (17). Verbs and pronouns were deleted from sentences, and the subjects were to select the appropriate verb-pronoun pair from a field of six to complete the sentences. The choices included preverbal and postverbal pronouns. These items are shown in the Appendix.[9] As soon as a test item was displayed, a timer using 1/60th-second increments was activated. When the mouse was clicked in response to the test item, the timer stopped, and responses and response times were recorded.[10]

Some controls were added to minimize the effect of potential nuisance variables. First, all items from all variables were generated randomly for all subjects to avoid carry-over effect. Second, the total number of characters per variable was held constant to within 2% difference so that response time was not affected by reading time. Finally, the correct response appeared in the same position among distractors for all items so that its positioning would

---

[8]A cautionary note is in order. All of the native Spanish speakers also spoke English as a second language, albeit with varying degrees of fluency. A respectable theory of SLA should have something to say about multilinguals as well as bilinguals, though it is not at all clear how the former could be incorporated into a parameter model.

[9]This approach is somewhat different from that utilizing traditional grammaticality judgment tasks in which subjects are asked only to declare a sentence well formed or ill formed. The format used here should not cause concern, however. I am merely assuming that a subject, by declaring a pronoun appropriate in some structure, is explicitly declaring that structure to be well formed and implicitly declaring others to be ill formed. The format used here is preferable because, among other things, subjects may reject sentences like (17) for reasons having nothing to do with what is being studied (e.g., they may reject such sentences because they believe that the verb doesn't agree with the subject).

[10]Testing took place in a computer lab on a set of Macintosh SEs with one megabyte RAM each. Subjects responded by moving the cursor to the verb-pronoun combination and clicking the mouse.

TABLE 4.2
Means and Standard Deviations for Responses and Response Times

English L1 (n = 47)

Label	VP-type	REFL	Measure	Mean	SD
$V1_{gj}$	BASE	+	G-judgment	1.87	1.44
$V2_{gj}$	ADVP	+	G-judgment	1.26	1.17
$V3_{gj}$	BASE	−	G-judgment	1.30	1.56
$V4_{gj}$	ADVP	−	G-judgment	0.87	1.01
$V1_{rt}$	BASE	+	R-time	4015.38	1697.99
$V2_{rt}$	ADVP	+	R-time	4052.74	1969.83
$V3_{rt}$	BASE	−	R-time	3903.74	1416.09
$V4_{rt}$	ADVP	−	R-time	4267.62	1491.69

Spanish L1 (n = 29)

Label	VP-type	REFL	Measure	Mean	SD
$V1_{gj}$	BASE	+	G-judgment	3.00	1.13
$V2_{gj}$	ADVP	+	G-judgment	1.66	1.26
$V3_{gj}$	BASE	−	G-judgment	2.34	1.40
$V4_{gj}$	ADVP	−	G-judgment	1.45	1.45
$V1_{rt}$	BASE	+	R-time	3626.83	1328.84
$V2_{rt}$	ADVP	+	R-time	4912.03	1806.53
$V3_{rt}$	BASE	+	R-time	3788.07	1142.06
$V4_{rt}$	ADVP	−	R-time	4271.66	1364.57

Note. G-judgment = grammaticality judgment, R-time = response time.

not affect response times.[11] Means and standard deviations for variables $V1_{gj}$ through $V4_{rt}$ are shown in Table 4.2.

As an initial step the data were factor analyzed much as they were in Hagen (1990). Four factors were requested, allowing one for each method (grammaticality judgment/response time) and one for each syntactic feature we manipulated in (17) (REFL/~REFL and BASE/ADVP). The best fit of the data came from a Harris–Kaiser rotation, which produced oblique or correlated factors. The results are shown in Table 4.3. In a factor matrix like the one in Table 4.3, we expect to find some variance due to method alone. Indeed, Factor 1 shows its highest loadings on grammaticality judgment variables, and Factor 2 shows its highest loadings on response time variables (cf. the

---

[11]The test battery also included nine diversionary items, for instance, *Est-ce qu'il prend une tasse de café le matin avant de se laver?* 'Does he have a cup of coffee in the morning before bathing himself?', *Avant de regarder les informations, habille-toi.* 'Before watching the news, dress yourself', *Avant de regarder les informations, est-ce que tu les habilles toi-même?* 'Before watching the news, do you dress them yourself?', so as not to cue the subjects that the same choice was required in every instance.

TABLE 4.3
Rotated Factor Matrix of Correct Answers and Response Times

Label	VP	REFL	Measure	Factor[a] 1	2	3	4
$V1_{gj}$	BASE	+	G-judgment	.26	−.05	**.95**	.36
$V2_{gj}$	ADVP	+	G-judgment	**.98**	−.08	.29	.47
$V3_{gj}$	BASE	−	G-judgment	**.39**	−.16	.64	**.83**
$V4_{gj}$	ADVP	−	G-judgment	**.45**	−.22	.26	**.92**
$V1_{rt}$	BASE	+	r-time	−.19	**.82**	−.34	−.20
$V2_{rt}$	ADVP	+	r-time	−.12	**.84**	.11	−.09
$V3_{rt}$	BASE	−	r-time	−.01	**.87**	−.10	**−.30**
$V4_{rt}$	ADVP	−	r-time	−.10	**.84**	.02	−.23

[a]Highest loadings are shown in boldface.

loadings in boldface in Table 4.3). Notice, however, that in the case of Factor 1 some of these loadings are fairly weak in magnitude.

We should also expect to find some variance corresponding to the hypothesized first-language effects postulated in (9) and (11). This too is supported somewhat by the factor matrix in Table 4.3. Factor 3 has by far its highest loadings on grammaticality judgments of base VPs, whereas Factor 4 has its highest loadings on grammaticality judgments of nonreflexive pronouns (though note as well the moderate loadings on $V2_{gj}$). Recalling what was said earlier about explicit knowledge and negative correlations between response times and grammaticality judgments, on Factor 3, $V1_{gj}$ and $V3_{gj}$ show some signs of an inverse relation with their corresponding response times. That is, the highest magnitude negative loadings on response times correspond to the highest magnitude positive loadings on grammaticality judgments. The same is true of $V3_{gj}$, $V4_{gj}$, $V3_{rt}$, $V4_{rt}$ in Factor 4, consistent with Krashen's claims about monitoring. However, considering the relatively low-magnitude loadings overall on response times for Factors 3 and 4, the relationship is not compelling. At any rate, there are no indications of adverse effect of explicit knowledge or monitoring on the grammaticality judgment tasks in Table 4.3. On the contrary, if Factor 3 represents the Spanish-as-L1 effect postulated in (11), and if Factor 4 represents the English-as-L1 effect in (9), then our hypotheses are right on target so far.

The matrix from the factor analysis in Table 4.3, however, is not nearly as perspicuous as the one in Hagen (1990), most likely because the subjects in Hagen's study were quite homogeneous with respect to L1 background, whereas those in the present study were not. Thus, let us consider another method of analysis. The experimental design is illustrated in (19):

(19)   V1   V2   V3   V4

L_{English} S1   S1   S1   S1
                    S2   S2   S2   S2

. . .

L_{Spanish} Sm   Sm   Sm   Sm
                    Sn   Sn   Sn   Sn

We have dependent samples, and a simple ANOVA is thus inappropriate. We use instead a repeated-measures ANOVA and a General Linear Models procedure for unequal group size.

There are three sources of variance in this design: (a) group effect, (b) treatment effect, and (c) group-treatment interaction. The first will tell us if, setting aside differences between the sentence types in (17), the two L1 groups represent the same distribution of means. Similarly, the second will tell us if, setting aside L1, the results from the four sentence types represent the same distribution of means. Finally, the third will tell us if the two L1 groups respond in a significantly different fashion to the different sentence types. Variance due to group effect is of only marginal interest because it is amenable to too many explanations (e.g., the Spanish speakers are somewhat more proficient, they take research projects more seriously, or they study more). Variance due to treatment is of some interest because it tells us whether or not we have gained anything at all by manipulating syntactic features in the manner shown in (17). However, it alone will not reveal a great deal more than the factor analysis in Table 4.3. In short, testing for statistically significant differences of means between groups or between treatments will not in itself surmount the problems of confounding aggregate results and individual results that Eckman discussed in his study.

Variance due to group-treatment interaction, on the other hand, will tell us whether or not Spanish and English speakers differ significantly in their grammaticality judgments for base/adjunct VPs and reflexive/nonreflexive pronouns. With this in mind, let us repeat our original hypotheses and spell out what sort of results will support them:

H1: The morphological identity between reflexive and nonreflexive pronouns in French is a source of error only for English-speaking learners of French (predicting treatment effect for English speakers only on a comparison of REFL/∼REFL variables, thus significant treatment by group interaction).

H2: The pro/enclitic parameter in Spanish is a source of error only for Spanish-speaking learners of French (predicting treatment effect for Spanish speakers only on a comparison of BASE/ADVP variables, thus significant treatment by group interaction).

H3: For all second-language speakers, r-pronouns in NNGs are bound in base VPs as they are in adjunct VPs, by virtue of a nonviolable principle (predicting no treatment effect for English speakers on a comparison of BASE/ADVP variables, thus significant treatment by group interaction).

RESULTS

The results of the repeated measures ANOVA are shown in Tables 4.4 and 4.5. There is overall significance ($p = .0001$) for treatment or sentence type effect on grammaticality judgments but none for interaction ($p = .1055$); Spanish and English speakers responded in essentially the same fashion to the different sentence types.

This trend, illustrated in Figs. 4.1 and 4.2, is confirmed by pairwise post hoc comparisons. For instance, Table 4.5a shows that when a pronoun is reflexive, there is a statistically significant difference between the variable measuring adjunct VPs and the one measuring base VPs. Table 4.5b shows the same sort of statistical significance when the pronoun is not reflexive. This holds for both L1 groups. By the same token, Tables 4.5c and 4.5d show statistically significant differences between reflexives and their nonreflexive counterparts, and again this is true for both L1 groups. Although we had expected the REFL/~REFL distinction to be a source of error for English speakers only, the pairwise comparisons show no signs of interaction. The comparison of reflexives to nonreflexives among base VPs is significant for

TABLE 4.4
Comparison of Means: Grammaticality Judgments

Source: Treatment (Sentence Type)

df	Type III SS	Mean Square	F	p
3	65.03	21.68	19.82	0.0001*

Source: Interaction (Sentence Type by L1)

df	Type III SS	Mean Square	F	p
3	6.78	2.26	2.07	0.1055

Source: Error

df	Type III SS	Mean Square
222	242.76	1.09

Note. General Linear Models Procedure. Repeated Measures Analysis of Variance. Univariate Tests of Hypotheses for Within Subject Effects.
*Significant when $\alpha = .0001$.

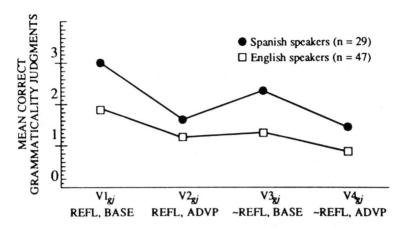

FIG. 4.1. Correct grammaticality judgments by sentence type.

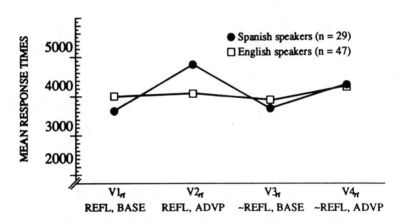

FIG. 4.2. Response times (in $\frac{1}{60}$th second increments) by sentence type.

TABLE 4.5a
Adjunct VPs Compared to Base VPs When a Pronoun is Reflexive

Source: Treatment (Sentence Type)

df	Type III SS	Mean Square	F	p
1	69.02	69.02	27.51	0.0001*

Source: Interaction (Sentence Type by L1)

df	Type III SS	Mean Square	F	p
1	9.49	9.49	3.79	0.05555

*Significant when α = .0001.

TABLE 4.5b
Adjunct VPs Compared to Base VPs When a Pronoun is Nonreflexive

Source: Treatment (Sentence Type)

df	Type III SS	Mean Square	F	p
1	31.35	31.35	18.38	0.0001*

Source: Interaction (Sentence Type by L1)

df	Type III SS	Mean Square	F	p
1	3.98	3.98	2.33	0.1309

*Significant when α = .0001.

TABLE 4.5c
Reflexives Compared to Nonreflexives When a VP is a Base Clause

Source: Treatment (Sentence Type)

df	Type III SS	Mean Square	F	p
1	27.12	27.12	11.80	0.0010*

Source: Interaction (Sentence Type by L1)

df	Type III SS	Mean Square	F	p
1	0.12	0.12	0.05	0.8222

*Significant when α = .001.

TABLE 4.5d
Reflexives Compared to Nonreflexives When a VP is an Adjunct Clause

Source: Treatment (Sentence Type)

df	Type III SS	Mean Square	F	p
1	6.24	6.24	3.73	0.0573

Source: Interaction (Sentence Type by L1)

df	Type III SS	Mean Square	F	p
1	0.56	0.56	0.33	0.566

all subjects ($p = 0.0001$), but the F value for interaction is not ($p = 0.8222$). The same comparison among adjuncts shows nearly the same results: Treatment effect is marginally significant ($p = .0573$), but the F value for interaction is well short of significance ($p = 0.566$).

All of this means that neither L1 nor UG offers an especially good account of the data. The pro/enclitic distinction, whether or not it is considered a matter of parametric variation, predicts differential responses among Spanish speakers only. Similarly, the reflexive/nonreflexive distinction in English morphology should be a source of error for English speakers only. The significant within-subject variance that turns up in the grammaticality judgment tasks is not due to L1 differences: English speakers are as likely as Spanish speakers to respond differentially across-the-board. Moreover, setting aside the results from the Spanish-speaking group, Fig. 4.1 and its corresponding statistics from Table 4.5d show that differential responses between base VPs and infinitival VPs that did not turn up in Hagen (1990) are in fact evident here. In other words, r-binding does not extend into adjuncts in the NNGs of the English speakers. Thus there is no support for any of the hypotheses in (9), (11), and (13).

DISCUSSION

Now let us sum up the major points of this study. We set out to identify those aspects of parameter models of SLA that are likely to be problematic as the details of theory construction are worked out. I have focused on three aspects.

First, these models have so far taken for granted that the constructs to be studied have already been laid out correctly in GB theory. There are, nonetheless, counterclaims from other theories that have a direct bearing on the issues raised in SLA research and that need to be taken seriously. Newmeyer (1987) made this point some time ago:

> The dominant trend [in SLA] has been to adopt the assumptions of GB, paralleling the fact that within linguistic theory itself, GB has considerably more supporters than the other models. But still a lingering, and entirely understandable, feeling persists that if so many questions about linguistic theory are still up for grabs, then the results of an allied field which are based on a specific set of assumptions internal to one particular theoretical framework can hardly be secure. (p. 4)

Admittedly, Newmeyer's tone was more optimistic than that in the present discussion. In any event, regardless of whether one prefers GB or GPSG as a point of departure, SLA theory construction will require a thorough accounting of the facts regarding NNGs through systematic data gathering. There is no reason why anyone cannot or should not construct a general account of those data quite apart from any prepackaged theory from generative syntax. Surely any points of convergence between SLA and theoretical syntax would be all the more compelling if they were motivated independently of one another.

Second, even in cases where there is essential agreement among competing syntactic theories as to the nature of L1s, SLA research needs to sharpen its research methods if it chooses to do reliable empirical data analysis involving NNGs. With some modifications and improvements, the methods presented in this chapter show promise for measurement validation as well as for hypothesis testing. Factorial ANOVAs like the one used here permit greater precision in pinpointing differences between L1 groups, as Flynn's (1984, 1989) research has already demonstrated. However, the computer-driven format has the additional merits of permitting (a) repeated-measures designs, and (b) measurement of response times. Repeated-measures designs have the advantage of allowing the researcher to control for within-subject differences while substantially reducing the number of subjects required in experiments (Pedhazur, 1982). Traditionally, they have been used sparingly because they are susceptible to carry-over effects when "treatments administered earlier in the sequence continue to affect the behavior of subjects while they are being administered a subsequent treatment" (Pedhazur, 1982, p. 553). Latin Square Designs circumvent this problem by alternating the order of presentation of experimental treatments for all subjects (Tabachnick & Fidell, 1983), so that any inherent ordering effects will merely inflate the error term. Complete randomization of stimuli by computer accomplishes the same objective more thoroughly while doing away with a slew of logistical problems involved in staggering the order of many stimuli for many learners and reassembling the results afterwards. Once an experiment is moved into computer format, it is easy enough to keep track of response times, which, as we noted earlier, allow for hypothesis testing regarding the use of conscious or explicit grammar rules during grammaticality judgment tasks.

Third, the results of the study discussed here show that neither parametric variation nor the parochial first-language principles that were investigated worked as explanations for errors in grammaticality judgments for the stimulus sentences. Among other things, this means that the rather strong claim in Hagen (1990)—that the structure of pronominal systems in NNGs can be explained by first-language principles—is wrong. In fact, not even the "nonviolable" principle of r-binding worked well as an explanatory construct in this study, because the judgments of English speakers regarding the acceptability of locally bound reflexives did not extend to adjunct VPs. Thus the results point to an issue of substance that has already come up in work by Clahsen (1988), Bley-Vroman (1989), and others: "UG principles available to L1 learners are not available to adults" (Clahsen, 1988, p. 69). If further research supports this proposal, an explanation of this fundamental difference between L2s and L1s will be in order.

APPENDIX: STIMULUS SENTENCES

V1.
1. Before listening to the radio in the morning do you get up?
   Avant d'écouter la radio le matin est-ce que tu te lèves?
2. Before having a cup of coffee do you bathe?
   Avant de prendre une tasse de café est-ce que tu te laves?
3. Before preparing breakfast in the morning do you fix your hair?
   Avant de préparer le petit déjeuner le matin est-ce que tu te coiffes?
4. Before watching the news on TV do you get dressed?
   Avant de regarder les informations à la télé est-ce que tu t'habilles?

V2.
1. Do you listen to the radio before getting up in the morning?
   Est-ce que tu écoutes la radio avant de te lever le matin?
2. Do you have a cup of coffee before bathing?
   Est-ce que tu prends une tasse de café avant de te laver?
3. Do you prepare breakfast before fixing your hair?
   Est-ce que tu prépares le petit déjeuner avant de te coiffer?
4. Do you watch the news on TV before getting dressed?
   Est-ce que tu regardes les informations à la télé avant de t'habiller?

V3.
1. Before listening to the radio in the morning do I get you up?
   Avant d'écouter la radio le matin est-ce que je te lève?
2. Before having a cup of coffee, do I bathe you?
   Avant de prendre une tasse de café est-ce que je te lave?
3. Before preparing breakfast, do I fix your hair?
   Avant de préparer le petit déjeuner est-ce que je te coiffe?
4. Before watching the news on TV do I dress you?
   Avant de regarder les informations à la télé est-ce que je t'habille?

V4.
1. Do I listen to the radio in the morning before getting you up?
   Est-ce que j'écoute la radio le matin avant de te lever?
2. Do I have a cup of coffee before bathing you?
   Est-ce que je prends une tasse de café avant de te laver?
3. Do I prepare breakfast before fixing your hair?
   Est-ce que je prépare le petit déjeuner avant de te coiffer?

4. Do I watch the news on TV before dressing you?
Est-ce que je regarde les informations à la télé avant de t'habiller?

REFERENCES

Bès, G. (1986). Cliticos en frances y modelos lingüísticos [French clitics and linguistic models]. *Revista Argentina de Lingüística 2, 2,* 246–265.

Bès, G. (1988). Clitiques et constructions topicalisées dans une grammaire GPSG du français [Clitics and topicalized constructions in a GPSG grammar of French]. *Lexique, 6,* 55–81.

Bley-Vroman, R. (1989). What is the logical problem of foreign language learning? In S. Gass & J. Schachter (Eds.), *Linguistic perspectives on second language acquisition* (pp. 41–68). Cambridge: Cambridge University Press.

Chomsky, N. (1980). *Rules and representations.* New York: Columbia University Press.

Chomsky, N. (1981). *Lectures on government and binding.* Dordrecht: D. Reidel.

Chomsky, N. (1986). *Knowledge of language.* New York: Praeger.

Clahsen, H. (1988). Parameterized grammatical theory and language acquisition: A study of the acquisition of verb placement and inflection by children and adults. In S. Flynn & W. O'Neill (Eds.), *Linguistic theory and second language acquisition* (pp. 47–75). Dordrecht: Kluwer Academic Publishers.

Cohen Sherman, J., & Lust, B. (1986). Syntactic and lexical constraints on the acquisition of control in complement sentences. In B. Lust (Ed.), *Studies in the acquisition of anaphora: Vol. 1. Defining the constraints* (pp. 279–310). Dordrecht: D. Reidel.

Cook, V. J. (1985). Chomsky's universal grammar and second language learning. *Applied Linguistics, 6,* 2–18.

Felix, S. (1988). UG-generated knowledge in adult second language acquisition. In S. Flynn & W. O'Neill (Eds.), *Linguistic theory and second language acquisition* (pp. 277–294). Dordrecht: Kluwer Academic Publishers.

Finer, D. (1982). A non-transformational relation between causatives and non-causatives in French. In D. Flickenger, M. Macken, & N. Weigard (Eds.), *Proceedings of the First West Coast Conference on Formal Linguistics* (pp. 47–57). Stanford: Stanford Linguistics Association.

Flynn, S. (1983). Similarities and differences between first and second language acquisition: Setting the parameters of universal grammar. In D. Rogers & J. Sloboda (Eds.), *The acquisition of symbolic skills* (pp. 485–499). New York: Plenum.

Flynn, S. (1984). A universal in L2 acquisition based on a PBD typology. In F. Eckman, L. Bell, & R. D. Nelson (Eds.), *Universals of second language acquisition.* Rowley, MA: Newbury House.

Flynn, S. (1987a). *A parameter-setting model of L2 acquisition.* Dordrecht: D. Reidel.

Flynn, S. (1987b). Second language acquisition of pronoun anaphora: Resetting the parameter. In B. Lust (Ed.), *Studies in the acquisition of anaphora* (Vol. 2, pp. 227–246). Dordrecht: D. Reidel.

Flynn, S. (1988). Nature and development in L2 acquisition and implications for theories of language acquisition in general. In S. Flynn & W. O'Neill (Eds.), *Linguistic theory and second language acquisition* (pp. 76–89). Dordrecht: Kluwer Academic Publishers.

Flynn, S. (1989). The role of the head-initial/head-final parameter in the acquisition of English relative clauses by adult Spanish and Japanese speakers. In S. Gass & J. Schachter (Eds.), *Linguistic perspectives on second language acquisition* (pp. 89–108). New York: Cambridge University Press.

Gazdar, G., Klein, E., Pullam, G., & Sag, I. (1985). *Generalized phrase structure grammar.* Cambridge, MA: Harvard University Press.

Gregg, K. (1989). Second language acquisition theory: The case for a generative perspective. In S. Gass & J. Schachter (Eds.), *Linguistic perspectives on second language acquisition* (pp. 15–40). New York: Cambridge University Press.

Hagen, L. K. (1990). The representation of clitics in the lexicons of English-speaking learners of French. Doctoral dissertation, University of Illinois at Urbana-Champaign.

Hulk, A. (1991). Parameter setting and the acquisition of word order in L2 French. *Second Language Research, 7*, 1–34.

Krashen, S. (1985). *The input hypothesis: Issues and implications*. New York: Longman.

Krashen, S. (1982). *Principles and practices in second language acquisition*. Oxford: Pergamon Press.

Liceras, J. (1985). The value of clitics in non-native Spanish. *Second Language Research, 1*, 151–168.

Liceras, J. (1988). L2 learnability: Delimiting the domain of core grammar as distinct from the marked periphery. In S. Flynn & W. O'Neill (Eds.), *Linguistic theory and second language acquisition* (pp. 199–224). Dordrecht: Kluwer Academic Publishers.

Lust, B. (1988). Universal grammar in second language acquisition: Promises and problems in the critically relating theory and empirical studies. In S. Flynn & W. O'Neill (Eds.), *Linguistic theory and second language acquisition* (pp. 309–328). Dordrecht: Kluwer Academic Publishers.

Lust, B., Solan, L., Flynn, S., Cross, C., & Shuetz, E. (1986). A comparison of null pronoun anaphora in first language acquisition. In B. Lust (Ed.), *Studies in the acquisition of anaphora: Vol. 1. Defining the constraints* (pp. 245–277). Dordrecht: D. Reidel.

Newmeyer, F. (1987). The current convergence in linguistic theory: Some implications for second language acquisition research. *Second Language Research, 3*, 1–19.

Pedhazur, E. (1982). *Multiple regression in behavioral research: Explanation and prediction* (2nd ed.). New York: Holt, Rinehart & Winston.

Pollard, C., & Sag, I. (1983). Reflexives and reciprocals in English: An alternative to the binding theory. In M. Barton, D. Flickenger, & M. Westcoat (Eds.), *Proceedings of the West Coast Conference on Formal Linguistics* (Vol. 2, pp. 189–203). Stanford: Stanford Linguistic Association.

Pollard, C., & Sag, I. (1987). *Information-based syntax and semantics*. Stanford: Center for the Study of Language and Information.

Ritchie, W. (1983a). Second language acquisition: Introduction. In D. Rogers & J. Sloboda (Eds.), *The acquisition of symbolic skills* (pp. 471–472). New York: Plenum.

Ritchie, W. (1983b). Universal grammar and second language acquisition. In D. Rogers & J. Sloboda (Eds.), *The acquisition of symbolic skills* (pp. 473–483). New York: Plenum.

Roeper, T. (1986). How children acquire bound variables. In B. Lust (Ed.), *Studies in the acquisition of anaphora: Vol. 1. Defining the constraints* (pp. 191–200). Dordrecht: D. Reidel.

Schachter, J. (1989). Testing a proposed universal. In S. Gass & J. Schachter (Eds.), *Linguistic perspectives on second language acquisition* (pp. 73–88). New York: Cambridge University Press.

Sells, P. (1985). *Lectures on contemporary theories of syntax*. Stanford: Center for the Study of Language and Information.

Tabachnick, B., & Fidell, L. (1983). *Using multivariate statistics*. New York: Harper & Row.

van Riemsdijk, H. (1986). Crossover between acquisition research and government and binding theory. In B. Lust (Ed.), *Studies in the acquisition of anaphora: Vol. 1. Defining the constraints* (pp. 311–318). Dordrecht: D. Reidel.

Verheijen, R., & Beukema, F. (1988). Anaphors and free adjuncts: A GPSG account. *Folia Linguistica: Acta Societatis Linguisticae Europaeae, 24*, 393–412.

Wexler, K., & Chien, Y.-C. (1985). The development of lexical anaphors and pronouns. *Papers and reports on child language development* (pp. 138–149). Stanford: Stanford University.

CHAPTER

5

TOWARD AN ETHNOMETHODOLOGICAL RESPECIFICATION OF SECOND-LANGUAGE ACQUISITION STUDIES

Numa P. Markee
University of Illinois at Urbana-Champaign

How well do applied linguists and second-language acquisition (SLA) researchers understand theory construction in our field? As attested by a number of books, edited collections, journal articles, and a recent conference devoted to theory construction, SLA researchers are becoming increasingly sophisticated in such matters. We have not only reached the stage where we are actively exploring what philosophy of science has to say about theory construction; we are also defining the goals of SLA research ever more precisely.

These developments are welcome signs that SLA studies are coming of age. However, this sense of growing maturity is being achieved at some cost to the field. As even a casual reading of the SLA literature will attest, the overwhelming majority of SLA studies are of the logico-deductive, experimental variety. Thus, whether they recognize this or not, most SLA researchers subscribe to a nomothetic epistemology that has, in my opinion, prematurely achieved the status of a dominant orthodoxy.

Although the results of nomothetic science are in many instances impressive, we should not be seduced into accepting the validity of this epistemological position without question. I therefore first present a critique of the current nomothetic orthodoxy in SLA research from an ethnomethodological perspective and then demonstrate how Conversation Analysis may be used to motivate the theoretical position that conversation is the sociocultural context of second-language learning.

A CRITIQUE OF THE CURRENT ORTHODOXY
IN SLA RESEARCH

Let me begin with a summary of some technical terms. Ochsner (1979) differentiates between nomothetic and hermeneutic scientific traditions by noting that the former is concerned with explaining and predicting how natural phenomena work, whereas the latter focuses on understanding and interpreting how these phenomena are organized. More specifically, nomothetic science (the Greek prefix *nomo* means "lawful") assumes the existence of a single, discoverable reality that causally obeys the laws of nature. In contrast, hermeneutics (meaning "the art of interpretation") assumes that multiple realities exist and that human events in particular can be interpreted only according to their outcomes. In terms of research methodology, an experimental, quantitative methodology is associated with the nomothetic tradition, and a naturalistic, qualitative methodology is associated with the hermeneutic tradition.

As I noted earlier, the dominant paradigm[1] in SLA research today is that of nomothetic science. The value of this tradition has been forcefully, even relentlessly, articulated by Mike Long and various colleagues and collaborators (see Crookes, 1991, 1992; Larsen-Freeman & Long, 1991; Long, 1985, 1990, in press, among others). Specifically addressing issues of theory construction, Larsen-Freeman and Long (1991) differentiated between two types of theories in nomothetic science. These are *causal-process* theories and *sets-of-laws* theories. They noted that sets-of-laws theories consist of collections of (often) unrelated generalizations or laws regarding SLA that are based on observed and tested relationships between variables. The problem with this type of research, according to the authors, is that it does not provide an explanation for the processes being studied; it merely establishes that they are in need of explanation. On the other hand, causal-process theories consist of definitions and operationalizations of abstract theoretical constructs, existence statements, and deterministic and/or probabilistic statements, which are mathematically tested to explain how and why SLA occurs. Larsen-Freeman and Long therefore argued that causal-process theories are the most desirable type of theory from a theory construction perspective because they lead to predictions and generalizations of great explanatory power.

A few writers, principally Schumann (1983, in press), supported by Candlin (1983), Guiora (1983), and van Lier (1988), have valiantly attempted to stem the nomothetic tide. But the debate has unfortunately been somewhat

---

[1]As Ochsner (1979) correctly noted, most of the social sciences (including SLA) are actually preparadigmatic and are likely to remain so for quite some time. For this reason, following Giddens (1988), I prefer to speak of a tradition rather than a paradigm.

lopsided. For the most part, these have been voices crying in the applied linguistic wilderness.

Various statements by Crookes, Larsen-Freeman and Long give a flavor of the confidence with which the nomothetic cause is being advanced in SLA studies. Thus, Crookes (1991) stated: "It may be that SL production research is at the point where the field is ready to move from primarily descriptive research to greater use of experimental investigations of a more obviously hypothesis-testing, theory-developing nature" (p. 125). Similarly, although acknowledging the utility and necessity of descriptive studies as a means of establishing baseline data, Larsen-Freeman and Long (1991) labeled these studies as limited and maintained that only a causal-process approach to theory construction can explain SLA.

I disagree with these statements for two reasons. First, although nomothetic science does not preclude descriptive studies, these statements have the undesirable (if unintentional) effect of severely undercutting the viability of hermeneutics in SLA studies by pinning a negative (and incorrect) label ("limited") on qualitative research.[2] And second, these statements gloss over the fact that a nomothetic epistemology is itself open to serious criticism, a fact that its proponents rarely mention, much less address in any serious fashion.[3]

Before I develop this latter point, I should make it clear that I am not interested in reopening the argument whether qualitative and quantitative approaches to SLA research are mutually exclusive. There is, in fact, considerable agreement, among SLA researchers on both sides of the methodological divide, that qualitative and quantitative studies are in reality complementary ways of creating new knowledge (see Allwright & Bailey, 1991; Chaudron, 1988; Cohen & Olshtain, this volume, chapter 8; Ellis, 1984; Grotjahn, 1991; Larsen-Freeman & Long, 1991; Long, 1983; Selinker & Douglas, this volume, chapter 6; Shohamy, this volume, chapter 7; van Lier, 1988; and Watson-Gegeo, 1988). I wholeheartedly endorse this assessment. What I wish to do in this chapter is reexamine the relative value that we currently

---

[2]In this regard, Long (in press) called for a culling of existing theories of SLA so that the field can progress to a period of paradigmatic stability, in which a so-called Dominant Theory will rule the SLA roost, and demanded that relativists explain why such a culling should not take place (see also Beretta, 1991). As mentioned earlier, we need only look at the preponderance of experimental research published in SLA journals to realize that a culling of SLA theories probably has already taken place. More specifically, the dominant nomothetic paradigm has in fact preempted the development of hermeneutic theories of SLA before their potential worth could be evaluated. This is a loss to the field, not an indication of theoretical maturity, because researchers (particularly doctoral students, on whom the field's capability for self-renewal rests) are thereby subtly discouraged from committing themselves to nonexperimental research.

[3]Thus, Crookes (1992) mentioned in passing that there are objections to experimental research but does not say what they are. And Larsen-Freeman and Long (1991) referred to hermeneutics only three times (in notes) in their entire book, never considering the possibility that hermeneutics can offer an explanatory theory of SLA.

ascribe to understanding versus explaining SLA phenomena and question whether explanation can be achieved only through a causal-process approach to SLA theorizing.

What are the weaknesses of a causal-process approach to SLA? I address this question from the perspective of ethnomethodology, a radical sociology in the hermeneutic tradition proposed by the sociologist Harold Garfinkel, who defined ethnomethodology as "the investigation of the rational properties of indexical expressions and other practical actions as contingent ongoing accomplishments of organized artful practices of everyday life" (Garfinkel, 1967, p. 11).

The ethnomethodological critique of nomothetic science focuses crucially on experimentalists' rejection of ordinary language and day-to-day experience as valid ways of knowing and organizing the world,[4] both these ways of accessing knowledge are viewed by experimentalists as too value-laden and subjective to be useful tools for science, which must above all else be value-free and objective. In order to go beyond the perceived inadequacies of the lay talk of ordinary social actors and the "shallow" explanations of social phenomena that a dependence on ordinary language generates, experimentalists have developed a highly technical language to describe their subject matter and to provide "deeper" explanations that are cast in terms of underlying causes and effects. Thus, they attempt to define and operationalize abstract theoretical constructs and develop logico-deductive hypotheses about a given phenomenon (such as SLA), which they then set out to falsify using the pure, value-free language of mathematics. But in their efforts to develop this objective, value-free language, experimentalists are confronted with the contradiction that the technical language and causative explanations of social science cannot be anything but parasitic upon the ordinary language of social actors and their lay explanations of everyday experience (Giddens, 1988).

More specifically, I wish to develop the following theses: The operationalization of constructs and the technical definitions that experimentalists develop are contaminated by the notion of *reasonable agreement* concerning the defining characteristics of a given phenomenon (Lynch, 1991).[5] Furthermore, experimentalists depend on lay talk as a component of any technical

---

[4]Of course, I do not mean to imply that experimental research on classroom discourse is not based on transcripts of actual classroom interaction. But these transcripts are merely the raw material for the subsequent coding and statistical analyses, which become the primary data for the experimental researcher.

[5]In his critique of orthodox social science, Lynch (1991) pointed out that for Kuhn (1961), " 'the only possible criterion' for assessing the agreement between the accepted numbers and observed measures 'is the mere fact that they appear, together with the theory from which they are derived, in a professionally accepted text' " (p. 78). For example, physicists can decide, given current measurement techniques, that a discrepancy between the predicted and actual orbit of

definition (Coulter, 1991) and/or depend on highly metaphorical language to develop their arguments. In addition, the degree to which a discipline has been mathematized (i.e., the extent to which it routinely uses inferential statistics to test predicted interactions between variables) is not necessarily an indication of maturity. Not only can the use of some statistical procedures result in unnecessarily opaque discourse whose actual conclusions may in the end be comparatively meager, but the supposed objectivity of such discourse also frequently camouflages the many practical decisions, judgments, and subjective interpretations that inform this attempt to objectivize the language of science (see Benson & Hughes, 1991; Sharrock & Button, 1991). Therefore, there can be no absolute guarantee that an abstract, mathematical explanation of a phenomenon is necessarily superior to a hermeneutic explanation that is constructed in terms of lay participants' real-time understanding of the same phenomenon[6] (Sharrock & Button, 1991).

Let me now illustrate what I mean by critiquing some undeniably good examples of recent experimental SLA research. This research has been selected to show that, notwithstanding its careful research design and attention to detail, it is nonetheless vulnerable to the criticisms outlined previously.

In line with the position developed by Long (1983), Long and Porter (1985) and Porter (1986) used the qualitative work on conversational repair in Schegloff, Jefferson, and Sacks (1977) to generate their own operational definition of repair as a prelude to quantification and experimentation. Briefly, Long and Porter defined repair as a composite variable consisting of six subcategories including confirmation checks, clarification requests, comprehension checks, verifications of meaning, definition requests, and expressions of lexical uncertainty. They used this new definition of repair to test hypotheses about the relative importance of different types of input and interaction that native and nonnative speakers provide to each other in task-centered talk. These hypotheses were inspired by Long's (1981) hypothesis that negotiated comprehensible input is the necessary and sufficient cause of language learning.

The first problem that Long and Porter came up against was that their operationalization of the construct of repair was based on the notion of reasonable agreement. That is, they accepted that Schegloff et al.'s treatment of repair was an accurate and trustworthy account of how participants actually

---

a planet is acceptably accurate or that this discrepancy is due to the effect of gravitational forces from an as yet undiscovered planet, only on the basis of what other respected researchers have said on the subject. For the purposes of this chapter, I maintain that the notion of reasonable agreement underlies all attempts to infer, interpret, or argue a particular point of view.

[6]See the second part of this chapter (in particular, footnote 23) for a discussion of the methodology that is used to identify participants' understanding of the conversations they construct. I wish to emphasize that the methodology of Conversation Analysis does not use the kind of triangulated self-report procedures that are a familiar part of ethnographic research.

achieve repair. Note that I am not denying the high quality of Schegloff et al.'s work here (which would be foolish, because it constitutes a foundation for the analysis presented in the second part of this chapter). What I am pointing out is that, in terms of their own epistemology, the supposedly objective research enterprise described by Long and Porter in their various papers is founded on the quicksand of opinion, however well informed this opinion may be. The ostensibly scientific definition of the composite variable of repair that they propose cannot escape being contaminated by the so-called imprecisions of everyday language, because our understanding of notions like comprehension checks and clarification requests (as shown by the italicized turns in the following extracts) must necessarily depend ultimately on examples of ordinary talk extracted from transcripts of the participants' original conversations:

Comprehension check

L: To sin- uh . . . to sink
N: *Do you know what that is?*
L: To go uh-
N: To go under . . .

Definition request

L: . . . *what is the meaning of research?*
N: Um, study? You study a problem and find an answer.
(Porter, 1986, p. 207, emphasis original)

With respect to the question of camouflage in this particular research, notice that the statistical analyses reported later to test the hypotheses of the study depend crucially on such categories as comprehension checks and definition requests being objectively distinct. But what Porter's analysis glosses over is that, from a participant's intersubjective perspective, these categories have little or no psychological validity. They are in fact superficial artifices of the analyst that distort the pragmatic intent of the participants. More specifically, there is no real-world justification for treating these two categories as discrete illocutionary acts. The interlocutors in both extracts orient to (a) a need to resolve some trouble in their conversation, and (b) a resolution by means of some definitional work on the lexical items that are problematic. Arguably, therefore, the single category of *defining*, in which the meaning that the participants themselves attach to what they are doing is intersubjectively constructed over several turns, seems better motivated by the data than the two categories proposed by Porter. The analyst's subjective and unwarranted decision to treat these categories as discrete entities therefore inevitably taints the subsequent statistical analysis.

I wish to emphasize that these kinds of problems are not peculiar to the particular research I have just reviewed. For example, with respect to the issue of how important it is to mathematize a discipline if it is to have anything worthwhile to say, the work of Bayley (this volume, chapter 9) also illustrates some of the problems faced by researchers who work in the nomothetic tradition rather well.

Bayley explained the interlanguage variation exhibited by Mandarin Chinese speakers of English as a second language with respect to their use of the phonetic form of the past tense and their use of grammatical aspect by using the method of *maximum likelihood estimation*, a form of multivariate statistical analysis. This is expressed by the following mathematical formula:

$$\frac{P}{1-P} = \frac{Po \times Pi}{1-Po} \times \frac{PJ}{1-Pj} \times \cdots \times \frac{Pn}{1-Pj}$$

The exact meaning (or, rather, the lack of meaning to perhaps the majority of his readers) of this supposedly objective but hardly very transparent equation required Bayley to devote about a quarter of his chapter to explaining what all this actually means. Yet, in order to explain this highly abstract communication, Bayley had to explain himself through language!

The persistent reader was rewarded with the conclusion that "variation in interlanguage tense marking is indeed systematically conditioned by a range of linguistic, social, and developmental factors" (which are then outlined in greater detail). I leave it to readers to decide whether their investment of time and energy into an understanding of the statistical procedure was worth the conclusions that Bayley reached.

Finally, the question of metaphor in "objective" research is highly problematic for the nomothetic tradition (and indeed for researchers who work in the more logical-deductive tradition that informs much formal linguistic research). Consider the following citation from Bley-Vroman and Chaudron (this volume, chapter 13), in which the authors set out their ideas on how language is stored in the brain:

In keeping with nearly all present thinking on language processing, we assume that, in the native speaker, the language processor automatically and obligatorily produces representations of the input and does not itself require the use of short-term memory. To borrow the evocative allusion of Fodor (1983), parsing is·not "sicklied o'er with the pale cast of thought" (p. 64). In the conception of current generative linguistics, the language processor is "encapsulated" in a language module (see Garfield, 1987, for papers in this tradition). Parsing thus cannot affect imitation accuracy directly by "filling up" short-term memory. It is important to be clear about this matter. The claim is not that the parser has no memory store: No doubt it has at least some sort of "look-ahead buffer" (Berwick & Weinberg, 1984). Rather, whatever the store used by the parser, it is

not the same short-term store that is used by a subject in remembering what
was said in order to repeat it. (quotation marks original)

What is remarkable about this extract is that it draws on no less than three
different metaphors in one paragraph to clarify the authors' position. These
metaphors are identified explicitly by the use of quotation marks. First, there
is the Shakespearean metaphor, which is used throughout the chapter to provide one explanation of how short-term memory may work. Second, there
is the formalist metaphor of generative linguistics, which suggests that the
language processor (whatever that is, neurobiologically) is "encapsulated"
in something called a language module (again, whatever this might be, from
a neurobiological perspective). And third, there are the artificial intelli-
gence/computer science metaphors of "filling up" memory banks and putative "look-ahead buffers."

The reader may wonder which of these three metaphors is the most important in these authors' discussion. Furthermore, it is instructive to consider
that if this chapter had been written in the 17th century, we most likely would
have been presented with a metaphor involving language as a well-regulated
mechanism that could be explained by analogy with the chronometer (the
dominant metaphor of the day, used by Newton and others to explain the
universe). Thus, a fundamental epistemological question for researchers working in this kind of tradition is: Does the use of such metaphors serve to clarify the phenomenon of SLA or does it serve merely to obfuscate it?

Experimental researchers interested in developing causative theories of
SLA may reply that these kinds of issues are merely technical problems that
should not sidetrack us from the real business of SLA research, which is to
provide causative explanations of SLA. Furthermore, so the argument runs,
many of these objections can be met by developing better coding procedures.

The development of better coding procedures is indeed always a possibility. However, the elaboration per se of better analytical categories does not
circumvent the basic problem of "objective" technical definitions being dependent on "subjective" lay talk and/or on the inescapable use of metaphor.
But even if we accept the technocratic argument that these deeper epistemological matters can be set aside temporarily in the interests of scientific
progress (an argument that, of course, I do not accept), it is by no means
an irrefutable, objective fact that only nomothetic science can explain SLA
phenomena.

As we have seen, the categories that constitute Porter's composite variable of repair by themselves tell us next to nothing about the fundamental
properties of second-language learning. For example, we do not know
whether, by repairing their speech, the learners in the two extracts actually
understood, much less learned, what the words *to sink* or *research* mean.
Thus, the use of quantified data cannot tell us whether a particular conversa-

tional mechanism (such as turn-taking or repair) is actually available as a resource for second-language learning; it merely tells us how often this mechanism occurs in a conversation and whether this frequency of occurrence is statistically significant. Thus, SLA researchers are left in the peculiar position of positing that negotiated comprehensible input is an important variable in SLA, without really knowing on the basis of empirical evidence what successful input (i.e., input that results in demonstrable learning) actually looks like in context. Ironically, therefore, the kind of *predictive explanation* (Watson-Gegeo, 1988) that researchers working in the nomothetic tradition seek to construct seems to be quite limited in its ability to capture the essence of the phenomena I have just been discussing.

In contrast, the originality of the ethnomethodological respecification of social science (and therefore of SLA studies) offered by Giddens (1988) and others is that this respecification (a) problematizes the methodological assumptions in traditional social science about the process of theory construction as intersubjectively achieved phenomena that are worthy of analysis in their own right; and (b) embraces ordinary language as the indispensable medium for analyzing participants' constructions of their everyday experience, whether this analysis is done by participants or by analysts. Thus, as Benson and Hughes (1991) put it, ethnomethodology is an attempt to make the world investigable in the participants' own terms. Consequently, from an ethnomethodological perspective, the scientific rigor of a study is not evaluated in terms of the sophistication of the statistical techniques that might be employed, because ethnomethodologists rarely use such techniques. Rather, a study is rigorous to the extent that it explains the intersubjective achievement in which participants understand the locally recognizable and locally adequate turns-at-talk that they engage in to organize their world.

At the risk of being accused of setting up a straw man and/or of being redundant, I predict that many experimentalists will raise the familiar objections: (a) such a program of research is useful only to describe baseline SLA phenomena but, cannot explain SLA for the reason given in (b); (b) ethnomethodologists do not attempt to make a priori predictions that can be falsified experimentally; and (c) ethnomethodologists do not work with large groups of subjects, which is the only methodology that can explain SLA phenomena in such a way that the results can be generalized from the subjects tested to a broader population of learners.

It should be obvious by now that I believe that objections of this kind entirely miss the point of the arguments developed in this chapter. Perhaps an example from anatomy will demonstrate the fallacy of such arguments. It would be a very strange version of anatomy indeed that insisted that the function of the human heart as a pump could be reliably explained only by dissecting a large number of hearts to check whether the pumping hypothesis was true of a statistically significant sample of hearts, so that this fact could be generalized to the entire population of human beings. Dissecting a single cadaver is sufficient to demonstrate (i.e., explain) that the heart does indeed function as a pump. Similarly, researchers interested in the "anatomy" of conversation (i.e., its structure) can make valid generalizations from single cases to the broader population because, as Benson and Hughes (1991) argued, "the point of working with 'actual occurrences,' single instances, single events, is to see them as the products of 'machinery' that constituted members' cultural competence enabling them to do what they do, produce the activities and scenes of everyday life . . . the explication, say, of some segment of talk in terms of the 'mechanism' by which *that* talk was produced *there* and *then*, is an explication of some part of culture" (p. 130, emphasis original). Thus, although the explanation is of a different type (what Watson-Gegeo, 1988, p. 576, calls "interpretive explanation"), it is no less powerful and generalizable in its own terms than is predictive explanation.

AN SLA PHENOMENON RESPECIFIED:
A CONVERSATION-ANALYTIC EXPLICATION
OF SPOKEN DEFINITIONS

I now demonstrate how Conversation Analysis (CA), a manifestation of ethnomethodology that has already been successfully used in SLA research (see van Lier, 1988, and others), can be used to provide an interpretive explanation of the mechanisms that enable language learners to use spoken definitions as a resource for language learning. Four basic assumptions govern CA work (Heritage, 1988):[7] (a) conversation has structure; (b) conversation is its own autonomous context—that is, the meaning of a particular utterance is shaped by what immediately precedes it and also by what immediately follows it; (c) there is no a priori justification for believing that any detail of conversation, however minute, is disorderly, accidental, or irrelevant; and (d) the study of conversation requires naturally occurring data.

Because the rules of evidence used by conversation analysts are not as well understood as those used by experimental researchers, let me briefly review what counts as evidence in CA and the kinds of claims made by conversation analysts (in this regard, see Jacobs, 1986, 1987, whose work forms the basis of the following summary). The methodology of CA is qualitative and subject to the usual evaluation criteria for qualitative research. Beyond this, however, the methodology of CA attempts to explicate the lay knowledge of conversationalists by "unpacking" examples that demonstrate the participants' orientations to the conversations they construct in real time. Such

---

[7]See also Jefferson and Schenkein (1978), Levinson (1983), Hopper (1988), Hopper, Koch, and Mandelbaum, (1988), McLaughlin (1988), and Zimmerman (1987) for comprehensive accounts of CA.

examples provide the primary evidence for the asserted existence of particular conversational mechanisms identified by analysts; a case is convincing to the extent that it is directly motivated by the conversational data presented for analysis. Thus, CA makes no appeal to ethnographic knowledge to make an argument. Furthermore, conversation analysts do not develop arguments about the structure of conversation on the basis of quantitative analyses of frequency data, because such analyses cannot tell us anything about the underlying structure of conversation per se.[8] Instead, conversation analysts seek to demonstrate that conversation could not be conversation if such universal interactional resources for constructing meaning as turn-taking, repair, or preference rules[9] did not exist.

In order to demonstrate the existence of such phenomena, conversation analysts use prototypical examples[10] that give discursive form to the phenomenon being analyzed. But such examples are not by themselves sufficient to make a convincing argument. Analysts must be able to corroborate their claims by pointing to a convergence of different types of textual evidence or by showing that a single structure identified by the analyst plays a role in different types of cases. Note that the use of convergent evidence, like the use of related data, is a particularly important resource in countering the charge that an analysis is merely an artifact of the examples collected and chosen for presentation to readers. Thus, for example, a preceding preinvitation turn shows that reading the following turn as an invitation is contextually warranted. Finally, analyses must be subject to critical falsification. That is, analysts must demonstrate that potential counterexamples and different accounts for the same data set have been anticipated and that other researchers can replicate findings with different transcripts. Let us now move on to an analysis of classroom data that demonstrates how CA might be used to motivate an ethnomethodological respecification of SLA studies.

THE DATABASE

The complete database for this project consists of 14 lower-intermediate to upper-intermediate English as a Second Language (ESL) classes at a large research university located in the Midwest of the United States. These classes were video- and audiotaped during spring semester, 1990. Each class lasted

---

[8]Of course, this does not mean that CA researchers never report regularities in behavior (see Heritage & Greatbatch, 1986, and Jefferson, 1988) or that some researchers do not follow up their initial studies with experimental research (see Wilson & Zimmerman, 1986).

[9]For an account of preference rules in CA, see Bilmes (1988).

[10]I prefer this term (which is used by Jacobs, 1986) to the notion of a *paradigm case* (used by Jacobs, 1987).

50 minutes. Currently, the conversations of 3 teachers and 33 learners (11 in Class 1, 10 in Class 2, and 12 in Class 3) interacting in ordinary classrooms[11] have been fully transcribed, using transcription conventions that are based on those developed by Jefferson (1978) and van Lier (1988) (see Appendix). The data analyzed in this chapter come from Class 2 only.

DATA COLLECTION PROCEDURES

Two video cameras were used to film the participants, who were visually identified by a number pinned to their clothing (i.e., L1, L2, L3, etc.); the video signals were fed into an electronic switcher operated by an assistant. Camera 1 (the main camera) recorded learners interacting in groups or whole class activities, and Camera 2 filmed teacher-fronted activities and/or presentations by students using the blackboard or overhead projector. These video recordings were used primarily to check visually who was speaking to whom when this information could not be determined from the audio data (see Fig. 5.1 for a graphic representation that shows the layout of the class, the position of the two cameras, and the composition of the groups in Class 2).

The audio recordings are the primary sources of data. Each participant was issued a numbered Walkman-sized stereo cassette recorder and a lapel microphone. The number on each recorder (and on each cassette) corresponded to the number pinned to a participant's clothing. This set-up allowed the analyst to identify participants visually on the videotape and aurally on their audiotapes. The portability of this equipment also enabled teachers and students to move around the class without having to worry about problems like tripping over cables. The availability of multiple audio recordings meant that such technically significant information as the difference between pauses and inhaled or exhaled breaths, the specific number of laughter tokens, the precise onset and resolution of overlaps, and the content of muttered commentaries could be distinguished and therefore transcribed with a high degree of confidence. Transcripts for each group and teacher in every class were produced on the basis of these multiple recordings; in the case of Class 2, this yielded a total of six transcripts for the lesson (four parallel transcripts for the four groups, one teacher's transcript, and one transcript consisting of collections of definitions excerpted from the class interaction).

---

[11]That is, the teachers could teach what they wanted, how they wanted. This contrasts with the more experimental nature of much classroom research, in which the kinds of activities teachers use are prespecified and variables such as the composition of groups (in terms of characteristics like gender and proficiency level) are carefully controlled by the researcher.

(Front)

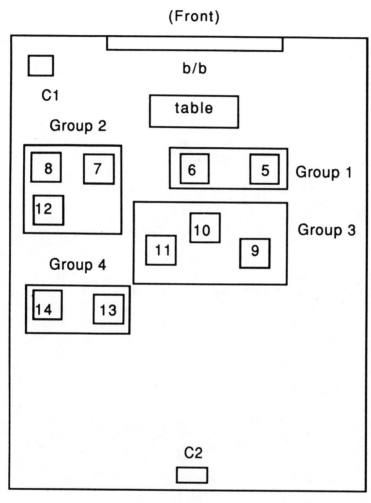

(Back)

C1 = camera 1 (main camera)
C2 = camera 2 (secondary camera)
b/b = blackboard

FIG. 5.1. Seating plan.

THE TASKS

The tasks learners had to complete in Class 2 involved an open-ended four-way exchange of information. Students first read and discussed, in four small groups, one of four thematically-related magazine articles on the greenhouse effect. A representative or representatives from each group then presented the information contained in each reading with an overhead projector in an oral, whole-class activity. The end product was some written work, which was done in a later class that was not recorded. Approximately 30 minutes (which included 5 to 10 minutes of silent reading, depending on the group) were allocated to small group discussion and about 20 minutes were given over to three oral presentations. The first seven excerpts cited here were produced collaboratively by Group 3 during the group work phase, and Excerpt 8 was produced by L10 (an erstwhile member of Group 3) as part of the oral report to the whole class.

THE DATA

Excerpt I: Group Work Phase

```
1 L10:   <hh> hhhh what is th- what is the (+) coral (+) what's ((whis-
2        per)) (+) I don't know (h)
3 L11:   just- look at it (+) as a (+) an m- material that's all
4        (+)
5 L9?:   uhm don't worry about it
6        (+)
```

Excerpt 2: Group Work Phase

```
1 L10:   excuse me what is c-o-r-a-l ((L10 spells out the word))
2        (+)
3 T:     can I: (+) open //(h)// <h> (+ +) get an idea (+) see where's that
4 L10:              //(h)//
5 L10:   <h> I don't know whether the-
6        (+)
7 T:     corals (+) does anyone know? (+) where you find corals?
8 L9:    corals (+) u- underwater //you mean? under the-//
9 T:                        //uh huh,//
10       (+)
```

11 T: that's right yeah some-
12 L9:   //under// the sea? //in the sea//
13 T: //down-//
14 L10:   //oh hh//
15 T: ex- counting some shells o//:r I don't// know s-
16 L9:   //shells yeah//
17   (+)
18 L10: **at the bottom of the of the s- (+) sea?**
19   (+)
20 T: yeah
21   (+)
22 L9:   **at the bottom**
23 L10: o:h
24 L9:   //yes//
25 L10: //oh// ok oh I see (+) thank you <h>

Excerpt 3: Group Work Phase

1 T: ok when you're explaining that to the: uh to the class or (+)
2   whoever is <h> probably //you'll// have to
3 L9:   //((unintelligible whisper))//
4 T: say (+) what corals (+) are //= because//
5 L10:   //what is// corals
6 T: yeah give a definition of //uh of corals//
7 L10:   //oh okay what is corals maybe uh//
8   (+)
9 L10:   or say-
10 T: or give an example say //for// instance in //Austra://lia (+)
11 L9:   //((unintelligible whisper))//
12 L10:   //oh yeah,//
13 T: around Australia you get lots of barrier reefs
14 L9:   (barrier reefs)
15 T: //o//therwise people might not kno:w (+) might not be
16 L10: //oh//
17 T: f//amiliar with that word//
18 L10: //oh ok, ok **coral reefs**//
19   (1)

Excerpt 4: Group Work Phase

1 L10:   what is uh corals I don't know
2 L11:   did you read (in) about corals

3 L9?:   no
4   (+ +)

Excerpt 5: Group Work Phase

1 L10:   both of them what they say
2   (1.3)
3 L10:   coral. what is corals
4   (4)
5 L9:   <hh> do you know the under the sea, under the sea,
6 L10:   un-
7 L9:   there's uh:: (+) //how do we call it//
8 L10:   //have uh some coral//
9 L9:   ah yeah (+) coral sometimes
10   (+)
11 L10:   eh includ[ə]s (+) uh includes some uh: somethings uh-
12   (+ +)
13 L10:   //the corals,// is means uh: (+) s somethings **at bottom of**
14 L9:   //((unintelligible))//
15 L10:   //**the**// **sea**
16 L9:   //yeah,//
17 L9:   **at the bottom of the sea,**
18*L10:   ok uh:m also is a food for is a food for fish uh and uh
19   (+)
20 L9:   food?
21   (+)
22 L10:   foo-
23*L9:   no it is not a food it is like a stone you know?
24*L10:   oh I see I see I see I see I see I know I know (+) I see (+) a
25*   whi- (+) a kind of a (+) white stone <h> //very beautiful//
26*L9:   //yeah yeah// very
27*   big yeah //sometimes very beautiful and// sometimes when
28*L10:   //I see I see I ok//
29*L9:   the ship moves ship tries ((unintelligible)) I think it was the
30*   ((unintelligible; the final part of this turn is overlapped by
31   L10's next turn as shown by // //))
32*L10:   //oh I see (+) I see the Chinese is uh (+)// [sanku]
33   (+ +)
34 L11:   uh?
35*L10:   [sanku]

36   (+)
37 L9:   what
38*L10:   c//orals//
39*L11:   //corals//
40 L9:   corals oh okay
41 L10:   yeah

Excerpt 6 (simplified): Group Work Phase

1 L10:   **fis[ə]I** (+ +) **fis[ə]I** ((whisper)) (+) <h> **I think (+) the**
2   **coral is also is a fis** (("fis" is whispered)) **is a fi-**
3   **f::** ((unintelligible whisper))
4 L9:   fi-shing?
5 L10:   if- (1) how to s- how to spell <hhh>
6   (1)
7 L10:   //**fis-**//
8 L9:   //**foss**//**il** (+) **fossil**

Excerpt 7 (simplified): Group Work Phase

1 L11:   ok (+) excuse me (+) uh: what what does it mean hab- (+)
2   habi-
3   . . .
4 T: <h> yeah what would be another word for a **habitat** then
5   (+) it's like (1) //it's hli-//
6 L11:   //I ha//ve no idea
7 L9:   //situation//
8 T: //'s like the whole// (+) situation (+) //**home**//
9 L10:   //**home**//

Excerpt 8: Whole Class Oral Discussion Phase

1 L10:   <h> in my section I think the main point is the: <hh> raising of
2   the sea (+) sea level <hh> we are accompanied uh global
3   tempera increasing <hh> (+) so these (+) put the co[I]al (+) at
4   [I]isk. <h> **I think the co[I]al is the kind of fossil** (+) <h>
5   **fossil at the: botto of the sea.** <hh> **the: co[I]al reef**
6   you are one of the imp- very important, <hh> **habitats** (+)
7   fo:r fish that support th[ə]:m more than (+) <h> one (+) more

8   than one third of topic- topical species. <hh> the **habitats**
9   is the: **home** (+) is the **home** for animal living <hh> so this is
10   very important (+) very important <hhh> so: now, the
11   conversationalist uh want to find some [v]ay: (+) to save
12   these uh (+) to: (+) solve this problem.

A DEFINITION OF SPOKEN DEFINITIONS

For the purposes of the analysis of the larger corpus from which these data
were taken, the defining characteristics of spoken definitions[12] were determined not on the basis of a priori categories but on the basis of an analysis
of the interaction in all three fully transcribed classes. Thus, spoken definitions are not defined here as linguistic products (see Watson, 1985, for an
analysis of the linguistic structure of definitions) or as logical forms (see Flowerdew, 1991, 1992, for an analysis of definitions inspired by speech act theory). Rather, they are defined as any turn(s)-at-talk that are hearable by
participants as explanations of lexical items or phrases whose meaning is actually or potentially unclear.[13] More specifically, participants achieve definitions by simultaneously orienting to the resources of turn-taking and repair
available to them as conversationalists and using a range of vocabulary elaboration strategies (Chaudron, 1982) to resolve the problem they are confronted with. These strategies (which may be used singly or in combination) include
the use of iconic, nonverbal means of defining, such as pointing, acting, drawing, and showing pictures. They also may be explicit verbal strategies such
as simplification, synonymy, antonymy, classification, approximation, exemplification, comparison, and translation. Finally, these explicit strategies are
complemented by such implicit verbal elaboration strategies as apposition,
parallelism, and paraphrase.[14]

---

[12]Field notes indicate that although definitions are not unknown in ordinary conversations
between fully competent native speakers, they are infrequent. For example, an analysis of three
transcripts of native-speaker ordinary conversation, "Two Girls," "SN-4," and "Auto discussion,"
showed that no definitions occurred in these conversations. But the present data indicate that
they can be frequent in SL classrooms. Definitions may therefore be understood as a typically
pedagogical form of talk.

[13]Note that for a stretch of talk to count as a definition, analysts cannot rely on their subjective impressions regarding participants' possible psychological motivations for doing a definition. They must be able to show, on the basis of empirical data from the transcript, that the
participants are demonstrating to each other (and thus to the analyst) that a term is actually
or potentially problematic and that it therefore needs to be explained.

[14]All of these elaboration strategies are attested in the three classes that have been fully
transcribed. In the eight related examples given in the previous section of this chapter, we find
a more restricted subset of these strategies, which includes the use of categorization in Excerpt
1 (line 3); exemplification in Excerpt 2 (lines 7–22) and Excerpt 3 (lines 10–18); synonymy in
Excerpt 6 (line 2); comparison in Excerpt 7 (lines 7–9); a combination of simplification (lines 11–17),

PROCEDURES USED TO IDENTIFY
THE CONVERSATIONAL STRUCTURE
OF SPOKEN DEFINITIONS

The data were first examined to establish the prototypical conversational structure of definitions. Prototypical definitions are achieved as sequences that consist of a question-and-answer adjacency pair (Sacks & Schegloff, 1973), followed by an evaluation turn in which participants indicate whether they have understood the definition. In the question turn(s) of the adjacency pair, participants predominantly use *wh*-questions such as *what does X mean*, *what's the meaning of X*, *what is X*, (or interlingual variations thereof) to initiate definitions; however, a number of other forms (such as *yes/no* questions or plain *X* with rising intonation) are also found. In the answering turn(s), participants define problematic terms using the kinds of elaboration strategies identified by Chaudron (1982). And in the third and final commenting turn(s), participants typically use change-of-state tokens like *oh (ok)*, which assert understanding and which may close the sequence (Heritage, 1984).

In order to guard against inadvertent analyst bias, the data were also checked (a) to see if participants achieved definitions in ways that did not conform to this prototypical pattern, and (b) to confirm that participants did indeed orient to sequences that superficially conformed to the prototypical pattern as bona fide definitions. As the teacher's talk in Excerpt 3 (lines 1–10) demonstrates, Excerpt 8 includes talk (at lines 4–9) that is intended by L10 to be heard as a definition, even though it is not done as a sequence and does not display the three-part structure I have just alluded to.[15] And with respect to the issue of talk that superficially resembles prototypical definitions, untaped classroom observations and field notes from a fourth class that is not fully transcribed at the present time indicate that sequences that begin with a *What is X* turn followed by the prototypical answering and commenting turns need not necessarily count as definitions of unknown terms. More specifically, a learner in this fourth class (which was discussing euthanasia) rhetorically asked, "What is death?" His interlocutor initially oriented to this question as a request to define this word and began to provide a definition in his answering turn. But it immediately became clear, when the first student interrupted this definition-in-progress with his own answering turn, that he asked this question so that he could develop his own views on this subject, not because he did not know the meaning of *death*. The final comment-

---

classification (lines 18–23), comparison (line 23), exemplification (lines 24–30), and translation (lines 32, 35, and 38–39) in Excerpt 5; and a combination of classification (line 4–5) and synonymy (line 9) in Excerpt 8.

[15]Three other definitions that display a structure similar to that of the definition in Excerpt 8 were found in the three classes, though not all occurred in the same environment as the one in Excerpt 8.

ing turn of the second student confirmed the rhetorical nature of this definition, because he indicated that he understood that the first learner was not
in fact asking for help in understanding the meaning of *death*.

On the basis of these procedures, a total of 82 attempted and/or completed spoken definitions[16] have been identified in the three classes that constitute the current database in the larger corpus. The eight definitions cited in
the data section are representative of the range of definition types used in
the database as a whole.

ANALYSIS

The first question we might ask ourselves is what conversational resources
L10 draws on in Excerpts 1–8, first to understand what *coral* means, and ultimately to explain this word to her fellow students. The definitions in Excerpts 1–7 are not planned.[17] They are locally occasioned (i.e., they are
constructed in real time by interlocutors who use the resource of turn-taking
to develop a definition sequence cooperatively). And they are also done as
repairs.[18] Following Schegloff et al. (1977) and other writers,[19] repair consists
of any work participants engage in to clear up conversational trouble as it

---

[16]Preliminary counts of the number of attempted and/or completed spoken definitions instantiated in the data indicated that a total of 80 definitions had been produced in the three
classes, of which 79 were associated with target words or phrases that occurred in the original
source readings. Thus, only one definition focused on a word or phrase that had been locally
occasioned by the talk itself. This occurred in Class 3 during a short period of time when the
composition of the groups was being reconstituted and two students briefly engaged in light-
hearted banter, which included a word that one of the participants did not understand. Because
the preponderance of definitions done on words or phrases from the source readings across the
three classes was surprising, the data were checked again a number of times to make sure that
this figure was accurate. These checks identified two more definitions of words that were locally occasioned by the talk itself in Class 3, but which themselves defined material offered as a
paraphrase of a phrase from one of the source readings. This lopsided distribution is probably
caused by the way in which the tasks were set up by the teachers, who focused the learners'
attention on the importance of understanding the source readings and thereby unconsciously
directed the learners to organize their talk around these readings.
[17]Note that this does not mean that these definitions are unplanned, because the recipient
design of a conversation ensures that all talk is constructed so as to be relevant to what has
just been said and to what a conversationalist demonstrably believes his/her interlocutor(s) to
know.
[18]I do not mean to imply that all spoken definitions must occur as repairs in all conversational contexts in order to count as definitions. What I am claiming is that repair is so relevant
to achieving spoken definitions that, at least, in the present database from the three classes,
all definitions were achieved as repairs. This may be a function of the way in which the tasks
were set up.
[19]See Gaskill (1980), Schwartz (1980), Kasper (1985), Varonis and Gass (1985), van Lier (1988),
and McHoul (1990).

occurs. This work usually involves a switch in the focus of the discourse and is often signaled by the presence of such lexical devices as *well, you know, I mean* and by repetitions and/or reordering of syntactic units; furthermore, nonlexical devices such as silences, pauses, false starts, cut-offs, lengthenings, emphatic stress, hesitation markers such as *uh* or *uhm*, gestures, and other paralinguistic phenomena are also frequently present. Finally, participants may modulate repairs by laughing or by using modal verbs or question forms to make themselves sound more tentative, and therefore less challenging, to their interlocutors. The greater the number of these microlevel signals of repair found in a stretch of talk, the stronger the evidence that participants are repairing the interaction.[20]

Notice that if we look at the first 24 lines of Excerpt 5, we can find several of the technical signals of repair mentioned earlier. More specifically, there is a switch in the focus of the discourse at line 1 (where L10 is reading from the article to herself) from reading for information to asking about the meaning of *coral* at line 3. Interturn silences occur at lines 2 and 4; interturn pauses are found at lines 10, 12, 19, and 21; and intraturn pauses occur at lines 7, 9, 11, 13, and 24. We also find multiple instances of various hesitation markers at lines 7, 8, 11, 13, and 18; cut-offs at lines 6, 11, and 22; and syllable lengthenings at lines 7, 11, 13, and 18. Furthermore, L9 constructs her turns at lines 5, 20, and 23 as questions. Finally, notice that repetition occurs not only at lines 13, 14, and 17 but also across excerpts in L10's repeated requests for an explanation of what *coral* means. Thus, there can be no doubt that these participants are repairing their talk in this excerpt (as in the other excerpts cited).

But how can we demonstrate that repaired conversations are actually a resource for language learning? More specifically, what evidence can we use to show that the conversational resources of turn-taking and repair not only help L10 to understand what *coral* means but also promote some kind of learning, as opposed to mere short-term, localized understanding?

First, let us discard the kind of evidence that we should not rely on to answer these questions. Notice that L10 repeatedly uses the change-of-state token *oh* in Excerpts 2 and 3 and actually closes these sequences with the combined tokens *oh ok* at lines 25 (in Excerpt 2) and 18 (in Excerpt 3).[21]

---

[20]Repair is also analyzed in terms of who initiates and who completes a repair, with participants orienting to preference rules that vary according to the turn-taking system in operation at any given time (see the references given in footnote 14). However, there is no structural evidence that by orienting to a particular preference rule, learners are provided with superior opportunities for language learning. Thus, no analysis of the preference structure of definitions is offered in this chapter.

[21]Notice incidentally that Heritage (1984) demonstrated that one of the environments in which such change-of-state tokens occur is in the context of other-initiated repair, as in these two extracts. The use of such change-of-state tokens provides the type of independent corroborating evidence called for by Jacobs (1986, 1987), evidence that repair is a mechanism that is relevant to spoken definitions.

Because the teacher does not pursue this matter any further, we have reason to believe that he or she interprets L10's use of these tokens (particularly at line 25 of excerpt 2, where she says, "Oh ok oh I see thank you") as evidence that L10 has understood what *coral* means. But such a reading (on the part of either the teacher or the analyst) of what L10 means by these final tokens would be erroneous, because L10 subsequently initiates two more sequences on the same word. I suggest that in Excerpt 2, L10 is only indicating that she understands that corals are found at the bottom of the sea, and in Excerpt 3, that a definition of what *coral* means must be provided in the subsequent whole-class activity. But for the reasons already outlined, L10 cannot have fully understood what *coral* means by the end of Excerpt 3. These "appropriate" answers therefore do not constitute sufficient evidence of understanding (see also Hawkins, 1985, on the difficulty of interpreting learners' appropriate answers).

What evidence, then, should we rely on to demonstrate localized understanding and perhaps even learning? The most important evidence that we can point to in this regard occurs in the marked turns of excerpt 5 (lines 18, 23–30, 32, 35, 38–39). At line 23, in response to L10's question at line 18 asking whether coral is food for fish, L9 replies that coral is like stone. This information seems to trigger a breakthrough in understanding for L10. More specifically, L10 vehemently asserts at line 24 that she has understood (which indicates at least that L10 is rather confident that she has indeed understood this word and is willing to expose herself to a potential loss of face if she turns out to be wrong). At line 25, she independently provides the extra information that coral is very beautiful, which L9 corroborates at line 27. At lines 27, 29, and 30, L9 provides more descriptive information about coral, which L10 overlaps with further assertions that she has understood, at lines 28 and 32. In addition, in the last part of her turn at line 32 and also at line 35, L10 again goes further by providing a translation of this word into Chinese. Because L9 is not a Chinese speaker, she does not understand these translations; consequently, L10 translates the Chinese term back into English by saying "coral" at line 38. The correctness of this translation is corroborated by L11 (who is also a Chinese speaker), who overlaps L10 at line 39 by also saying "coral." We may therefore conclude that L10 has indeed understood what *coral* means.[22]

---

[22]Notice that no attempt was made to use self-report procedures or thinking-aloud protocols to obtain the kind of triangulated data (i.e., where the investigator checks his or her interpretations against those of the teacher and student) used by Hawkins (1985) and advocated by Cohen and Olshtain (this volume, chapter 8) and Selinker and Doublas (this volume, chapter 6). The reason for this is that ethnomethodology discounts the use of ethnographic data unless there is internal evidence in the conversational data themselves warranting their introduction (Schegloff, 1987). Once a text has been produced, the analyst is said to be as well placed to analyze the data as the individual(s) who first produced the text. In this regard, the production of other texts

We now need to demonstrate that these sequences actually contribute to learning that goes beyond a mere understanding of *coral* in its immediate local context in the interaction. Finding evidence of this kind in data that are transcribed from a single lesson is difficult, because learning is not necessarily public and occurs over extended periods of time. Fortunately, however, the data in Excerpt 8, which L10 produced during her oral report to the rest of the class some 10 minutes after the end of Excerpt 5, provides the kind of internal textual evidence we need. These data include L10's definition for her peers of the word *coral*, which, as we have just seen, she had only just learned. As we have already noted, we can be sure that the highlighted parts of Excerpt 8 are intended by L10 to be understood as a definition, because the teacher had requested Group 3 to give a definition of *coral* in Excerpt 3. To the extent that this definition is conversationally adequate, therefore, the evidence in Excerpt 8 suggests that L10 has actually learned this word and uses this new knowledge for her own purposes in a different part of the conversation.

Notice, too, that the more planned definition found in Excerpt 8 is also done as a repair (in this regard, note the same kinds of technical signals of repair I have already remarked on, distributed throughout this excerpt). More specifically, L10 borrows the highlighted parts of Excerpts 2, 3, 5, 6, and 7 and recombines these elements to produce her own original definition of *coral* in excerpt 8.[23] Thus, "at the bottom of the sea" first occurs at lines 18 and 22 of Excerpt 2; this phrase reappears at lines 13, 15, and 17 of Excerpt 5 and again at line 5 of Excerpt 8. "Coral reefs" is borrowed from line 13 of Excerpt 3 and also reappears at line 5 of Excerpt 8; and the remaining components of the definition found in Excerpt 8 ("fossil" in lines 4 and 5, "habitat" in lines 6 and 8, and "home" in line 9) are borrowed from Excerpt 6 (lines 1, 2, and 7–8) and Excerpt 7 (lines 4, 8, and 9).

Finally, notice that the definition that L10 produces in lines 4–9 of Excerpt 8 is a planned definition (see also Crookes, 1989). That is, it contains many of the elements of logical definitions, which are often constructed as three-

---

by the original participants, as they explain or comment on what they really meant in the primary text, only serves to confuse the issue.

However, notice that the analysis offered in this chapter is internally triangulated insofar as three different sets of publicly available evidence in the conversations of the participants are analyzed. As pointed out by Jacobs (1986, 1987), it is the sum of these converging pieces of evidence that allows us to conclude that L10 has understood what *coral* means. Thus, although there are some rare instances in which ethnographic triangulation might be the most convenient means of understanding what participants meant (see the *strawberry* example cited by van Lier (1988), where the highly idiosyncratic use of this word can be understood only by having access to a previous conversation or, failing this, by asking participants what they meant), such external triangulation is unnecessary in this case because sufficient text-internal evidence exists to make the argument stick.

[23]Thus, Excerpts 1 and 4 do not provide L10 with any data useful for learning.

part statements (Abelson, 1967) like the following: An A is a B, which does C. Thus, *coral* would fit in the A part of this statement, the information classifying coral as a type of fossil found at the bottom of the sea would fit in the B part of the statement, and the information about coral being an important habitat or home for fish would fit into the C part of the statement. This more formal and complex definition also provides internal textual evidence that L10 has actually learned the meaning of *coral*.

CONCLUSION

I have demonstrated two things in the preceding paragraphs. In the first part of this chapter, I showed that the nomothetic characterization of descriptive studies as limited and non-theory-generating need not be unquestioningly accepted. Interpretive explanations, inspired by hermeneutics, of ordinary data have considerable theoretical power, which may be generalized beyond the single events on which they are based. And in the second part, I applied CA to explain how the mechanisms of turn-taking and repair may be used as resources for successful second-language learning.[24]

If these proposals for respecifying SLA studies have any merit, our notions of what constitutes the most valuable kind of research will have to be reassessed. This does not mean that I believe that research in the nomothetic tradition has no value. As I indicated at the beginning of this chapter, I acknowledge that qualitative and quantitative research represent complementary paths to new knowledge about the phenomenon of SLA and that the results of nomothetic research are in many ways impressive. But it does mean that researchers will have to reevaluate whether the current dominance of the nomothetic tradition is entirely beneficial to the field. At a time when epistemology and theory construction are high on the SLA research agenda, I believe that an ethnomethodological respecification of the process of SLA research is of the essence because it simultaneously problematizes the way in which we try to theorize SLA and provides a distinctive methodology for analyzing this complex phenomenon. Thus, in my opinion, the value of ethnomethodology lies in the fact that it provides the field with opportunities for critically reevaluating its dominant epistemology and also for reassessing the criteria by which it measures its level of success as a scientific endeavor. These are matters that a maturing discipline cannot afford to ignore.

---

[24]Although I have confined myself here to analyzing how the mechanisms of turn-taking and repair are used to learn new lexis, there is no reason why this approach might not also be used to analyze the acquisition of phonology or syntax. In this regard, see Hatch (1978) and Hawkins (1988) for a discourse-analytic account of the effect of scaffolded talk on the development of syntax-in-conversation. This research could easily be reanalyzed in conversation-analytic terms.

ACKNOWLEDGMENTS

I would like to thank Susan Gonzo, Ron Cowan, Barbara O'Keefe, and John Schumann for their comments on earlier drafts of this chapter. The errors it contains are of course my own.

APPENDIX: Transcription Conventions:
Adapted from van Lier (1988)

T	teacher
L1, L2	identified learner
L	unidentified learner
L3?	probably learner 3 (L3)
LL	several or all learners simultaneously
//yes//yah//ok//	overlapping or simultaneous listening
///huh?///oh///	responses, brief comments, etc., by two, three, or an unspecified number of learners
=	a) turn continues at the next identical symbol b) if inserted at the end of one speaker's turn and the beginning of the next speaker's adjacent turn, it indicates that there is no gap at all between the two turns
(+) (+ +) (1)	pauses; (+) = a pause of between .1 and .5 seconds; (+ +) = a pause of between .6 and 9 seconds; and (1) (2) (3) = pauses of 1, 2, or 3 seconds, respectively
?	rising intonation, not necessarily a question
!	strong emphasis with falling intonation
ok. now. well.	a period indicates falling (final) intonation
so, the next thing	a comma indicates low-rising intonation, suggesting continuation
e:r, the:::	one or more colons indicate lengthening of the preceding sound
emphasis	italic type indicates marked stress
SYLVIA	capitals indicate increased volume
°the next thing	degree sign indicates decreased volume
. . . . (radio)	single parentheses indicate unclear or probable item
((coughs))	double parentheses indicate comments about the transcript and note nonverbal actions
((unintelligible))	indicates a stretch of talk that is unintelligible to the analyst

no-	a hyphen indicates an abrupt cut-off, with level pitch
Peter	capitals are used only for proper names, not to indicate beginnings of sentences
[si:m]	square brackets indicate phonetic transcription
<hhh>	in-drawn breath
hhh	exhaled breath
(hhh)	laughter tokens

REFERENCES

Abelson, R. (1967). Definition. In P. Edwards (Ed.), *The encyclopedia of philosophy* (Vol. 2, pp. 314–324). London: MacMillan and Free Press.

Allwright, R., & Bailey, K. M. (1991). *Focus on the language classroom*. Cambridge: Cambridge University Press.

Benson, D., & Hughes, J. (1991). Method: Evidence and inference for ethnomethodology. In G. Button (Ed.), *Ethnomethodology and the human sciences* (pp. 109–136). Cambridge: Cambridge University Press.

Beretta, A. (1991). Theory construction in SSLA: Complementarity and opposition. *Studies in Second Language Acquisition, 13*, 493–512.

Berwick, R. C., & Weinberg, A. S. (1984). *The grammatical basis of linguistic performance: Language use and acquisition*. Cambridge, MA: MIT Press.

Bilmes, J. (1988). The concept of preference in conversation analysis. *Language in Society, 17*, 161–181.

Candlin, C. N. (1983, April). *Plenary address given at the Second Language Research Forum*, University of Southern California, Los Angeles, CA.

Chaudron, C. (1982). Vocabulary elaboration in teachers' speech to L2 learners. *Studies in Second Language Acquisition, 4*, 170–180.

Chaudron, C. (1988). *Second language classrooms: Research on teaching and learning*. Cambridge: Cambridge University Press.

Coulter, J. (1991). Logic: Ethnomethodology and the logic of language. In G. Button (Ed.), *Ethnomethodology and the human sciences* (pp. 20–50). Cambridge: Cambridge University Press.

Crookes, G. (1989). Planning and interlanguage variation. *Studies in Second Language Acquisition, 11*, 367–383.

Crookes, G. (1991). Second language speech production research: A methodologically-oriented overview. *Studies in Second Language Acquisition, 13*, 113–132.

Crookes, G. (1992). Theory format and SLA theory. *Studies in Second Language Acquisition, 14*, 425–449.

Ellis, R. (1984). *Classroom second language development*. Oxford: Pergamon.

Flowerdew, J. (1991). Pragmatic modifications on the 'representative' speech act of defining. *Journal of Pragmatics, 15*, 253–264.

Flowerdew, J. (1992). Definitions in science lectures. *Applied Linguistics, 13*, 202–221.

Fodor, J. A. (1983). *Modularity of mind: An essay on faculty psychology*. Cambridge, MA: MIT Press.

Garfield, J. L. (Ed.). (1987). *Modularity in knowledge representation and natural-language understanding*. Cambridge, MA: MIT Press.

Garfinkel, H. (1967). *Studies in ethnomethodology*. Englewood Cliffs, NJ: Prentice Hall.

Gaskill, W. (1980). Correction in native speaker–non-native speaker conversation. In D. Larsen-Freeman (Ed.), *Discourse analysis in second language research* (pp. 125–137). Rowley, MA: Newbury House.

Giddens, A. (1988). The orthodox consensus and the emerging synthesis. In B. Dervin, L. Grossberg, B. O'Keefe, & E. Wartella (Eds.), *Rethinking communication: Paradigm issues* (Vol. 1, pp. 53–65). International Communication Association.

Grotjahn, R. (1991). The research programme subjective theories: A new approach in second language research. *Studies in Second Language Acquisition, 13,* 187–214.

Guiora, A. Z. (1983). The dialectic of language acquisition. *Language Learning, 33,* 3–12.

Hatch, E. (1978). Discourse analysis and second language acquisition. In E. Hatch (Ed.), *Second language acquisition: A book of readings* (pp. 402–435). Rowley, MA: Newbury House.

Hawkins, B. (1985). Is an 'appropriate' response always so appropriate? In S. Gass and C. Madden (Eds.), *Input in second language acquisition* (pp. 162–178). Rowley, MA: Newbury House.

Hawkins, B. (1988). Scaffolded classroom interaction and second language acquisition for language minority students (Doctoral dissertation, University of California at Los Angeles, 1988). *Dissertation Abstracts International,* DEV88-10213.

Heritage, J. (1984). A change-of-state token and aspects of its sequential placement. In J. Atkinson & J. Heritage (Eds.), *Structures of social action: Studies in conversation analysis* (pp. 299–345). Cambridge: Cambridge University Press.

Heritage, J. (1988). Current development in conversation analysis. In D. Roger & P. Bull (Eds.), *Conversation* (pp. 21–47). Multilingual Matters: Clevedon.

Heritage, J. & Greatbatch, D. (1986). Generating applause: A study of rhetoric and response at party political conferences. *American Journal of Sociology, 92,* 110–157.

Hopper, R. (1988). Conversation analysis and social psychology as descriptions of interpersonal communication. In D. Roger & P. Bull (Eds.), *Conversation* (pp. 48–65). Multilingual Matters: Clevedon.

Hopper, R., Koch, S., & Mandelbaum, J. (1988). Conversation analysis methods. In D. G. Ellis & W. A. Donohue (Eds.), *Contemporary issues in language and discourse processes* (pp. 169–186). Hillsdale, NJ: Lawrence Erlbaum Associates.

Jacobs, S. (1986). How to make an argument from example. In D. G. Ellis & W. A. Donohue (Eds.), *Contemporary issues in language and discourse processes* (pp. 149–167). Hillsdale, NJ: Lawrence Erlbaum Associates.

Jacobs, S. (1987). Commentary on Zimmerman: Evidence and inference in conversation analysis. *Communication Yearbook, 11,* 433–443.

Jefferson, G. (1978). Sequential aspects of story-telling in conversation. In J. Schenkein (Ed.), *Studies in the organization of conversational interaction* (pp. 219–248). New York: Academic Press.

Jefferson, G. (1988). Preliminary notes on a possible metric which provides for a 'standard maximum' silence of approximately one second in conversation. In D. Roger & P. Bull (Eds.), *Conversation* (pp. 167–196). Multilingual Matters: Clevedon.

Jefferson, G., & Schenkein, J. (1978). Some sequential negotiations in conversation: Unexpanded and expanded versions of projected action sequences. In J. Schenkein (Ed.), *Studies in the organization of conversational interaction* (pp. 155–172). New York: Academic Press.

Kasper, G. (1985). Repair in foreign language teaching. *Studies in Second Language Acquisition, 7,* 200–215.

Kuhn, T. S. (1961). The function of measurement in modern physical science. *Isis, 52,* 161–193.

Larsen-Freeman, D., & Long, M. H. (1991). *An introduction to second language acquisition research.* London: Longman.

Levinson, S. (1983). *Pragmatics.* Cambridge: Cambridge University Press.

Long, M. H. (1981). Input, interaction and second language acquisition (Doctoral dissertation, University of California at Los Angeles, 1981). *Dissertation Abstracts International,* DDJ81-11249.

Long, M. H. (1983). Inside the "black box": Methodological issues in classroom research on language learning. In H. W. Seliger & M. H. Long (Eds.), *Classroom oriented research in second language acquisition* (pp. 3–35). Rowley, MA: Newbury House.

Long, M. H. (1985). Input and second language acquisition theory. In S. Gass & C. Madden (Eds.), *Input in second language acquisition* (pp. 377–393). Rowley, MA: Newbury House.

Long, M. H. (1990). The least a second language acquisition theory needs to explain. *TESOL Quarterly, 24,* 649–666.

Long, M. H. (1993). Assessment strategies for second language acquisition theory. *Applied Linguistics, 14,* 225–249.

Long, M. H., & Porter, P. (1985). Group work, interlanguage talk, and second language acquisition. *TESOL Quarterly, 19,* 207–228.

Lynch, M. (1991). Method: Measurement—ordinary and scientific measurement as ethnomethodological phenomena. In G. Button (Ed.), *Ethnomethodology and the human sciences* (pp. 77–108). Cambridge: Cambridge University Press.

McHoul, A. (1990). The organization of repair in classroom talk. *Language in Society, 19,* 349–377.

McLaughlin, M. (1988). The analysis of action sequences in conversation: Some comments on method. In D. G. Ellis & W. A. Donohue (Eds.), *Contemporary issues in language and discourse processes* (pp. 187–200). Hillsdale, NJ: Lawrence Erlbaum Associates.

Ochsner, R. (1979). A poetics of second language acquisition. *Language Learning, 29,* 53–80.

Porter, P. (1986). How learners talk to each other: Input and interaction in task-centered discussions. In R. Day (Ed.), *Talking to learn* (pp. 200–222). Rowley, MA: Newbury House.

Sacks, H., & Schegloff, E. (1973). Opening up closings. *Semiotica, 8,* 289–327.

Schegloff, E. (1987). Between macro and micro: Contexts and other connections. In J. Alexander, B. Giesen, R. Munch, & N. Smelser (Eds.), *The micro–macro link* (pp. 207–234). Berkeley: University of California Press.

Schegloff, E., Jefferson, G., & Sacks, H. (1977). The preference for self-correction in the organization of repair in conversation. *Language, 53,* 361–382.

Schumann, J. (1983). Art and science in second language acquisition research. *Language Learning, 33,* 49–75.

Schumann, J. (1993). Falsification: Has it ever happened in second language acquisition? *Applied Linguistics, 14,* 295–306.

Schwartz, J. (1980). The negotiation for meaning: Repair in conversations between second language learners of English. In D. Larsen-Freeman (Ed.), *Discourse analysis in second language research* (pp. 138–153). Rowley, MA: Newbury House.

Sharrock, W., & Button, G. (1991). The social actor: Social action in real time. In G. Button (Ed.), *Ethnomethodology and the human sciences* (pp. 137–175). Cambridge: Cambridge University Press.

van Lier, L. (1988). *The classroom and the language learner.* London: Longman.

Varonis, E. M., & Gass, S. (1985). Non-native/non-native conversation: A model for negotiation of meaning. *Applied Linguistics, 6,* 71–90.

Watson, R. (1985). Towards a theory of definition. *Journal of Child Language, 12,* 181–197.

Watson-Gegeo, K. (1988). Ethnography in ESL: Defining the essentials. *TESOL Quarterly, 22,* 575–592.

Wilson, T. P., & Zimmerman, D. (1986). The structure of silence between turns in two-party conversation. *Discourse Processes, 9,* 375–390.

Zimmerman, D. (1987). On conversation: The conversation analytic perspective. *Communication Yearbook, 11,* 406–432.

METHODOLOGIES FOR ELICITING AND ANALYZING LANGUAGE IN CONTEXT

6

RESEARCH METHODOLOGY IN CONTEXT-BASED SECOND-LANGUAGE RESEARCH

Dan Douglas
Iowa State University

Larry Selinker
University of London

In 1989, we suggested a combined research methodology for studying second-language acquisition (SLA) in real-life and important contexts (Selinker & Douglas, 1989). The combined research methodology we suggested there integrated features from three fields: grounded ethnography, subject-specialist informant (SSI) procedures in language for specific purposes (LSP), and rhetorical/grammatical (R/G) strategies in discourse analysis.

In this chapter, we wish to do two things. First, we review several of the major features of our earlier proposal, and second, we extend the methodology as a result of two case studies where transcripts of subjects' responses to specific purpose (SP) English tests are analyzed as interlanguage (IL) discourse.

We also have some questions about context that are related to questions about Universal Grammar (UG). We are interested in the integration of these concerns with problems of understanding language transfer and fossilization. The SP contexts we are most interested in here are those in which a great deal of adult SLA takes place. In these contexts there is also a strong possibility of IL fossilization. In fact, the SP input may even guide the learner into fossilizing particular IL structures, at least in those contexts, which are contexts where the learner is apparently encouraged by the input to fossilize certain formulaic patterns (see the references in Selinker & Douglas, 1989). Also, if "internal-IL transfer" occurs from one domain/genre to another in such cases, there may be real problems. We return to this point.

TYPES OF IL DATA

In our empirical research, we are interested in understanding the ability of a nonnative speaker to use English in talking about and writing about a technical field. Thus, we are surely interested in the IL associated with that context, but there may be new and unresearched types of questions that arise in such contextually based IL work, for example, the *degree of precision*[1] that the learner's IL allows in attempted and successful communication in that field in technical interactions with experts. We are also interested in the IL created by the same learner but associated with a range of nontechnical contexts, as well as in how the ILs in the various sets of contexts interrelate. This actually constitutes a new type of IL contrastive analysis.

Primary and Secondary Data

In terms of the research methodology we are suggesting, we first make a distinction that we have found to be very useful in our work: the distinction between *primary data* and *secondary data*. First, we note the following definition:

  (1) a. *Primary data:*   The interlanguage talk or writing we wish to study.

The talk is often recorded on video tape to facilitate the analysis. We define *secondary data* as follows:

  (1) b. *Secondary data:*   Commentary on the primary data.

There are two categories of secondary data: first, audio tapes of retrospective commentaries on the primary data by the coparticipants themselves, and second, audio tapes of various types of expert commentaries on these primary data. We have used the following types of expert reviewers: other linguists, ethnographers and ethnomethodologists, and subject specialist informants, each of whom brings to bear on the primary data their various perspectives and methods.

The reader should note at this point that we have here three separable forms of data, each contributing to our understanding of context in inter-

---

[1]Note that the notion *degree of precision* must be kept separate from the notion *targetlike*. That is, the precise IL necessary for a particular context (vs. the IL necessary for another context) need not be the same as the more targetlike (vs. less targetlike) IL in a context. In fact, we can imagine situations where a less targetlike IL may produce more precision in a particular context.

Concerning this distinction between *precision* and the notion *targetlike*, Lakshmanan has asked us whether Kellerman's (1989) results involving, as she put it, Dutch learners "making English more perfect than it is," would also instantiate precision. We think they do; thus IL precision need not be restricted to LSP domains "but can be extended to other general spheres as well" (U. Lakshmanan, personal communication, October 10, 1991).

language studies: primary data, retrospective commentary by the coparticipants, and expert commentary on the primary data.

METHODOLOGICAL PRINCIPLES

The primary IL texts are the objects of analysis. By themselves, however, these primary IL texts often lend themselves to ambiguity, which leads to a general methodological principle for studying IL in context:

> (2) a. Primary interlanguage data are always ambiguous; at a minimum, one needs to gain access to interlanguage intention.

(2a) articulates the fundamental notion that data by themselves do not compel any particular conclusions. IL phenomena (like other socially-constructed human phenomena) need to be studied and understood in the participants' own terms (cf. Garfinkel, 1967). For example, in one of the case studies in Selinker and Douglas (1989), the researcher, in reviewing the primary data of a Chinese graduate student, pointed out to the subject that his use of pronoun gender was quite targetlike in one context although it had not been targetlike in another context. The subject indicated that he had been "thinking about it" and cleared up the issue for us in terms of categories related to his native culture.

Regarding the second type of secondary data, that is, the expert commentary, a methodological problem we have run into, which only a subject-specialist informant can help with, involves the common case where we do not understand a piece of technical IL discourse that occurs either in spontaneous IL speech or writing, or in a language test situation. In such a case, we need to ask: Is the nonnative speaker (NNS) producing only IL-particular semantics and rhetorical structure? Or is he/she producing semantics and rhetorical structure related to the discipline and only partially IL-particular? It appears that the IL-particular nature of such material can become confounded by a semantic and rhetorical structure peculiar to a particular discipline. This problem may be a partial explanation for, or source of, some of the ambiguity we see in the primary IL data.

This latter phenomenon may be cross-cultural and international in scope and may be at least partially independent of the languages involved. In this case, there is no doubt that we have new combinations of R/G correspondences in oral or written IL texts, hitherto undescribed in the literature, which may be affecting in unclear ways the meaning and the social significance of those texts. This leads to a second IL methodological principle:

> (2) b. To disambiguate interlanguage technical texts in their contexts, subject-specialist informant procedures are necessary.

For example, in reviewing data provided by an instructor of statistics, the statistics subject-specialist informant revealed for us the underlying technical principle that the instructor was dealing with. The instructor herself had not commented on that aspect of the data, believing that her treatment of it had been clear enough (Douglas, 1989).

One should note that for our purposes of investigating IL in real-life and important contexts, we need to augment the primary IL data in one significant way. In order to gain necessary technical and rhetorical information about the content and organization of the IL talk or writing we wish to understand, we need to add a modified form of the SSI procedures in the study of LSP.[2]

For example, if we are going to study the IL development (or lack of it) of a foreign engineering student in the United States and, perhaps, study that development in a testing situation, we may need to know what an engineering professor understands to be the meaning of a particular engineering text that the student will discuss using a technical IL. We may also need to know details of the rhetorical or organizational structure of both the technical written piece and the technical IL involved (see Selinker & Douglas, 1985).

A further problematic feature of the study of SLA in context is that discourse takes place in real time. That is, in doing contextualized IL research there must be a strong focus on the actual construction of texts in real interactional time (see, for example, Frankel & Beckman, 1982). We need to account for various real-time factors that can influence the construction of IL texts. One reason for this is that, by definition, second-language acquisition takes place over time, and there is enough evidence in the literature (see the summary material in Larsen-Freeman & Long, 1991) to suggest that at least some parts of IL grammar are learned from ongoing discourse in real time. This perspective leads to a third IL methodological principle:

(2) c. In addition to studying the occurrence of features of an interaction, it is necessary to study the relationship between these features as they unfold in real time.

One thing we are trying to capture here is the dynamic nature of conversational interaction, the fact that the contexts are, socially and culturally, constructed in interaction (cf., for example, Frankel, 1984).

A fourth feature of the study of contextualized IL data is that language users assess, and thus respond to, the mutually constructed context from often divergent underlying assumptions. This is particularly true of NS/NNS inter-

---

[2]One can find detail concerning the SSI procedures in a number of papers (e.g., Bley-Vroman & Selinker, 1984; Cohen, Glasman, Rosenbaum-Cohen, Ferrara, & Fine, 1979; Huckin & Olsen, 1984; Selinker, 1979, 1991; Swales, 1986; Tarone, Dwyer, Gillette, & Icke, 1981).

actions. A problem is that the underlying assumptions crucial to an understanding of the interaction are not necessarily available to researchers or apparent from a direct analysis of the primary text itself. For context-based SLA researchers, the point made by Frankel and Beckman (1982) is that the assumptions of each of the coparticipants may have real-world significance beyond the communicative event itself. They relate this significance to the training of physician residents through an understanding of the underlying assumptions made by the coparticipants in medical encounters. Frankel and Beckman's observation holds for the two case studies presented in Selinker and Douglas (1989), one involving a mathematics teaching assistant (TA) and the other, a chemistry TA. It is our experience that divergent secondary data accounts of the primary IL data provide insights into IL-particular semantics and rhetorical structure.

To summarize, then, diverging accounts of the primary data by the coparticipants may point to different sets of underlying assumptions about the nature of the interaction, which leads to principle (2d):

(2) d. Divergent secondary data accounts of the primary interlanguage data provide insights into interlanguage-particular semantic and rhetorical structure.

Concerning the detail of subject-specialist informant work, we have no space to discuss this material here and refer the interested reader to Selinker and Douglas (1989) where such detail and many references can be found. Some principles follow here:

(2) e. Concerning the subject-specialist informant procedure: The procedure, with its classic concentration on written language for specific purposes, must be adapted to apply to the talk that helps to produce those texts and is produced during their use. The procedure must be part of a research strategy (called an *optimal research strategy*) consisting of three phases: the prerequisite phase, the analysis phase, and the application/use phase. The procedure should concentrate on *highly valued texts* as those texts that are central to a field and central to the acculturation of neophytes in that field.[3]

Regarding the actual R/G analysis, an important principle is stated as (2f):

(2) f. When rhetorical/grammatical distinctions show up in IL technical talk, they may not show up in other domains of IL talk (i.e., internal IL transfer may not have occurred).

---

[3]These procedures were originally presented in Selinker (1979) and were revised in terms of the concepts of optimal research strategy and highly valued texts in Bley-Vroman and Selinker (1984).

That is, when R/G distinctions (such as precise classificational structure) show up in IL technical talk, at least some NNSs who gain this sort of R/G link will do so only in talk about work and not in other domains of talk. We adduce such cases in several places. One of the clearest examples involves a Korean teaching assistant who showed strong classificational structure in talk about work but not in other domains (see Selinker & Douglas, 1989).

Note that this result is probably what is desired and that those NNSs who produce internal-IL transfer and transfer this sort of distinction to other domains of talk could very well produce nontargetlike talk in those other domains. Thus, this is a conclusion that surely has important pedagogical ramifications: Internal-IL transfer in many LSP/IL situations may not be what is desired.

This conclusion leads to the SLA hypothesis (Selinker & Douglas, 1985) that language transfer concerns on a rhetorical level are related to restricted genre and domain considerations. The grammatical choices that would be related to rhetorical strategies would have to be language-specific, so it is an interesting question whether, in the creation of IL texts, learners produce a domain-bound universality at one level with a language-specific transferability at another.

In our use of the R/G tradition in analyzing IL texts, we keep in mind an inventory of rhetorical strategies such as stating purpose, definition, classification, cause and effect, comparison and contrast, linear development of ideas, and concentric development; Selinker and Douglas (1989) provided a more complete listing.

We also consider whether these strategies are explicitly produced or whether there are implicit elements lacking in the IL text; Tyma (1981) provided criteria for distinguishing explicit from implicit rhetorical functioning. We also note Bley-Vroman's (1978) strictures that an adequate theory of rhetorical functioning would have to involve several aspects: an inventory of rhetorical purposes, the devices used to instantiate them, and those grammatical choices associated with the various rhetorical strategies. Finally, we look at rhetorical paragraphing or discourse chunking and the explicit linguistic signals that often occur.

APPLICATION OF THE PRINCIPLES

Now we come to the second section of our chapter: a description of our first attempts to integrate language testing into concerns of IL in context. We do this to combine SLA methodology, as it relates to theory, with language testing methodology as it relates to what is, unfortunately, often a quite different sort of theory. This point was made forcefully and clearly by Shohamy (this volume, chapter 7). It has been noted (e.g., Bachman, 1988) that SLA and language testing concerns have often diverged in terms of theoretical perspective, focus, and methodology.[4] One central objective in our contextually based SLA research is to work toward integrating language testing principles and approaches into concerns of SLA and IL in context, with intended benefits both ways.

Specifically, in our empirical research, we borrow from Bachman where he presented conclusions on the *method effect* in testing theory: "While it is generally recognized that (specification of the test domain) usually involves specification of the ability domain, what is often ignored is that examining content relevance also requires the specification of the test method factors" (Bachman, 1990, p. 244). Bachman quoted Cronbach:

> A validation study examines the procedure as a whole. Every aspect of the setting in which the test is given and every detail of the procedure may have an influence on performance and hence on what is measured. . . . Changes in procedure . . . lead to substantial changes in ability-test . . . performance, and hence in the appropriate interpretation of test scores. (Cronbach, 1971, p. 449)

This seems to us another point of view on what we have called in several places the discourse domains approach to interlanguage. Namely, any factor one changes in the test environment—personnel, physical conditions, time, organization, instructions, level of precision, or propositional content—can lead to changes in learner perceptions and assessment of communicative situation, and thus to changes in interlanguage performance on a test. Elsewhere (Douglas & Selinker, 1992), we related the concept of discourse domains in SLA (Selinker & Douglas, 1985) to that of contextualization cues in ethnomethodology (Gumperz, 1976) and hence to the concept of method facets in language testing (Bachman, 1990). We feel that this sort of addition to our conception of research methodology in SLA is important because tests (as defined by Carroll, 1968, as "procedure[s] designed to elicit certain behavior from which one can make inferences about certain characteristics of an individual" [p. 6]) of one sort or another are commonly used in SLA research,

---

[4]More recently, there has been a recognition on the part of SLA and language testing researchers that questions of mutual interest might be addressed more convergently. We have already noted Bachman (1988) and also note, for example, the Invitational Symposium on Language Acquisition and Language Assessment held at the Educational Testing Service in 1989 and the construction of a language assessment procedure based on an understanding of possible developmental stages of acquisition (Pienemann, Johnston, & Brindley, 1988). Also, at the 1992 AAAL conference in Seattle, a special panel was organized to look at how the two theories and methods might interrelate, and a volume of papers emerged from that meeting (Bachman & Cohen, 1993).

regardless of the particular theory being explored. Thus, we add the methodological principle (2g) for the study of IL in context:

(2) g. SLA research should proceed by investigating the effect on acquisition of the manipulation of method facets in the elicitation of interlanguage data.

General Versus Field-Specific Language Tests: MATHSPEAK

In the past four years, in relating interlanguage studies to language testing, we have been concerned with the problem of performance on general versus field-specific tests of speaking proficiency. Here we briefly describe the applied problem we have been dealing with. (Interested colleagues should consult Douglas & Selinker, 1992, 1993.)

Users of the oral English test in the TOEFL program, called the Test of Spoken English (TSE) or SPEAK, have frequently suggested that the test is too general to be used for a valid assessment of an international teaching assistant's ability to use English in fields such as mathematics, chemistry, or physics, although this type of assessment is among the stated purposes of the test. This is the applied linguistics problem we have responded to. In the first study, we created a field-specific mathematics version of SPEAK, which we called MATHSPEAK. Then the SPEAK and the MATHSPEAK were given to NNS mathematics TAs.

In Douglas and Selinker (1993), in terms of the discourse domains hypothesis in contextually-based interlanguage research, we were trying to set up a situation where the field-specific test was conducted so as to give the testees oral interlanguage experience in talking about mathematics during the testing session. Our methodological goal was that the only difference between the two tests be one of domain of discourse, as defined by test method facets. In that study we focused on both a statistical (quantitative) and a rhetorical (qualitative) comparison of IL performance on SPEAK with that on MATHSPEAK. We then attempted to replicate the procedure with a test in a chemistry domain. Details of this study may be found in Douglas and Selinker (1992).

With regard to the focus on test method as a distinguishing feature of performance, we refer to what Bachman (1990) called "the dilemma of language testing" (p. 287)—language is both the object and the instrument of measurement. For Bachman, a way out of the dilemma is to understand more explicitly both the nature of language ability and the nature of test methods, so that we can "minimize the effect of test method" (p. 12) in our interpretation of results as indicators of language abilities. Our perspective is focused differently: Rather than attempting to minimize the method effects, we capitalize on them to produce tests, useful in both language testing and SLA empirical research, that would provide information interpretable as evidence of language ability in SP contexts.

However, in our experiment with MATHSPEAK, we found statistically significant differences between SPEAK and MATHSPEAK in grammar and fluency subscores, and a number of rhetorical differences in the responses. Where the raters claimed the differences in talk about math were grammatical, we did not find such evidence. We looked through the transcripts ourselves and also submitted them to expert informants. None found consistent IL grammatical differences. This is important from a testing point of view because the raters gave the math testees higher ratings on grammar in MATHSPEAK. We concluded that the raters were responding to something else and calling it grammar. One thus has to be wary of subjective gross ratings and provide R/G IL analysis. This leads to principle (2h):

(2) h. Rhetorical/grammatical interlanguage analysis may be necessary to disambiguate subjective gross ratings on tests as well as subjective gross interpretations of elicited IL data (e.g., imitation or grammaticality judgment tasks).

In applying this principle to the technical case of MATHSPEAK,[5] we found that the knowledge of technical math allowed the IL speakers to use metaphors where the IL speakers without the technical knowledge could not produce them. We saw more rhetorical complexity, that is, more embedding of content information in larger rhetorical structures, by the technically competent. Another result showed no interlanguage differences in terms of necessity or obligation language but did show differences due to test prompt.

**General Versus Field-Specific Language Tests:
CHEMSPEAK**

Concerning the testing/IL study in the domain of chemistry talk, as measured by a field-specific chemistry test called CHEMSPEAK, we looked at discourse markers in the oral production of chemistry majors and found that IL rhetorical complexity was independent of the use of discourse markers, but that it was not the case that IL talk based on CHEMSPEAK was always more complex. One important misunderstanding of the discourse

---

[5]This principle may be useful not only to contextually based IL studies, but to UG SLA studies, as well. For example, it should be particularly useful for researchers conducting UG studies that rely on language tests (e.g., Flynn, 1989; Zobl, 1989) to be aware of the tricky problem of different sorts of knowledge, possibly reflecting different proficiency levels.

domains idea is the view that talk about work will always be more complex. What we found in that study was IL difference by domain. In one significant case, however, a chemistry major used targetlike talk in referring to general topics, but less targetlike talk in discussing chemistry topics. This finding relates to the point made earlier, that the notion of a targetlike IL is independent of the notion of precision of the IL for a particular purpose in a particular context.

Furthermore, with this study, concentration on methodological issues seemed to help in clarifying a theoretical point. Through the work reported on in this section, we came to realize that there was a strong and a weak version of the discourse domains hypothesis. The weak version of the hypothesis is that there will be IL differences by domain, not a startling view, given what we know about variation in IL. The stronger version of the discourse domains hypothesis is concerned with the direction of IL change, that is, the directions that internal-IL transfer will take. Interestingly, we have received help from a UG colleague on this point. H. Zobl (personal communication, October 6, 1991) has suggested that an important area of study based on this work is the directionality of the transferability between "the results of 'general' ESL courses and LSP courses." He predicted that IL elements will transfer from the former context to the latter, but not vice versa. We have tested this claim. In one of the case studies in Selinker and Douglas (1989), we first showed more evidence for the weak hypothesis, in the case that IL modal use is domain-specific. We then attempted to test Zobl's suggestion informally. Given the subject's life story, which we acquired as a domain of IL talk, we were able to conclude that Zobl's suspicion was correct for that case, in that general courses occurred first in his life. If it turns out that Zobl's hypothesis has widespread application, it could prove important for practical work as well as for SLA theory and methodology in general. Directionality of internal-IL transfer is one of those issues that SLA theory should be intimately concerned with. It is an interesting question whether, in the creation of IL texts, as suggested previously, learners produce a domain-bound universality at one level with a language-specific transferability at another.

CONCLUSION

One of our conclusions from the IL methodological paper just referred to (Selinker & Douglas, 1989) is the following: We do not wish to leave the reader with the conclusion that we believe that all SLA is contextually based and that the search for core universals is a chimera. We believe that the two approaches are complementary but feel that it is time that UG researchers integrate into their research the results of contextually based efforts, especially, as mentioned earlier, those concerning the methodological constraints of tests that UG researchers often use to establish levels of IL knowledge. Most importantly, the two approaches need to search for situations where language transfer and fossilization effects intersect. Some examples are provided in Selinker and Lakshmanan (1990), where multiple effects on IL form were documented. We note again the interesting study by St. John (1987), which has been ignored to date in the UG SLA literature. In that study, Spanish scientists needed to write in technical IL English. This is the quintessential highly contextualized LSP situation. Learners in this context appeared to produce fossilized formulaic IL in one section of a technical report (Procedures), but to develop IL composing strategies in other sections (especially Conclusions). If it turns out that Lakshmanan (1987) was correct, regarding this situation, that in certain Spanish LSP domains, pronoun subjects are usually retained, it means that *pro*-drop is the marked category for some contexts. The property of *pro*-drop may therefore be less likely to transfer in those contexts, which, as we concluded in 1989, gives the parameter a contextual dimension, an important result for UG concerns.[6]

To summarize the principles we have proposed for the study of SLA in field-specific contexts, we have described three types of IL data (primary data, coparticipant commentary, and expert commentary) and eight methodological principles, repeated below as (3a–h):

(3) a. Primary IL data are always ambiguous.

   b. Subject specialist informant procedures are necessary to disambiguate IL technical texts.

   c. Interactional features and the relationships among them in real time must be studied.

   d. Divergent interpretations of primary data provide insights into IL-particular structures.

   e. SSI procedures must be adapted to the study of specific purpose talk concerning highly valued texts, in an optimal research strategy.

   f. Rhetorical/grammatical distinctions in IL technical talk may not transfer to other domains of IL talk.

---

[6]In the oral presentation of this paper, Long, noting the strong possibility of the IL results by context suggested here, asked where attested SLA developmental effects fit in. It is our speculation that it is not unreasonable to suggest that UG and developmental constraints may apply only up to a certain stage in IL development. That is, it may be the case, as L. Trimble advocated (personal communication, August 5, 1985), that with advanced LSP concerns, language transfer effects and other SLA effects do not apply very much. What is more important, he claimed, was lack of knowledge of target texts and contexts. If empirical refinement of these ideas proves empirically correct, then we would guess that contextualized IL results as they might affect parameter setting need not upset basic core grammar UG concerns very much. This would indeed be a nice result, leading, we predict, to much fruitful cooperation.

g. SLA research needs to consider the effect on acquisition of the manipulation of method facets in elicitation procedures.

h. Rhetorical/grammatical interlanguage analysis may be necessary to disambiguate subjective gross ratings on tests as well as subjective gross interpretations of elicited IL data (e.g., imitation or grammaticality judgment tasks).

We claim that the methodological principles that appear here, and in the references cited, reduce problems of extrapolation by more directly relating empirical results to real-life and important contexts where much SLA takes place. This is so, we claim, whether the research purpose is to understand those contexts in depth, for practical purposes or for their own sake, or to look at the IL features hypothesized to be part of core grammar by UG theory.

REFERENCES

Bachman, L. F. (1988). Language testing—SLA research interfaces. *Annual Review of Applied Linguistics, 9*, 193–209.

Bachman, L. F. (1990). *Fundamental considerations in language testing.* Oxford: Oxford University Press.

Bachman, L. F., & Cohen, A. D. (1993). *Interfaces between SLA and language testing research.* Manuscript submitted for publication.

Bley-Vroman, R. (1978). Purpose, device and level in rhetorical theory. In R. M. Todd Trimble, L. P. Trimble, & K. Drobnic (Eds.), *English for specific purposes: Science and technology.* Corvallis, OR: Oregon State University.

Bley-Vroman, R., & Selinker, L. (1984). Research design in rhetorical/grammatical studies: A proposed optimal research strategy. *English for Specific Purposes Newsletter, 82/83*, 1–4; and 84, 1–6.

Carroll, J. B. (1968). The psychology of language testing. In A. Davies (Ed.), *Language Testing Symposium: A psycholinguistic perspective* (pp. 46–69). London: Oxford University Press.

Cohen, A., Glasman, H., Rosenbaum-Cohen, P., Ferrara, J., & Fine, J. (1979). Reading English for specific purposes: Discourse analysis and the use of student informants. *TESOL Quarterly, 13*, 551–564.

Cronbach, L. J. (1971). Validity. In R. L. Thorndike (Ed.), *Educational measurement* (2nd ed., pp. 443–597). Washington, DC: American Council on Education.

Douglas, D. (1989, March). *The notion of "motivation" in ITA training.* Paper presented at International TESOL Convention, San Antonio.

Douglas, D., & Selinker, L. (1992). Analyzing oral proficiency test performance in general and specific purpose contexts. *System, 20*, 317–328.

Douglas, D., & Selinker, L. (1993). Performance on general versus field-specific tests of speaking proficiency. In D. Douglas & C. Chapelle (Eds.), *A new decade of language testing research* (pp. 235–256). Alexandria, VA: Teachers of English to Speakers of Other Languages.

Flynn, S. (1989). The role of the head-initial/head final parameter in the acquisition of English relative clauses by adult Spanish & Japanese speakers. In S. Gass & J. Schachter (Eds.), *Linguistic perspectives on second language acquistion* (pp. 89–108). Cambridge: Cambridge University Press.

Frankel, R. (1984). From sentence to sequence: Understanding the medical encounter through microinteractional analysis. *Discourse Processes, 7*, 135–170.

Frankel, R., & Beckman, H. (1982). IMPACT: An interaction-based method for preserving and analyzing clinical transactions. In L. Pettigrew (Ed.), *Explorations in provider and patient transactions* (pp. 71–85). Memphis, TN: Humana.

Garfinkel, H. (1967). *Studies in ethnomethodology.* Englewood Cliffs, NJ: Prentice-Hall.

Gumperz, J. (1976). Language, communication and public negotiation. In P. R. Sanday (Ed.), *Anthropology and the public interest* (pp. 273–292). New York: Academic.

Huckin, T., & Olsen, L. (1984). On the use of informants in LSP discourse analysis. In J. M. Ulijn & A. K. Pugh (Eds.), *Reading for professional purposes* (pp. 120–129). Leuven, Belgium: ACCO.

Kellerman, E. (1989). The imperfect conditional. In K. Hyltenstam & L. K. Obler (Eds.), *Bilingualism across the lifespan: Aspects of acquisition, maturity, and loss* (pp. 87–115). Cambridge: Cambridge University Press.

Lakshmanan, U. (1987). *Second language acquisition and LSP.* Unpublished manuscript, University of Michigan, Ann Arbor.

Larsen-Freeman, D., & Long, M. (1991). *An introduction to second language acquisition research.* London: Longman.

Pienemann, M., Johnston, M., & Brindley, G. (1988). Constructing an acquisition-based procedure for second language assessment. *Studies in Second Language Acquisition, 10*, 121–143.

Selinker, L. (1979). On the use of informants in discourse analysis and 'language for specific purposes'. *International Review of Applied Linguistics, 17*, 189–215.

Selinker, L. (1991). *Fachsprachentheorie: How we gain our special information.* Paper presented at the Seventh European Symposium Workshop on Language for Specific Purposes, Jerusalem.

Selinker, L., & Douglas, D. (1985). Wrestling with "context" in interlanguage theory. *Applied Linguistics, 6*, 75–86.

Selinker, L., & Douglas, D. (1989). Research methodology in contextually-based second language research. *Second Language Research, 5*, 93–126.

Selinker, L., & Lakshmanan, U. (1990, March). *Consciousness-raising strategies in the rhetoric of writing development.* Paper presented at the 24th Annual Convention of Teachers of English to Speakers of Other Languages, San Francisco.

St. John, M. J. (1987). Writing processes of Spanish scientists publishing English. *English for Specific Purposes, 6*, 113–120.

Swales, J. (1986). A genre-based approach to language across the curriculum. In M. L. Tickoo (Ed.), *Language across the curriculum* (pp. 10–22). Singapore: Regional English Language Centre.

Tarone, E., Dwyer, S., Gillette, S., & Icke, V. (1981). On the use of the passive in two astrophysics journal papers. *The ESP Journal, 1*, 123–140.

Tyma, D. (1981). Anaphoric functions of some demonstrative noun phrases in EST. In L. Selinker, E. Tarone, & V. Hanzeli (Eds.), *English for academic purposes: Studies in honor of Louis Trimble* (pp. 65–75). Rowley, MA: Newbury House.

Zobl, H. (1989). Canonical typological structures and ergativity in English second language acquisition. In S. Gass & J. Schachter (Eds.), *Linguistic perspectives on second language acquisition* (pp. 109–123). Cambridge: Cambridge University Press.

7

THE ROLE OF LANGUAGE TESTS IN THE CONSTRUCTION AND VALIDATION OF SECOND-LANGUAGE ACQUISITION THEORIES

Elana Shohamy
Tel Aviv University

Language testing plays a role in three major contexts:

1. An external context where standardized tests are used for making decisions about individuals and programs regarding, for instance, certificates, diplomas, acceptance, rejections, and placement into language programs. Examples of external tests are the TOEFL (Test of English as a Foreign Language), the SAT (Scholastic Aptitude Test) matriculation examinations given at the end of high school in many countries, diploma and certificate tests, and placement and entrance exams.

2. The classroom context, where tests are used as part of the teaching and learning process.

3. The Second Language Acquisition (SLA) research context, where language tests are used as tools for collecting language data in order to answer and test SLA research questions and hypotheses.

Although these three contexts differ from one another with respect to conditions, purposes, procedures, and the type of decisions that are made based on test results, the external testing context has been the most dominant and influential paradigm of language testing in all three contexts. Thus, it is not uncommon to come across situations where the TOEFL is used as the main instrument for collecting language data in SLA research, whereas multiple-choice questions are used as part of classroom testing, where they are generally unsuitable. Yet the language testing discipline rarely addresses issues related to either classroom testing or tests in SLA research.

There are many reasons for the prestige and influence that external tests hold on the general testing scene. One is the power of external tests to affect the lives of individuals; another is the lack of training in testing methods on the part of both teachers and researchers; yet another is that external tests are promoted by testing companies with economic interests. The focus of this chapter is the role of language tests within the context of SLA research.

Before addressing the specific contribution of language testing to SLA research, it is important to note that the external testing context differs from the SLA research context in a number of ways. Thus, testing is used in SLA research to provide evidence for theories or research questions, but tests are used in the external context to arrive at decisions about individuals' futures. Consequently, testing in research does not have a direct impact on test takers' lives, whereas results obtained from external tests do. Also, in many SLA studies, tests are not the only devices used for collecting data; rather, multiple procedures such as questionnaires, observations, and interviews are employed. In most external testing contexts, tests are the only procedures used for obtaining information on the subjects' language ability.

In spite of these differences, it is clear that language tests (LT) can contribute to SLA theories and research in a number of ways: (a) defining and identifying means of measuring language ability (the dependent variable in SLA research), (b) improving the quality of the data collection instruments used in SLA research, and (c) identifying and testing hypotheses for SLA research. On the other hand, there are also a number of ways in which SLA research and theory can contribute to language testing: (a) identifying areas to be tested and perspectives for analyzing the language samples, (b) proposing a variety of tasks useful in the collection of language data (not just tests), and (c) alerting language testers as to potential differences in performance due to the first language (L1) of the respondents. Each of these contributions is now discussed in detail.

THE CONTRIBUTION OF LT TO SLA

Defining and Identifying Means
of Measuring Language Ability

Much of the work in LT in the past two decades has been devoted to defining language ability, under the rationale that if there is clear identification of the structure of language, it will be possible to design tests to match such descriptions. In the early work of Oller (1983), language was viewed as a unitary factor underlying language behavior competence, based on the learner's pragmatic expectancy of grammar operationalized through integrative tests such as cloze and dictation. Canale and Swain (1980) hypothesized that language competence comprises four competencies—linguistic, sociolinguistic, discourse, and pragmatic—implying that a valid language measure needs to include these components.

More recently, Bachman (1990) offered his model of language ability, concentrating on organizational and pragmatic competencies. In this model, organizational competence involves grammatical and textual competencies, and organizational competence involves illocutionary and sociolingistic competencies.

The main contribution of the different models to SLA theory and research is in providing a framework for measuring the dependent variable, that is, language ability. After all, SLA researchers must test their hypotheses about SLA (regarding, for example, the acquisition processes, factors interacting with and affecting SLA, strategies used by learners in SLA) in relation to language ability. These models can thus provide information on what constitutes language ability and how it can be validly measured. For example, given current models, it would be unwise for SLA researchers to measure the dependent variable of language via a cloze test, whereas 15 years ago it would have been acceptable. Today, it is clear that to measure language in SLA one must focus on a number of components—linguistic, sociolinguistic, discourse, and pragmatic, to use the Canale and Swain model. Alternatively, the focus must be on organizational (grammatical and textual) and pragmatic (illocutionary and sociolinguistic) competence, as in Bachman's model.

However, the contribution of LT to SLA research in this area of measuring language ability is still limited, because many of these models have not yet been validated empirically. It is not known, for example, whether the different components are independent of one another and what is the relationship between them in testing situations. Some work in this area has been done by Harley, Cummins, Swain, and Allen (1990), in which they examined whether grammatical, discourse, and SL competence can be distinguished empirically. Factor analysis failed to confirm the hypothesized three-trait structure of proficiency. In other studies there was support for the existence of separate grammatical and discourse components, whereas evidence for the existence of a separate sociolinguistic competence was not as strong (Milanovic, 1988; Swain, 1985). The Bachman model has not been validated empirically, although it is based on a previous study by Bachman and Palmer (1982) showing that language ability consists of one factor plus a number of unique abilities.

But there is yet another problem that limits the contribution of LT to SLA research. Testers rely on tests as the exclusive procedures for validating their models and as the only way of obtaining data. But language ability is a broad and complex construct that cannot be fully measured by tests. Thus, much as language testers would like to contribute to the definition of language ability, as long as they continue to obtain their data exclusively from tests, their contribution to SLA research and theory will be limited. Only when language testers begin to explore the use of other assessment procedures, especially those that are less testlike and more ethnographic (for example, observation or analysis of natural occurring documents) will they be in a position to contribute more substantially to SLA theory and research by providing more valid information about language ability and ways of assessing it.

Related to this problem of reliance on tests is another problem that originates from a conflict existing between the construct of language and the procedure of test analysis. Most current techniques for analyzing testing data, such as Item Response Theories (IRT) and latent trait models, are based on the assumption of unidimensionality. However, because language is clearly not a unidimensional construct, a serious conflict and a mismatch exist between the domains of LT and SLA. Specifically, how can LT analyses contribute to SLA research when they are based on different assumptions?

This is clearly a problem that has not yet been resolved and is a point of ample discussion in the field of language testing. One perspective on this issue is provided by Henning (1992), who attempted to resolve the problem by arguing that the effort to equate psychometric reality with psychological reality is mistaken. Henning argued that the two must be viewed as representing separate and distinct realities—a psychological reality and a psychometric one. These can be better referred to as a psychometric reality and a language (or second language) reality. Thus, testers should try to identify not what knowing a language means but rather what knowing a language means in testing situations. According to this approach, the contribution of LT to SLA will lie in providing information on the performance of test takers in testing situations and not in language in general. Performance on tests can therefore be considered a subset of general language performance. For example, if the SLA researcher is studying the area of communicative strategies, the use of such strategies in SL tests may be considered to be one subset of more general use of such strategies. Any results are therefore not necessarily generalizable to nontesting situations. Thus, the contribution of language testing to SLA lies in defining the dependent variable, though at this point the definition applies only to testlike situations.

Improving the Quality of SLA Data Collection Instruments Used in SLA Research

It was mentioned earlier that the results of external tests have a major impact on the lives of the test takers. Due to this responsibility, external tests should be of high quality and must pass strict quality criteria. These requirements (for example, that external tests be reliable and valid, that items and tasks be pretested and piloted before the actual administration, that bad items be revised or removed, that cultural and contextual biases be avoided), as imposed by the field of psychometrics, could be adopted by SLA research to improve research instruments.

Although tests in SLA research do not have a direct impact on the test takers' lives, they do have an indirect impact insofar as they contribute to an increased understanding of the theory of SLA, as well as to practical conclusions and implications. Thus, the inappropriateness of tests in research and the lack of quality criteria for instruments are likely to lead to a misunderstanding of SLA phenomena and to mistaken conclusions regarding new programs, new teaching methods, and new curricula.

SLA researchers often use tasks and not tests, but here quality criteria are equally important. Several SLA studies that examined communicative strategies reached conclusions that could be challenged because they had no test–retest or parallel form reliability information. Test–retest reliability provides information on whether similar results would be obtained had the tests been administered on a different occasion, and parallel form reliability shows whether the use of a similar version of the instrument will result in the same data. Similar criticism applies to work on variation, introspection, and pragmatics. The type of reliability (for example, internal consistency, test–retest, or parallel forms) depends, of course, on the specific instrument used. Ethnographic procedures should not be exempt from scrutiny as to quality control. Seliger and Shohamy (1989) outlined specific ways of examining quality criteria in relation to the specific research questions and type of data collection procedures used.

Instruments used in SLA research need to be tested for their validity as well. Evidence of construct validity needs to be obtained in order to show that the instruments measure the construct in light of current theories. This type of validity is different from the pragmatic validity that is required of external tests. Pragmatic validity is related to real life as it questions whether the test predicts well (predictive validity) or whether it correlates with another test and can therefore serve as a substitute (concurrent or criterion validity).

The impact that tests have on the lives of individuals is not very relevant for tests used in SLA research. These tests are generally one-shot events in which control over all the variables of the study may affect the validity of the results. However, an area that is gaining importance in external testing is that of fairness and ethics in testing; this aspect is currently being viewed as a new type of validity. This type of validity is certainly relevant to the SLA researcher as well, because it applies to the protection of the subjects of research studies.

In reading SLA research, however, too often it is found that quality criteria were not applied. Specifically lacking is information about the process of test development and about the different types of reliability and validity. It is apparent that many of the tests used are inappropriate for the specific research questions being studied and that often tests designed for making decisions about individuals are used for answering research questions. It often seems that the researchers simply had easy access to certain tests and used them without giving serious consideration as to their appropriateness for the specific research questions.

One study that illustrates the consequences of using instruments of doubtful quality was reported by Rosansky (1979). She provided convincing evidence that the Bilingual Syntax Measure (BSM) tests in the morpheme acquisition studies that led to a whole new policy for limited English speakers were based on instruments that had no reliability or validity. She demonstrated how major decisions were based on studies that used inappropriate and inaccurate tests and that led to invalid theoretical conclusions and implications and to inappropriate language teaching programs. She cautioned, "Continued use of the BSM as a research tool, with its questionable validity, leaves many otherwise well-designed research studies subject to serious criticism at their very core—the data base. Continued placement of children in bilingual programs on the basis of the BSM, with its limited sample of items and fuzzy proficiency level assignments, is risky" (Rosansky, 1979, p. 134). By applying some of the procedures used by language testers, SLA researchers are likely to obtain data that are more reliable and valid.

Related to the issue of the data collection instruments is that of the ample research available to language testers about language tests and the language testing process. In LT research, as distinguished from LT development, researchers examine questions concerning the testing process, the effect of testing methods, or the effect of contextual variables on test takers' scores.

One illustrative example involves the effect of the method of testing on test scores. Results of certain studies show that the method of testing, that is, the procedure used for collecting the data, the type of instrument, or even the type of questions (multiple-choice versus open-ended) (Gordon, 1987; Shohamy, 1984; Shohamy, Reves, & Bejerano, 1986) affect the scores obtained on language tests. Similar studies showed that familiarity with topic (Douglas & Selinker, 1990), genre (Shohamy & Inbar, 1991), and a variety of other contextual variables affect the test taker's scores.

Interestingly, the work of Tarone (1983) on elicited versus spontaneous tasks, which indicated that task and context have an effect on the language samples obtained, is a method effect study. Yet one wonders if Tarone's conclusions can be interpreted as an indication of variation or of testing method effect. Here, again, LT research can be instrumental in interpreting findings. In the testing literature there are procedures for finding out whether differences are a result of the method of eliciting the data regarding the trait (that is, method) or the language (that is, the trait). This is a very important area in which language testers can contribute to SLA research by virtue of their own research and experience in applying different validation methods such as multitrait multimethod in a number of major studies.

Thus, language testing can contribute to improved data collection procedures in SLA research by applying psychometric criteria and by applying the results obtained in LT research, especially in the area of different elicitation tasks. (See also chapter 12 in this volume, by Munich, Flynn, & Martohardjono, on the use of elicited imitation and chapter 13, by Bley-Vroman & Chaudron, which emphasizes the need to use instruments with more caution.)

Identifying and Testing Hypotheses for SLA Research

Advances in testing using procedures such as Differential Item Functioning (DIF) and latent trait may have an effect on SLA research. Through the DIF procedure, for example, it is possible to find out that certain items on tests function differently for certain groups of test takers. This procedure is especially powerful in tests such as the TOEFL, where it is possible to observe that certain ethnic groups, for example, behave differently than do other groups. Information of this sort can be valuable for second-language researchers in constructing hypotheses from language data. Pollitt (1991) reported recently on a study in which a group with a certain L1 performed differently on the Cambridge test than did other test takers. In analyzing the specific items, he identified those that discriminated against this group because of idiosyncracies in their L1. The fact that specific psychometric techniques such as DIF are capable of identifying different linguistic behaviors is important because it can provide SLA researchers with a variety of new hypotheses in SLA.

Furthermore, language testers, especially those in large testing agencies, often have vast amounts of data. These data are a powerful resource for confirming and testing hypotheses, regarding, for instance, the success on tests of test takers who have different language learning backgrounds (that is, formal vs. informal), the possibility of a natural developmental process in acquiring a language, or the question whether teaching makes a difference.

THE CONTRIBUTION OF SLA TO LT

Identifying Areas to Be Tested and Perspectives for Analyzing Language Samples

The major contribution of SLA research to LT is in identifying the construct of language acquisition that the language tester needs to consider in the construction of second-language tests. There are endless examples of this: The most striking ones are those involving analysis of reading comprehension (RC) or the writing processes. The fact that RC involves different types of schema, that it is an interactive process, and that different strategies play a role in language processing would make it imperative that language testers incorporate this information into their tests. An awareness on the part of testers of how writing is a process that requires revision would serve to remind them that they cannot administer a one-shot-type test, but rather must use a test in which test takers have the opportunity to revise their writing samples before the final assessment is made.

Unfortunately, a large number of testers do not utilize this information and as a result, the tests do not have construct validity. In a recent article on discourse analysis and language testing, it was pointed out that language testers have overlooked the vast work done in discourse analysis (Shohamy, 1990). As a prominent example, the American Council of the Teaching of Foreign Language guidelines did not consider the work in SLA; rather, they were based on a view of language that was unitary, hierarchical, and homogeneous, and therefore detached from current understanding of language and especially from findings concerning language variation. Similar claims can be made regarding the TOEFL and other tests. Clearly, those working on the development of tests for decision making are often not aware of and do not apply the findings of SLA research.

Proposing a Variety of Tasks, Not Just Tests

SLA researchers have long been collecting data using different types of procedures and have not limited themselves to tests. Language testers could begin to expand their repertoire of procedures for collecting language data beyond the traditional test approach. This is an area where language testers can benefit from the experience of language researchers and begin to use procedures such as judgment tests, observation of natural language use, documents, and self-assessments (cf. Larsen-Freeman & Long, 1991, for a list of available instruments commonly used in SLA research).

Alerting Language Testers to Potential Differences in Performance Due to Ll

On the basis of their findings, SLA researchers can forewarn the language tester as to possible problem areas. If SLA research has concluded that the L1 makes a difference in SLA, then the language tester cannot treat test takers from different L1 backgrounds in the same way. If different learners process language differently, attempts should be made to give different tasks to different learners. The evidence that the type of elicitation task has a significant impact on the language elicited should be of equal interest to language testers and to SLA researchers.

CONCLUSIONS

In this chapter, an attempt was made to point out ways in which language testing can contribute to SLA research and SLA research can contribute to LT. It was shown that although language testers and SLA researchers have different purposes, there are many areas where they can contribute to one another. If testers use creative tasks invented by SLA researchers they may enrich the pool of testing tasks and improve both test quality and the accuracy of decisions based on these tools. At the same time, SLA researchers should know which tools to use to obtain reliable and valid research results.

It is also important for SLA researchers to demand that language testers pay attention to their research findings. By the same token, those working in SLA research could turn to language testers to ensure that their instruments, whether tests or other elicitation tasks, are of high quality. At the same time, SLA researchers can help to interpret language test results on the basis of their research and can alert testers as to where problems may be expected to occur.

It is clear that researchers who collect language data and testers who make decisions about the language of individuals must begin to pay more attention to one another, thus making it possible for researchers to arrive at more valid theories and for testers to make sounder decisions about the future of individuals.

REFERENCES

Bachman, L. (1990). *Fundamental considerations in language testing.* Oxford: Oxford University Press.

Bachman, L., & Palmer, A. (1982). The construct validation of some components of communicative proficiency. *TESOL Quarterly, 14*, 449–465.

Canale, M., & Swain, M. (1980). Theoretical bases of communicative approaches to second language teaching and testing. *Applied Linguistics 1*, 1–47.

Douglas, D., & Selinker, L. (1990, March). *Performance on a general vs. a field specific test of speaking proficiency by international teaching assistants.* Paper presented at the 12th Language Testing Research Colloquium, San Francisco, CA.

Gordon, C. (1987). *The effects of testing method on achievement in reading comprehension tests in English as a foreign language.* Unpublished master's thesis, Tel Aviv University.

Harley, B., Cummins, J., Swain, M., & Allen, P. (1990). The nature of language proficiency. In B. Harley, P. Allen, J. Cummins, & M. Swain (Eds.), *The development of second language proficiency* (pp. 7–25). Cambridge: Cambridge University Press.

Henning, G. (1992). Dimensionality and construct validity of language tests. *Language Testing, 9*, 1–11.

Larsen-Freeman, D., & Long, M. (1991). *An introduction to second language acquisition research.* New York: Longman.

Milanovic, M. (1988). *The construction and validation of a performance-based battery of English language progress tests.* Unpublished doctoral dissertation, University of London.

Oller, J. (1983). *Issues in language testing research*. Rowley, MA: Newbury House.

Pollitt, A. (1991, August). *Construct validation of some cloze tests*. Paper presented at the East/West Symposium, Jyvaskyla.

Rosansky, E. (1979). A review of the bilingual syntax measure. In B. Spolsky & R. Jones (Eds.), *Advances in language testing series* (pp. 116–135). Arlington, VA: Center for Applied Linguistics.

Seliger, H., & Shohamy, E. (1989). *Second language research methods*. Oxford: Oxford University Press.

Shohamy, E. (1984). Does the testing method make a difference? The case of reading comprehension. *Language Testing, 1*, 147–180.

Shohamy, E. (1990). Discourse analysis and language testing. *Annual Review of Applied Linguistics, 11*, 115–131.

Shohamy, E., & Inbar, O. (1991). Construct validation of listening comprehension tests: The effect of text and question type. *Language Testing, 8*, 23–40.

Shohamy, E., Reves, T., & Bejerano, Y. (1986). Introducing a new comprehensive test of oral proficiency. *English Language Teaching Journal, 40*, 212–220.

Swain, M. (1985). Communicative competence: Some roles of comprehensible input and output in its development. In S. Gass & C. Madden (Eds.), *Input and second language acquisition*. Rowley, MA: Newbury House.

Tarone, E. (1983). On the variability of interlanguage systems. *Applied Linguistics, 4*, 143–163.

8

RESEARCHING THE PRODUCTION OF SECOND-LANGUAGE SPEECH ACTS

Andrew D. Cohen
University of Minnesota

Elite Olshtain
Hebrew University

Speech acts have been investigated and described from a variety of perspectives: philosophical, social, cultural, and linguistic. In the last 15 years or so, there has been an interest in collecting empirical data on the perception and production of speech acts by learners of a second or foreign language, at varying stages of language proficiency, and in different social interactions. This work has included efforts to establish both cross-language and language-specific norms of speech act behavior, norms without which it would be impossible to understand and evaluate interlanguage behavior.

EMPIRICAL VALIDATION OF SPEECH ACT SETS

Given a speech act such as apologizing, requesting, complimenting, or complaining, the first concern of second-language acquisition (SLA) researchers has been to arrive at the set of realization patterns typically used by native speakers of the target language, any one of which would be recognized as the speech act in question when uttered in the appropriate context. We have referred to this set of strategies as the speech act set of the specific speech act (Olshtain & Cohen, 1983).

In order to arrive at a speech act set, it is necessary to define the preconditions and interactional goals of the speech act in question and to identify performative and semantic prerequisites for the realization of these goals. If we take the act of apologizing, for example, we could stipulate that an apology is called for when there is some behavior that violates social norms. When an action or an utterance (or the absence of either) results in the fact that one or more persons perceive themselves as deserving an apology, the culpable person(s) is (are) expected to apologize. According to Searle (1979), a person who apologizes for doing A expresses regret at having done A. Thus, the apology act takes place only if the speaker believes that some act A has been performed prior to the time of speaking and that this precondition has resulted in an infraction that affected another person who now deserves an apology. Furthermore, the apologizer believes that he or she was at least partly responsible for the offense (Fraser, 1980), so that making amends is an interactional goal.

In the case of the apology, it is necessary to separate the performatives (e.g., *I'm sorry*) from other semantic formulas by which an apology can be realized, such as an explanation and justification for the offense (e.g., *The bus was late and so I couldn't possibly get here on time*) or an offer of repair (e.g., *I'll do it tomorrow*). The speech act set of apologizing has been found to consist of at least the following main strategies or semantic formulas (Cohen, Olshtain, & Rosenstein, 1986):

1. An expression of an apology, whereby the speaker uses a word, expression, or sentence that contains a relevant performative such as *apologize, forgive, excuse, be sorry.*
2. An explanation or account of the situation that indirectly caused the apologizer to commit the offense, used by the speaker in an indirect speech act of apologizing.
3. Acknowledgment of responsibility, whereby the offender recognizes his/her fault in causing the infraction.
4. An offer of repair, whereby the apologizer makes a bid to carry out an action or provide payment for some kind of damage that resulted from the infraction.
5. A promise of non-reoccurrence, whereby the apologizer commits him/herself to preventing a reoccurrence of the offense.[1]

In order to investigate the speech act of requesting, it was necessary to validate empirically a scale of imposition—from the most direct and imposing request to the most indirect and least imposing one (Blum-Kulka, 1989;

---

[1]As more empirical investigation of apologies is conducted, further main strategies are suggested for the speech act set. Whereas Cohen, Olshtain, and Rosenstein (1986) categorized comments such as *How could I* and *Are you O.K.?* as modifications of apology strategies, Frescura (1993) would subsume these under a main strategy that she labels appeals. There are problems with this categorization, such as whether an appeal standing alone would constitute an apology. The point here is that empirical work continues to refine the categorizations in use.

Olshtain & Blum-Kulka, 1984; Weizman, 1989). Perhaps the earliest empirical SLA research on requests involved having natives and nonnativies of English rank order the degree of politeness of a series of request strategies in the context of making a purchase (Carrell & Konneker, 1981). The request strategies themselves came from a theoretical claim that in making requests, imperatives are less polite than declaratives, which are in turn less polite than questions (Lakoff, 1977). For the natives, five levels of politeness were empirically validated, from the elliptical imperative (*steak and fries*) and the imperative (*give me steak and fries*) on the lower or least polite end to the past tense interrogative model (*could you give me steak and fries?*) on the upper or most polite end. The nonnatives generally agreed with these rankings, although they reversed the order of two lower level requests. (The natives rank ordered the declarative with no modal, *I want steak and fries*, lower than the declarative using a present tense modal, *I'll have steak and fries*, whereas the nonnatives reversed this ordering.)

One of the most comprehensive empirical studies of speech act behavior, both for its breadth and depth, has been that of the Cross-Cultural Speech Act Research Project (CCSARP) (Blum-Kulka, House, & Kasper, 1989), which compared speech act behavior of native speakers of a number of different languages with the behavior of learners of those languages. The CCSARP has also produced useful instruments for data collection and a coding scheme that has been widely replicated in other speech act studies. In addition, several excellent surveys of the research literature have appeared, which help to define and shape the field of investigation with respect to speech act research (e.g., Kasper & Dahl, 1991; Wolfson, 1989).

SOCIOCULTURAL AND SOCIOLINGUISTIC ABILITIES

What has emerged both from the large-scale empirical studies and from the comprehensive reviews of the literature is that successful planning and production of speech act utterances depend on certain sociocultural and sociolinguistic abilities. Speakers and hearers are successful speech act users when they have mastery over the speech act sets for speech acts in the language in which they converse. Such mastery calls for the ability to provide both socioculturally and sociolinguistically appropriate behavior.

Sociocultural ability refers to the respondents' skill at selecting speech act strategies that are appropriate given (a) the culture involved, (b) the age and sex of the speakers, (c) their social class and occupations, and (d) their roles and status in the interaction. For example, in some cultures (such as U.S. culture) it may be appropriate for speakers, as a repair strategy, to suggest to the boss when to reschedule a meeting that they had missed through their own negligence. However, in other cultures (such as Israeli culture) this type of repair strategy might be considered out of place in that it would most likely be the boss who determines what happens next. Thus, the sociocultural ability is what determines whether a speech act set is used and which members of the set are selected for use.

Sociolinguistic ability refers to the respondents' skill at selecting appropriate linguistic forms to express the particular strategy used to realize the speech act (e.g., expression of regret in an apology, registration of a grievance in a complaint, specification of the objective of a request, or the refusal of an invitation). Sociolinguistic ability reflects the speakers' control over the actual language forms used to realize the speech act (e.g., *sorry* vs. *excuse me*, *really sorry* vs. *very sorry*), as well as their control over register or formality of the utterance, from most intimate to most formal language. For example, when students are asked to dinner by their professor and they cannot make it, the reply *No way!* would be a *possible* form to use with the semantic formula "refusal." The problem is that sociolinguistically, this phrase would constitute an inappropriate refusal, unless the students had an especially close relationship with their professor and the utterance were made in jest.

SELECTING THE APPROPRIATE SPEECH ACT STRATEGY AND THE FORMS FOR REALIZING IT

The process of selecting the socioculturally appropriate strategy and the appropriate sociolinguistic forms for that strategy is complex, because the selection is conditioned by the social, cultural, situational, and personal factors already indicated. Strategy selection and selection of forms often depend on the social status of the speaker and the hearer, because in most societies deference toward a person of higher status, for instance, is realized via linguistic features (e.g., using *vous* rather than *tu*) or via modification of the main speech act strategies (e.g., adding intensity to the apology or purposely refraining from cursing). Thus, coming late to a meeting might evoke a more intensified and possibly invective-free apology when the apologizee is the boss, rather than a friend. Other factors such as age and social distance are part of the social set of factors that might play a significant role in strategy selection.

It has been found that situational factors also play an important role in strategy selection. Some situations generalize across cultures and hence will elicit similar strategies in different languages, whereas other situations are more culture-specific and are likely to cause cross-cultural problems. In one of the situations involving apology that was used in the CCSARP, a waiter brought the customer the wrong order. The waiters in all the languages under investigation avoided the expression of personal responsibility, perhaps because admitting such a mistake might cost them their job. On the other hand, the cross-cultural study of complaints showed that noise made by neighbors is perceived as a serious offense that warrants a complaint within some cultures whereas in other cultures it is viewed as a less significant offense. Furthermore, it has been found that situational circumstances are more likely to lead to personal variation than are social or pragmatic factors (Olshtain & Weinbach, 1993).

FOCUSING ON SPEECH ACT PRODUCTION

Research has demonstrated that in speech act behavior, as in other language areas, there is a discrepancy between a learner's perceptive and productive abilities. Thus, in a study done with immigrants in Israel it was found that although it might take 8 years to acquire nativelike perception of speech acts, a nonnative learner may never truly acquire nativelike production of such utterances (Olshtain & Blum-Kulka, 1984). As Kasper and Dahl (1991) noted, most of the early studies of speech act behavior (from the late 1970s) investigated the nonnatives' perception of speech acts carried out in the second language. Perhaps the very complexity involved in production then prompted a major focus on the production of speech acts.

Once again the research focus is shifting back toward perception of production, but this time with more sophisticated studies involving video taping. Most recently there have been two doctoral dissertations completed on this theme, one dealing with perceptions of L1 apologies (Edmundson, 1992) and one dealing with perceptions of L2 apologies, requests, refusals, and complaints (Zuskin, 1993). Yet, although the focus on perception may be in the process of renewal, there are still areas concerning the production of speech acts, particularly the cognitive processing aspect, that are in need of further investigation. In the present chapter we discuss methodological issues in researching the cognitive processes involved in the production of speech acts in a second language.

METHODS FOR COLLECTING SPEECH ACT DATA

The complexity of speech act realization and of strategy selection requires very careful development of research methods for describing speech act production. In the field of language assessment, there is a current emphasis on the multimethod approach. The consensus is that no single method will thoroughly assess the behavior in question. In speech act investigations, the challenge is, likewise, to find some means of combining different approaches to describe a single speech act among natives and nonnatives of a language. The ideal cycle of data collection has been perceived as one that includes different collection techniques (Olshtain & Blum-Kulka, 1985).

Investigators would start with the generation of initial hypotheses based on observational data from natural speech in L1 and L2, whether collected initially in L1 or simultaneously in both languages. Then we would elicit simulated speech such as that in role-plays, to test the initial hypotheses. From there we might go on to a paper-and-pencil task such as discourse completion (Blum-Kulka, 1982) in order to focus on specific realizations and manipulate the social and situational variables. If we are concerned with the perlocutionary aspect of speech acts, we might want to use acceptability checks in order to validate the range of acceptability within a speech community. Finally, we might be advised to validate the findings by means of further naturalistic, observational data (see Fig. 8.1).

Discussions of the relative strengths and weaknesses of each of these research methods have appeared elsewhere (Beebe & Takahashi, 1989; Blum-Kulka, House, & Kasper, 1989; Hartford & Bardovi-Harlig, 1992; Kasper & Dahl, 1991; Wolfson, Marmor, & Jones, 1989), and so we will not discuss them here. Unfortunately, it is difficult to obtain extensive observational data on speech acts across languages because the speech act being studied may not often appear naturally. As for discourse completion, it is a projective measure of speaking and so the cognitive processes involved in producing utterances in response to this elicitation device may not truly reflect those used when having to speak relatively naturally.

Although we mention discourse completion data, we focus this chapter on the more direct method for studying how complex speech acts like apologies, complaints, and requests are produced, namely, the role-play interview. We enumerate certain pitfalls associated with this method. But by the same token, there are a number of benefits. For one thing, it is possible to simulate conversational turns and to have the interlocutor apply conversational pressures that are not present in discourse completion tasks, even if rejoinders

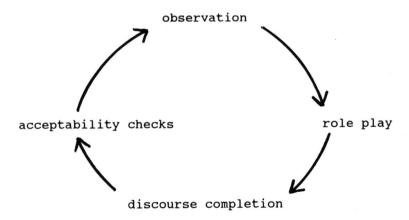

FIG. 8.1. The cycle of speech act research methods.

are added around which respondents must write in what they would be likely to say.

THE USE OF VERBAL REPORT
IN STUDYING SPEECH ACT PRODUCTION

In an effort to understand better the choices made by respondents when engaged in a speech act production task (naturalistic, role-play, or discourse completion) or a perception task (acceptability checks), we could make use of verbal report techniques. The cognitive processes that learners go through in order to produce or perceive speech acts are not available to outside observers and are usually not even attended to by the learners themselves. It would appear that only through verbal report are researchers able to tap some of these cognitive processes by calling the learners' attention to them. (For a discussion of the strengths and weaknesses of verbal report, see Cohen, 1991.) We could, thus, add verbal report to Fig. 8.1 by including it within an inner concentric circle, to indicate that it could be used with any form of speech act production or with perception (see Fig. 8.2).

To our knowledge there have as yet been only four studies of speech act production behavior using verbal report. Two of these used discourse completion as the data elicitation format, and two of them involved role-plays. The first, by Motti (1987), involved 10 intermediate EFL university students in Brazil who, after filling out a discourse completion task calling for apologies in English, were asked to retrospect individually in Portuguese regarding a series of variables, including their depth of analysis of the situation before response and the extent to which they thought in the foreign language, English, or in Portuguese L1 while preparing and writing their responses. Motti found that respondents thought slightly more in English than in Portuguese in the planning and execution of their utterances and were preoccupied with

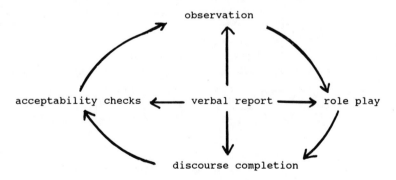

FIG. 8.2. Verbal report in speech act research.

correctness. They also reported paying more attention to another's status than to age.

In the second study, Robinson (1991) had 12 native Japanese-speaking females respond to six written discourse completion items calling for refusals of requests and invitations in English. The respondents were asked to think aloud as they filled out the task, and their verbal reports were tape-recorded. Immediately after completing the task, the researcher interviewed the subjects individually for 20 to 30 minutes regarding the content of their utterances from the think-aloud session, playing back the tape-recording to remind the respondents of specific thoughts. Although they were given the option of responding in Japanese, all the respondents performed their verbal reports in English. The investigator interpreted this use of English for verbal reporting as a result of her inability to speak Japanese. The use of verbal report in this case helped to reveal a sociocultural problem, namely, that Japanese girls are brought up to say yes, or at least not to say no. Therefore, the task of refusing was difficult for them to perform.

Although it is unreasonable to ask speakers to provide such data while they are engaged in speaking—given the intrusive nature of verbal report techniques—it is possible to obtain retrospective verbal report either between tasks or immediately after the tasks. A recent study that called for role playing and then verbal report after all the tasks had been completed was that of Frescura (1993). Role-play data on apologies were tape-recorded from native Italian speakers in Italy, native English speakers in Canada, Italians residing in Canada, and English-Canadian learners of Italian. After being tape-recorded in six role-play interactions, the respondents were asked to listen to all six recordings and to provide retrospective verbal report on: (a) how close to real life they felt their performance to be, (b) how dominant they felt their interlocutor was, (c) their sensitivity to the severity of the offense and to the tone of the complaint, and (d) (for Italians in Canada and learners of Italian) their possible linguistic difficulties. Frescura's use of verbal report helped her establish, among other things, that the learners of Italian tended to think in English first before responding to the role-plays.

The first study to combine verbal report with role-play is that of Cohen and Olshtain (1993). The study sought to describe ways in which nonnative speakers plan and execute speech act utterances. The subjects, 15 advanced English foreign-language learners, were given six speech act situations in which they were to role-play along with a native speaker. The interactions were videotaped, and after each set of two situations of the same type, the tape was played back and the respondents were asked both fixed and probing questions regarding the factors contributing to the production of their response to that situation.

In the administration of the role-play interview, the interlocutor gave the respondents an opportunity to read the descriptions of two brief role-play situations at a time (two apologies, two complaints, and two requests in all). Then she slowly read each situation out loud, gave the respondent time to think of a response, and then gave her an opener and had the respondent role-play with her. The interaction was videotaped and audiotaped as well. In a previous study where the verbal interaction had been recorded only on audiotape—the structure was fixed—an opener was followed by a single response from the respondent (Cohen & Olshtain, 1981). In this case, flexible structuring of the role-play was used. The native English-speaking interlocutor determined whether the interaction had reached its natural and logical end—usually after four or five exchanges.

The probing interviews conducted after each set of two speech act situations were intended to employ retrospective self-observation in order to obtain verbal report data about the cognitive processes that went into the production of speech act realizations. The interviewer's probes were conducted in what was the native language for 11 of the respondents, and a language of greater proficiency than English for the other 4 respondents. An effort was made to have the respondents be precise and to give examples where possible. The subjects were interviewed in three sessions—after the apology, complaint, and request situations—instead of waiting until after all six speech act situations, in order to obtain a more accurate retrospective report of behavior. It was feared that the delaying of the verbal report would reduce the reliability of the protocols, even using the videotaped behavior as a memory aid. When the respondents were not sure as to what they did and why, the interviewers played the relevant portion of the videotaped session a second or even a third time. This usually helped to jog the respondent's memory.

THE ROLE-PLAY INTERVIEW AS A RESEARCH METHOD: INSIGHTS FROM VERBAL REPORT

The use of the role-play interview—in other words, an oral and/or written prompt regarding a given situation and then role-play—as a simulation of actual behavior needs to be examined closely in each research context. To what extent are any such research instruments really semiethnographic or reflective of natural behavior, as suggested by Olshtain and Blum-Kulka (1984)? The remainder of the chapter deals with issues that verbal report techniques have highlighted with regard to the use of role-plays in collecting speech act data.

Cultural and Personal Reactions to the Situations

Whereas an effort may be made to select situations that are cross-culturally appropriate (i.e., that have the same cultural weight in different cultures, such as a neighbor playing loud music late at night), it is possible that one or another of the situations could still be viewed by the given respondent as not constituting a sociocultural infraction. For example, being half an hour late to meet a friend to study for an exam may not be considered an offense in Latin America or in the Middle East. In fact, it may be considered rude or unusual behavior to appear right on time (Hall, 1963).

On the personal level, respondents may point out that a given role-play situation occurs all the time. They may, in fact, indicate that they had performed that speech act in that very same situation the previous day (e.g., requesting that a neighbor turn down loud music late at night). In other cases, respondents may make it clear that they have never had to perform that speech act in that situation. In instances where the respondent has never had to react in such a situation (e.g., apologizing for keeping a classmate's book two weeks beyond the agreed date), it could be argued that the instrument is forcing unnatural behavior and that if the respondent is not a good actor, the results might be problematic. In cases where the respondents are asked to play a role that is out of character for them, the challenge for the researcher is to distinguish the respondents' sociolinguistic proficiency from their situational adeptness.

One way to handle this would be to allow respondents to opt out of the speech act (Bonikowska, 1988), as we do in real life. If they deflected the stimulus, the interlocutor would not pursue the issue. This is often the case in the real world, where a person may opt not to apologize, complain, or request something. Allowing for opting out, however, leaves holes in the data, and so researchers and evaluators tend to request that respondents produce an answer for each situation—even in face-threatening situations (Brown & Levinson, 1987).

The use of verbal report in the Cohen and Olshtain (1993) study revealed the degree of planning that certain situations may activate in the speaker. In other words, the situation itself may have properties that cause it to stimulate planning more than do other situations, regardless of the personal characteristics of the speaker. For example, students' asking their teacher for a lift home—where the inequality of status was found to play an important role in the mind of the respondent—was shown to prompt a conscious style shift, at least after the teacher pretended that she did not hear and replied, "What?" In addition, if they felt that they were in the right, as in a complaint situation, then some of the respondents reported planning less than when they felt the need to make amends, as in the apology situations.

The Language for the Task Description and for the Prompts

If the role-play situations are written in the target language, this procedure usually provides sociolinguistically appropriate words and phrases that can be copied directly into the response—if the respondents pick up on this. In the Cohen and Olshtain (1993) study, for instance, several respondents reported taking phrases directly from the text that described the situation—phrases that were only partially in or absent from their productive knowledge. For example, in the "lift" situation, a respondent noted that she took "my bus has just left" directly from the text. Also, whereas she would ordinarily say "token," she requested a "phone token" in the "token" situation because that was written in the text. In that same situation, several respondents reported that they had used the word *urgent* only because "it was included in the situation." They noted that they would not have used it otherwise.

Sometimes the process was a bit more complex and involved the combining of the respondent's own material with that in the text. So, in the "lift" situation, a respondent described how he arrived at asking the teacher, Debbie, "Can I come by your car?":

> First I thought "with your car, with you" and that I would not mention the car because I didn't know how to indicate *hamixonit shelax* 'your car' [in Hebrew]. I worried that she would think I wanted to go for a ride with her. "To get a ride with you" would be an expression I wouldn't know how to use. "Can I come" are words that I know how to use. After I heard Debbie read "by car," I said "by your car." (Cohen & Olshtain, 1993, p. 48)

In addition, there were numerous cases where respondents did not make use of clues that were in the written descriptions of the situation. For example, in the situation calling for a request from the teacher for a "lift" home, there were respondents who reported that they disregarded this clue and had difficulties finding a word in English for this request. The Semi-direct Oral Proficiency Interview (SOPI) (Stansfield, Kenyon, Paiva, Doyle, Ulsh, & Cowles, 1990), for example, gives the prompts in the native language of the respondent rather than in the target language being assessed. Consequently, no clues are given for the response.

The Validity of Verbal Report for Speech Act Research

There is always the danger that if the interviewer makes leading suggestions in an effort to elicit verbal report, the respondents may fabricate inaccurate descriptions of what they did to produce utterances (Cohen, 1991). Also, there is the possibility that the interviewer might make false assumptions based on intuitions regarding the verbal report and might put words in the respondent's mouth, as in the following case from Cohen and Olshtain (1993): "I could see you were focusing on grammar." In this instance, the informant indicated that he was not doing so. On the plus side, verbal report interviews provide feedback from respondents regarding aspects of their behavior that would otherwise be left to the intuitions and speculations of the investigator.

Likewise, there is the concern that reported behavior may not truly reflect actual behavior. The use of immediate retrospection (immediate playback of the tape after two situations) may help to diminish the likelihood of the retrospections being fabricated, but there is still this possibility. In the Cohen and Olshtain (1993) study, no effort was made to investigate the relationship, for example, between the report of planning and actual evidence of planning (e.g., pauses in delivery). It has been suggested that looking for tangible signs of planning in the videotaped role-play interactions could serve as a means for corroborating verbal report data indicating that planning was going on (B. Spolsky, personal communication, May 16, 1991).

Finally, in the Cohen and Olshtain (1993) study, the question arose as to when to stop the role-play in order to have the respondents retrospect. It was decided that if the retrospection had been delayed until the end of the session, then valuable verbal report data would have been lost, even with the replaying of the videotaped role-play interactions to help jog the memory. Yet by having the retrospection come at three intervals during the role-plays, there was a possibility that efforts taken to heighten awareness about a particular processing strategy could have inadvertently triggered that strategy, as respondents progressed from the first response session to the second and the third. Thus, asking respondents to indicate the language in which they were thinking may have stimulated the respondents—especially the trilingual ones—to think in a language in which they had not been thinking previously.

DISCUSSION AND CONCLUSIONS

The chapter began by noting that, although much work has been accomplished with respect to the empirical validation of speech act sets, much work still remains to be done. It was also noted that speech act behavior is so complex because the performance of any given respondent is dependent on a host of sociocultural and sociolinguistic abilities, each of which calls for a sensitive measurement effort. We pointed out that, although the field of speech act investigation began with studies of perception, moved to production, and now is swinging back to more sophisticated studies of perception, there are still numerous areas for investigation with regard to speech act production. This chapter focused on one of these.

The research cycle of observation, role-play, discourse completion, and acceptability checks was presented. We indicated that each of these data collection techniques has its own merits, but that it is the use of more than one technique that provides us with important triangulation. We suggested that in addition to considering the techniques that are useful for the description of speech act behavior within a group, the researcher of speech act behavior also needs to understand better the choices made by individuals. It is here that verbal reports can be most valuable—in order to understand further the cognitive processing involved in producing speech act utterances. The last portion of the chapter raised some issues about the use of the role-play interview, which were brought to the fore through the use of verbal report. The concerns raised with regard to the use of verbal report, such as the relative benefits of immediate versus delayed retrospection, simply underscore the need to carry out more empirical research on the use of verbal report in investigating complex language tasks such as speech acts.

Because the field of speech act research is still fledgling compared to other fields of investigation, we have not reached the point of mandating one or another research method for one or another purpose. The safest way to proceed is to use multiple measures, in order to triangulate the measurement of the speech act phenomena in question. No doubt we need to continue to conduct studies utilizing the various measures and to continue to scrutinize each one in some detail. Hence, we had no intention of arriving at pronouncements about the preferred use of role-play measures. We simply assert that researchers need to use such measures with a keen awareness as to their potential strengths and weaknesses.

REFERENCES

Beebe, L. M., & Takahashi, T. (1989). Sociolinguistic variation in face-threatening speech acts: Chastisement and disagreement. In M. R. Eisenstein (Ed.), *The dynamic interlanguage: Empirical studies in second language variation* (pp. 199–218). New York: Plenum.

Blum-Kulka, S. (1982). Learning to say what you mean in a second language: A study of the speech act performance of learners of Hebrew as a second language. *Applied Linguistics, 3*, 29–59.

Blum-Kulka, S. (1989). Playing it safe: The role of conventionality in indirectness. In S. Blum-Kulka, J. House-Edmondson, & G. Kasper (Eds.), *Cross-cultural pragmatics: Requests and apologies* (pp. 37–70). Norwood, NJ: Ablex.

Blum-Kulka, S., House-Edmondson, J., & Kasper, G. (Eds.). (1989). *Cross-cultural pragmatics: Requests and apologies*. Norwood, NJ: Ablex.

Bonikowska, M. P. (1988). The choice of opting out. *Applied Linguistics, 9*, 169–181.

Brown, P., & Levinson, S. (1987). *Politeness: Some universals in language usage*. Cambridge: Cambridge University Press.

Carrell, P. L., & Konneker, B. H. (1981). Politeness: Comparing native and nonnative judgments. *Language Learning, 31*, 17–30.

Cohen, A. D. (1991). Feedback on writing: The use of verbal report. *Studies in Second Language Acquisition, 13*, 133–159.

Cohen, A. D., & Olshtain, E. (1981). Developing a measure of sociocultural competence: The case of apology. *Language Learning, 31*, 113–134.

Cohen, A. D., & Olshtain, E. (1993). The production of speech acts by ESL learners. *TESOL Quarterly, 27*, 33–56.

Cohen, A. D., Olshtain, E., & Rosenstein, D. S. (1986). Advanced EFL apologies: What remains to be learned? *International Journal of the Sociology of Language, 62*, 51–74.

Edmundson, R. J. (1992). *Evidence for native speaker notions of apologizing and accepting apologies in American English.* Unpublished doctoral dissertation, Indiana University, Bloomington.

Fraser, B. (1980). On apologizing. In F. Coulmas (Ed.), *Conversational routines* (pp. 259–271). The Hague: Mouton.

Frescura, M. A. (1993). *A sociolinguistic comparison of reactions to complaints: Italian L1 vs. English L1, Italian as a community language, and Italian as a second language.* Unpublished doctoral dissertation, University of Toronto.

Hall, E. T. (1963). *The silent language.* New York: Premier Books.

Hartford, B. S., & Bardovi-Harlig, K. (1992). Experimental and observational data in the study of interlanguage pragmatics. In L. F. Bouton & Y. Kachru (Eds.), *Pragmatics and language learning* (Monograph No. 3, pp. 33–52). Urbana, IL: Division of English as an International Language, University of Illinois at Urbana-Champaign.

Kasper, G., & Dahl, M. (1991). Research methods in interlanguage pragmatics. *Studies in Second Language Acquisition, 13,* 215–247.

Lakoff, R. (1977). What you can do with words: Politeness, pragmatics and performatives. In A. Rogers, B., Wall, & J. Murphy (Eds.), *Proceedings of the Texas conference on performatives, presuppositions, and implicatures* (pp. 79–105). Arlington, VA: Center for Applied Linguistics.

Motti, S. T. (1987). Competência comunicativa em lingua estrangeira: O uso de pedido de disculpas. Unpublished manuscript, Pontifícia Universidade Católica de São Paulo, Program in Applied Linguistics, São Paulo, Brazil.

Olshtain, E., & Blum-Kulka, S. (1984). Cross-linguistic speech act studies: Theoretical and empirical issues. In L. Mac Mathuna & D. Singleton (Eds.), *Language across cultures* (pp. 235–248). Dublin: Irish Association for Applied Linguistics.

Olshtain, E., & Blum-Kulka, S. (1985). Crosscultural pragmatics and the testing of communicative competence. *Language Testing, 2,* 16–30.

Olshtain, E., & Cohen, A. D. (1983). Apology: A speech act set. In N. Wolfson & E. Judd (Eds.), *Sociolinguistics and language acquisition* (pp. 18–35). Rowley, MA: Newbury House.

Olshtain, E., & Weinbach, L. (1993). Interlanguage features of the speech act of complaining. In S. Blum-Kulka & G. Kasper (Eds.), *Interlanguage pragmatics* (pp. 108–122). New York: Oxford University Press.

Robinson, M. (1991). Introspective methodology in interlanguage pragmatics research. In G. Kasper (Ed.), *Pragmatics of Japanese as native and target language.* (Technical Report Vol. 3, pp. 29–84). Honolulu, HI: University of Hawaii, Second Language Teaching and Curriculum Center.

Searle, J. R. (1979). *Expression and meaning: Studies in the theory of speech acts.* Cambridge, England: Cambridge University Press.

Stansfield, C. W., Kenyon, D. M., Paiva, R., Doyle, F., Ulsh, I., & Cowles, M. A. (1990). The development and validation of the Portuguese speaking test. *Hispania, 73,* 641–651.

Weizman, E. (1989). Requestive hints. In S. Blum-Kulka, J. House-Edmondson, & G. Kasper (Eds.), *Cross-cultural pragmatics: Requests and apologies* (pp. 71–95). Norwood, NJ: Ablex.

Wolfson, N. (1989). *Perspectives: Sociolinguistics and TESOL.* Cambridge, MA: Newbury House.

Wolfson, N., Marmor, R., & Jones, S. (1989). Problems in the comparison of speech acts across cultures. In S. Blum-Kulka, J. House-Edmondson, & G. Kasper (Eds.), *Cross-cultural pragmatics: Requests and apologies* (pp. 174–196). Norwood, NJ: Ablex.

Zuskin, R. (1993). *L2 Learner interpretations of the DCT prompt: Sociolinguistic inference generated from context.* Unpublished doctoral dissertation, University of New Mexico, Albuquerque.

CHAPTER

9

INTERLANGUAGE VARIATION AND THE QUANTITATIVE PARADIGM: PAST TENSE MARKING IN CHINESE-ENGLISH

Robert Bayley
University of Texas at San Antonio

Variation in the speech of language learners has become an important concern in second-language acquisition research, as many scholars have come
to the conclusion that understanding variation is essential to understanding
acquisition (see, e.g., Adamson, 1988; Preston, 1989; Tarone, 1988). Although
scholars are far from unanimous in their opinions about the relationship between studies of second-language (L2) variation and second-language acquisition theory (see, e.g., Eckman, this volume, chapter 1; Gregg, 1990),[1] in

---

[1]Eckman (this volume, chapter 1) summarizes the debate between variationists such as Ellis
(1990) and Tarone (1990) and their critics, principally Gregg (1990), and argues that the burden of
showing that studies of interlanguage variation may contribute to SLA theory lies with the variationists. Scholars such as Gregg, however, who argue that SLA theory should follow the lead of
formal linguistics and focus only on competence, are left without data with which to test the
claims of competing theories, unless they take account of variability either in grammaticality judgments or in actual speech. Formal linguists who are interested only in competence can, after all,
rely on speaker grammaticality judgments, which tend to be quite stable, at least for speakers of
standard dialects. SLA researchers have no such recourse, however, because learner grammaticality judgments are themselves highly variable, as Ellis (1991) has recently shown. Moreover, the
validity of learner grammaticality judgments has also been challenged. Goss, Zhang, and Lantolf
(this volume, chapter 14), for example, suggest that learners rely on "translation and pedagogical
rules to determine the grammaticality of sentences in their L2" rather than on linguistic knowledge. Finally, recent work by Gass (this volume, chapter 16) suggests that learner grammaticality
judgments vary in a systematic way. Gass shows that judgments become more reliable the higher
one moves on a relative clause accessibility hierarchy. Given the nature of learner grammaticality judgments, then, the choice in SLA is not between studying a presumably invariant competence and studying variable performance. The choice is, rather, between testing our theories
on variable grammaticality judgments and testing them on variable performance.

157

recent years researchers have examined L2 variation at the level of phonology (e.g., Adamson & Regan, 1991; Dickerson, 1974), morphology (e.g., Bayley, 1991; Hatfield, 1986; Tarone, 1985; Wolfram & Hatfield, 1984, 1986;
Young, 1988, 1991), syntax (e.g., Hyltenstam, 1977), and discourse (e.g.,
Kumpf, 1984; Tarone & Parrish, 1988). Numerous explanations of observed
variation have been advanced, including, for example, the Labovian construct
of attention to speech (Tarone, 1979), planning time (Ellis, 1987), L1 transfer
(Flashner, 1989), language contact (Trudgill, 1989), and proposed language
universals such as the primacy of aspect (Robison, 1990). Researchers have
also suggested social, affective, and developmental explanations for L2 variation, including the learner's accommodation to the interlocutor (Beebe &
Zuengler, 1983), the learner's emotional investment in the topic (Eisenstein
& Starbuck, 1989), and age (Wode, 1989). Indeed, Tarone (1988), noting the
multiplicity of competing models and explanations, has called for a comprehensive theory to account for all the known causes of interlanguage variation.

A call for a theory that encompasses all known causes of variation may
well be premature. As Scarcella (1991) recently observed, the study of interlanguage variation is still in its infancy. Indeed, no single theory is likely to
account for the "fifty some-odd categories" that Preston (1986) identified as
influences on variation. In cases where the limits to variability can be specified with sufficient precision, however, current sociolinguistic methods do
provide a way to model the effects of the multiple independent factors that
have been proposed to account for observed variation. These methods therefore permit us to test the predictions of different theories. This study, based
on nearly 5,000 past-reference verbs extracted from sociolinguistic interviews
with 20 adult Chinese learners of English, uses the multivariate technique
of variable rule analysis developed by researchers working within the Labovian quantitative tradition to examine the effects of multiple constraints on
interlanguage past tense marking. The results of variable rule analysis using
Macvarb (Guy, 1989), a Macintosh version of the VARBRUL 2 computer program developed by Rousseau and Sankoff (1978), show that interlanguage
past tense marking is indeed systematic and subject to multiple linguistic,
social, and developmental factors. Moreover, the study shows that the variable rule model (Cedergren & Sankoff, 1974; Guy, 1988; Rickford, 1991; Rousseau & Sankoff, 1978; Sankoff, 1988) that underlies studies of native language
variation provides an effective means of accounting for the factors that influence interlanguage production.

This chapter focuses on the two main linguistic factors that constrain interlanguage past tense marking—saliency and aspect. Both have been suggested as possible universal constraints on language change as well as
language and dialect acquisition (Antinucci & Miller, 1976; Bardovi-Harlig,
1987, 1992, chapter 3 in this volume; Bloom, Lifter, & Hafitz, 1980; Bronckart

& Sinclair, 1973; Guy, in press; Robison, 1990; Trudgill, 1986). Researchers in second-language acquisition, however, have tended to slight either one or the other of these factors. Hatfield (1986), for example, in a study of the English spoken by Vietnamese refugees in the United States, acknowledged that the Vietnamese aspectual marking system might have had an effect on the informants' English past tense marking. Hatfield chose, however, not to explore this possibility in the greater part of the corpus, concentrating instead on lower level phonetic and phonological factors. Other researchers who have investigated interlanguage tense marking have focused almost exclusively on the influence of higher level factors such as aspect. Flashner (1989), for example, concluded on the basis of a relatively small number of narratives from three adult Russian learners of English that tense marking in the interlanguage of her informants could be accounted for by transfer from the Russian aspectual system.

The results of the present study provide additional evidence in support of Wolfram and Hatfield's (1986) argument that any adequate account of interlanguage verbal morphology must consider the effects of lower level factors such as the phonetic form of the past tense. The results also indicate, however, that lower level factors alone do not fully account for variable tense marking in Chinese–English interlanguage. Grammatical aspect also systematically constrains past tense marking, along with social and developmental factors.

METHODS

Speakers

The data reported here have been extracted from sociolinguistic interviews with 20 adult native speakers of Mandarin living in California. Their social characteristics are summarized in Table 9.1.

Speakers varied greatly both in English proficiency and in the degree to which they participated in English-speaking social networks. At the time of the first interview, 15 speakers had taken the Test of English as a Foreign Language (TOEFL). 10 speakers had received scores of 550 or higher and 5 had scored between 410 and 510. The 5 speakers who had not taken TOEFL were studying ESL in preuniversity or adult school programs. For the purposes of this study, speakers were divided into two proficiency groups: TOEFL 550 or higher, and TOEFL lower than 510 or pre-TOEFL.

The social networks of nine speakers, five from the lower and four from the higher proficiency group, were predominantly or exclusively Chinese. These speakers lived with other Chinese and, if employed, worked with other Chinese. Their opportunities for acquisition of English outside of the language

TABLE 9.1
Speaker Social and Demographic Characteristics

Pseudonym	English Proficiency	Age	Sex	Time in U.S. (months)	Occupation	Social Network
Guo Chang	H	32	M	54	Grad. stu.	Mixed
Susan	H	29	F	48	Computer salesperson	Mixed
Helen	H	40	F	36	Grad. stu.	Mixed
Tom	H	31	M	18	Grad. stu.	Mixed
Nan	H	26	F	18	Grad. stu.	Mixed
Hsiao Lan	H	25	F	18	Grad. stu.	Mixed
David	H	25	M	9	Grad. stu.	Chinese
Mei	H	30	F	6	Library assistant	Chinese
Jim	H	33	M	18	Grad. stu.	Chinese
Peter	H	30	M	61	Undergrad.	Chinese
Ai Hua	L	25	F	3	ESL stu.	Mixed
Cora	L	40	F	18	ESL stu.	Mixed
Francis	L	25	F	9	ESL stu.	Mixed
Louis	L	26	M	6	ESL stu.	Mixed
Will	L	30	M	9	ESL stu.	Mixed
Mike	L	29	M	9	ESL stu.	Chinese
Ella	L	18	F	6	ESL stu.	Chinese
Beth	L	26	F	9	ESL stu.	Chinese
Ronald	L	30	M	2	ESL stu.	Chinese
Lisa	L	34	F	9	Restaurant worker/ ESL stu.	Chinese

Note. H: TOEFL 550 +; L: TOEFL 510—or enrollment in TOEFL preparation class.
Note. The following abbreviations are used: Grad. stu.: Graduate student, Undergrad.: Undergraduate, ESL stu.: ESL student.

classroom were severely restricted. Eleven other speakers, six from the high and five from the lower proficiency group, had extensive opportunities for informal acquisition, having either lived or worked with native speakers of English for at least 6 months before the first interview.

Data Elicitation

Speakers were interviewed twice for approximately 1 hour each time. Normally, no more than a week or two elapsed between interviews. Participants in the first interviews were the informant and the researcher, a non-Chinese native speaker of English. The second interviews involved three-way conversations among two informants and the researcher. Interviews included the usual demographic questions as well as discussion of a wide variety of topics. Discourses ranged from stereotypical accounts of the difficulties of learning English to intensely involved narratives of experiences during the Bay Area earthquake of October, 1989 and eyewitness descriptions of the events of June 4, 1989 at Tiananmen.

Data Reduction

Past-reference verbs were transcribed in standard orthography, along with sufficient contextual information to establish temporal reference and aspectual class. Provided the data set is large enough, VARBRUL enables a researcher to test whether any number of factors significantly influence observed patterns of variation. In this study, I tested the effects of seven factor groups: (a) verb type, or phonetic form of the past tense; (b) the preceding segment (applies only to regular nonsyllabics and some replacives); (c) the following segment (applies to regular nonsyllabics and some replacives); (d) grammatical aspect; (e) English proficiency (TOEFL 550+, TOEFL 510−); (f) participation in English-speaking social networks (mixed social network, predominantly or exclusively Chinese social network); and (g) interview type (individual, paired). The three developmental and social factor groups, discussed in detail in Bayley (1991), were coded as simple binary oppositions. The coding system used for the dependent variable and the four linguistic factor groups is as follows.

The Dependent Variable.   In English, tense is marked on the main verb or the first auxiliary. The nearly 5,000 verbs in the corpus for the present study that require past tense marking in standard English were coded as (a) unmarked, (b) marked as in standard English, (c) regularized (e.g., *runned*), (d) marked but in nonstandard English (e.g., *I seen him last week*), or (e) marked as present by affixation of third-person singular *-s*. Because this study is concerned with the presence or absence of past tense marking rather than the use of standard morphology, verbs that were regularized (8 tokens) or marked in some other nonstandard manner (49 tokens) were counted as marked, and verbs referring to the past but marked as third-person singular present (107 tokens) were counted as unmarked. Verbs that have identical forms in the past and the present (e.g., *hit*, *put*) and regular nonsyllabics followed by homorganic stops or interdental fricatives were excluded from the corpus.

Verb Type (Phonetic Form of the Past Tense).   The first factor group, the verb type, was designed to test the hypothesis that the more salient the difference between the present and past tense forms, the more likely a past-reference verb is to be marked. Saliency is defined in phonic terms: "Greater stress and material substance (i.e., more features or segments) lend an element greater salience" (Guy, in press). For example, a past form such as *left* (Factor 2 in the following) is considered more salient than a past form such as *came* (Factor 3 in the following). The past form *left* differs from the present *leave* with respect to three features or segments (internal vowel change, devoicing of /v/, addition of a final stop), whereas *came* differs from present tense *come* with respect to only one segment (internal vowel change). A modified version of the classification system used by Wolfram and Hatfield (1984), the coding system used here includes eight factors that form a saliency hierarchy:

1. The suppletives *go, went* and *am, was.*
2. Verbs that form the past tense by means of an internal vowel change and affixation of *-t,d* (doubly marked or semiweak verbs, e.g., *leave, left*) and verbs that form the past by means of an internal vowel change, deletion of the final segment(s), and affixation of *-t,d* (e.g., *bring, brought*).
3. Strong verbs that form the past tense by an internal vowel change (e.g., *come, came*).
4. Copula forms other than the first-person singular. These forms, although usually classified as suppletives, were coded separately from the first-person singular because, viewed in terms of the present rather than the base, they do not form true suppletives. Unlike the first-person singular copula, the past tense forms *was* and *were* have one segment in common with the present.
5. Replacives (e.g., *have, had; send, sent*).
6. Regular nonsyllabics (e.g., *play, played; talk, talked*).
7. Regular syllabics (e.g., *want, wanted*).
8. The modals *can, could* and *will, would.* Considered strictly in phonetic terms, modals belong with Factor 2, verbs that form the past by an internal vowel change and affixation of *-t,d.* However, *could* and *would* may refer to the present or the past (e.g., *When I was a boy, we would go to the park every Sunday* and *I would go today if I could*). Because their temporal function is opaque, these forms represent the least salient verb class.

Preceding and Following Segments.   The preceding and following segments affect tense marking of forms where the past tense morpheme may be lost as a result of the phonological process of consonant cluster reduction (i.e., regular nonsyllabics and some replacives such as *send, sent*). This study controlled for the effects of preceding vowels, liquids, and obstruents and following pauses, vowels or glides, and consonants or liquids. A more detailed discussion of the phonetic and phonological constraints on marking of regular nonsyllabics is contained in Bayley (1991, 1992).

Grammatical Aspect.   Verbs may be marked for tense and/or aspect. Tense refers to the deictic relationship between an event or state and the moment of speaking. Aspect refers to the internal temporal constitution of a situation. In many languages, the perfective–imperfective opposition prevails over finer distinctions (Comrie, 1976). According to Comrie, "perfectivity indicates the view of a situation as a single whole, without distinction of the various separate phases that make up that situation; while the imperfective pays essential attention to the internal structure of the situation" (1976, p. 16). Examples (1) and (2) illustrate the distinction:

(1) *I was driving* to work today when I suddenly *remembered* our appointment.

(2) John *continued talking* after Mary *left* the room.

All the verbs in the examples are in the past tense. Only *remembered* and *left*, however, are aspectual perfectives. They present my remembering the appointment and Mary's leaving the room as single events and include the beginning, middle, and end. In contrast, *was driving* and *continued talking* are imperfectives. They express the ongoing nature of the actions without reference to their inception or completion.

Languages differ as to whether and how they mark the basic conceptual distinction between perfectivity and imperfectivity. In English, for example, neither the perfective nor the imperfective constitutes a separate morphological category. Rather, English marks the distinctions between a temporally restricted state, the nonprogressive, and a temporally nonrestricted state, the progressive, and between the habitual and nonhabitual past. In addition, English marks the distinction between perfect and nonperfect meaning (Comrie, 1976). Despite their similarity, however, the terms *perfect* and *perfective* refer to very different concepts. Most commonly, the perfect indicates the current relevance of a past event or relative time. It does not provide any information about the internal constitution of the event. In contrast, perfectivity is one way of viewing an event's internal constitution.

Mandarin Chinese, in contrast to English, grammaticalizes aspectual distinctions, although not tense (Li & Thompson, 1981). Of particular relevance for the study of Chinese learners, the perfective is the marked member of the perfective–imperfective opposition. Chinese marks the perfective by the clitic particle *-le*,[2] as in the following examples from Li and Thompson, 1981, pp. 186, 189.

---

[2]The grammatical status of *-le* is one of the more problematic questions in Chinese linguistics. Although most scholars (e.g., Chao, 1968; Li & Thompson, 1981) have viewed *-le* as a perfective marker, Shi (1989) recently challenged the traditional analysis. Shi argues that "LE after the verb but before the verb complement in modern Chinese should have two functions: one as a relative anteriority marker and the other as a phrase complement [of the resultative construction]. Previous accounts . . . cannot explain why LE sometimes occurs in imperfective sentences" (p. 112). A resolution of the question, however, is not essential to this study because the influence of aspect does not depend solely on transfer from the first language. The perfective is the marked member of the perfective–imperfective opposition in many of the world's languages (Dahl, 1985). On typological grounds alone, then, there is reason to suspect that it may influence patterns of interlanguage tense marking.

(3) a. ta   shui *-le*   san   -ge zhongtou.
       3 sg sleep -PFV three -CL hour.
       'S/He slept for three hours.'

    b. Zhangsan zai bowuguan men-kou   deng Lisi, deng-*le*
       Zhangsan at museum   door-mouth wait Lisi wait-PFV
       san   -shi fenzhong.
       three -ten minute.
       'Zhangsan waited for Lisi at the entrance to the museum for thirty
       minutes.'

In recent decades, considerable attention has been paid to the influence
of lexical and grammatical aspect on the acquisition of tense marking systems
(Antinucci & Miller, 1976; Slobin, 1985; Weist, Wysocka, Witkowska-Stadnick,
Buczowska, & Konieczna, 1984). Researchers in first-language acquisition have
shown that children acquiring native languages that grammaticalize both tense
and aspect tend to mark aspectual oppositions before verb tenses. Bronckart
and Sinclair (1973), for example, found that children acquiring French used
the present tense to describe events of long duration with no clear conclusion and the past tense to describe shorter, perfective actions. Berman (1985)
found that children acquiring Hebrew initially use the present tense for durative statives and statives and the past tense for end-state or punctual verbs.
De Villiers and de Villiers (1985) also found that children acquiring English
as a first language initially use the past tense to mark perfective and punctu-
ate actions.

Research in second-language acquisition has also suggested that learners
of English initially mark aspectual rather than tense distinctions. These suggestions, however, have often been based on small amounts of data from
very few speakers (e.g., Flashner, 1989; Robison, 1990). The data for this study,
extracted from approximately 30 hours of speech by 20 native speakers of
Mandarin, offer the opportunity for a more comprehensive examination of
the relationship between tense and grammatical aspect in learner speech.

In this study, past-reference verbs have been coded as perfective or imperfective to test the hypothesis that the convergence of the informants' first-
language aspectual marking system and the tendency of first and second learners to favor marking of perfective verbs, previously reported by Weist et al.
(1984) and Flashner (1989), results in a greater likelihood of past tense marking for perfectives than for imperfectives.

Analysis

Data were analyzed with Macvarb (Guy, 1989), a Macintosh version of VAR-
BRUL 2 (Rousseau & Sankoff, 1978). Although sociolinguists have long used
successive versions of VARBRUL to analyze variation in native languages,

the program has seldom been used even in naturalistic studies of second-language variation. This section, then, outlines the basic assumptions of variable rule analysis. More detailed treatments may be found in the extensive literature on variable rule analysis and the VARBRUL program (e.g., Cedergren & Sankoff, 1974; Guy, 1988; Preston, 1989; Rousseau, 1989; Rousseau & Sankoff, 1978; Sankoff, 1988; Sankoff & Labov, 1979; Young, 1988, 1991).

Originally developed as a method of analyzing phonological variation, variable rule analysis offers researchers a method to account for rule-governed variation in language use at all levels of the grammar. Rule-governed variation is distinguished from random or free variation because it "regularly shows greater or lesser rates of occurrence in particular environments or . . . regularly predominates among particular social groups or in particular speech styles" (Guy, 1988, p. 124). For example, speakers of African American Vernacular English (AAVE) are more likely to omit the copula when it is followed by *gon(na)* or by a present participle than when it is followed by a locative, predicate adjective, or noun phrase (Baugh, 1983). These patterns of variation are not random, although such general statements do not constitute a descriptively adequate account of the variable. Rather, an adequate account "should precisely define the nature and extent of each of these conditioning effects, and allow us to probabilistically 'predict' the approximate rate of use of . . . [the variable] by an individual, given certain information about the social characteristics of the person, the social situation and the linguistic environment" (Guy, 1988, p. 124). VARBRUL analysis enables us to accomplish this task.

The basic statistical problem in variable rule analysis arises from the fact that the data are not collected in controlled experiments. Every instance of a variable form occurs in a particular linguistic environment and a particular speech situation and, because our data consist of transcriptions of natural speech, the numbers of tokens represented in different environments are usually highly unequal. Moreover, both the linguistic environment and the speech situation vary in multiple independent ways. We cannot, therefore, examine only one factor group at a time, for example, speech style or grammatical aspect, and expect to achieve useful results. Rather, our analysis must be multivariate, "an attempt to model the data as a function of several simultaneous, intersecting, independent forces, which may be pulling in different directions" (Guy, 1988, p. 125). From such an analysis, we derive a numerical measure of the strength (promoting or inhibiting use) of each factor.

VARBRUL calculates the numerical measures of the strength of the different factors by the method of maximum likelihood estimation. Observed variation is modeled using equation (4):

$$(4) \quad \frac{1}{1-p} = \frac{1}{1-p_o} \times \frac{1}{1-p_i} \times \frac{1}{1-p_j} \times \ldots \times \frac{1}{1-p_n}.$$

In this equation, p is the probability that a rule will apply, p_i, p_j, ... p_n are the effects of factors $i, j, \ldots n$, and p_o is an input probability, a measure of the likelihood that the rule will apply regardless of the presence or absence of any other factor (Young, 1991). Factors $i, j \ldots n$ may be any linguistic or social influences that the researcher has reason to believe may affect the presence or absence of the form under investigation. For example, in a study of the acquisition of sociolinguistic norms on IN/ING alternation by Vietnamese and Cambodian immigrants to the United States, Adamson and Regan (1991) examined linguistic influences such as grammatical category and following phonological environment and social factors such as speaker gender. To find the probability that, say, a female immigrant will use the IN variant in a progressive verb form followed by a vowel, we need to model the effects of three simultaneously occurring factors and include a measure of the general tendency of the speaker to use IN rather than ING. In equation (4), the factors for grammatical category (progressive), following phonological environment (vowel), and gender (female) would be expressed by the terms p_i, p_j, and p_n, and the overall tendency of the speaker to use IN would be expressed by the term p_o.

The effect of each factor is expressed as a value (p_i)[3] between 0 and 1. A value of 1 indicates that the rule always applies when a particular factor is present in the environment; a value of 0 indicates that the rule never applies. Values between .5 and 1 indicate that the factor promotes rule application; values between 0 and .5 indicate that the factor inhibits application. In addition, VARBRUL estimates the input probability (p_o), a measure of the overall tendency of a variable rule to apply. VARBRUL also provides a measure of how well the model fits the data, the log likelihood statistic. The lower the log likelihood, the better the fit.

Significance Testing. With VARBRUL 2, the researcher may test for the significance of entire factor groups and of individual factors within groups. Commonly used instantiations of the program include a step-up step-down procedure analogous to the forward and backward selection procedures for doing multiple regression. The output includes a measure of the statistical significance of each factor group.

Perhaps because the step-up step-down procedure is widely available, researchers commonly report significance levels for factor groups, but numerous studies report results for individual factors within groups that do not differ significantly from one another. Provided that factors may be grouped in linguistically more general combinations, however, we may easily test the

---

[3]The term *probabilities* is often used to refer to the relative strengths, or factor values, calculated by VARBRUL. To avoid confusion for those accustomed to more conventional statistical techniques, I have used the terms *factor weight* or *factor value* throughout this study.

significance of difference between factors within groups by combining them, remodeling the data, and applying the log likelihood test. Twice the difference between the logs of the two likelihoods is equal to a chi-square measure of the differences between the models (with degrees of freedom calculated as the difference in total degrees of freedom, i.e., number of factors minus number of factor groups for the two runs).

Variable Rule Analysis and Second-Language Acquisition. Variable rule analysis involves a number of theoretical assumptions about the relationship between variation in performance and grammatical competence and about the nature of speech communities (Cedergren & Sankoff, 1974; Sankoff, 1988; Sankoff & Labov, 1979). Two of these are critical for applying the variable rule model to second-language acquisition (Guy, 1991):

1. Individual speakers may differ in their basic rate of use of a variable rule, that is, in their input probability for the rule.
2. Individuals should be similar or identical in the factor values assigned to linguistic constraints on the rule. (The assumption is usually qualified to apply just to people who belong to the same speech community.)

Evidence that linguistic factors have different effects on performance, then, indicates that speakers have different internal grammars and so belong to different speech communities.[4] For example, Guy (1980) found that a following pause has a different effect on the likelihood of -*t,d* deletion in the speech of New Yorkers and Philadelphians. He argued that the different factor weights for a following pause represented a dialectal difference between the two groups of speakers.

The principle that speakers who possess substantially identical internal grammars may vary in their frequency of application of a variable rule, but not in the constraints upon application, provides a means to test whether second-language acquisition involves repeated structurings, as Huebner's (1983) form–function model suggested, or whether it proceeds gradually along a multidimensional continuum. If second-language acquisition is characterized by restructuring, the results of VARBRUL analyses of longitudinal data or the results for speakers of different levels of L2 proficiency should show

---

[4]The application of the Labovian notion of the speech community to groups of language learners, even learners such as those in the present study who share an L1 and a target dialect, raises a number of questions. Unlike the Harlem gangs Labov (1972a) studied, who were characterized by densely interwoven social networks, speakers in most SLA studies, including this study, do not form a community in any conventional sense of the term. Classroom-based studies, however, would seem to be exceptions to this generalization. It may be best to think of learners who share the same patterning of constraints on a variable form as analogous to a speech community as it is usually conceived in sociolinguistics, rather than as an actual community.

that different factor groups constrain rule application and/or that the same factors have substantially different effects for low- versus high-proficiency learners. On the other hand, if acquisition proceeds gradually along a multidimensional continuum, with each factor group representing a single dimension, then once a rule has entered the grammar, both factor groups and individual factors within groups should have very similar effects on the performance of speakers at different stages of acquisition.

The hypothetical data in Tables 9.2 and 9.3 illustrate the quantitative consequences of restructuring and of variable rule models of second-language acquisition. Assume that the interlanguage variable under study is the realization of an obligatory target language inflectional morpheme. In that case, we would expect variable rule analysis to show that the target language rule has a greater tendency to apply (p_o) in the speech of high-proficiency learners, regardless of whether speakers restructure their internal grammars as acquisition proceeds. If, however, restructuring takes place, that is, if the variable is used to mark different linguistic functions in early and late acquisition, we would expect the factors that affect realization of the target language rule to differ in low (L) and high (H) proficiency speech. Furthermore, in this model, factors that significantly affect the likelihood of rule application in the speech of low-proficiency learners might have no effect on the speech of high-proficiency learners and vice versa. Table 9.2 illustrates what the factor values for speakers of different proficiency levels might look like if learners restructure their grammars as acquisition proceeds.

In contrast to a model that involves restructuring, a variable rule model of second-language acquisition predicts that factors and factor groups should have the same or similar effects on speakers of different proficiency levels, or on the same speaker at different stages of acquisition. That is, if acquisition involves a gradual increase in the likelihood that a target language rule will apply, the results of a variable rule analysis of low- and high-proficiency speakers should look approximately like the hypothetical data in Table 9.3.

Assume that the three hypothetical factor groups represent different types of factors. Let Group X represent a universal articulatory constraint (e.g., the tendency to reduce final consonant clusters before obstruents). Neither a re-

TABLE 9.2
Quantitative Consequences of Model of SLA Involving Restructuring
(Hypothetical Data)

Factor Group X			Factor Group Y			Factor Group Z		
	L	H		L	H		L	H
factor a	.38	.40	factor c	.67	.33	factor f	.40	ns
factor b	.62	.60	factor d	.50	.67	factor g	.60	ns
			factor e	.33	.50			

TABLE 9.3
Quantitative Consequences of a Variable Rule Model of SLA
(Hypothetical Data)

Factor Group X			Factor Group Y			Factor Group Z		
	L	H		L	H		L	H
factor a	.43	.39	factor c	.67	.67	factor f	.40	.38
factor b	.57	.61	factor d	.50	.53	factor g	.60	.62
			factor e	.33	.32			

structuring nor a variable rule model would predict much change in the ordering or values of such universally constrained factors. Let Groups Y and Z represent factors that would be affected if speakers restructured their internal grammars so that identical forms fulfilled different functions as acquisition proceeded. For these kinds of factors, for example, a form's grammatical function or semantic features, the two models would predict very different outcomes for factor weights and/or the significance of factor groups.

In summary, a variable rule model of second-language acquisition makes very explicit predictions. Crucially, it predicts that the factors that influence realization of a targetlike variant should have similar effects for learners at different stages of acquisition. The utility of the VARBRUL program, however, is not predicated on acceptance of a variable rule model. By enabling researchers to use production data to test the predictions of competing theories of SLA, VARBRUL analysis may contribute to the task of theory culling that Beretta (1991) has advocated.

RESULTS AND DISCUSSION

The results of VARBRUL analysis, summarized in Table 9.4, show that past tense marking is indeed highly systematic and subject to multiple linguistic, developmental, and social conditioning factors. Note that the Varbrul weights, or factor values, here labeled p_i, are not probabilities of occurrence. Rather, they are measures of the strength of factors within a group relative to other factors in the group. In a binary factor group, for example, where factor a has a value of .75 and b has a value of .25, a rule is approximately three times as likely to apply when a is present as when b is present. The actual number of rule applications, however, is constrained by the input probability (p_o in conventional notation), a measure of the overall strength of the rule, as well as by the effects of other independent factors that co-occur with a and b. In the present analysis, the step-up step-down procedure indicates that all factor groups tested significantly affect the likelihood that a past-reference verb will be marked for tense ($p < .01$). I shall restrict the dis-

TABLE 9.4
Past Tense Marking in Chinese–English Interlanguage:
Combined Results for 20 Speakers

Factor Group	Factor	p_i	% Marked	N
1. Verb type	Suppletive	.75	66	509
	Internal vowel change + suffix	.70	58	954
	Internal vowel change	.57	56	885
	Copula (except ls)	.55	35	865
	Replacive	.47	32	393
	Weak nonsyllabic	.42	34	855
	Weak syllabic	.27	22	259
	Modal *could, would*	.27	11	197
2. Preceding segment	Vowel	.59	38	208
	Liquid	.49	40	94
	Obstruent	.42	31	553
	Not applicable	—	47	4062
3. Following segment	Pause	.61	46	127
	Vowel or glide	.52	36	398
	Obstruent or liquid	.37	25	330
	Not applicable	—	47	4062
4. Aspect	Perfective	.67	61	2262
	Imperfective	.33	30	2655
5. Proficiency	High	.66	54	3097
	Low, intermediate	.34	28	1820
6. Social network	Mixed	.55	48	2955
	Chinese	.45	39	1962
7. Interview type	Paired	.53	48	1386
	Individual	.47	43	3531
TOTAL	Input probability (p_o)	.38	44	4917

Note. From Bayley (1991), p. 49.

cussion, however, to the linguistic factors because they have the greatest bearing on SLA theory.

Verb Type: The Effect of Phonetic Saliency

The results for verb type support Wolfram and Hatfield's (1984) hypothesis that the more salient the phonetic difference between the past and present tense forms of the verb, the more likely a past-reference verb is to be marked for tense. The closeness of the values for some factors suggests, however, that not all of the differences between verb types reported in Table 9.1 may be significant. The difference between the factor values for strong verbs like *come* and copulas other than the first-person singular, for example, is only .02 (.57 − .55). The difference between replacives and weak nonsyllabics is only .05 (.47 − .42). Moreover, in both instances, there are sound justifications for combining factors. Past tense formation of strong verbs like *come* and copulas other than the first-person singular is similar in that the past tense forms of both verb types involve a vowel change without affixation of a regular past tense marker (e.g., *come* → *came*; *is* → *was*). Moreover, past tense formation of replacives and weak nonsyllabics involves a change in the final segment (e.g., *send* → *sent*; *show* → *showed*; *walk* → *walked*). As the results in Table 9.5 indicate, combining similar factors results in a more efficient analysis. Furthermore, a comparison of the logs of the two likelihoods shows that the two analyses do not differ significantly with respect to goodness of fit ($p > .25$).

In these results, only weak syllabics appear to contradict the saliency hypothesis. A complete syllable, after all, would seem to be more salient than a final segment, particularly a segment that is usually the final element of a consonant cluster and therefore subject to deletion. In most common regular nonsyllabics, however, *-t,d* is affixed to a stressed syllable. This is true of 85% of the nonsyllabics in the present corpus. In contrast, the *-ed* suffix is always unstressed. Stress syllables are, of course, more salient than unstressed syllables. The greater saliency of stressed syllables, then, accounts for the difference between the values for the regular verb types.

Saliency and L2 Proficiency. The foregoing analysis indicates that saliency constrains acquisition. The role of saliency can be seen even more clearly, however, when separate analyses are run by proficiency level, as shown in Table 9.6.

Apart from the nonsignificant reversal of syllabics and modals in the high group and of verbs that undergo an internal vowel change and those that undergo a change in the final segment in the lower group, these results show that the ordering of constraints remains constant when high- and low-proficiency speakers are analyzed separately. For both groups, the more salient verb types—suppletives, doubly marked verbs, and other strong verbs—favor marking, whereas the less salient types—syllabics and modals—

TABLE 9.5
Saliency Constraint on Past Tense Marking in Chinese–English Interlanguage:
Revised Analysis

Factor	p_i	% Marked	N
Suppletive	.75	66	509
Doubly marked	.70	58	954
Internal vowel	.56	46	1750
Change in final	.46	33	1248
Weak syllabic	.27	22	259
Modal	.27	11	197

Note. From Bayley (1991), p. 53.

TABLE 9.6
Past Tense Marking in Chinese–English Interlanguage by
Verb Type and Proficiency Level

Verb Type	Lower Proficiency			High Proficiency			% Gain
	p_i	%	N	p_i	%	N	
Suppletive	.69	43	185	.79	80	324	+37
Doubly marked	.66	36	360	.71	71	594	+35
Internal vowel							
(+ copula except ls)	.42	27	588	.56	55	1162	+28
Change in final	.53	23	501	.44	40	747	+17
Regular syllabic	.36	16	104	.23	26	155	+10
Modal	.25	5	82	.27	16	115	+11
Input (p_o)	.22	28	1820	.58	54	3097	+26

Note. From Bayley (1991), p. 54.

disfavor marking. Furthermore, although high-proficiency speakers mark verbs of all types more frequently than do lower proficiency speakers, the increase in past tense marking does not proceed evenly across verb types. Rather, the more salient verb types lead. In fact, a comparison of percentages of marking by proficiency group shows that the higher a verb type is on the saliency hierarchy, the greater the increase in marking. Advanced learners, for example, marked 80% of suppletive verbs. Their less advanced counterparts marked only 43%, a difference of 37%. The advanced speakers, however, marked only 26% of weak syllabics, compared to a rate of 16% for the lower proficiency speakers, a difference of only 10%. Figure 9.1 illustrates percentages of past tense marking by verb type and proficiency level. Although less reliable than VARBRUL weights, percentages are used because VARBRUL normalizes values around an average of .50. The greater spread in the factor values among high-proficiency speakers (Table 9.6) reflects their greater gains in the more salient verb types. Percentages, however, show absolute gains in marking of all verb types.

The results for tense marking by verb type clearly show that the saliency of the difference between the present and past tense form of the verb not only influences early acquisition of second-language morphology but also continues to influence even very advanced learners. As a consequence of the uneven rate of acquisition across morphological classes, variability increases as acquisition proceeds. Setting aside modals because of their special characteristics, the difference between the percentages of marked nonsyllabics (16%), the least salient verb type, and suppletives (43%), the most salient type, is only 27% in the speech of the lower proficiency learners. In the speech of the advanced learners, however, the difference is 54% (80% for suppletives minus 26% for nonsyllabics).

In sum, past tense marking in Chinese–English interlanguage is strongly

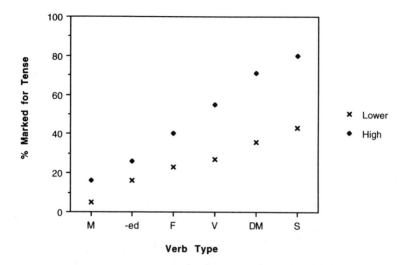

Key: M - modal; -ed - weak syllabic; F - change in final segment (replacives and weak nonsyllabics); V - internal vowel change (including copulas other than 1 s); DM - doubly marked (internal vowel change + suffix); S - suppletive

FIG. 9.1. Past tense marking in Chinese–English interlanguage by verb type and proficiency level. (From Bayley, 1991, p. 55.)

constrained by the salience of the difference between the present and past tense forms of the verb. More salient verb types are more likely to be marked in the informal speech of Chinese learners, regardless of their level of proficiency. Moreover, past tense marking remains highly variable even in the speech of very advanced learners. In fact, in the speech of the high-proficiency informants, marking of only one verb type, suppletives, reaches the 80% criterion for acquisition commonly accepted in second-language acquisition research.

The Effect of the Phonological Environment on Marking of Nonsyllabics

Regular nonsyllabic verbs, in addition to being subject to factors that affect all verbs regardless of their morphological class, are also subject to systematic -t,d deletion, a process that has been well documented in both native and nonnative varieties of English (e.g., Guy, 1980; Labov, 1989; Wolfram & Hatfield, 1984). In native speaker varieties, -t,d is more likely to be omitted if it is preceded by an obstruent rather than by a liquid or vowel. Native speakers of English, for example, are more likely to pronounce -d in *cold* than -t in *last*. Final -t,d is also more likely to be deleted if the following word begins

TABLE 9.7
Past Tense Marking of Regular Nonsyllabic Verbs in Chinese–English
Interlanguage by Preceding Segment and Proficiency Level

	Lower Proficiency			High Proficiency			Combined		
	p_i	%	N	p_i	%	N	p_i	%	N
Vowel	.47	23	128	.66	61	80	.59	38	208
Liquid	.57	31	29	.46	45	65	.49	40	94
Obstruent	.46	23	213	.38	36	340	.42	31	553

Note. From Bayley (1991), p. 70.

with an obstruent or a liquid rather than a glide or vowel. For example, -t
is more likely to be deleted from last in the phrase last night than in the phrase
last one.

If, then, past tense marking of regular verbs in learner speech is influenced
by variable -t,d deletion, the preceding and following segments should have
effects similar to those reported for other dialects of English. As Tables 9.7
and 9.8 indicate, the speakers in this study generally replicate the native speaker pattern. The only exception is that the preceding segment does not significantly affect lower proficiency speakers. These nonsignificant values are
italicized.

The results of the analysis of the pooled data show that a preceding vowel
favors tense marking, a preceding liquid is neutral, and a preceding obstruent
disfavors marking. Tense marking is also favored by a following pause or
a vowel and disfavored by a following obstruent or liquid.

Separate analyses by proficiency level show that for less advanced speakers the preceding segment, a relatively weak constraint according to Labov
(1989), does not significantly affect tense marking. The following segment,
however, a stronger constraint, has a similar effect for both high and lower
proficiency speakers. The difference between the two groups, reflected in
the fact that the preceding segment does not significantly affect past marking for the lower proficiency speakers, may be a result of the influence of
Mandarin, which lacks final stops. The data from the lower proficiency speakers contain many examples of postvocalic -d deletion before pauses (e.g., I
was driving on the /lo/ [road]). These cases suggest that at least some of the
less advanced speakers, for whom the effect of the first language phonological system is greatest, had not yet acquired final stops.[5]

---

[5]A separate analysis of the interaction of the convergent processes of past tense marking
and -t,d deletion among the same speakers reported here (Bayley, 1991, 1992) shows that the
higher proficiency learners have indeed begun to acquire the native speaker pattern of phonological constraints, in which a preceding obstruent favors and a preceding liquid disfavors -t,d
deletion.

TABLE 9.8
Past Tense Marking of Regular Nonsyllabics:
Following Segment by Proficiency Level

	Lower Proficiency			High Proficiency			Combined		
	p_i	%	N	p_i	%	N	p_i	%	N
Pause	.61	38	52	.59	52	75	.61	46	127
Vowel or glide	.52	27	169	.52	44	229	.52	36	398
Obstruent or liquid	.37	15	149	.39	34	181	.37	25	330

Note. From Bayley (1991), p. 70.

Grammatical Aspect and Past Tense Marking

The binary perfective–imperfective aspectual opposition strongly affects the likelihood that verb forms of all morphological classes will be marked for tense. Perfective aspect favors ($p_i = .68$) and imperfective aspect disfavors ($p_i = .32$) past tense marking. Moreover, the effect of the perfective–imperfective opposition remains constant across proficiency levels and even across individual speakers. Table 9.9 shows the results of analyses for the pooled data and for speakers of different levels of proficiency.

For adult second-language learners, perfectivity favors verb marking, as Flashner (1989) and Robison (1990) have suggested, but it does not fully explain it. All speakers in this study marked more perfectives than imperfectives; however, all speakers marked past-reference verbs belonging to both aspectual classes.

Moreover, as with saliency, the tendency of perfectives to favor marking extends well into the advanced stages of acquisition. For speakers at the levels of acquisition studied here, an increase in the input probability (p_o), an overall measure of the tendency to mark past-reference verbs, does not result in a change in the values (p_i) for perfective and imperfective aspect. On this dimension, speakers representing a range of proficiency levels merely turn up the input probability as they move in the direction of target language norms.

TABLE 9.9
Past Tense Marking in Chinese–English Interlanguage by
Aspectual Category and Proficiency Level

	Lower Proficiency			High Proficiency			Combined		
	p_i	%	N	p_i	%	N	p_i	%	N
Perfective	.67	42	856	.69	73	1406	.68	61	2262
Imperfective	.33	15	964	.31	38	1691	.32	30	2655

Note. From Bayley (1991), p. 72.

Figure 9.2 shows the relationship between the factor values for perfectives and the input probabilities for the 15 speakers who supplied sufficient data for individual analysis. Only the values for perfectives are shown because, in a binary factor group, the values for the second factor are simply the reciprocals of the first. A regression line fitted to the dispersion is included in the figure. The line is nearly level, with a correlation of .038 for the values for perfective marking and input probability. Note that the regression line for perfectives would approach .50 for the advanced learners if the effect of the aspectual constraint were weakening as the likelihood of marking past-reference verbs increased.

These results strongly support a variable rule model for the acquisition of second-language morphology. Indeed, judged by the effect of the aspectual constraint on their patterns of past tense marking, these Chinese learners of English approach "the uniformity of abstract patterns of variation which are invariant in respect to particular levels of usage" (Labov, 1972b, p. 121) by which Labov defines a speech community. For speakers at the levels of proficiency studied here, acquisition, or movement toward target language norms, consists of adjusting the input probability, or "particular level of usage." Such adjustments do not perturb "the uniformity of the abstract patterns of variation."

The Convergence of the LI Aspectual System and the Prototypical Meaning of Perfectivity.   The discussion so far has shown that multivariate analysis is required in order to model linguistic variation. Frequently, multiple explanations are also required in order to account for the quantitative results generated by VARBRUL. The regularity of the effect of grammatical aspect shown in Fig. 9.2, for example, may best be explained as a consequence of the convergence of the speakers' first-language aspectual marking system, in which the perfective is the marked member of the perfective–imperfective opposition, and the prototypical meaning of perfectivity, which is summarized by Dahl: "For all languages it holds that 'past time reference' characterizes prototypical uses of PFV [perfectivity]—single, completed events will in the 'typical cases' be located in the past. Languages will differ, however, in the extent to which they allow uses of PFV with non-past time reference" (1985, p. 79). In contrast, the ongoing nature of the event or situation rather than past-time reference characterizes prototypical uses of imperfectivity.

In Chinese–English interlanguage, then, perfectives are more likely to be marked for tense because they are prototypically past. Past-reference imperfectives are less likely to be marked for tense because the core meaning of imperfectivity includes the unmarked tense, the present. This tendency for perfectivity to favor past tense marking is reinforced for native speakers of Chinese by the first-language aspectual marking system, where perfectives are marked by the clitic -le. As a result of the convergence of a typological

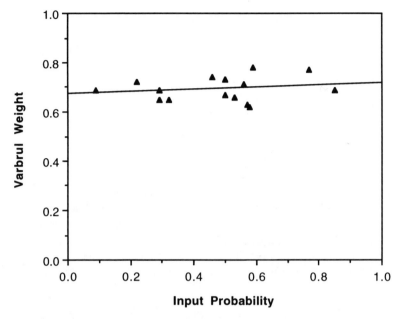

FIG. 9.2.   Past tense marking of perfective verbs in Chinese–English interlanguage: VARBRUL weights for 15 speakers. (From Bayley, 1991, p. 75.)

universal and the L1 aspectual system, perfectives strongly favor—and imperfectives strongly disfavor—past tense marking in the conversation of even
the most highly proficient speakers in this study.

CONCLUSION

The results of this study indicate that variation in interlanguage tense marking is indeed systematically conditioned by a range of linguistic, social, and
developmental factors. Moreover, when considered together with the results
of previous studies of second-language acquisition and language change (e.g.,
Bardovi-Harlig, 1992; Flashner, 1989; Guy, in press; Wolfram & Hatfield, 1984),
the results reported here suggest that the two main linguistic factors, saliency and aspect, may well be universal constraints on second-language acquisition. Language learners appear more likely to mark more salient forms and
aspectual perfectives; they are less likely to mark less salient forms and aspectual imperfectives.

The results also suggest that the acquisition of past tense marking may
best be described as proceeding along a continuum. The continuum, however,
is not one-dimensional or linear. Rather, it is multidimensional, with the
perfective–imperfective aspectual opposition, phonetic saliency, phonological

processes (such as -*t,d* deletion) that converge with marking of particular morphological classes, and social and developmental factors constituting the different dimensions. Finally, the results suggest that variable rule analysis, which enables us to account for the multiple independent factors that affect speakers' choices of variable linguistic forms, provides a richer and more comprehensive picture of L2 variation on which to base theories than models that posit a single overriding cause of interlanguage variation.

ACKNOWLEDGMENTS

The research reported here was undertaken as part of my doctoral dissertation, completed at Stanford University in 1991. I wish to thank my advisor, Kenji Hakuta, and committee members, Gregory Guy and John Rickford, for their many contributions. John Baugh, Sik Lee Cheung, Peter Patrick, and Elaine Tarone also provided valuable comments and suggestions. Any faults that remain are of course my own.

REFERENCES

Adamson, H. D. (1988). *Variation theory and second language acquisition*. Washington, DC: Georgetown University Press.

Adamson, H. D., & Regan, V. (1991). The acquisition of community speech norms by Asian immigrants learning English as a second language. *Studies in Second Language Acquisition, 13*, 1–22.

Antinucci, F., & Miller, R. (1976). How children talk about what happened. *Journal of Child Language, 3*, 167–189.

Bardovi-Harlig, K. (1987). Markedness and salience in second language acquisition. *Language Learning, 37*, 385–408.

Bardovi-Harlig, K. (1992). The relationship of form and meaning: A cross-sectional study of tense and aspect in the interlanguage of learners of English as a second language. *Applied Psycholinguistics, 13*, 253–278.

Baugh, J. (1983). *Black street speech: Its history, structure, and survival*. Austin: University of Texas Press.

Bayley, R. (1991). *Variation theory and second language learning: Linguistic and social constraints on interlanguage tense marking*. Unpublished doctoral dissertation, Stanford University, Stanford, CA.

Bayley, R. (1992). Production as a reflection of acquisition: Past marking and -*t,d* deletion in Chinese-English. In D. Staub & C. Delk (Eds.), *The Proceedings of the Twelfth Second Language Research Forum* (pp. 397–415). East Lansing, MI: Papers in Applied Linguistics—Michigan.

Beebe, L. M., & Zuengler, J. (1983). Accommodation theory: An explanation for style shifting in second language dialects. In N. Wolfson & E. Judd (Eds.), *Sociolinguistics and language acquisition* (pp. 195–213). Rowley, MA: Newbury House.

Beretta, A. (1991). Theory construction in SLA: Complementarity and opposition. *Studies in Second Language Acquisition, 13*, 413–512.

Berman, R. A. (1985). The acquisition of Hebrew. In D. I. Slobin (Ed.), *The crosslinguistic study of language acquisition* (Vol. 1, pp. 255–372). Hillsdale, NJ: Lawrence Erlbaum Associates.

Bloom, L., Lifter, K., & Hafitz, J. (1980). Semantics of verbs and the development of verb inflection in child language. *Language, 56,* 386–412.

Bronckart, J. P. & Sinclair, H. (1973). Time, tense and aspect. *Cognition, 2,* 107–130.

Cedergren, H., & Sankoff, D. (1974). Variable rules: Performance as a statistical reflection of competence. *Language, 50,* 333–355.

Chao, Y. R. (1968). *A grammar of spoken Chinese.* Berkeley: University of California Press.

Comrie, B. F. (1976). *Aspect.* Cambridge: Cambridge University Press.

Dahl, Ö. (1985). *Tense and aspect systems.* Oxford: Basil Blackwell.

deVilliers, J. G., & deVilliers, P. A. (1985). The acquisition of English. In D. I. Slobin (Ed.), *The crosslinguistic study of language acquisition* (Vol. 1, pp. 27–140). Hillsdale, NJ: Lawrence Erlbaum Associates.

Dickerson, L. (1974). *Internal and external patterning of phonological variability in the speech of Japanese learners of English.* Unpublished doctoral dissertation, University of Illinois, Champaign-Urbana.

Eisenstein, M., & Starbuck, R. (1989). The effect of emotional investment of L2 production. In S. Gass, C. Madden, D. R. Preston, & L. Selinker (Eds.), *Variation in second language acquisition: Vol. 1. Psycholinguistic issues* (pp. 125–140). Clevedon: Multilingual Matters.

Ellis, R. (1987). Interlanguage variability in narrative discourse: Style shifting in the use of the past tense. *Studies in Second Language Acquisition, 9,* 1–20.

Ellis, R. (1990). A response to Gregg. *Applied Linguistics, 11,* 384–391.

Ellis, R. (1991). Grammaticality judgments and second language acquisition. *Studies in Second Language Acquisition, 13,* 161–186.

Flashner, V. (1989). Transfer of aspect in the English oral narratives of native Russian speakers. In H. W. Dechert and M. Raupach (Eds.), *Transfer in language production* (pp. 71–98). Norwood, NJ: Ablex.

Gregg, K. R. (1990). The variable competence model of second language acquisition and why it isn't. *Applied Linguistics, 11,* 364–383.

Guy, G. R. (1980). Variation in the group and the individual: The case of final stop deletion. In W. Labov (Ed.), *Locating language in time and space* (pp. 1–36). New York: Academic Press.

Guy, G. R. (1988). Advanced varbrul analysis. In K. Ferrara, B. Brown, K. Walters, & J. Baugh (Eds.), *Linguistic change and contact: Proceedings of the Sixteenth Annual Conference on New Ways of Analyzing Variation* (pp. 124–136). Austin: University of Texas, Department of Linguistics.

Guy, G. R. (1989). *Macvarb.* [Computer program]. Stanford, CA: Stanford University, Department of Linguistics.

Guy, G. R. (1991). Explanation in variable phonology: An exponential model of morphological constraints. *Language Variation and Change, 3,* 1–22.

Guy, G. R. (in press). Saliency and the direction of syntactic change. *Journal of Pidgin and Creole Studies.*

Hatfield, D. (1986). *Tense marking in the spoken English of Vietnamese refugees.* Unpublished doctoral dissertation. Georgetown University, Washington, DC.

Huebner, T. G. (1983). *A longitudinal study of the acquisition of English.* Ann Arbor, MI: Karoma.

Hyltenstam, K. (1977). Implicational patterns of interlanguage syntax variation. *Language Learning, 27,* 383–411.

Kumpf, L. (1984). Temporal systems and universality in interlanguage: A case study. In F. R. Eckman, L. H. Bell, & D. Nelson (Eds.), *Universals of second language acquisition* (pp. 132–143). Rowley, MA: Newbury House.

Labov, W. (1972a). *Language in the inner city: Studies in the Black English Vernacular.* Philadelphia: University of Pennsylvania Press.

Labov, W. (1972b). *Sociolinguistic patterns.* Philadelphia: University of Pennsylvania Press.

Labov, W. (1989). The child as linguistic historian. *Language Variation and Change, 1*, 85–98.

Li, C. N., & Thompson, S. A. (1981). *Mandarin Chinese: A functional reference grammar.* Berkeley: University of California Press.

Preston, D. (1986). The fifty some-odd categories of language variation. *International Journal of the Sociology of Language, 57*, 9–47.

Preston, D. (1989). *Sociolinguistics and second language acquisition.* Oxford: Basil Blackwell.

Rickford, J. R. (1991). Variation theory: Implicational scaling and critical age limits in models of linguistic variation, acquisition, and change. In T. G. Huebner & C. A. Ferguson (Eds.), *Crosscurrents in second language acquisition and linguistic theory* (pp. 225–245). Amsterdam: John Benjamins.

Robison, R. E. (1990). The primacy of aspect: Aspectual marking in English interlanguage. *Studies in Second Language Acquisition, 12*, 315–330.

Rousseau, P. (1989). A versatile program for the analysis of sociolinguistic data. In R. W. Fasold & D. Schiffrin (Eds.), *Language change and variation* (pp. 395–409). Amsterdam: John Benjamins.

Rousseau, P., & Sankoff, D. (1978). Advances in variable rule methodology. In D. Sankoff (Ed.), *Linguistic variation: Models and methods* (pp. 57–69). New York: Academic Press.

Sankoff, D. (1988). Variable rules. In U. Ammon, N. Dittmar, & K. J. Mattheier (Eds.), *Sociolinguistics: An international handbook of the science of language and society* (Vol. 2, pp. 984–997). Berlin: deGruyter.

Sankoff, D., & Labov, W. (1979). On the uses of variable rules. *Language in Society, 8*, 189–222.

Scarcella, R. (1991). Review of S. Gass et al. (Eds.), *Variation in second language acquisition. Language in Society, 20*, 483–491.

Shi, Z. Q. (1989). The grammaticalization of the particle le in Mandarin Chinese. *Language Variation and Change, 1*, 99–114.

Slobin, D. I. (1985). Crosslinguistic evidence for the language-making capacity. In D. I. Slobin (Ed.), *The crosslinguistic study of language acquisition* (Vol. 2, pp. 1157–1256). Hillsdale, NJ: Lawrence Erlbaum Associates.

Tarone, E. (1979). Interlanguage as chameleon. *Language Learning, 29*, 181–191.

Tarone, E. (1985). Variability in interlanguage use: A study in style-shifting in morphology and syntax. *Language Learning, 35*, 373–403.

Tarone, E. (1988). *Variation in interlanguage.* London: Edward Arnold.

Tarone, E. (1990). On variation in interlanguage: A response to Gregg. *Applied Linguistics, 11*, 392–399.

Tarone, E., & Parrish, B. (1988). Task-related variation in interlanguage: The case of articles. *Language Learning, 38*, 21–44.

Trudgill, P. (1986). *Dialects in contact.* Oxford: Basil Blackwell.

Trudgill, P. (1989). Interlanguage, interdialect, and typological change. In S. Gass, C. Madden, D. Preston, & L. Selinker (Eds.), *Variation in second language acquisition: Vol. 2. Psycholinguistic issues* (pp. 243–253). Clevedon: Multilingual Matters.

Weist, R. M., Wysocka, H., Witkowska-Stadnick, K., Buczowska, E., & Konieczna, E. (1984). The defective tense hypothesis: On the emergence of tense and aspect in child Polish. *Journal of Child Language, 11*, 347–374.

Wode, H. (1989). Maturational changes in language acquisitional abilities. In S. Gass, C. Madden, D. R. Preston, & L. Selinker (Eds.), *Variation in second language acquisition: Vol. 2. Psycholinguistic issues* (pp. 176–188). Clevedon: Multilingual Matters.

Wolfram, W., & Hatfield, D. (1984). *Tense marking in second language learning: Patterns of spoken and written English in a Vietnamese community.* Washington, DC: Center for Applied Linguistics.

Wolfram, W., & Hatfield, D. (1986). Interlanguage fads and linguistic reality: The case of tense marking. In D. Tannen & J. E. Alatis (Eds.), *GURT '85. Languages and linguistics: The interdependence of theory, data, and application* (pp. 17–34). Washington, DC: Georgetown University Press.
Young, R. (1988). Variation and the interlanguage hypothesis. *Studies in Second Language Acquisition, 10*, 281–302.
Young, R. (1991). *Variation in interlanguage morphology.* New York: Peter Lang.

III

METHODOLOGIES FOR ELICITING AND ANALYZING SENTENCE-LEVEL DATA

CHAPTER

10

Preferences Versus Grammaticality Judgments: Some Methodological Issues Concerning the Governing Category Parameter in Second-Language Acquisition

Usha Lakshmanan
Southern Illinois University at Carbondale

Keiko Teranishi
Southern Illinois University at Nakajo

Recently, there has been a great deal of interest in the interpretation of reflexives by second-language (L2) learners of English. Specifically, some second-language acquisition (SLA) researchers have sought to address the question whether L2 learners of English, whose first languages (L1s) treat reflexives differently from the way they are treated in English, interpret English reflexives in the same way that native speakers of English interpret them or in a manner consistent with the interpretation of reflexives in their first language. In these previous L2 studies, L2 learners' intuitions about the behavior of English reflexives were obtained through either a picture identification task or a multiple-choice task. A major conclusion of these previous studies was that L2 learners fail to judge English reflexives in a manner that is consistent with the target language. Instead, their interpretation of the L2 reflexives is consistent with the interpretation that these would have in a larger or a superset grammar, such as that of the learners' L1. In other words, these studies indicate that the Subset Principle (see the following), which is claimed to be operative in L1 acquisition, is not operative in L2 acquisition.

In this chapter, we argue that the findings of these earlier studies are questionable because of certain methodological problems. Specifically, we claim that the methodologies used in these studies provide information about the L2 learners' preferred interpretations or about their use of a nongrammatical strategy but not about their grammatical knowledge. We then report on the results of a recent study that attempted to overcome some of these methodological problems through the use of an alternative methodology. We argue that this alternative methodology provides us with a clearer picture of L2 learners' grammatical knowledge with respect to the behavior of reflexives. Finally, we suggest a way by which the effects of the Subset Principle are successfully overcome by L2 learners.

BINDING PRINCIPLE A AND THE GOVERNING CATEGORY PARAMETER

Reflexives, along with reciprocals, constitute the class of anaphors, which are said to obey Principle A of the binding theory (see (1a)).

(1) *Binding Principles* (Chomsky, 1981):
   a. Binding Principle A: An anaphor must be bound in its governing category.
   b. Binding Principle B: A pronoun must be free in its governing category.
   c. Binding Principle C: An R-expression must be free.

According to Binding Principle A, an anaphor must be bound in its governing category. It must be c-commanded by and coindexed with its antecedent contained in its governing category. Although Principle A is said to be a universal property of anaphors, languages can vary with respect to what they take to be their governing category. In order to account for this variation, Wexler and Manzini (1987) proposed a Governing Category Parameter (GCP) that is associated with five values. The five values of the GCP as proposed by Wexler and Manzini are shown in (2).[1]

(2) *Governing Category Parameter* (Wexler & Manzini, 1987): B is the governing category for A iff B is the minimal category that contains A and a governor for A and has
   a. a subject; or
   b. an INFL; or
   c. a tense; or
   d. a "referential" tense (=indicative mood); or
   e. a "root" tense.

---

[1]For an alternative view of the parametric variation in the behavior of reflexives, see Cole, Hermon, and Sung (1990) and Katada (1991).

The reflexive in English instantiates value (2a); it must be bound in the minimal/nearest clause containing it, a governor, and a subject. In other words, the antecedent of the reflexive must occur in the minimal clause containing the reflexive and a subject. For example, in (3a) the reflexive *himself* can refer only to *Bill*, that is, the subject of the embedded clause; it cannot refer to *John*, which is the subject of the matrix clause.

(3) a. John$_j$ said that Bill$_i$ saw himself$_i$/$_{*j}$ in the mirror.

In contrast to English, Japanese has several reflexive forms. One of these reflexive forms is a morphologically simple form *zibun* 'self', Japanese also has morphologically complex forms, such as *zibun-zisin* 'self-self', *kare-zisin* 'he-self' and *kanojo-zisin* 'she-self'. The morphologically simple form *zibun* is associated with value (2e). The governing category for *zibun* is the matrix clause. As (3b) indicates, *zibun* can refer to either *Bill* (the subject NP in the embedded clause) or *John*, the subject of the matrix clause. In other words, (3b), in the absence of additional context, is ambiguous. On the other hand, the morphologically complex reflexive forms appear to instantiate the same GCP value as the English reflexive. As (3c) and (3d) indicate, they can take only the embedded clause subject and not the matrix clause subject as their antecedent.

(3) b. John$_j$-wa [Bill$_i$-ga kagami-no naka-de   zibun$_i$/$_j$-o mita to] itta
      John-Top Bill-Nom mirror-Gen inside-Loc self-Acc   saw   that said
      'John said that Bill saw self in the mirror'

     c. John$_j$-wa [Bill$_i$-ga kagami-no naka-de zibun-zisin $_i$/$_{*j}$ mita to] itta
      'John said that Bill saw himself in the mirror'

     d. John$_j$-wa Bill$_i$-ga kagami-no naka-de kare-zisin$_i$/$_{*j}$ mita to itta (= 3c)

Wexler and Manzini (1987) proposed the Lexical Parameterization Hypothesis, which states that the values of the GCP are not set for the language as a whole but are associated with particular lexical items. The Lexical Parameterization Hypothesis is given in (4).

(4) *Lexical Parameterization Hypothesis* (Wexler & Manzini, 1987, p. 55): Values of a parameter are associated not with particular languages, but with particular lexical items in a language.

As can be seen from the Japanese data in (3b–d), the simple form is associated with value (2e) of the GCP, whereas the complex forms are associated with value (2a) of the GCP.

THE SUBSET PRINCIPLE AND THE GCP

Wexler and Manzini (1987) claimed that the different values of the GCP are
in a nested subset–superset relationship. As Fig. 10.1 illustrates, value (2a)
of the GCP is embedded inside value (2b), which is in turn embedded inside
the next larger value, value (2c), and so on. This means that the grammar
of a language that instantiates a larger parametric value includes the grammar of a language generated by the smaller value. As we saw earlier, the
English reflexive is associated with the smallest value of the GCP, value (2a).
Its c-commanding antecedent, with which it is coindexed, must be present
in the nearest clause. The Japanese reflexive *zibun*, on the other hand, is
associated with value (2e), which generates a larger grammar. As we saw
earlier, *zibun* can take a local NP (i.e., an NP in the minimal clause containing *zibun*) or a nonlocal NP (an NP outside the minimal clause) as its antecedent. In other words, the English value, which generates the smallest possible
grammar, can be said to be embedded inside the Japanese value of the GCP
for *zibun*, which generates a larger grammar.

    In the acquisition literature, it is generally assumed that positive evidence
but not negative evidence is available to the learner. Given the five different
values of the GCP, the following question may be posed: How does the learner
arrive at the correct GCP values for the reflexives in the language being acquired? The learnability problem for those cases where the values of a
parameter are in a subset–superset relationship is that if the learner over-
generalizes, that is, selects a grammar that produces too large a language,
then no amount of positive evidence can cause the learner to arrive at the

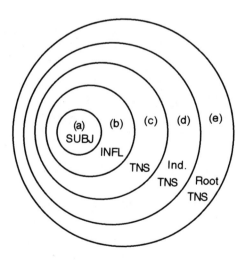

FIG. 10.1. Governing Category Parameter. *Note.* Ind. = indicative.

correct grammar, because all such positive data will be generated by the over-generalized grammar. On the other hand, if the learner undergeneralizes, that is, chooses a smaller grammar (which is a subset of the correct grammar), then positive evidence will indicate to the learner that the grammar selected is not the correct one.

Wexler and Manzini (1987) proposed a principle known as the Subset Principle to account for the learnability problem in those cases where the parametric values are in a subset–superset relationship. The Subset Principle is given in (5).

(5) *Subset Principle* (Wexler & Manzini, 1987, p. 61): The learning function maps the input data to that value of a parameter that generates a language:
a. compatible with the input data; and
b. smallest among the languages compatible with the input data.

The Subset Principle states that given two or more values of a parameter, the child will initially select the value that yields the smallest language. In regard to the GCP, an English-speaking child will initially select value (2a) of the parameter, which generates the smallest language. Because the child is not likely to encounter evidence that suggests that value (2a) is not the correct one, the child will remain with the value initially selected. However, if the child initially selects value (2e), which is consistent with the largest grammar, then he/she will never be able to move back to the smallest grammar (i.e., the correct grammar) on the basis of positive evidence alone, because the grammar generated by value (2e) includes the grammar generated by value (2a). In the case of the Japanese-speaking child, even if value (2a) is selected first for the simple reflexive form *zibun*, positive evidence that value (2e) is the correct one for this particular lexical item will be encountered in the input, and thus the child will be able to switch to the parametric value that is consistent with the larger grammar.

In general, studies on the acquisition of reflexives by child L1 learners suggest that the Subset Principle is operative in L1 acquisition. In other words, child L1 learners appear to set the GCP, initially, to the value that is consistent with the smallest grammar (see, for example, Chien & Wexler, 1987; Lee & Wexler, 1987). In the case of adult L2 acquisition, there appear to be at least two possibilities. One possibility is that the Subset Principle is operative. Under this scenario, we would expect all L2 learners of English, for example, to select the smallest value of the GCP, initially, regardless of what the value is for the reflexive element(s) in their L1. A second possibility is that the Subset Principle is not operative in adult L2 acquisition. In this case, we would expect L2 learners of English initially to transfer the value from the L1 to their English interlanguage. In those instances where the reflexive in the L1 is associated with the same value as in English (i.e., the subset value), there will be no problem, as the learners will remain with the value selected. However, in those cases where the reflexive in the L1 is associated with a superset value, the L1 value will initially be transferred to their English interlanguage. However, assuming that, as in the case of the child L1 learner, direct negative evidence is not available to the L2 learner, the L2 learners who select the larger value will never be able to arrive at the correct GCP value for English.

Let us now turn to the findings of previous research on the interpretation of reflexives by L2 learners of English.

PREVIOUS L2 RESEARCH

As stated earlier, a number of SLA researchers have studied how L2 learners acquire the target value of the GCP in those cases where it does not match the GCP value in their L1 (Finer, 1991; Finer & Broselow, 1986; Hirakawa, 1990; Thomas, 1989, 1990). (For a detailed review of these studies see Teranishi, 1991.) The overall findings of these L2 studies suggest that the Subset Principle is no longer operative in adult L2 acquisition.

Finer and Broselow (1986) investigated the acquisition of English reflexives by six adult native speakers of Korean. Korean, like Japanese, has both simple and complex reflexive forms. The simple reflexive *caki*, like *zibun*, is associated with the largest value of the GCP (i.e., value (2e)). A picture identification task was used to verify the L2 learners' interpretations of the English reflexive contained in finite embedded clauses and in nonfinite embedded clauses. The results indicated that local antecedents were strongly favored in sentences with finite embedded clauses, such as *Mr. Fat thinks that Mr. Thin will paint himself.* However, in those sentences where the reflexive was contained in the nonfinite embedded clause, such as *Mr. Fat asks Mr. Thin to paint himself*, nonlocal responses, that is, responses indicating that the matrix clause subject was interpreted as the antecedent, were very frequent, although a majority of the responses were of the local-only type. Finer and Broselow argued that the results indicated that the L2 learners did not obey the Subset Principle. Nor, according to the authors, did they transfer the value from Korean. Instead, Finer and Broselow proposed that the L2 learners initially selected an intermediary value of the GCP, value (2c), on the grounds that they treated finite and nonfinite embedded clauses differently. In the case of finite embedded clauses, 92% of the responses were consistent with the interpretation where the antecedent was a local NP, and only 8% of the responses indicated that the nonlocal NP was selected as the antecedent of the reflexive. In contrast, in the case of nonfinite embedded clauses, only 58% of the responses were of the local type, and 38% of the responses were of the nonlocal type.

However, we suggest that the picture identification task used by Finer and Broselow is methodologically questionable. Subjects can be successful on this task by selecting the picture of what can be termed a reflexive action. In other words, simply by knowing that the sentence names an action of self-painting, for example, the subjects would be able to pick the right picture every time to match the sentence provided. Thus, their choice of the correct picture may have been the result of adopting a nongrammatical strategy and may not have been based on their grammatical knowledge at all (see Grimshaw & Rosen, 1990, for a similar view regarding the methodological problems involved in using a picture identification task for testing children's knowledge of the Binding Principles).

Eckman (this volume, chapter 11) also used a picture identification task similar to the one used in the Finer and Broselow study. The task was used to gather data concerning the interpretation of reflexives by L2 learners of two target languages (English and Japanese) as well as data from native speakers of these two languages. The subjects in the English L2 group included native speakers of Arabic, Spanish, Japanese, and Mandarin. Eckman's results regarding the GCP differed from the results reported in the Finer and Broselow study. Specifically, Eckman found that the L2 learners' interpretation of the English reflexive did not differ depending on whether the embedded clause was a tensed clause or an infinitival clause. In both domains, all the L2 learners, except for one Arabic subject and one Spanish subject, bound the reflexive locally.

One possible reason for the difference in the results of the two studies is that the English L2 subjects in Eckman's study were at a more advanced level than the L2 subjects in the Finer and Broselow study. A more reasonable explanation may lie in the way the results were reported. As Eckman observed, the findings of L2 studies on binding, as well as other aspects of Universal Grammar (UG), have been based largely on group results rather than on results for individuals. Recall that in the Finer and Broselow study, a majority of the total responses in the infinitival embedded clause domain were of the local type, whereas 38% of the responses in the same domain were of the nonlocal type. In contrast to the Eckman study procedure, group results rather than results for individuals were reported by Finer and Broselow. Therefore, we do not in fact know whether all the nonlocal responses were made by the same few individuals. If this is indeed the case, then one would have to conclude that the asymmetry observed by Finer and Broselow in the interpretation of the reflexive in tensed embedded clauses and infinitival embedded clauses might not in fact characterize the individual data from many of their subjects.

Thomas (1989) examined the interpretation of English reflexives by native speakers of Spanish and native speakers of Chinese. Her findings suggested that the L2 learners initially set the GCP value for English wider than it should have been, allowing nonlocal antecedents in many cases. Thomas concluded that the Subset Principle was not operative because the subjects failed to choose the most restricted value.

Hirakawa (1990) studied the acquisition of English reflexives by native speakers of Japanese. She examined these L2 learners' interpretation of reflexives contained in finite and nonfinite embedded clauses of biclausal and triclausal sentences. As in the case of the previous studies, Hirokawa concluded that the Subset Principle was not operative in L2 acquisition, because her subjects selected a nonlocal NP as the antecedent for the reflexive in several cases. She argued that the Japanese L2 learners had set the parameter at the largest value, allowing nonlocal antecedents not only in the case of nonfinite embedded clauses but also in the case of finite embedded clauses.

Unlike Finer and Broselow or Eckman (this volume, chapter 11), Hirakawa (1990) and Thomas (1989) did not use a picture identification task. Instead, they used a multiple-choice format for testing their subjects' interpretation of the reflexive. An example from Hirakawa is shown in (6):

(6) John said that Bill hit himself.
   a. John
   b. Bill
   c. either John or Bill.
   d. someone else.
   e. don't know.

The subjects were presented with a sentence containing the reflexive and were asked to indicate who *himself* referred to by circling one of the given choices. The task appears to be methodologically flawed in that the subjects were required to identify who the reflexive could refer to, but not who the reflexive could not refer to. In other words, the task required the subjects to interpret the sentence in a way that made them think about what could be a possible antecedent for the reflexive but not about what could not be an antecedent. So it is possible that the subjects did not consider all possible options before arriving at their interpretations. In other words, a multiple-choice task such as the one listed in (6) may be tapping only subjects' preferences when interpreting reflexives and not their syntactic judgments.

Hirakawa (1990) used the multiple-choice task even in the case of the L1 Japanese-speaking controls who participated in her study. Thomas (1990) investigated the interpretation of the Japanese reflexive *zibun* by native speakers of Chinese, native speakers of English, and Chinese–English and Korean–English bilinguals—all of whom were learning Japanese in Japan. In her study, Thomas used a similar multiple choice task. In addition to the Japanese L2 subjects, a group of native speakers of Japanese, who served as the native speaker controls, also completed the task. Both Hirakawa and

TABLE 10.1
Interpretation of *Zibun* in Biclausal Tensed Sentences by
Native Speakers of Japanese

Study	n	Nonlocal	Local	Either
Hirakawa (1990)	22	62.73%	26.36%	9.10%
Thomas (1990)	10	67.5%	2.50%	30.00%

Thomas reported that the Japanese controls showed a strong preference for nonlocal antecedents in their interpretation of *zibun*.[2] It is interesting that Eckman (this volume, chapter 11), reported similar results with respect to his native Japanese-speaking control group, although the task used in his study was a picture identification task and not a multiple-choice one. The figures obtained by Thomas and Hirakawa are shown in Table 10.1.

The results shown in Table 10.1 contradict linguists' accounts of the properties of the Japanese reflexive *zibun*. If *zibun* really does instantiate the superset value, which includes the subset values, we would expect close to 100% or at least a majority of the native speakers of Japanese to allow either the local or the nonlocal NP as the antecedent. In other words, we would expect them to have interpreted the sentences containing *zibun* as ambiguous.

One reason for these results may have been that the verbs in the embedded clause of many of the sentences used in these studies tended to bias the informant in favor of the nonlocal NP as the antecedent, even though either the local or the nonlocal NP could theoretically be the antecedent of the reflexive. Consider, for example, sentence (7).

(7) John-wa   Bill-ga   zibun-o   nagutta to   itta.
    John-Top   Bill-Nom   self-Acc   hit-past comp said.
    'John said that Bill hit self.'

It is theoretically possible for *zibun* in (7) to refer to either *John* or *Bill*. But the verb in the embedded clause, *nagutta* 'hit', appears to introduce a semantic bias in favor of the nonlocal antecedent, and this may account for the tendency on the part of native speakers of Japanese to select the nonlocal NP as the antecedent for *zibun* (in the absence of a preceding context). Other examples of semantically biasing verbs are *love* and *hate*, which appear to be more naturally related to long-distance antecedents for native speakers of Japanese, in the absence of additional context.

Apart from the semantic bias introduced by the verbs in the sentences used in the interpretation task, another circumstance may also have been

---

[2]Finer (1991) likewise reported that the native speakers of Japanese who participated in his study also strongly favored a nonlocal NP as the antecedent of *zibun*.

responsible for the results observed. The task used with the Japanese controls in the studies by Hirakawa and Thomas was a multiple-choice type, which, as discussed earlier, does not require learners to think about what the reflexive cannot refer to. The results of previous studies may thus be questionable in that, as stated earlier, they may have tapped only the preferences of the subjects and not their syntactic judgments.

THE STUDY

The present study sought to overcome some of the methodological problems of the previous studies that investigated the role of the GCP in the acquisition of reflexives by L2 learners of English. The specific research questions addressed in this study are as follows:

1. Is the Japanese reflexive *zibun* associated with the widest value of the GCP? In other words, do native speakers of Japanese allow *zibun* to be bound by either a local or a nonlocal antecedent—that is, do they interpret sentences containing *zibun* as ambiguous?

2. Is the Subset Principle operative in adult L2 acquisition of English reflexives? In other words, do native speakers of Japanese acquiring English as a second language initially select the value consistent with the most restrictive grammar or do they transfer the superset value associated with *zibun* to their English interlanguage?

3. If Japanese L2 learners of English initially apply the superset value of the GCP associated with *zibun* to the English reflexive, will they, despite the predictions of the Subset Principle, be able to reset the GCP to the value that is appropriate for English?

METHODOLOGY

Subjects

Two groups of subjects participated in the study. A native English-speaking control group consisted of 11 subjects, all of whom were undergraduate students at Southern Illinois University. The experimental group included 34 native speakers of Japanese who were acquiring English as a second language. These subjects were students at Southern Illinois University at the time the study was conducted. Twenty-three of the 34 subjects were enrolled in the intensive English program at the Center for English as a Second Language. Eleven subjects were enrolled in Linguistics 105 and Linguistics 290, which are required composition classes for nonnative speakers enrolled in the University's undergraduate and graduate programs. The 23 students in the intensive English program had been assigned to four different levels (Level 1: beginning level, Level 2: low intermediate, Level 3: upper intermediate, and Level 4: advanced level). The placement of the students at the different levels was done on the basis of the scores they had received on the institutional TOEFL test taken upon their arrival at the university.

There was no separate native Japanese-speaking control group; the 34 L2 learners of English served as their own L1 Japanese controls. This was done in order to compare each subject's interpretations of *zibun* in the sentences in the Japanese L1 test with his/her interpretation of the reflexive in the sentences in the English L1 test.

The Sentence Interpretation Tests

There were two interpretation tests: an English test that was taken by the native speakers of English and the Japanese L2 learners of English, and a Japanese version of the same test for the Japanese L2 learners of English. Each test included written instructions and ten biclausal sentences. Each of the sentences contained the reflexive element in the embedded clause. Each sentence was followed by two statements concerning the interpretation of the reflexive in the sentence. The order of presentation of these statements was randomized. Examples from the Japanese test and the English test are given in (8) and (9):

(8) Taroo-wa Jiroo-ga kagami-no naka-de zibun-o mita to itta.
    1. zibun cannot be Taroo.   agree   disagree
    2. zibun cannot be Jiroo.   agree   disagree

(9) John said that Bill saw himself in the mirror.
    1. 'Himself' cannot be John.   agree   disagree
    2. 'Himself' cannot be Bill.   agree   disagree

Subjects were asked to consider each statement and indicate whether they disagreed or agreed with the statement by circling the relevant option. Subjects were informed that agreement with one option did not necessarily exclude agreement with the second statement. Instead, they were to think about each statement separately. For a detailed discussion of how the test instrument was developed, see Teranishi (1991).

There are at least four ways in which subjects could respond to the sentences shown in (8) and (9):

1. They could agree with statement 1 and disagree with statement 2. (This would be coded as local response only.)

2. They could disagree with statement 1 and agree with statement 2. (This would be coded as nonlocal only.)

3. They could disagree with both statement 1 and statement 2. (This would be coded as either local or nonlocal, i.e., the sentence is ambiguous.)

4. They could agree with both statements. (This would be coded as neither local nor nonlocal, i.e., the reflexive is not bound in the sentence.)

Insofar as it was possible, an attempt was made to avoid a semantic bias toward one of the two NPs (i.e., the local or the nonlocal NP) through the use of neutral verbs. However, this was a difficult task, as many verbs tend to introduce a bias in favor of either the local or the nonlocal antecedent. The English test was an equivalent translation of the Japanese test, except for the difference between the interpretation of the reflexive in the English sentences and the interpretation of the reflexive *zibun* in the Japanese sentences. The English and the Japanese test sentences are provided in Appendix A and Appendix B, respectively.[3]

The English test was first given to the Japanese L2 learners of English. They took 10 to 15 minutes to complete the English L2 test. One week later, the Japanese L1 test was administered to the same group of subjects. The English test was also administered to the native English-speaking group. All subjects answered all of the items on the two tests.

Let us now turn to the results of the study. In what follows, we first present the results of the Japanese L1 test and then report on the results of the English L2 test.

RESULTS

Results of the Japanese L1 Test

In Table 10.2, the responses of the Japanese L2 learners of English to the L1 Japanese test are presented.

As discussed earlier, previous L2 studies found that native speakers of Japanese strongly preferred a reading where *zibun* was bound to a nonlocal antecedent, although in theory either the matrix clause subject or the embedded clause subject can serve as an antecedent for *zibun*. However, as can

---

[3]In addition to the 10 sentences, the Japanese test also included 2 sentences in which the embedded clause was fronted. These 2 sentences were included in order to investigate the effects of word order on the interpretation of *zibun*. However, the results from these 2 sentences, where the embedded clause appears first, will not be reported here. For information about these results, the reader is directed to the detailed discussion in Teranishi (1991).

TABLE 10.2
Responses of the Native Speakers of Japanese to the Japanese Test (*n* = 34)

Response Type	Number of Responses (%)
local	72 (21.2%)
nonlocal	70 (20.6%)
either	197 (57.9%)
neither	1 (.3%)

be seen from Table 10.2, our subjects did not display a preference for the nonlocal antecedent. Instead, a majority of their responses were consistent with the reading wherein *zibun* is bound by either the local or the nonlocal NP (i.e., the reference of *zibun* is ambiguous). Our results suggest that the test used in our study may have been more effective than the instrument used in previous studies in tapping the subjects' syntactic knowledge (as opposed to their preferences).

Table 10.3 displays the frequency of "either"-type responses of the L2 subjects to each sentence in the L1 Japanese test. The frequencies indicate the degree of bias for each sentence; the lower the frequency, the greater the degree of bias. The results in Table 10.3 indicate that some sentences introduce more bias than do others. Let us consider two extreme cases, sentences 1 and 4. The test sentences 1 and 4 are presented in (10a) and (10b).

(10) a. Masao-wa Toshihiko-ga   zibun-no shashin-o   mitsuketa to   itta
       Masao-Top Toshihiko-Nom self-Gen picture-Acc found   that said
       'Masao said that Toshihiko found a picture of self'

   b. Kenji-wa Ryoohei-ga   zibun-o Yoko-ni   shookaishita to   itta.
      Kenji-Top Ryoohei-Nom self-Acc Yoko-Dat introduced   that said
      'Kenji said that Ryoohei introduced self to Yoko'

For sentence (10a), 25 of the 34 subjects gave "either"-type responses, whereas for sentence (10b), only 12 of the 34 subjects allowed both the local and the nonlocal NPs to serve as possible antecedents. Most of the subjects interpreted the nonlocal NP as the antecedent of *zibun* in (10b). The verb in the embedded clause in the sentence in (10b) is *shookaisuru* 'to introduce', which, judging from the responses of the subjects, appears to introduce a bias in favor of the nonlocal antecedent.

There appear to be two possible explanations for the bias with respect to the verb *shookaisuru*. One explanation involves Japanese culture. Self-introduction is not as common in Japan as it is in some societies. Therefore, it is possible that the subjects, when interpreting sentence (10b), may not have thought of a situation where someone performs a self-introduction. A second (and more plausible) explanation is related to the form of the verb that is

TABLE 10.3
Frequency of "Either"-Type Responses for Each Sentence in the Japanese Test

Sentence	Frequency (%)
1	25 (73.5%)
2	19 (55.9%)
3	20 (58.8%)
4	12 (35.3%)
5	23 (67.6%)
6	24 (70.6%)
7	17 (50.0%)
8	19 (55.9%)
9	22 (64.7%)
10	16 (47.1%)

used. In Japanese, the verb *jiko-shookaisuru* 'to self-introduce' is often used instead of *shookaisuru*. It may be that for some Japanese speakers *shookaisuru* is used exclusively when a nonlocal NP is the antecedent, whereas *jiko-shookaisuru* is used exclusively in contexts where the local NP is the antecedent.

Results of the English L2 Test

The results of the English L2 test are presented in Table 10.4. The results obtained for the native English-speaking control group are also provided. As stated earlier, the L2 learners of English also served as the L1 Japanese-speaking controls. The results of the Japanese L1 test are repeated in Table 10.4 for ease of exposition.

As can be seen from Table 10.4, the native English-speaking group predominantly chose local antecedents. This is consistent with what the GCP predicts: English instantiates the subset value of the GCP, allowing only local

TABLE 10.4
Responses of the L2 Learners and Native Speakers of English to the English Test and Responses of the Native Speakers of Japanese to the Japanese Test

Response Type	A Native Speakers of English (n = 11)		B L2 Learners (n = 34)		C Native Speakers of Japanese (n = 34)	
Local	106	(96.4%)	265	(77.9%)	72	(21.2%)
Nonlocal	0	(0 %)	24	(7.1%)	70	(20.6%)
Either	3	(2.7%)	48	(14.1%)	197	(57.9%)
Neither	1	(.9%)	3	(.9%)	1	(.3%)

antecedents. When we examine the responses of the Japanese English-as-a-second-language (ESL) learners, we notice that most of their responses were correct; that is, they chose the local NP as the antecedent of the reflexive. The response pattern of the L2 learners in the English test resembles that of the native speakers of English more than it does their response pattern in the Japanese L1 test. These results suggest that these L2 learners, considered as a group, were not treating the English reflexive like Japanese *zibun*.

Table 10.5 displays the responses to the English L2 test from the ESL learners at different levels of proficiency. The responses of the ESL learners in CESL Levels 1 and 2, and in CESL Levels 3 and 4, have been collapsed because of the small number of subjects. Likewise, the responses of the L2 learners enrolled in the English Composition courses Linguistics 105 and Linguistics 290 have been considered together.

As can be seen from Table 10.5, the ESL learners at Levels 1 and 2, considered as one group, gave a higher percentage of incorrect responses than did the learners at the higher levels. Their incorrect responses included both nonlocal and "either"-type responses. When we compare the responses of the subjects in CESL Levels 3 and 4 with the responses of the subjects in Linguistics 105 and 290, we notice that their behavior with respect to the number of correct responses is very similar. However, when we examine the number of incorrect responses, we notice that the subjects in Linguistics 105 and 290 did not make any nonlocal response, unlike the learners in CESL Levels 3 and 4. All of their incorrect responses except for one instance were "either"-type.

Not all of the L2 learners chose an incorrect response. Of the 34 L2 subjects, 14 subjects chose local antecedents only for all 10 sentences in the English L2 test. This suggests that these 14 subjects have successfully fixed the value of the GCP that is appropriate for the English reflexive. The responses of these 14 subjects on the L1 Japanese test were not similarly consistent; 99 of 140 responses (70.7%) were "either"-type, 23 of 140 (16.4%) were for the local antecedent only, and 18 responses (12.9%) were of the nonlocal

TABLE 10.5
Responses to the English Test by L2 Learners at Different Levels

Response Type	A CESL Level 1 & 2 (n = 8)		B CESL Level 3 & 4 (n = 15)		C Ling. 105 & 290 (n = 11)	
Local	51	(64.0%)	125	(83%)	89	(81%)
Nonlocal	14	(17.5%)	10	(7%)	0	(0%)
'Either'	13	(16.0%)	15	(10%)	20	(18%)
'Neither'	2	(2.5%)	0	(0%)	1	(1%)
X̄ (correct responses)	6.38		8.33		8.09	

type. Nine of the 34 subjects chose only local antecedents for 8 or 9 of the 10 sentences in the English L2 test.

For the remaining individuals, their incorrect responses to each sentence on the English L2 test were examined and compared with their responses to the corresponding sentences on the Japanese L1 test. Recall that except for the differences in the interpretation of the reflexive element, the English L2 test and the Japanese L1 test were equivalent. An interesting picture emerges from such a comparison. Only 7 of a total of 12 possible patterns were observed, as can be seen in Table 10.6.

Seven of the 10 responses shown in Pattern 1, where a local antecedent was chosen for the Japanese sentences and a nonlocal antecedent was chosen for the equivalent English sentences, were made by the same subject. Because this subject appears to have been behaving very differently from the rest of the group, Pattern 1 may be ignored. The predominant pattern is 8, where an "either" choice (i.e., either a local or a nonlocal antecedent) was made for the equivalent sentences in both the L1 Japanese test and the L2 English test. Those individuals whose responses were consistent with Pattern 8 may be argued to have transferred the syntactic value (i.e., the GCP value) for the Japanese reflexive *zibun* to the English reflexive. The other two major patterns are Pattern 4 and Pattern 5. As can be seen from Table 10.6, in Pattern 4, a nonlocal antecedent was selected for both the Japanese reflexive *zibun* and the English reflexive. In the case of the responses consistent with Pattern 4, we can hypothesize that the semantic bias from the L1 was transferred to the English interlanguage. Furthermore, it may be that the L2 learners, in this case, had not figured out the correct value of the GCP for the English reflexive. As for Pattern 5, a nonlocal antecedent was selected for

TABLE 10.6
Patterns of Incorrect Responses

| Pattern | Pattern Type | | Frequency |
	Japanese L1 Test	English L2 Test	
1	local	nonlocal	10
2	local	either	5
3	local	neither	0
4	nonlocal	nonlocal	10
5	nonlocal	either	10
6	nonlocal	neither	3
7	either	nonlocal	4
8	either	either	33
9	either	neither	0
10	neither	nonlocal	0
11	neither	either	0
12	neither	neither	0

zibun and an "either" choice was made for the English reflexive. It may be that the L2 learners whose responses were consistent with Pattern 5 had transferred the semantic bias for a nonlocal antecedent from their L1 to their English interlanguage. At the same time, it may be that they knew the appropriate value of the GCP for the English reflexive. In other words, a local NP was selected as the antecedent for a syntactic reason and a nonlocal NP was selected for a semantic reason.

DISCUSSION AND CONCLUSION

In Table 10.6, we noted that 33 of the incorrect responses in the English L2 test were consistent with the "either" choice. In other words, the subjects appear to have transferred the GCP value that is associated with *zibun* to the English reflexive. At the same time, however, we observed that 14 of the 34 L2 learners had successfully arrived at the correct GCP value for the English reflexive. Recall that the Subset Principle predicts that although it would be possible to move from a smaller grammar to a larger grammar, it would be impossible to move from a larger (superset) grammar to a smaller grammar. Given that the highest number of incorrect responses in the English L2 test were consistent with the "either" choice, it is possible that during a previous stage, these 14 successful L2 learners were operating with a nontargetlike grammar. In other words, they too may have initially set the GCP value for the English reflexive in a way that would be consistent with the superset grammar. The following question may then be posed: How did they come to reset the GCP value correctly for the English reflexive, even though this would have necessitated their moving from a larger grammar to a smaller grammar? In other words, why are the predictions of the Subset Principle not borne out?

Because these L2 learners were acquiring English in an instructional setting, it may be that direct negative evidence was available to them. In other words, they may have received overt instruction about the behavior of English reflexives. However, because the linguistic property in question is a complex one, it is not very likely that negative evidence was indeed available to these learners.

A more plausible explanation for the successful resetting of the GCP value from one that is consistent with the superset grammar to one that is consistent with the subset grammar entails an important role for *interlingual identifications* (Weinreich, 1953, as discussed in Selinker, 1991). Recall that in addition to the morphologically simple reflexive form *zibun*, Japanese also has morphologically complex forms such as *zibun-zisin* 'self-self', *kare-zisin* 'he-self', *kanojo-zisin* 'she-self', and *karera-zisin* 'they-self'. In contrast to *zibun*, these morphologically complex forms can take only a local NP as their antecedent. In other words, as in the case of the English reflexives, which are also morphologically complex, the morphologically complex reflexive forms in Japanese are associated with the value of the GCP that is consistent with the most restrictive grammar, not the superset grammar. They cannot take a nonlocal NP as their antecedent.

It is possible that the Japanese L2 learners of English initially associate the English reflexives in the input, such as *himself* and *herself*, with the morphologically simple form *zibun*. So during this initial stage, the English reflexive is perhaps analyzed as a simple form rather than as a complex form. In other words, the focus of the learners may be only on *self* in *himself/herself*. There is some evidence from child L2 production data that the English reflexive may be initially perceived as a simple form. The evidence comes from Uguisu, a 5-year-old native speaker of Japanese who acquired English as a second language in the United States. The relevant data on Uguisu, which were reported in Hakuta (1976), are presented in Table 10.7.

As can be seen from the data in Table 10.7, Uguisu initially produced only the morphologically simple form of the reflexive (i.e., self). The morphologically complex form emerges in sample 12. However, it does not match the target form exactly and instead is realized in forms such as *he-self* and *their-selfs*. Because all the utterances containing the reflexive element are monoclausal sentences, we cannot tell from the data what the exact GCP

TABLE 10.7
List of Reflexives Used by Uguisu

Sample	Utterance
Sample 11	You have to do self, because remember I do self?
	I will do it self.
	I can do it self.
	Give me that, I can do it self.
	You have to make it self, it's not hard to make.
Sample 12	He did it he-self.
Sample 20	He did he-self.
	They have to do it with their-selfs.
	The shoes is walking with their-selfs.
Sample 23	Make it with your-self over here.
	You can write it with your-self.
	You could drive with your-self.
Sample 25	You can drive with your-self, couldn't you?
Sample 27	I can make toast with my-self.
Sample 29	He's scared of self.
	His-self because he's scared of dog.

Note. From "A Case Study of a Japanese Child Learning English as a Second Language" by K. Hakuta, 1976, *Language Learning, 26*, p. 345. Reprinted with permission.

value of the simple and the complex reflexive forms is, in Uguisu's developing L2 grammar. However, the data do support our prediction that initially native speakers of Japanese may perceive and analyze the English reflexive as a simple rather than a complex form. More important, the data from Uguisu suggest that there is both a negative and a positive role for interlingual identification and that interlingual identification can overcome the effects of the Subset Principle.

As we noted earlier, the English reflexive is analyzed initially as a morphologically simple form. This results in an association between the English reflexive and the Japanese simple reflexive form *zibun*, which in turn leads to the transfer of the GCP value for *zibun* (i.e., the value consistent with the superset grammar) to the reflexive in the English interlanguage.[4] Later, when the L2 learners realize that words such as *himself/herself* are morphologically complex reflexives, there is an association between these complex forms in the interlanguage and the complex forms in the L1 like *kare-zisin* and *kanojo-zisin*. But as we saw earlier, these complex forms in the L1 are associated with the value of the GCP that is consistent with the most restrictive grammar. As a result of the identification, the subset value is transferred to the complex forms in the interlanguage and thus the effects of the Subset Principle are overcome. In other words, it appears that through a process of interlingual identification, L2 learners can successfully move from a superset grammar to a subset grammar.[5]

However, certain conditions will need to be met in order to make such movement possible. With respect to native speakers of Japanese acquiring English as the L2, the L1 (Japanese) has both types of reflexives, the morphologically complex and the simple forms, the former associated with the subset value of the GCP and the latter, with the superset value of the GCP. If, on the other hand, the L1 has simple forms but no complex forms, or if it has simple and complex forms that are both associated with the superset value of the GCP, perhaps the effects of the Subset Principle cannot be overcome on the basis of positive evidence alone. This is clearly a matter for further research.

---

[4]In Gass's (1988) terminology, this would be an example of "apperceived input."

[5]It may be that the GCP, in its current formulation, does not accurately capture the cross-linguistic properties of the reflexive. Katada (1991) proposed that the morphologically simple form *zibun* is a raising anaphor and that it raises at the level of Logical Form (LF). The morphologically complex forms in Japanese (and English), on the other hand, are, according to Katada, nonraising anaphors, which, unlike *zibun*, do not raise at LF. Assuming Katada's analysis, we may reinterpret the role of interlingual identification in the interpretation of the English reflexive by Japanese L2 learners in the following way. Initially, the morphologically complex reflexive form in English is perceived as a simple form and, as a result of the association with the simple form *zibun*, it is analyzed as a raising anaphor. Later, when it is perceived correctly as a complex reflexive form, it is associated with the complex forms in Japanese (i.e., *zibun-zisin*, *kare-zisin*, etc.), and this results in a reanalysis of the English reflexive as a nonraising anaphor.

ACKNOWLEDGMENTS

The research reported here is partly based on the second author's master's thesis, submitted to the Department of Linguistics at Southern Illinois University. An earlier version of the paper was presented by both authors at the Conference on Theory Construction and Methodology in SLA held at Michigan State University, East Lansing, in October 1991. We are grateful to the editors, Andrew Cohen, Susan Gass, and Elaine Tarone, for their comments.

APPENDIX A: SENTENCES IN THE ENGLISH L2 TEST

1. Jeff said that Tom found a picture of himself.
2. John said that Bill saw himself in the mirror.
3. Mary thinks that Ann is proud of herself.
4. David said that Bob introduced himself to Sally.
5. Barbara thinks that Lisa understands herself well.
6. Janet thinks that Patricia often talks about herself.
7. Greg knows that Steve blamed himself for the accident.
8. Jack said that Ron wrote about himself in the letter.
9. Diane knows that Shirley was thinking about herself during the party.
10. Mark thinks that Eric is ruining himself.

APPENDIX B: SENTENCES IN THE JAPANESE L1 TEST

1. Masao-wa Toshihiko-ga   zibun-no shashin-o   mitsuketa to   itta.
   Masao-Top Toshihiko-Nom self-Gen picture-Acc found   Comp said.
   'Masao said that Toshihiko found a picture of self.'
2. Hiroaki-wa Kazuyoshi-ga   jiko-no   ato   zibun-o
   Hiroaki-Top Kazuyoshi-Nom accident-Gen after self-Acc
       semeteita   no-o   shitteiru.
       was blaming Comp-Acc   know
   'Hiroaki knows that Kazuyoshi was blaming self after the accident.'
3. Hisashi-wa Saburoo-ga   zibun-no   koto-o   tegami-ni
   Hisashi-Top Saburoo-Nom self-Gen   matter-Acc letter-Loc
       kaiteita   to   itta.
       was writing Comp   said
   'Hisashi said that Saburoo was writing about self in the letter.'
4. Kenji-wa Ryoohei-ga   zibun-o Yoko-ni   shookaishita to   itta.
   Kenji-Top Ryoohei-Nom self-Acc Yoko-Dat introduced Comp   said
   'Kenji said that Ryoohei introduced self to Yoko.'

5. Hanako-wa Kyoko-ga zibun-o hokorashikuomotteiru to
   Hanako-Top Kyoko-Nom self-Acc be proud of Comp
   omotteiru.
   think
   'Hanako thinks that Kyoko is proud of self.'

6. Taroo-wa Jiroo-ga kagami-no naka-de zibun-o mita
   Taroo-Top Jiroo-Nom mirror-Gen inside-Loc self-Acc saw
   to itta.
   Comp said
   'Taroo said that Jiroo saw self in the mirror.'

7. Etsuko-wa Sachiko-ga zibun-no koto-o yoku wakatteiru
   Etsuko-Top Sachiko-Nom self-Gen matter-Acc well understand
   to omotteiru.
   Comp think
   'Etsuko thinks that Sachiko understands self well.'

8. Junko-wa Ritsuko-ga zibun-no koto-o yoku hanasu to
   Junko-Top Ritsuko-Nom self-Gen matter-Acc often talk Comp
   omotteiru.
   think
   'Junko thinks that Ritsuko talks a lot about self.'

9. Mariko-wa Yoshiko-ga paatii-de zibun-no koto-o
   Mariko-Top Yoshiko-Nom party-Loc self-Gen matter-Acc
   kangaeteita no-o shitteiru.
   was thinking Comp-Acc know
   'Mariko knows that Yoshiko was thinking about self during the party.'

10. Manabu-wa Kazuo-ga zibun-o damenishiteiru to
    Manabu-Top Kazuo-Nom self-Acc is ruining Comp
    omotteiru.
    think
    'Manabu thinks that Kazuo is ruining self.'

11. Hiroshi-ga jiko-no ato zibun-o semeteita
    Hiroshi-Nom accident-Gen after self-Acc was blaming
    no-o Junji-wa shitteiru.
    Comp-Acc Junji-Top know
    'Junji knows that Hiroshi was blaming self after the accident.'

12. Michiko-ga zibun-no koto-o tegami-ni kaiteita
    Michiko-Nom self-Gen matter-Acc letter-Loc was writing
    to Masako-wa itta.
    Comp Masako-Top said
    'Masako said that Michiko was writing about self in the letter.'

Note. Sentences 1–10 are in the basic word order; sentences 11 and 12 represent the altered word order with the embedded clause fronted. The order in which the sentences appear is not the order in which the sentences were presented to the subjects. That is, the sentences in 11 and 12 (where the embedded clause is fronted) were not presented consecutively, as shown here.

REFERENCES

Chien, Y., & Wexler, K. (1987). Children's acquisition of the locality condition for reflexives and pronouns. *Papers and Reports on Child Language Development, 26*, 30–39.

Chomsky, N. (1981). *Lectures on government and binding.* Dordrecht: Foris.

Cole, P., Hermon, G., & Sung, L. (1990). Principles and parameters of long-distance reflexives. *Linguistic Inquiry, 21*, 1–22.

Finer, D. (1991). Binding parameters in second language acquisition. In L. Eubank (Ed.), *Point/counterpoint: Universal Grammar in the second language.* Amsterdam: John Benjamins.

Finer, D., & Broselow, E. (1986). Second language acquisition of reflexive binding. *Proceedings of the North Eastern Linguistic Society, 16*, 154–168.

Gass, S. (1988). Integrating research areas: A framework for second language studies. *Applied Linguistics, 9*, 198–217.

Grimshaw, J., & Rosen, S. (1990). Knowledge and obedience: The developmental status of the binding theory. *Linguistic Inquiry, 21*, 187–222.

Hakuta, K. (1976). A case study of a Japanese child learning English as a second language. *Language Learning, 26*, 321–351.

Hirakawa, M. (1990). A study of the L2 acquisition of English reflexives. *Second Language Research, 6*, 60–85.

Katada, F. (1991). The LF representation of anaphors. *Linguistic Inquiry, 22*, 287–313.

Lee, H. S., & Wexler, K. (1987, October). *The acquisition of reflexives and pronouns in Korean from a crosslinguistic perspective.* Paper presented at the 12th Annual Boston University Conference on Language Development, Boston, MA.

Selinker, L. (1991). *Rediscovering interlanguage.* London: Longman.

Teranishi, K. (1991). The acquisition of reflexive pronouns by L2 learners. Unpublished master's thesis, Southern Illinois University, Carbondale, IL.

Thomas, M. (1989). The interpretation of English reflexive pronouns by non-native speakers. *Studies in Second Language Acquisition, 11*, 281–303.

Thomas, M. (1990). Acquisition of the Japanese reflexive *zibun* by unilingual and multilingual learners. In H. Burmeister & P. Rounds (Eds.), *Variability in second language acquisition: Proceedings of the 10th meeting of the Second Language Research Forum* (pp. 701–718). Eugene: University of Oregon, Department of Linguistics.

Weinreich, U. (1953). *Languages in contact.* The Hague: Mouton.

Wexler, K., & Manzini, R. (1987). Parameters and learnability in binding theory. In T. Roeper & E. Williams (Eds.), *Parameter setting* (pp. 41–76). Dordrecht: Reidel.

CHAPTER

11

LOCAL AND LONG-DISTANCE ANAPHORA IN SECOND-LANGUAGE ACQUISITION

Fred R. Eckman
University of Wisconsin—Milwaukee

This chapter reports the analysis of some second-language acquisition (SLA) data on the binding of reflexives (anaphors) in interlanguages. This study builds in two ways on a growing body of literature in this area (e.g., Broselow & Finer, 1991; Cook, 1990; Finer, 1991; Finer & Broselow, 1986; Hirakawa, 1990; Thomas, 1989, 1991). First, the present study considers the question of the binding of reflexives with respect to two parameters of Universal Grammar (UG): the Governing Category Parameter (GCP) and the Proper Antecedent Parameter (PAP); and second, it considers this question from the viewpoint of two target languages: English and Japanese.

The central problem to be addressed in this chapter is whether the grammars of interlanguages (IL) adhere to the constraints of UG, or whether in some cases they fall outside of these constraints. A related problem to be addressed involves the type of data and argumentation that bear on this problem. Much of the literature on the central problem, whether ILs obey UG, claims that L2 grammars do conform to the principles of UG, though there has been room for disagreement (e.g., Schachter, 1988; Hagen, this volume, chapter 4). The vast majority of studies addressing the related question, that of the type of data needed to support the claim, have reported aggregate data rather than data from individuals. In this chapter, it is argued that data from individuals, rather than group data, are necessary to test whether IL grammars adhere to the principles of UG.

The results of the present study suggest that, other research notwithstanding, some IL grammars apparently do fall outside the boundaries of UG.

However, the existence of such violations is not, in itself, a threat to the position that ILs are governed by UG, because it may in fact be possible to predict these violations. Thus, if it is shown that some IL grammars violate principles of UG, the task is to explain why the particular ILs in question violate UG principles, and why the violations happen in just the way that they do.

The organization of this chapter is as follows. First, I briefly describe the Binding Principles, the associated parameters, and their relationship to some previous work in SLA. I then lay out the rationale and methodology for the present study and report the results. Finally, I discuss these results and their implications for SLA theory.

BACKGROUND: UG, BINDING, AND SLA

UG, as put forth in Chomsky (1981) and elsewhere, is a set of abstract and general principles assumed to be adequate for characterizing the core grammars of all natural languages. The central goal, under Chomsky's approach, is to account for the systematic variation found among the world's languages, and the relative speed and uniformity with which children acquire their native language. To this end, UG is postulated as basic to the innate human language faculty. UG consists of principles that form the basis for all languages. The observed systematic variability found among languages is accounted for by hypothesizing that some principles of UG permit variation along certain well-defined parameters. These parameters can be viewed as principles containing variables whose values must be filled in. Primary language acquisition takes place, according to this view, as the child-learner molds these principles of UG into the native-language grammar by determining the values of the various parameters.

Two such parameters are the Governing Category Parameter and the Proper Antecedent Parameter, both of which are associated with the Binding Conditions, shown in (1):

(1) *Binding Conditions:*
    a. An anaphor is bound in its governing category.
    b. A pronominal is free in its governing category.
    c. R(eferring) expressions are free.

These principles determine when expressions in a sentence are properly bound (i.e., coreferential). For the purposes of this chapter, we will concern ourselves only with Principle A, involving the binding of reflexives, also known as anaphors. The Binding Conditions specify the structural configurations for coreference in terms of the notion *governing category*, which for English is, roughly speaking, a minimal category containing a subject.

Thus, for example, *himself* in (2a) must be bound by *John* because both of these expressions are contained in the same minimal category containing a subject, namely, the subordinate clause. On the other hand, *herself* in (2b) cannot be bound by *Mary* because these two expressions are not contained in the same minimal category containing a subject, namely, the subordinate clause.

(2) a. Bill knew that John$_i$ hit himself$_i$.
    b. *Mary$_i$ knew that John hit herself$_i$.

Although sentence (2b) is not grammatical in English, this sentence type is grammatical in some languages. The Binding Conditions allow for this possibility through parametric variation. The relevant parameter, stated in (3), specifies the various domains in which binding can take place in any given language by specifying the structure that defines a governing category for that language.

(3) *Governing Category Parameter (GCP):* gamma is a governing category for alpha iff gamma is the minimal category that contains alpha, a governor for alpha, and has

    a. a subject; or   English
    b. an INFL; or   Italian
    c. a TNS; or   Russian
    d. an indicative TNS; or   Icelandic
    e. a root TNS   Korean/Japanese

The GCP is essentially a hierarchy that divides languages into types according to how close two expressions in a sentence can or must be in order to be properly bound. English-type languages are the strictest in that they require local binding in which the reflexive and its antecedent must be in the same simple clause. Korean and Japanese, on the other hand, are less strict and allow nonlocal binding in which antecedents of reflexives can be indefinitely far away in the sentence; other languages fall between these extremes. The difference between languages of type (3a) and those of type (3e) with respect to the GCP can be illustrated using the sentence in (4), whose clausal structure is roughly that in (5a).

(4) Bill persuaded Charlie to consider Mick fond of himself.

(5) Binding possibilities in Japanese and English
   a. $_{S1}$ [NP$_i$ V $_{S2}$[NP$_j$ V $_{S3}$[NP$_k$ V refl]$_{S3}$]$_{S2}$]$_{S1}$
   b.   i   j   k   i/j/k/   (Japanese)
   c.   i   j   k   *i/*j/k   (English)

In an English sentence like (4), *himself* can refer only to *Mick*, the NP that is a clausemate of the reflexive, and not to *Charlie* or *Bill*. However, in the Japanese equivalent of a sentence like (4), the reflexive can refer to *Mick*, *Charlie*, or *Bill*. Thus, the governing category in a Japanese-type language is much wider than that in English.

The other parameter in question, the Proper Antecedent Parameter, shown in (6), has two values that specify whether the reflexive must be bound by a subject NP or can be bound by any NP within the governing category.

(6) *Proper Antecedent Parameter (PAP):*
   A proper antecedent for A is
   a. a subject NP
   b. any NP whatever

The English setting for this parameter is (6b), as is shown by sentence (7), in which either the subject or the indirect object NP may bind the reflexive, yielding two possible interpretations.

(7) John showed Bill a picture of himself.

In Japanese, which is set for value (6a) on the PAP, the counterpart of this sentence has only one interpretation, namely, the one in which the reflexive is bound by the subject NP.

Manzini and Wexler (1987) pointed out that there appears to be a correlation between the GCP and the PAP, such that languages that have the unmarked setting (3a) on the GCP have the marked setting (6b) on the PAP, and conversely, that languages that set the GCP for the marked value (3e) have the unmarked setting (6a) on the PAP. In other words, languages that allow nonlocal binding require the antecedent to be a subject NP, whereas languages that restrict binding to a local domain allow the antecedent to be any NP. What is apparently excluded by the two parameters are languages that are too liberal in that they permit binding to be both long-distance and local while allowing both subject and nonsubject orientation, and languages that are too restrictive in that they allow only local binding and only subject orientation. The allowed and disallowed possibilities are summarized in (8).

(8) Logically possible combinations of binding domains and antecedents:

	Local	*Local & Nonlocal*
Subject only	Type A (unattested)	Type B
		(Japanese, Korean)
Subjects &	Type C	Type D
nonsubjects	(English)	(unattested)

As mentioned earlier, a number of recent articles have studied the role of these two parameters in the grammars of interlanguages. Because space does not permit an extensive review of this literature, I recapitulate some of the salient points of this body of work.

The first SLA study in this area was a pilot by Finer and Broselow (1986), which used a picture identification task to elicit interpretations of coreference from six Korean subjects on English sentences containing the two types of complement clauses exemplified in (9).

(9) a. Mr. Fat believes that Mr. Thin will paint himself.
      b. Mr. Fat asked Mr. Thin to paint himself.

The subjects had to determine which of two pictures corresponded to the sentence in question. Given a sentence such as (9a), for example, subjects had to choose between two pictures, one in which Mr. Thin was painting himself and one in which Mr. Thin was painting Mr. Fat.

Finer and Broselow reported that the subjects, as a group, assigned local coreference in sentences like (9a) and nonlocal coreference in sentences like (9b). They drew the following conclusions: (a) the subjects had not yet learned the more restrictive English setting for the GCP, (b) their subjects did not simply transfer the Korean setting of the GCP, and (c) the Korean subjects, as a group, used a setting of the GCP in between that of English and Korean, somewhere around the (3c) or (3d) value.

This pilot study by Finer and Broselow was followed up by a number of studies that expanded on it (Broselow & Finer, 1991; Finer, 1991; Hirakawa, 1990; Thomas, 1989). These later studies, with the exception of Hirakawa (1990), supported the finding of the Finer and Broselow pilot that L2 subjects tended to bind reflexives locally in tensed embedded clauses, and nonlocally in infinitival clauses. Hirakawa (1990), in contrast, reported that her subjects made many more errors on sentences containing tensed complement clauses than did Finer and Broselow's subjects. Thus, Hirakawa argued that her subjects did not adopt an intermediate value for the GCP but instead set the GCP for their ILs at the widest possible value (that is, (3e)).

Studies that have considered the Proper Antecedent Parameter have shown consistently that L2 subjects generally bind the reflexive to a subject NP more often than to a nonsubject.

Thomas (1991) looked at nonnative binding with respect to two target languages. She considered Japanese and Spanish ESL learners, on the one hand, and English and Chinese L2 learners of Japanese on the other. She found that most English subjects bound the Japanese reflexive locally, although some nonlocal binding was allowed by subjects with higher proficiency. Interestingly, about half of the Chinese subjects bound the Japanese reflexive only nonlocally.

One of the goals of this research on binding in SLA has been to determine whether the IL grammars involved adhere to the principles of UG. In general, the findings of these studies have been the following: (a) the IL settings for each parameter are not merely transferred from the native language (NL) but are set at a value somewhere between that of the NL and the target language (TL) (though see Hirakawa, 1990 for a different result), and (b) the IL settings for each parameter are squarely within the limits prescribed by UG.

Some dissension on this second point has come from Thomas (1991), who argued that the findings of Finer (1991) and Hirakawa (1990) run contrary to UG on two counts. First, both Finer and Hirakawa reported that in 20% of the L2 responses, a reflexive was bound by the object in a sentence such as (10).

(10) Mr. Fat gives Mr. Thin a picture of himself.

And second, both studies reported that English reflexives in complement clauses were bound only by the subject of the matrix clause in 2% to 38% of L2 responses. Thomas cited this as a problem, claiming that UG principles do not sanction either of these response types.

The problem I adduce here is not limited to the findings reported in the Finer and Hirakawa studies but is endemic in all of the research reported thus far on L2 binding and much of the research attempting to test UG principles in SLA. The problem is twofold: First, previous research in this area has reported aggregate results rather than results for individuals, and second, principles of UG have been interpreted directly with respect to data instead of with respect to IL grammars. I will take up each of these points in turn.

Consider first the question of group results. It has never been shown, or even argued, that IL grammars reflect the linguistic knowledge of groups of learners; rather, it has been assumed, perhaps tacitly, that IL grammars pertain to individual learners. Thus, in testing whether principles of UG hold for IL grammars, there is a problem with reporting results for groups rather than individuals, namely, that it thereby becomes impossible to determine whether the UG principles in question are being adhered to. What has to be determined from the reported data is whether the individual IL grammar of each of the subjects adheres to the constraints imposed by UG. To the extent that this is true, it can be successfully argued that UG governs ILs.

However, if a study reports that one of the L2 groups gave local responses on English reflexives in 80% of the cases, as does Thomas (1991), this result does not tell us whether the principles of UG are being obeyed unless we know how those responses are distributed across the subjects. Clearly, the case for UG can be made if all of the subjects scored 80%. If, on the other hand, the 80% group result is a consequence of subjects' compiling many different scores, some of which indicate systematic adherence to UG principles and others that either are unsystematic or indicate nonadherence to UG, then the case for UG governing SLA is not at all clear.

This brings us to the second point. One cannot determine whether UG constraints have been violated simply by examining the errors. This is because the principles and parameters of UG do not directly constrain utterances but instead constrain grammars, in this case, IL grammars. What is crucial, therefore, is not the errors themselves but the analysis of those errors. Thus, Thomas' (1991) claim that the responses of Finer's and Hirakawa's subjects for sentences such as (10) are problematic for UG cannot be upheld unless it can be shown that the IL grammars that produced these responses are not in conformity with UG. And this, in turn, cannot be determined unless we know how the deviant responses were distributed across the subjects.

To sum up this section, previous research on binding has reported group rather than individual results, making it impossible to determine the extent to which UG constraints have been followed or violated. In the present study, therefore, the results will be presented for individuals.

METHODOLOGY

The present study builds in part on the methodology of two previous studies: that of Finer & Broselow (1986), who used a picture identification task, and that of Thomas (1991), who gathered data from two target languages, English and Japanese.

The subjects for this study were drawn from four groups. The L2 groups included 24 university-age native speakers of English learning Japanese as a foreign language and 25 ESL learners from four native-language backgrounds: Arabic, Japanese, Mandarin, and Spanish. The L2 Japanese group was drawn from students who were in their third and fourth year of studying Japanese. The L2 English group was drawn from students in the ESL Intensive Program at the University of Wisconsin at Milwaukee. The two L1 control groups consisted of 25 native speakers of English and 24 native speakers of Japanese.

Following Finer and Broselow (1986), a picture identification task was used in which the subjects had to match a picture with a sentence containing a reflexive. The subjects worked their way through a booklet, each page of which contained a pair of drawings with the target sentence typed across the top of the page. The directions told the subjects that they were to choose the picture that the sentence best described, and that it was possible for the sentence to describe only one of the pictures, neither of the pictures, or both of the pictures. To avoid certain methodological problems that have been ascribed to Finer and Broselow's picture identification task (see Lakshmanan & Teranishi, this volume, chapter 10), the instructions also reminded the subjects that, before choosing just one of the pictures as the answer, they should always check to see if both pictures corresponded to the sentence. To see whether the subjects understood the directions, they were given a short practice exercise. The test itself was not timed; the subjects were allowed to work at their own pace.

The sentence types used in this study are displayed in (11) and (12) and fall into four different categories.

(11) Type   Example
     a.   Mr. Small hit himself.
     b.   Mr. Small said that Mr. Big looked at himself.
     c.   Mr. Big asked Mr. Small to hit himself.
     d.   Mr. Big gave Mr. Small a portrait of himself.

(12) Type   Example
     a.   Big-san wa jibun wo mimashita.
     b.   Small-san wa Big-san ga jibun wo mita to iimashita.
     c.   Big-san wa Small-san ni jibun wo miruyo tanomimashita.
     d.   Big-san wa Small-san ni jubun no shozoga wo agemashita.

Type (a) includes simple sentences containing reflexives and object pronouns in which the reflexive must refer to the subject of the sentence. Type (b) includes sentences containing a complement clause where the clause boundary is clearly marked by the complementizer *that*. In sentences of type (b), the reflexive can refer only to the subordinate subject, and not to the superordinate subject or some entity outside the sentence. This is also true for type (c), except that in this case, the lower clause contains an infinitive instead of a tensed verb. Sentences of type (d) contain an object NP followed by a "picture" noun phrase containing a reflexive. (See Appendix for samples of the materials used.)

RESULTS

As discussed in the previous section, the objective of the study was to determine whether an individual's IL grammar adheres to the constraints of UG. Thus, the performance of each subject on a given sentence type was assessed as to whether or not the performance was systematic. Because there were four tokens of each sentence type (with the exception of Japanese type (d), which had only three tokens) it was decided that the threshold for systematicity was three out of four (two out of three for Japanese type (d)). Thus, for example, a subject's IL was deemed to have local binding in tensed clauses if that subject chose the pictures that represented local binding in three out of the four cases involving a sentence like (11b). Conversely, the subject's IL was deemed to have nonlocal binding if the subject chose the nonlocal picture in three out of four cases. The same criterion was applied to sentences like (11a) and (11c) for the determination of the binding domain and to sentence (11d) to determine whether the subject bound the reflexive only to subject NPs or to nonsubjects as well. If a subject did not reach the criterial threshold of three, the IL was deemed to be unsystematic with respect to that aspect of coreference assignment.

The results for all of the subjects are summarized in Table 11.1. The data for each group are reported in Table 11.2 for comparison with other studies; although there is some variation, the percentage of judgments for local binding and for subject orientation compare favorably with those in other studies.

Across the top of Table 11.1 are listed the possible binding domains: local only, nonlocal only, both local and nonlocal, and unsystematic. Within each domain, the orientation of the reflexive is listed, that is, whether the reflexive was bound only to a subject, whether it was bound to a subject or object, or whether the orientation was unsystematic. The first group listed is the native English control group, which uniformly bound the reflexive in a local domain. However, 15 of the 25 subjects bound this reflexive only to a subject NP, which accords with the findings of previous work (see Table 11.3).

TABLE 11.1
Number of Subjects in Each Combination of Binding Domain and Orientation

	Local Only			Nonlocal Only			Both Loc + Nonloc			Unsys
	S	S+O	Unsys	S	S+O	Unsys	S	S+O	Unsys	Unsys
L1E	15	6	4							
L2E										
Ar	6	3	2					1	1	
Mn	2		3							
J	4									
Sp	1		1							1
L2J	6		1	2		2	5	5	4	1
L1J	2			13		1	4	1	1	2

Note. Loc. = Local, Nonloc = Nonlocal, Unsys = Unsystematic, S = Subject, O = Object, E = English, Ar = Arabic, Mn = Mandarin, J = Japanese, Sp = Spanish.

TABLE 11.2
Group Results for Comparison with Previous Studies

	TL = English			
	Local Binding		*Orientation*	
Group	*Tensed Clause*	*Infinitive Clause*	*Subj Only*	*Subj & Object*
L1E	99%	98%	65%	35%
L2E	91%	82%	64%	34%
	TL = Japanese			
Group	*Nonlocal Binding*			*Subj Orientation*
L1J	88%			70%
L2J	65%			44%

Note. E = English, J = Japanese.

Six subjects allowed the reflexive to be bound by a subject or object, and 4 subjects were not systematic in their orientation.

The English L2 group was broken down according to NL background: There were 13 Arabic subjects, 5 Mandarin speakers, 4 Japanese speakers, and 3 native speakers of Spanish. The vast majority of these subjects bound the reflexive locally; one Arabic subject allowed both local and nonlocal binding and one Spanish subject performed unsystematically (see Table 11.4). It is interesting to note that the vast majority of L2 speakers whose performance was systematic permitted the reflexive to be bound only by a subject NP. Only four Arabic speakers allowed binding by either a subject or an object.

The native Japanese speakers also evinced some interesting patterns (see Table 11.5). Fourteen of the subjects bound the reflexive only to a nonlocal antecedent, 13 of these bound the reflexive to a subject, and one behaved unsystematically. Six subjects allowed both local and nonlocal binding and 2 allowed only local binding. The vast majority of the subjects whose IL showed systematicity bound the reflexive to a subject NP; only one allowed binding to a nonsubject also.

The group showing the most variability was that of English speakers learning Japanese (see Table 11.6). Seven speakers allowed only local binding and 2 evinced only nonlocal binding; 14 subjects bound the reflexive both locally and nonlocally. In the groups that bound the reflexive only locally or only nonlocally, the orientation, where systematic, was exclusively toward a subject antecedent. Where the binding was both local and nonlocal, the orientation was generally subject-only.

TABLE 11.3
Individual Results for Native English Speaker Control Group

		Locality			Orientation		
Speaker	Unsys	Loc Only	Nonloc	Both	Subj Only	Subj & Obj	Unsys
1		+			+		
8		+			+		
10		+			+		
11		+			+		
13		+			+		
15		+			+		
16		+			+		
17		+			+		
18		+			+		
19		+			+		
20		+			+		
21		+			+		
23		+			+		
24		+			+		
25		+			+		
5		+				+	
6		+				+	
7		+				+	
9		+				+	
12		+				+	
22		+				+	
2		+					+
3		+					+
4		+					+
14		+					+

Note. Unsys = Unsystematic, Loc = Local, Nonloc = Nonlocal.

In the next section I discuss the implications of these results.

DISCUSSION

In this section I consider whether the subjects' IL grammars are in conformity with the settings of the GCP and the PAP that are allowed by UG. In other words, we will be interested in how the ILs in question are distributed with respect to the typology of binding domains and reflexive orientation shown

TABLE 11.4
Individual Results for ESL Subjects

NL Speaker		Locality				Orientation		
		Unsys	Loc Only	Nonloc	Both	Subj Only	Subj & Obj	Unsys
Ar	1		tns	inf			+	
Ar	15		tns/inf				+	
Ar	17		tns/inf				+	
Ar	18		tns/inf			+		
Ar	19		tns/inf			+		
Ar	23		tns/inf				+	
Ar	24		tns/inf			+		
Ar	25		tns/inf			+		
Ar	26		tns/inf					+
Ar	27		tns/inf					+
Ar	28		tns/inf			+		
Ar	29		tns/inf				+	
Ar	30		tns/inf					+
Mn	3		tns/inf					+
Mn	7		tns/inf					+
Mn	8		tns/inf					+
Mn	9		tns/inf			+		
Mn	21		tns/inf			+		
Sp	10	tns	inf					+
Sp	12		tns/inf					+
Sp	14		tns/inf			+		
J	16		tns/inf			+		
J	20		tns/inf			+		
J	31		tns/inf			+		
J	32		tns/inf			+		

Note. tns = tensed clauses, inf = infinitival clauses, Ar = Arabic, Mn = Mandarin, Sp = Spanish, J = Japanese.

in (8). Our concern, therefore, will be only with those IL grammars that are systematic and not with those categorized as unsystematic.

The particular focus of this section is those ILs that appear not to adhere to the constraints of UG. The discussion of these grammars will approach this problem from two different points of view. When faced with ILs that appear not to conform to UG, we consider the implications for SLA theory, on the one hand, and for linguistic theory, on the other hand.

We first interpret the data from the SLA theory standpoint and consider the ESL group. Of the 25 subjects in this group, 17 performed systematically with respect to both binding domain and orientation of the reflexive. Of these,

TABLE 11.5
Individual Results for Native Japanese Speaker Control Group

	Locality				Orientation		
Speaker	Unsys	Loc Only	Nonloc	Both	Subj Only	Subj & Obj	Unsys
8		+			+		
10		+			+		
1			+		+		
5			+		+		
6			+		+		
7			+		+		
14			+		+		
15			+		+		
16			+		+		
17			+		+		
18			+		+		
20			+		+		
21			+		+		
23			+		+		
24			+		+		
13			+				+
4				+	+		
11				+	+		
12				+	+		
22				+	+		
3				+		+	
2				+			+
9	+				+		
19	+				+		

Note. Unsys = Unsystematic, Loc = Local, Nonloc = Nonlocal.

16 subjects bound the reflexive only locally, and one allowed both local and nonlocal binding. Now, of these 17 cases, only 3 fall into an attested category in (8), namely A, whereas 13 fall into type A and one falls into type D. Thus, only 3 of the 17 cases are Englishlike, whereas 13 would be classified as too restrictive and one would be considered too liberal. What is more interesting is that these cases cannot be explained as a consequence of NL interference, because both Japanese and Mandarin have nonlocal binding, and because both Arabic and Spanish allow subject and nonsubject antecedents for reflexives.

If we look at the native speaker controls, we see that similar orientation was also exhibited by the majority of speakers in this group. The native speakers were completely robust with respect to binding being only local; however, of the 21 subjects showing systematic performance regarding orientation, 15

TABLE 11.6
Individual Results for Native English Speakers Learning Japanese

Speaker	Locality				Orientation		
	Unsys	Loc Only	Nonloc	Both	Subj Only	Subj & Obj	Unsys
7		+			+		
15		+			+		
19		+			+		
20		+			+		
22		+			+		
24		+			+		
21		+					+
4			+		+		
10			+		+		
9				+	+		
5				+	+		
13				+	+		
14				+	+		
17				+	+		
2				+		+	
3				+		+	
8				+		+	
12				+		+	
23				+		+	
11				+			+
6				+			+
16				+			+
1				+			+
18	+					+	

Note. Unsys = Unsystematic, Loc = Local, Nonloc = Nonlocal.

(71%) bound the reflexive only by subject NPs. These results are in accord with those reported for the native control groups in Hirakawa (1990) and Thomas (1989, 1991), and for children learning English as their L1 in Read and Chou Hare (1979).

One possible explanation for this preference is the fact that the combination of local binding and subject-only antecedent is the least marked configuration: All languages apparently allow a reflexive to be locally bound, and all languages allow subjects to bind reflexives. The apparent problem arises in that this constellation of binding and orientation is not allowed by UG and is presumably not attested. One way around this quandary is to claim that the grammar of the English controls does in fact evince local binding with both subject and nonsubject orientation, but that speakers may employ a strategy that uses an unmarked configuration of these principles.

This same explanation could then be extended to the IL grammars of L2 learners. The claim would be that these IL grammars are unmarked variants of the target grammars, and that the IL grammars arise from the same strategy, perhaps a learning strategy, that we saw represented in the data from the native speakers. Under this scenario, the L2 learners construct an IL that makes use of the unmarked configuration of principles, even though the grammars of both the NL and the TL contain the more marked instantiations of these same principles. In sum, the explanation for why these IL grammars are of the unattested type A is that the learners construct a less marked version of the TL. A similar explanation was proposed for both negation and relative clause formation by Hyltenstam (1984).

We turn now to the L2 interpretations of Japanese reflexives by native speakers of English. Of the 24 subjects tested, 6 performed unsystematically: one with respect to the domain of binding and 5 with respect to orientation. Of the remaining 18, 6 interpreted coreference exclusively within a local domain and only with subject antecedents. This response pattern is the same as the one exhibited by many of the native speaker controls and has already been discussed. It is, grammatically speaking, similar to neither English nor Japanese.

There are two other Japanese L2 groups to be considered. In the first, two subjects bound the reflexive exclusively within a nonlocal domain, and only with subject antecedents. In the other, 10 subjects allowed both local and nonlocal binding; of these 10, 5 had subject orientation and 5 had both subject and object orientation. Only one of these configurations is allowed by UG, namely, type B in (8), which combines both local and nonlocal binding with subject orientation. The other two are apparently not allowed by UG and need to be explained.

The group that is easier to explain is the one allowing both types of binding and both subject and object orientation. This configuration characterizes the disallowed and apparently unattested type D language in (8). One plausible explanation for its occurrence is NL interference. The subjects have apparently learned that Japanese allows both local and nonlocal binding but have not yet learned that the antecedent in Japanese must be a subject. They consequently transfer the English principle, which allows binding by both a subject and an object. This hypothesis is supported by the findings in Thomas (1991), who reports that Chinese L2 learners of Japanese bind the reflexive extensively to a long-distance antecedent that is exclusively a subject. Because Chinese has setting (6a) on the PAP and English has setting (6b), transfer would seem to explain the differences between these two groups with respect to Japanese binding.

The responses of the other L2 Japanese group, the one containing the two subjects who preferred only long-distance binding, are not as easy to explain. Notice, in particular, that this type of binding was actually preferred by a majority of the native speaker controls for Japanese and is also reported as a preference for the controls in Hirakawa (1990) and Thomas (1991). It is, however, not allowed by the GCP, which claims that any language that allows reflexives to be bound over more than one clause, should also allow them to be bound within a single clause. Thomas proposes to explain these facts by showing that subjects underreport their intuitions. This is ultimately not an explanation because it begs the question why the subjects underreport in the way that they do and not in some other way.

One way to account for this behavior and still maintain the assumption that the Japanese subjects are employing an unmarked configuration of principles would be to speculate that the inclination to bind the reflexive only by a matrix antecedent in fact reflects a preference for the matrix subject as a binder over an embedded subject. Assuming that binding by only a subject NP is the unmarked case, then, in a language such as Japanese, which allows nonlocal antecedents, binding by the matrix subject, rather than one of the embedded subjects, could turn out to be the unmarked case. Under this view, which is admittedly speculation at this point, the anomaly of the exclusive nonlocal binding would reflect a preference for binding by the matrix subject.

Although this position is speculative at this point, it is nevertheless a testable position. If we hypothesize that the preference shown by some learners for binding by a nonlocal NP is in fact a preference for binding by a matrix subject, then we would predict that, in a three-clause sentence such as (4) (repeated for convenience as (13)), the NP *Bill* would be the preferred binder of the reflexive. Under the alternative hypothesis that only a nonlocal NP can be the binder, either *Bill* or *Charlie* should be a potential binder, but not *Mick*. Unfortunately, the evidence we have so far suggests that our hypothesis cannot be maintained. Hirakawa (1990) tested three-clause sentences and did not find a preference for binding by the matrix NP.

(13) Bill persuaded Charlie to consider Mick fond of himself.

Perhaps a better explanation is the one outlined by Lakshmanan and Teranishi (this volume, chapter 10), namely, that the verbs used in the test sentences introduce a semantic bias toward binding by the matrix NP. If this position can be maintained—Lakshmanan and Teranishi do give evidence in its support—then the results in question do not have to be explained on acquisition grounds, because the findings are apparently the consequence of a flaw in the test instrument.

Having discussed how the L2 binding patterns that do not conform to the configurations allowed by UG impinge on SLA theory, we turn our attention to the implications of these patterns for linguistic theory. The point to be made is the following. If interlanguages are in fact natural languages, as has been argued (Adjemian, 1976), then they should fall under the purview of linguistic theory. This being the case, the fact that our data reflect binding patterns not yet attested in L1s could indicate that such primary language types do in fact exist but have not yet been discovered or documented by linguists. In other words, under this view, interlanguages would serve as an indicator of the types of primary languages that one should expect to find. Along these lines, U. Lakshmanan (personal communication, May 1993) reports that Tamil has a reflexive that requires nonlocal binding, which is theoretically disallowed by the current formulation of the GCP.

The position that ILs may reflect the types of primary languages that linguists should expect to find is not unreasonable when one considers that only a handful of languages have been tested against the parameters in question, and only a few languages have been found for some values of the GCP. For example, Manzini and Wexler (1987) cite only Italian for value (3b), and only Icelandic *sig* and *hann* for values (3c) and (3d), respectively. To be sure, other languages have been adduced elsewhere; however, the point remains that, to date, there has been no published attempt that systematically characterizes a sizable number of languages with respect to the typology in (8). Thus, the fact that there exist some ILs that fall into unattested categories in (8) can be argued to be at least as much a problem for linguistic theory as it is for SLA theory.

CONCLUSION

In conclusion, we have presented data on L2 binding of reflexives with a view toward testing the hypothesis that UG principles hold for IL grammars. With respect to this position, we have argued that (a) this hypothesis can be tested most clearly by reporting data for individuals rather than for groups, and (b) at least two cases where the IL grammars conflicted with UG could be explained on other grounds, namely, in terms of markedness or in terms of the language-contact situation and NL transfer. We have considered some of the implications of these findings for both SLA theory and linguistic theory.

ACKNOWLEDGMENTS

This work was supported in part by a grant from the National Science Foundation (BNS 8213384), whose contribution is gratefully acknowledged. An earlier version of this paper was presented at the annual meeting of the American Association for Applied Linguistics, April 18, 1993, in Atlanta, Georgia. I would like to express my appreciation to the members of the audience for helpful feedback, and to Greg Iverson and Edith Moravcsik for comments and suggestions on earlier drafts of this paper. A special thanks to Jun Amano for assisting with the Japanese data and to Professors A. Miura and Natsuko Tsujimura for allowing me to use their third- and fourth-year Japanese classes to collect data.

APPENDIX: TASK INSTRUCTIONS

Directions

In this exercise you will be asked to look at a set of pictures about two main characters, Mr. Small and Mr. Big, and one minor character, some other man whose name we don't know.

On each page you will see two pictures. Across the top of each picture is a sentence. Read the sentence to yourself and then decide which picture the sentence can describe. There are three possibilities that you are to choose from: It may be that the sentence describes only one of the pictures, or that the sentence describes both of the pictures, or that it describes neither of the pictures.

If the sentence describes only one of the pictures, you are to say which picture the sentence describes by circling the correct choice, either "picture a" or "picture b" on the answer sheet. If the sentence describes neither of the pictures, you are to indicate this on the answer sheet by circling the words "neither picture." If the sentence can describe both of the pictures, please indicate this on the answer sheet by circling the words "both pictures." It is important that you pay attention to this last possibility; before choosing "picture a" or "picture b" as your answer, please check to see whether the sentence can describe both pictures.

Please mark all your answers on the answer sheet; do not write on the pictures in the test booklet.

Before you begin, be sure that you know each of the characters, and that you know the meanings of the following words:

hit   picture

tickle   portrait

look at

If there are other words that you do not know, please ask the test monitor.

We will begin with the set of practice sentences.

REFERENCES

Adjemian, C. (1976). On the nature of interlanguage systems. *Language Learning, 26*, 297–320.
Broselow, E., & Finer, D. (1991). Parameter setting in second language phonology and syntax. *Second Language Research, 7*, 35–59.
Chomsky, N. (1981). *Lectures on government and binding*. Dordrecht: Foris Publications.
Cook, V. (1990). Timed comprehension of binding in advanced L2 learners of English. *Language Learning, 40*, 557–599.
Finer, D. (1991). Binding parameters in second language acquisition. In L. Eubank (Ed.), *Point counterpoint: Universal grammar in the second language* (pp. 351–371). Amsterdam: John Benjamins.
Finer, D., & Broselow, E. (1986). Second language acquisition of reflexive binding. *NELS, 16*, 154–168.
Hirakawa, M. (1990). A study of the L2 acquisition of English reflexives. *Second Language Research, 6*, 60–85.
Hyltenstam, K. (1984). The use of typological markedness conditions as predictors in second language acquisition: The case of pronominal copies in relative clauses. In R. Andersen (Ed.), *Second Languages* (pp. 39–58). Rowley, MA: Newbury House.
Manzini, R., & Wexler, K. (1987). Parameters, binding theory and learnability. *Linguistic Inquiry, 18*, 413–444.
Read, C., & Chou Hare, V. (1979). Children's interpretation of reflexive pronouns in English. In F. Eckman & A. Hastings (Eds.), *Studies in first and second language acquisition* (pp. 98–116). Rowley, MA: Newbury House.
Schachter, J. (1988). Second language acquisition and its relationship to universal grammar. *Applied Linguistics, 9*, 219–235.
Thomas, M. (1989). The interpretation of English reflexive pronouns by nonnative speakers. *Studies in Second Language Acquisition, 11*, 281–303.
Thomas, M. (1991). Universal grammar and the interpretation of reflexives in a second language. *Language, 67*, 211–239.

12

ELICITED IMITATION AND GRAMMATICALITY JUDGMENT TASKS: WHAT THEY MEASURE AND HOW THEY RELATE TO EACH OTHER

Edward Munnich
Suzanne Flynn
Gita Martohardjono
Massachusetts Institute of Technology

The goal of psycholinguistic research is the empirical assessment of language abilities. Second-language (L2) acquisition research accomplishes this through the measurement and analysis of various modes of linguistic behavior. The tasks used to evaluate each of these modes include, for example, elicited imitation and sentence combining to measure production, act-out to evaluate comprehension, and grammaticality judgment to evaluate knowledge of grammaticality. All such tasks assume that the adult L2 learner's developing language ability does not match an adult native speaker's and that the linguistic behavior elicited from each learner with each task maps the territory lying between the target language grammar and the learner's developing grammar. In this way, evaluation of the variance in the learner's behavior allows us to measure development with respect to the native speaker's model (see related discussion for first-language (L1) acquisition in Crain, 1991; Lust, 1986; Lust, Chien, and Flynn, 1987; see Flynn, 1986, for an earlier discussion on L2 acquisition). Language ability in this sense is to be distinguished from competence in the sense used by Chomsky (1975). Thus, in Universal Grammar (UG)-based second language acquisition (SLA) research, it is hypothesized that the L2 learner's grammar and the native speaker's grammar are based on the same underlying competence for language, that is, on principles of UG, and that the variance in the learner's linguistic behavior is due to different levels of proficiency.

At the same time, such experiments allow us to evaluate what aspects of the incoming data language learners are sensitive to and use for the construction of the L2 grammar. However, given the task demands for each experimental test, how this evaluation is accomplished will vary from task to task.

Building on the results in Flynn (1986), the purpose of this chapter is to begin to specify what aspect of the learner's grammar each of two commonly used experimental tasks evaluate and to specify how each task relates to the other. In particular, we question whether L2 learners' responses to different task types reflect underlying competence in similar ways and how intervening performance factors influence the results. We are thus interested in how results converge as well as in how they diverge across tasks. In this preliminary study, we evaluated two production tasks—both an oral and a taped elicited imitation test—and two judgment tasks—a read and a taped grammaticality judgment test.

Results reported in this chapter indicate a certain convergence and comparability between the elicited imitation and the grammaticality judgment tasks with respect to the linguistic phenomena investigated. This finding suggests that both of these tasks evaluate developing language abilities in a similar manner while reflecting task-specific differences.

BACKGROUND

As is well known, experimental methods used to evaluate developing language ability only provide indirect measures of a learner's competence; from this, inferences are made about a learner's linguistic development. Within this context, the task demands of each experimental methodology chosen to test a hypothesis mediate this evaluation in unique ways. For example, Flynn (1986) compared results of an elicited imitation task (a learner was asked to repeat verbatim a stimulus sentence administered orally) and an act-out task (a learner was asked to manipulate plastic tokens to indicate the actions specified in a stimulus sentence). She found that, with respect to the particular phenomenon under investigation, that is, differences in direction of embedding of subordinate clauses, the elicited imitation task evoked more relevant and subtle linguistic information about the learner's developing language abilities than did the act-out task. Flynn argued that in an act-out task, a learner need not tap her structural knowledge to the degree necessary in production. In fact, structural competence can be by-passed in these types of comprehension tasks in a way that is impossible in elicited imitation tasks; extralinguistic knowledge and information available to the subject can be used to form a coherent interpretation of a stimulus sentence but cannot be exploited in the same way when formulating an utterance. Nonlinguistic strategies can therefore be used to a greater degree in comprehension than in certain production tasks.

Although at first glance this finding may seem simply to replicate something we already know, that is, that context is important in comprehension, Flynn's study empirically isolated an important new finding. Specifically, the results demonstrated exactly how and where the two types of tasks diverged. The results of the imitation task indicated a significant preference for forward rather than backward anaphora in postposed clauses at the intermediate level for adult speakers of Spanish learning English as a second language (ESL); results from the act-out task did not demonstrate this directionality effect at any of the three ESL levels tested.

Knowing precisely what aspect of language ability each experimental task evaluates is essential with respect to our choice of methodology for a particular study and with respect to an interpretation of the results elicited. Our understanding of how the results of one experimental study relate to the results of others also relies critically upon such knowledge.

The general question that we ask in this chapter is whether or not the grammaticality judgment test and the elicited imitation test produce significantly divergent or convergent sets of results.

Grammaticality Judgment Test

A priori, there are many reasons why the grammaticality judgment (GJ) test might not provide as sensitive an evaluation of a learner's developing linguistic abilities as the elicited imitation (EI) test. For example, the GJ test, like comprehension tasks, does not elicit linguistic behavior per se but rather a response indicating the learner's belief about the L2 grammar. A subject is asked to listen to or to read a particular sentence structure and evaluate whether or not the sentence is grammatical. In order to avoid learners' reliance on prescriptive grammar when using this task, most experimenters ask the subjects to indicate whether the sentences are "good" or "acceptable" rather than "grammatical." In some cases, the subject may be asked to rank a particular sentence in terms of degree of grammaticality. The methodology assumes that the subject's correct response on the test indicates that the subject has access to the linguistic knowledge sanctioning the structure of the target sentence, and the subject's incorrect response indicates the absence of that access. In a theory of UG, judgments of grammaticality have been argued to reflect an individual's linguistic competence (Chomsky, 1975). In UG-based experimental studies of both L1 and L2 acquisition, GJs have traditionally been the only task used to evaluate knowledge of ungrammaticality. This is because the goal of such studies is to assess a learner's knowledge of UG principles. Because such principles are formulated in terms of negative constraints on the grammar, eliciting a learner's beliefs about ungrammatical sentences has traditionally been the only way to assess this type of knowledge. Other tasks such as spontaneous speech, in which the experimenter examines the learner's utterances for violations of UG principles, are inadequate because the absence of such violations can never unequivocally be ascribed to a constraint that exists on the learner's grammar.

However, some researchers (Birdsong, 1989; Christie & Lantolf, 1992; Ellis, 1991; Martohardjono, 1993; Nagata, 1988; and in this volume, Cowan and Hatasa, chapter 15; Gass, chapter 16; Goss, Zhang, & Lantolf, chapter 14) have suggested that such a task is not devoid of extralinguistic factors. For example, responses might be influenced by an individual's prescriptive knowledge about language rules rather than being a measure of an individual's underlying competence.

Elicited Imitation

In EI tasks, subjects are asked to repeat selected sentences designed to manipulate certain grammatical factors relevant to the empirical questions being asked. With this task, a subject is assumed to reproduce the linguistic structure of the sentence he or she hears; thus, the utterance elicited is argued to reflect the degree to which a subject is able to assimilate the stimulus into an internal grammar. These sentences are controlled in terms of length for both number of words and syllables; this number always exceeds short-term memory capacity under the assumption that the task is reconstructive. In this task, a subject performs an analysis on each stimulus sentence, breaking it down into its semantic and syntactic parts. If the subject can analyze the sentence as would a native speaker, then, like the native speaker, the subject should be able to repeat the sentence without significant error. If significant errors occur, it is assumed that they reflect particular linguistic deficiencies on the part of the subject. The EI is reconstructive in nature; errors are traced to the grammatical abilities of the subjects rather than to chance. In contrast to the GJ task, which has been used to measure knowledge of ungrammaticality, this task has traditionally focused on the production of grammatical sentences.

It is clear that the basic structure of the GJ task is fundamentally different from that of the EI task. The GJ task elicits an L2 learner's belief about the target grammar, whereas the EI task elicits a linguistic utterance.

THE STUDY

Given the differences in the task demands for the two methodologies, one could reasonably hypothesize that each of these tasks provides distinct insights about the developing language base of the speaker. Alternatively, if one were to find similarities in the pattern of results for each of the two tasks, then this would suggest that both tasks might be evaluating a speaker's language abilities in a similar manner.

In this study, we sought to determine, with a select set of sentence structures, exactly how the elicited imitation task and the grammaticality judgment task relate to each other. Specifically, we asked whether the grammaticality judgment task and the elicited imitation task evaluate underlying competence in comparable ways. In addition, we sought to determine whether, within each task, different versions of the same test were equivalent, and whether these different versions related across tasks in a comparable manner. Thus, two versions of both of the tasks are evaluated.

We also sought to determine whether use of ungrammatical sentences in production would provide as insightful an evaluation of a learner's developing language abilities as the elicited imitation of grammatical sentences seems to provide. Finally, we sought to compare these results with those from GJ tasks involving ungrammatical sentences.

Design and Methodology

Twelve speakers of Japanese at an advanced level of ESL competence as measured by the Michigan Placement Test (overall mean score: 44, score range 0–50; mean score on the listening comprehension subtest: 17, score range 0–20) were evaluated on two types of elicited imitation and grammaticality judgment tasks. The subjects were graduate students at MIT at the time of testing.

Description of the Tasks

Grammaticality Judgment. The grammaticality judgment task involved both a timed read and a timed taped grammaticality judgment test. In the read version, the subject read a stimulus sentence from an individual card; she then recorded whether or not she believed the sentence to be grammatical. In the taped version, the subject listened to a recorded sentence and determined whether or not the sentence was grammatical. In both versions, the speakers were presented with a new stimulus sentence every 15 seconds. In order to avoid reliance on prescriptive grammar rather than on developing intuition, subjects were not allowed to refer back to previously read sentences or to listen to repeats of previously heard sentences.

Elicited Imitation. The elicited imitation tasks involved both an oral administration of a stimulus sentence that a subject was asked to repeat verbatim, and a taped presentation, in which the subject listened to a taped recording of a particular stimulus sentence and then repeated the stimulus sentence. In both versions of this task, the presentation of each utterance was followed by a 10-second pause in which the speaker was to repeat the stimulus sentence. The duration of presentation for each utterance in both versions of the EI task was also equated. No repeats were given for any of the stimulus items.

Task Sentences

For all of these tasks, subjects were administered stimulus sentences exemplified in (1).

(1) Examples of Stimulus Sentences
    a. Grammatical Sentences
        A. Object-Object (OO)
        The engineer answered the *gentleman* who the owner shoved Ø.
        B. Object-Subject (OS)
        The diplomat answered the *man* who Ø introduced the doctor.
    b. Ungrammatical Sentences
        C. Object-Object (OO)
        *The man greeted the *doctor* who the actor introduced *him*.
        D. Object-Subject (OS)
        *The lawyer questioned the *student* who *he* answered the owner.

These stimulus sentences were complex sentences with relative clauses.[1] The relative structures were either Object-Object (OO), as in A and C, or Object-Subject (OS), as in B and D. The grammatical sentences are shown in A–B; the ungrammatical sentences are shown in C–D. The ungrammatical sentences all involved a resumptive pronoun in the gap site in the relative clause. Object relative clauses were chosen as the focus of this study because results from Flynn (1989b), in which Japanese speakers were tested on four different types of relative clauses (Subject-Subject, Subject-Object, Object-Subject, and Object-Object), showed that differences between object- and subject-relativized noun phrases (NPs) were greatest for relatives with the head NP in object position. Thus, choice of these object relatives for this study seemed to be the most appropriate for investigation of potential subject/object differences across tasks.[2]

---

[1]Relative clause sentences were chosen because of a large body of literature available with respect to L2 acquisition (Gass, 1979; Gass & Ard, 1980; Hyltenstam, 1981; Ioup & Kruse, 1977; Schachter, 1974; Tarallo & Myhill, 1983), most specifically with respect to the elicited imitation of Restrictive Relative Clauses (RRCs) by Japanese speakers (Flynn, 1989b).

[2]The reason stated here for the choice of object relatives over subject relatives should answer the question raised by Bley-Vroman and Chaudron (this volume, chapter 13) with respect to our particular design.

Within each of the four experimental tasks administered, there were 12 sentences: 3 grammatical and 3 ungrammatical OO sentences, as in A and C, and 3 grammatical and 3 ungrammatical OS sentences, as in B and D. Thus, each speaker was tested on 48 sentences. The complete sentence batteries are shown in the Appendix.

All sentences used in the study were equalized in length (15 syllables) and (approximately) in number of words.[3] They were also controlled with respect to the pragmatics of the sentences so that atypical pairings of, for example, agents and patients were avoided. No repeats were given. The presentations were timed. All speakers were trained on the vocabulary items used in the stimulus sentences prior to the administration of the tasks. Sentences were randomized within the sentence batteries. The order of administration of the tasks was varied; one half of the subjects were administered the elicited production tests first and one half were administered the GJ tests first. In addition, within each of these two tasks, the ordering with respect to the two versions was varied for each subject.

RESULTS

Results are shown in Table 12.1. We first consider the overall results for the grammatical and ungrammatical sentences across tasks. We then consider

---

Sentences were also systematically randomized, as is standard in psycholinguistic experimentation.

In addition, Bley-Vroman and Chaudron suggested that all the stimulus sentences used in the EI tasks should be prerecorded and administered in a taped version to the subjects. We investigated this issue in our study, as a similar question had been previously raised by Eubank (1989). We found no significant difference between results from the oral presentation of the stimulus sentences and those from the taped presentation.

[3]One question recently raised is whether number of words rather than number of syllables should be exact. For example, L. Eubank (personal communication, February 1991) argued that if the number of syllables in each of two sentences matches but the number of words differs even by one, speakers will always find the sentence with the fewest number of words easier to imitate or comprehend. For a related discussion of these issues see Bley-Vroman and Chaudron (this volume, chapter 13).

However, Flynn (1989a), for example, has shown that this is not the case. In an L2 acquisition study that involved a test of sentences that were matched in number of syllables but differed by one in number of words, Flynn found that adult speakers of Japanese, Chinese, and Spanish learning English found sentences that had the greater number of words easier to imitate and to comprehend than those sentences that had one less word. In fact, all subjects converted the sentences that contained one less word to the sentence structure that involved one more word. This finding suggests that when sentences are equated in terms of number of syllables, it is the structure of the stimulus sentences rather than the number of words that determines the results.

TABLE 12.1
Mean Amount Correct

Sentence Type	EI Oral	EI Taped	GJ Cards	GJ Taped
		Test Type		
OBJ-OBJ GRAM				
M	.75	.42	1.00	1.67
SD	.75	.51	1.04	1.10
OBJ-OBJ UNGRAM				
M	.33	.17	2.83	2.50
SD	.65	.39	.39	.52
OBJ-SUBJ GRAM				
M	1.17	1.25	2.83	3.00
SD	1.02	1.05	.39	.00
OBJ-SUBJ UNGRAM				
M	.08	.33	2.83	1.58
SD	.29	.65	.58	1.10

Note. Score range = 0–3, N = 12.

results within tasks. Analyses were performed by Analysis of Variance (ANOVA).[4]

Across Tasks

Grammatical Sentences

First, between the two tasks tested, that is, EI and GJ, there was a significant overall effect of task [$F(1,11)$ = 46.301, p < .001]. Subjects performed better on the grammaticality judgment task than they did on the elicited imitation task. Second, there was an overall significant effect for clause type [$F(1,11)$ = 33.477, p < .001]; subjects in both tasks correctly repeated and judged sentences that contained OS relatives more often than they did sentences that contained OO relatives. This is an important result to which we will return. Third, there was a significant *task × clause type* interaction [$F(1,11)$

---

[4]The design for all of the statistical tests was factorial with repeated measures on the last factor in each case.

Test One:
    Overall Grammatical Sentences and Overall Ungrammatical Sentences. The factors were Task (Elicited Imitation or Grammaticality Judgment) × Clause Type (OS or OO).

Tests Two and Three: Within Tasks
    Elicited Imitation: Grammatical (Test Two) and Ungrammatical Sentences (Test Three). The factors were Task (Oral or Taped) × Clause Type (OS or OO).

Tests Three and Four: Within Tasks
    Grammaticality Judgment: Grammatical (Test Three) and Ungrammatical Sentences (Test Four). The factors were Task (Taped or Read) × Clause Type (OS or OO).

= 8.830, $p < .05$]. Superior performance for OS relative clauses was even more pronounced in the GJ than in the EI task.

Ungrammatical Sentences

First, within the ungrammatical sentences, there was a significant overall effect for task [$F(1,11)$ = 216.077, $p < .001$]. Speakers performed better on the grammaticality judgment task than they did on the elicited imitation task. Second, there was a significant effect for clause type [$F(1,11)$ = 5.5, $p < .039$]. For both the EI and GJ task, subjects correctly judged and repeated the ungrammatical OO relatives more often than they did the OS relatives, although within task, this effect did not hold for EI, as is discussed in the following section.

Within Tasks

Elicited Imitation

Grammatical Sentences. First, within the elicited imitation task, there was no significant difference between the taped and the oral presentations of the task for either grammatical or ungrammatical sentences. This suggests, contra Eubank (1989) and others, that a nontaped presentation of this task does not influence performance or introduce biasing factors that could significantly affect the results.

Second, within the grammatical sentences for EI, there was a significant preference for the OS structures [$F(1,11)$ = 6.395, $p < .028$]; this replicates the significant overall result for amount correct on these structures.

Ungrammatical Sentences. Within the ungrammatical sentences, there was no significant difference between the imitation of the OS and that of the OO sentence structures, nor was there any significant difference between the two versions of the task. In both cases, subjects found it difficult to repeat ungrammatical sentences, as the low scores in Table 12.1 indicate.

However, as is shown in Table 12.2, results of the error analyses did isolate more deletion of resumptive pronouns for the OS structures than for the OO sentences (21% vs. 2% overall). Recall that these relative clause structures were made ungrammatical by introducing a resumptive pronoun. Thus, a deletion of the resumptive pronoun in these sentences indicated that subjects spontaneously converted the ungrammatical sentences to grammatical ones. For example, when given the sentence example, *The man greeted the doctor who the actor introduced him*, a subject often repeated, *The man greeted the doctor who the actor introduced*. In this study, the subject corrected the ungrammatical sentences more often when the sentences involved an

TABLE 12.2
Error Analyses: Deletion of Resumptive Prounoun in Ungrammatical Sentences
of EI Task

Sentence Type[a]	Taped EI	Oral EI
OBJ-SUBJ	25.0%	16.7%
OBJ-OBJ	2.7%	0.0%

Note. $N = 12$.
[a]EXAMPLES:
OJB-SUBJ
Stimulus: *The man greeted the doctor who the actor reminded *him*.
Response: The man greeted the doctor who the actor reminded.
OBJ-OBJ
Stimulus: *The lawyer questioned the student who *he* answered the owner.
Response: The lawyer questioned the student who answered the owner.

OS structure; this finding is again consistent with the overall preference for OS shown in the amount correct. This finding also accounts for the better performance (that is, more repetition of ungrammatical sentences) on the OO structures.

Grammaticality Judgment

Grammatical Sentences. On grammatical sentences within the grammaticality judgment task, subjects found sentences with OS relatives significantly easier to judge as grammatical than those with OO relatives [$F(1,11) = 39.11$, $p < .001$]. This result once again conforms with the overall preference for OS structures. There was no significant difference between type of presentation with the grammatical sentences.

Ungrammatical Sentences. With ungrammatical sentences, there was a significant difference between the two types of GJ tasks [$F(1,11) = 8.503$, $p < .014$]. Speakers performed better on the read task than on the taped version. In addition, there was a significant interaction of *task type* × *clause type* [$F(1,11) = 5.863, p < .034$], indicating that on the taped version of the GJ task, subjects performed significantly better on the OO sentences than on the OS sentences. That is, they accepted ungrammatical OS sentences more often than they did ungrammatical OO sentences. On the read version they did not differentiate the sentence structures.

CONCLUSIONS AND DISCUSSION

The major results can be summarized as follows: First, the elicited imitation task can be used as an adequate measure of a learner's knowledge of the linguistic principles that both license grammatical strings and disallow ungrammatical ones for a particular language. That is to say, our results indicate that EI can be reliably used with both grammatical and ungrammatical sentence structures. This is an important finding because, prior to this study, it was unclear that knowledge of ungrammaticality could be measured with this task. There has been considerable discussion in the literature suggesting that EI is not reconstructive in nature but simply involves rote imitation. If this were so, then the EI task would, for example, not be adequate for measuring knowledge of principles of UG that are formulated in terms of negative constraints. Repetition of an ungrammatical sentence might only reflect the ability to "parrot" a sentence rather than showing the speaker's acceptance or rejection of a violation. The results we obtained for the ungrammatical sentences in this study strongly suggest that this is not the case. The speakers in this study converted ungrammatical sentences to grammatical ones (e.g., they converted an ungrammatical OS sentence to a grammatical OS sentence). These results suggest that EI is a powerful and sensitive instrument that can be used to measure knowledge of constraints on grammar. We can thus argue that EI provides a viable means with which to evaluate knowledge of UG constraints on the target grammar.

Bley-Vroman and Chaudron (this volume, chapter 13) raised a number of issues concerning this conclusion. For example, they stated that extragrammatical factors such as memory and proficiency level influence the results of this task. Insofar as this is true of most, if not all, experimental tasks used to evaluate grammatical knowledge, it is unclear why results of the EI task should be, as they recommended, interpreted with greater caution than the results of any other task. No one would ever claim that the EI task or any other task taps grammatical competence directly without some mediation by these factors.

Bley-Vroman and Chaudron also stated that the EI task is based on *chunking* and cited this as an objection to the use of this task. However, they themselves speculated that "chunking is mediated by a grammar-based sentence processor." Therefore, they seem to agree with us that grammatical knowledge *does* play a significant role in EI.

We wholeheartedly agree with Bley-Vroman and Chaudron that more cross-task comparisons are essential; this is precisely what we have attempted to contribute in this study. However, if we suspended the use of EI or any other task until we fully understood it, we would never make any advances in our understanding of the methodology or of the L2 acquisition process. It is only in the context of continued use and comparison that we are able to determine the parameters of each experimental methodology in any principled manner.

Another objection raised by Bley-Vroman and Chaudron was that EI has a narrow band of sensitivity. Thus, they conjectured that this task is "relatively insensitive to high-level syntax and semantic facts (binding relations, quantifier relations, and the like), but relatively sensitive to phrase-level aspects of syntax." Although such a statement is only speculation, this state of affairs, if true, makes EI an ideal task for studies such as ours, in which the object of study is phrase structure. In this context, Bley-Vroman and Chaudron claimed that Flynn's (1987) results "were attributable more to the differences in imitation ability between her two populations" than to differences in the (mis)match between L1 and L2 parameter settings. No such claim was ever made by Flynn. Readers are referred to Flynn and Lust (1990) for a detailed response to Bley-Vroman and Chaudron (1990) with respect to this issue.

One final point in this regard is that some of the objections raised by Bley-Vroman and Chaudron are based on results of studies investigating the recall of serial lists of digits, letters, and words. To construct such arguments based on these types of data fails to differentiate grammar-based sentence-level processing tasks from other nonlinguistic processing tasks (see Epstein, Flynn, & Martohardjono, 1993, for an extended discussion). In addition, Bley-Vroman and Chaudron claimed that the results isolated in this chapter can be accounted for in terms of *serial position*. However, results of other experimental studies (Flynn, 1989a, 1989b; Gair, Flynn, & Brown, 1993) do not support this conclusion. These results indicate that Spanish and Chinese speakers learning English as a second language do not find subject relatives significantly easier to imitate than object relatives. If Bley-Vroman and Chaudron's astructural explanation were correct, we would expect such a result to obtain for all L2 learners of English. Instead, the results isolated in this study and others demand a grammatical explanation (cf. Gair, Flynn, & Brown, 1993).

The second major finding is that with respect to grammatical sentence structures, the EI and the GJ tasks provide strikingly convergent results. There is an overall preference for OS sentence structures in both tasks.[5] This convergence across tasks is unexpected given the task demand differences—repetition in one case and judgment of grammaticality in the other.

Third, with respect to the ungrammatical sentence structures, the results for both of the elicited imitation tasks and the read grammaticality judgment task converge when we consider amount correct in judging ungrammatical sentences as ungrammatical. That is, none of these three tasks significantly differentiated the sentences with respect to their particular grammatical structure. However, this result is more complex than this finding alone suggests. This result does not indicate that these three tasks (that is, read GJ and both of the EI tasks) evaluate language abilities comparably at all levels when using ungrammatical sentences. In fact, results suggest that the EI and the taped GJ tasks might in fact provide a closer fit on ungrammatical sentences than do the EI results and those from the read GJ tasks. In order to understand

---

[5]This finding for the EI task replicates results reported earlier for the Japanese speakers (Flynn, 1989b; Flynn & Brown, 1988; Gair, Flynn, & Brown, 1993).

this tentative conclusion, we suggest the following: Consider again the fact that on grammatical sentences for all tasks, speakers preferred OS structures over OO structures.[6] With ungrammatical sentences, we argue, this preference for OS structures is still there, although it manifests itself differentially across the tasks.

In the EI task, subjects have recourse to correction in their production of ungrammatical sentences, as the results in Table 12.2 indicate. That is, given the nature of the task, EI provides us with more information than a GJ task even when subjects are asked to correct what they have judged to be ungrammatical. In its most basic form, the GJ task provides us only with an indication of the learner's beliefs with regard to grammaticality. When a correction is provided in GJ, it is still very different from the utterance provided in EI tasks. Because it is post hoc, we risk eliciting conscious knowledge (e.g., prescribed rules) about the L2 grammar rather than the unconscious, abstract grammatical knowledge that we want to investigate. Within EI, on the other hand, the learner produces an entire utterance which can subsequently be analyzed. The changes made in an EI are spontaneous and unconscious.

The OS preference in the EI tasks emerges in the fact that the speakers correctly delete the resumptive pronoun in the OS sentences significantly more often than in the OO structures. The same preference for OS structures is not as straightforward in the GJ tasks. We suggest that this is because of the restricted nature of the GJ task; it involves just a yes–no judgment. The OS preference does not emerge at all in the read GJ task. There was a suggestion that the preference for OS was neutralized by the reading task, which in some sense allows for more monitoring than does the taped GJ.[7] However, it does emerge in the taped version as a higher acceptance rate of the OS structures regardless of whether the sentences are grammatical or ungrammatical; a higher acceptance rate for ungrammatical OS sentences in the GJ tasks results in a low score for amount correct. The difference between the two GJ tasks suggests that the taped and, by extension, oral GJ task rather than the read GJ task may in fact be more sensitive to subtleties in developing language abilities. The read GJ task seems to introduce factors that neutralize this effect. However, it is important to note that such an in-

---

[6]We are thus suggesting, contra Bley-Vroman and Chaudron (this volume, chapter 13), that our results across the EI tasks and the taped GJ task are not strikingly divergent. In other words, as we have stated, the preference for the OS relative clause structures manifests itself in a higher overall acceptance rate of OS sentences, regardless of grammaticality. Although it is plausible that preference for a particular structure would aid subjects in error detection, we argue that this preference could also result in the OS structures being less marked than the OO structures for these subjects. This is manifested in the higher acceptance rate of such structures, independent of grammaticality, in the GJ task.

[7]This is not surprising given the relationship between level of reading ability in the L2 and level of proficiency in the target L2 (see, for example, McLaughlin, 1993).

terpretation of these seemingly anomalous results on the GJ tasks is possible only within the context of the EI results. If we had isolated the GJ task results, we might have arrived at a slightly different conclusion or left the results unexplained.

To conclude, results of this preliminary study indicate certain significant convergences between EI and GJ tasks that up until this time have been unattested. At the same time, results indicate the need for continued empirical comparison across methodologies in order that we be able to isolate precisely the nature and the properties of developing language abilities. Thus, we argue that these results underscore: (a) the need for multiple investigations of the same linguistic phenomena with distinct methodologies, namely, the use of EI and GJ together; (b) the complex and subtle nature of the acquisition data we need to investigate to arrive at a principled understanding of the L2 acquisition process; and (c) the need for the development of increasingly more sensitive instruments to evaluate linguistic development.

ACKNOWLEDGMENTS

Results reported in this chapter derive from Munnich (1991) and represent part of an ongoing study that investigates the relationship among various experimental methodologies. The authors thank the editors of this volume and the participants at the Conference on Applied Linguistics at Michigan State University, East Lansing, October 1991.

APPENDIX: STIMULUS SENTENCES

Grammatical Sentences

OO

1. The student reminded the doctor who the man instructed.
2. The professor told the architect who the lawyer answered.
3. The engineer answered the gentleman who the owner shoved.
4. The owner instructed the lawyer who the policeman called.
5. The janitor questioned the doctor who the student greeted.
6. The actor greeted the architect who the lawyer answered.
7. The man informed the architect who the doctor introduced.
8. The engineer instructed the student who the doctor told.
9. The professor introduced the lawyer who the actor called.
10. The foreman informed the architect who the engineer called.

11. The professor instructed the worker who the boss greeted.
12. The student greeted the doctor who the policeman questioned.

OS

1. The actor informed the engineer who criticized the boss.
2. The diplomat answered the man who introduced the doctor.
3. The doctor reminded the lawyer who answered the worker.
4. The gentleman greeted the doctor who answered the lawyer.
5. The owner questioned the businessman who greeted the worker.
6. The professor greeted the actor who called the janitor.
7. The student criticized the policeman who answered the boss.
8. The diplomat called the engineer who informed the doctor.
9. The actor instructed the student who questioned the lawyer.
10. The foreman questioned the architect who introduced the man.
11. The student instructed the lawyer who called the engineer.
12. The diplomat greeted the policeman who questioned the man.

Ungrammatical Sentences

OO

1. *The man greeted the doctor who the actor reminded him.
2. *The foreman questioned the engineer who the owner shoved him.
3. *The man informed the doctor who the lawyer reminded him.
4. *The diplomat instructed the doctor who the man shoved him.
5. *The student informed the engineer who the boss questioned him.
6. *The actor greeted the professor who the doctor called him.
7. *The doctor introduced the student who the actor shoved him.
8. *The actor shoved the man who the janitor instructed him.
9. *The owner called the actor who the lawyer instructed him.
10. *The diplomat questioned the man who the boss instructed him.
11. *The engineer greeted the man who the worker answered him.
12. *The actor informed the man who the engineer greeted him.

OS

1. *The man introduced the boss who he reminded the actor.
2. *The lawyer questioned the student who he answered the owner.
3. *The businessman greeted the man who he answered the doctor.
4. *The actor shoved the student who he greeted the architect.

5. *The boss introduced the man who he instructed the worker.
6. *The student informed the doctor who he answered the lawyer.
7. *The worker answered the diplomat who he told the student.
8. *The lawyer informed the architect who he shoved the student.
9. *The doctor instructed the lawyer who he answered the boss.
10. *The boss introduced the gentleman who he questioned the man.
11. *The worker questioned the student who he told the gentleman.
12. *The janitor criticized the actor who he told the boss.

REFERENCES

Birdsong, D. (1989). *Metalinguistic performance and interlinguistic competence.* Berlin: Springer-Verlag.

Bley-Vroman, R., & Chaudron, C. (1990). Second language processing of subordinate clauses and anaphora—First language and universal influences: A review of Flynn's research. *Language Learning, 40,* 245–285.

Chomsky, N. (1975). *Reflections on language.* New York: Pantheon.

Christie, K., & Lantolf, J. (1992). The ontological status of learner grammaticality judgments in UG approaches to L2 acquisition. *Rassegna Italiana di Linguistica Applicata, 3,* 31–57.

Crain, S. (1991). Language acquisition in the absence of experience. *Brain and Behavioral Sciences, 14,* 597–612.

Ellis, R. (1991). Grammaticality judgments and second language acquisition. *Studies in Second Language Acquisition, 13,* 161–187.

Epstein, S., Flynn, S., & Martohardjono, G. (1993). *Explanation in SLA: With a consideration of a case study in functional categories.* Manuscript submitted for publication.

Eubank, L. (1989). Parameters in L2 acquisition: Flynn revisited. *Second Language Research, 5,* 129–153.

Flynn, S. (1987). *A parameter setting model of L2 acquisition: Experimental studies in anaphora.* Dordrecht: Reidel.

Flynn, S. (1986). Production vs. comprehension: Differences in underlying competences. *Studies in Second Language Acquisition, 8,* 135–164.

Flynn, S. (1989a). Adult L2 acquisition of two distinct phonetic forms of anaphora. *Canadian Journal of Linguistics, 34,* 419–443.

Flynn, S. (1989b). The role of the head-initial/head-final parameter in the acquisition of English relative clauses by adult Spanish and Japanese speakers. In S. Gass & J. Schachter (Eds.), *Linguistic perspectives on second language acquisiton* (pp. 89–108). Cambridge: Cambridge University Press.

Flynn, S., & Brown, O. (1988). *Three types of adult second language learning.* Paper presented at the 13th Annual Boston University Conference on Language Development, Boston, MA.

Flynn, S., & Lust, B. (1990). In defense of parameter-setting in L2 acquisition: A reply to Bley-Vroman and Chaudron '90. *Language Learning, 3,* 419–449.

Gair, J., Flynn, S., & Brown, O. (1993). *Why Japanese learners object to objects.* Manuscript submitted for publication.

Gass, S. (1979). Language transfer and universal grammatical relations. *Language Learning, 29,* 327–344.

Gass, S., & Ard, J. (1980). L2 data: Their relevance for language universals. *TESOL Quarterly, 14,* 443–452.

Hyltenstam, K. (1981). *The use of typological markedness as predictors in second language acquisition.* Unpublished manuscript.

Ioup, G., & Kruse, A. (1977). Interference versus structural complexity as a predictor of second language relative clause acquisition. In C. Henning (Ed.), *Proceedings of the Second Language Research Forum* (pp. 22–35). Los Angeles: University of California at Los Angeles.

Lust, B. (1986). Introduction. In B. Lust (Ed.), *Studies in the acquisition of anaphora: Vol. 1. Defining the constraints.* Dordrecht: Reidel Press.

Lust, B., Chien, Y.-C., & Flynn, S. (1987). What children know: Methods for the study of first language acquisition. In B. Lust (Ed.), *Studies in the acquisition of anaphora: Vol. 2. Applying the constraints* (pp. 271–356). Dordrecht: Reidel Press.

Martohardjono, G. (1993). *Movement constraints on the acquisition of Wh questions.* Unpublished doctoral dissertation, Cornell University, Ithaca, NY.

McLaughlin, B. (1993). *Plenary address at Second Language Research Forum*, University of Pittsburgh, Pittsburgh, PA.

Munnich, E. (1991). *A comparison of methodologies used in assessing adult second language acquisition.* Unpublished bachelor's thesis. MIT, Cambridge, MA.

Myhill, J. (1981). The acquisition of complex sentences: A crosslinguistic study. *Studies in Second Language Acquisition, 4,* 2–19.

Nagata, H. (1988). The relativity of linguistic intuition: The effect of repetition on grammaticality judgments. *Journal of Psycholinguistic Research, 17,* 1–17.

Schachter, J. (1974). An error in error analysis. *Language Learning, 24,* 205–214.

Tarallo, F., & Myhill, J. (1983). Interference and natural language processing in second language acquisition. *Language Learning, 33,* 55–76.

CHAPTER

13

ELICITED IMITATION AS A MEASURE OF SECOND-LANGUAGE COMPETENCE

Robert Bley-Vroman
Craig Chaudron
University of Hawai'i

The application of first-language (L1)-based research methods to second-language acquisition (SLA) has led researchers to question assumptions of the methodologies, with respect, in particular, to their reliability and validity (for consideration of metalinguistic judgments, see, e.g., Birdsong, 1989; Chaudron, 1983). The connection between the data collection technique and a subject's behavior independent of the data collection context is always one that should concern the researcher. This chapter considers one recent methodology, the psycholinguistic technique of elicited imitation, in which a subject is presented with a spoken string of words in the language (usually a grammatical sentence) and asked to repeat it. The investigator records facts about the repetition and makes inferences about the state of the learner's knowledge of the language. The basic idea is that if the subject's grammar corresponds to the grammar used in producing the string, the imitation is more likely to be accurate. Specific inaccuracies may point to specific differences between the subject's grammar and the grammar of the target string. The technique has been used in studies both of child language development and of adult foreign-language learning (see Chaudron & Russell, 1990; Lust, Chien, & Flynn, 1987, for reviews), but the precise parameters of performance and valid interpretation of learner competence have not been fully determined. We regard it as premature to view elicited imitation as a proven method for inferring learner competence, because a considerable amount of research needs to be conducted to understand how performance under imitation conditions compares with other methods and with learner's underlying knowledge.

245

We outline our view of the nature of the elicited imitation process and the inferences that may be appropriately drawn from its use. We believe that developing a plausible account of the process must accompany an evaluation of its use in particular experimental contexts. In the first section we investigate some issues involved in developing such an account and outline our view of the process of elicited imitation. It is too grand to say that a theory is being proposed: We are telling what we hope is a plausible story. In the second section of the chapter, we consider the results of some experiments using elicited imitation in the context of the general picture we have developed. Our strongest result is that elicited imitation is a very delicate instrument, with strong floor and ceiling effects and a narrow band of extreme sensitivity to various interacting factors.

THE NATURE OF ELICITED IMITATION

Although it is clear that elicited imitation (EI) is more than mere rote repetition, little work has been done in attempting to work out, even speculatively, the precise process that might be involved. Slobin and Welsh (1973) suggested that "sentence recognition and imitation are filtered through the individual's productive linguistic systems" (p. 496). It has been proposed that EI uses a process of *reconstruction* (Lust, Chien, & Flynn, 1987). In reconstruction, the subject hears the sentence and, to the extent that the sentence is comprehended, reconstructs the meaning using his or her own grammar. This seems a plausible general approach. However, much remains to be worked out with respect both to comprehension and reconstruction.

We begin with certain prima facie facts about EI. In many cases the evidence is phenomenological and introspective. In other cases, research results back up the assertions. An account of EI must, at a minimum, explain the following facts:

1. Competent native speakers can often repeat grammatical sentences accurately. However, not all grammatical sentences are always accurately repeated: Even native speakers make errors. Likewise, a learner who can use a particular structure in free conversation will not always imitate that structure correctly in an EI task. (In these cases, scholars of language development may observe that "production precedes imitation," or that EI is a "regressive measure.") More generally, possessing the appropriate linguistic knowledge is not always sufficient for imitation accuracy.

2. Adult speakers can imitate ungrammatical strings (within limits). Learners can imitate accurately sentences with structural patterns that they have not yet mastered (or at least cannot use in free production). (Scholars of child language development may say that "imitation precedes production," or that

EI is a "progressive measure.") Clearly, possessing the appropriate linguistic knowledge is not always necessary; observations 1 and 2 are two sides of the same coin. They are not really surprising: They merely suggest that EI and productive use of grammar involve different processes.

3. Other things being equal, it appears easier to imitate grammatical sentences than ungrammatical strings of words. Thus, it appears that grammatical processing somehow aids repetition.

4. The longer a sentence is the less likely it is to be accurately repeated. This holds for both native speakers and learners, and it suggests that some sort of limited-capacity memory system is involved.

5. Sometimes, the message is not accurately repeated word for word, but the subject produces a different string that captures approximately the same message as the original. This suggests that an abstract message-meaning level can be accessed in EI.

6. Speakers can imitate strings of words (at least short strings) that do not have a coherent semantic interpretation. This suggests that the ability to construct sentence-level meaning is not a necessary condition for repetition.

7. Repetition is often accurate not just for gist but also for particular wording. Even particular aspects of the pronunciation (a funny accent, say) can sometimes be imitated. This suggests that a lower level of representation can be involved, one that includes more than just message meaning.

8. The more you know of a foreign language, the better you can imitate the sentences of the language. Thus, EI is a reasonable measure of global proficiency.

PROCESSING, CHUNKING, AND SHORT-TERM MEMORY

In developing an account that will be consistent with these general observations, we propose that EI crucially involves both the language-processing system and the memory system. In outline, EI involves the following:

1. The Speech comprehension system: The subject hears the input and processes it, forming a representation.
2. Representation: The resulting representation includes information at various levels.
3. Memory: The representation must be kept in short-term memory.
4. The Speech production system: The subject formulates a sentence based on the accessed representation. (There may also be monitoring of the phonetic plan, comparing it to the model.)

When the sentence is heard, it is processed, and then the output representation is stored in a limited-capacity memory. The subject then "reads out" this stored representation. This short-term memory is limited to about seven units, or *chunks* (Miller, 1956). The limited capacity of the memory in which representations are stored is central to our account. It explains why longer sentences, ceteris paribus, are harder to imitate accurately than shorter ones: The shorter ones take less memory space.

Obviously, sentences longer than seven or eight words can be imitated accurately (hence, in our account, stored in short-term memory). This is because the sentences are being chunked. We speculate that this chunking is mediated by a grammar-based sentence processor. If the grammar can reduce the number of units so that they can fit into short-term memory, then the sentence has a chance of being repeated accurately. A consequence is that grammatical sentences will on the whole be repeated more accurately than ungrammatical strings of equivalent length. *The old man saw the young woman in the park* will be repeated more accurately than *park old man the the saw woman in young the.* Chunking reflects the interaction of the grammar with the input side of the EI.

In keeping with nearly all present thinking on language processing, we assume that, in the native speaker, the language processor automatically and obligatorily produces representations of the input and does not itself require the use of short-term memory. To borrow the evocative allusion of Fodor, parsing is not "sicklied o'er with the past cast of thought" (1983, p. 64). In the conception of current generative linguistics, the language processor is encapsulated in a language module (see Garfield, 1987, for papers in this tradition). Parsing thus cannot affect imitation accuracy directly by filling up short-term memory. It is important to be clear about this matter. The claim is not that the parser has no memory store: It has at least some sort of "look-ahead buffer" (Berwick & Weinberg, 1984). Rather, whatever the store used by the parser, it is not the same short-term store that is used by a subject in remembering what was said in order to repeat it.[1]

In nonnatives, it is conceivable that language input processing is in fact "sicklied o'er with the pale cast of thought." Thus, processing might in principle place a load on working memory (which is equivalent to saying that the foreign–language–processing system is not fully encapsulated). If it does, then foreign-language learners will, in effect, have less memory available for the imitation task, hence their lowered performance. Also, as proficiency increases and input processing becomes more completely automatized, imitation accuracy should improve.

---

[1]Nor is it claimed that parsing difficulty cannot ever affect imitation accuracy; but if it does, it must be by some other route.

> 0: Visual
> 1: Letter
> 2: Syllable
> 3: Lexical
> 4: Phrasal
> 5: S-structure
> 6: Logical form
> 7: Interpretive

FIG. 13.1. Possible control levels. Adapted from Forster (1987).

CONTROL LEVELS AND THE EI TASK

The language processor itself consists of articulated components. As a result, it produces representations at various levels. Forster (1987), for example, proposed the levels given in Fig. 13.1.

Contemporary theorists agree that there are multiple levels of representation.[2] Alternatively (and equivalently) one can posit that a single shared representation encodes all kinds of information simultaneously (Frazier, 1987; see also Berwick, 1991; Levelt, 1989; and Pritchett, 1988, for related proposals). We display Forster's system because his conception of the way levels interact with psycholinguistic tasks is very close to that presented here.

To say that these levels exist is not to say that one somehow chooses which to produce. The competent native speaker cannot decide, say, to understand the meaning of the message without parsing it syntactically; nor can one decide to parse it and avoid trying to construct an interpretation. In general, the language processor automatically and obligatorily produces as complete a representation as possible and on as many levels as possible. To be sure, if a sentence cannot be processed at some level or can be only partially processed at that level, the representation will necessarily be deficient at that level. Such deficient representations result, for instance, when the grammar itself is deficient (as in the case of a learner), or when the sentence is ill formed. (These two cases are logically the same: There is a mismatch between mentally represented grammar and the linguistic structure of the stimulus.)

---

[2]There is some debate over whether information from one level can affect the formation of other levels during processing. This debate is orthogonal to our concern. (For one viewpoint, see Tannenhaus, Carlson, & Seidenberg, 1985; Tannenhaus, Dell, & Carlson, 1987; Lucas, Tannenhaus, & Carlson, 1990.)

The crucial question is what level (or levels) can control (Forster, 1987) the EI task. To be somewhat more concrete, consider two hypothetical possibilities. Perhaps the subject hears the sentence, processes it (successfully at all levels), and then says the same thing in his own words. In this case the controlling level for the task may be the highest level (7: the interpretive level). In Levelt's (1989) terms, the subject understands the message conceptually, and then the message is automatically and obligatorily run through the subject's fast, dumb formulator, where the subject's own system of grammatical rules are applied. EI controlled at the interpretive or conceptual level is one way of understanding what is meant by reconstruction as the term is used by Lust et al. (1987). At the other extreme, consider the possibility that EI is controlled at the lexical level. This is precisely the case of rote repetition or parroting, to use Lust et al.'s terms. Because there are many levels of representation, there are in principle many logically possible control levels for a task.[3]

The control level interacts with chunking, because the number of chunks is dependent on the level chosen. The higher the level the fewer the chunks. A string that consists of 14 word-chunks may consist of 4 phrase-chunks. There is a tension in the EI task between the need to reduce the number of chunks (which pushes to a higher level) and the need to be accurate word-by-word (which pushes to a lower level), and these considerations in turn interact with the length and structure of the stimulus sentence. Specifically, if the stimulus is short, it can be chunked in words, which means that it can be repeated accurately, even if no syntactic analysis is done—even if none can be done. Ungrammatical lists of unrelated words can be imitated accurately if there are less than about seven items.

On a priori grounds, our account would predict that for stimuli of the length and complexity typical in many EI experiments, the optimal control level is probably the phrase level or some other low syntactic level. A very high "gist" level is too inaccurate, and the lexical level is too low for stimuli over seven or eight words long. The controlling level might be that of the Φ-phrases of Gee and Grosjean (1983), the chunks of Abney (1991), or the first-level representation proposed by Weinberg (1987).

Weinberg argued that a related experimental task—sentence matching—operates at a level no higher than her first-level representation. In sentence matching, the subjects must determine whether two sentences displayed on a computer screen are word-by-word identical. (See Bley-Vroman & Masterson, 1989, for a description of the application of sentence matching to SLA

---

[3]For the sake of brevity, we do not explore the reasonable idea that several levels may be involved simultaneously: Perhaps there is a principal control level, but some reference may somehow be made to other levels. Likewise, we do not consider more elaborated production models, in which there could be a formulation of the message based on a high level and then a monitoring of the output by checking it against a lower level. See Levelt (1989) for discussion.

studies.) Weinberg interpreted the results of Freedman and Forster (1985) as demonstrating the insensitivity of sentence matching to binding constraints—the principles that govern the relationship of antecedents to pronouns and anaphors and to certain empty categories. On the face of it, it is hard to see why EI would optimally access a higher level than sentence matching, though empirical evidence is required to decide the issue.

VARIABILITY OF THE CONTROL LEVEL

Although one can speak in abstract terms of an optimal control level, given the character of the task and assuming all else is equal, in actual experiments with real subjects—especially learners—the control level may vary. "There are no good grounds for insisting that a particular level will always be the most efficient for all subjects on all occasions" (Forster, 1987, p. 74).

We have already mentioned the interaction of control level with stimulus length. In addition, the very availability of representational levels will clearly differ depending on level of language development. Assuming that the stimulus is well formed, the native speaker will produce complete representations on all levels, so that an optimal level (given the length and complexity of the stimulus) will be available.

But consider the case of a beginning learner. If the stimulus contains phrase-level structure that cannot be handled automatically by the learner's internal parser, then the learner cannot operate at the phrasal level, even though that level may be optimal. The learner may be able to handle the lexical level, but the stimulus may be too long at that level. Perhaps the learner gets some sort of message from the stimulus (forming a rough representation at a higher level that encodes thematic relationships). The learner will then try to run that message through the primitive grammar, and the result will be inaccurate. A slightly more advanced learner may be able to reduce the stimulus to a manageable number of chunks to fit into memory. Put somewhat differently, the effective length of the stimulus is literally subjective: dependent on subject. What is short for one is long for another. We submit that the connection between subjective length and learner proficiency and the connection between subjective length and memory capacity account for the correlation of imitation accuracy with measures of language proficiency.

Another factor affecting control level is the subject's own perception of the nature of the task. How does the subject interpret *say what I say*? Young children seem to interpret the task on the message level, accounting for their reconstructive imitations. How will a particular foreign-language learner approach a difficult imitation task? Will the learner try to produce accurately as many words as possible? Will the learner try to convey the approximate meaning? We expect that there may be a great deal of intersubject variation here, and that it may be strongly influenced by the nature of the instructions. Finally, for a given learner, the level may not even remain constant across a given stimulus set.

EXPECTED PATTERNS
AND EXPERIMENTAL RESULTS

Given our general account, what pattern of results are expected in the experimental data? First, because memory limitations are crucially involved, we expect accuracy when length is short. As length increases, accuracy will remain good until the limits of memory are approached. Then accuracy should fall rather quickly and remain low. Around the limits of memory, there should be a narrow band of sensitivity, where accuracy might be affected by details of the syntactic structure. Second, because EI is in part a recall task, we should see the range of effects associated with recall tasks, such as sensitivity of the task to serial position. Third, because effective length is a function of learner proficiency, we should see an analog to the band of sensitivity as proficiency varies. A given stimulus set will be insensitive to syntactic differences at too high a proficiency level (because performance will be at ceiling) and also insensitive at too low a level (because performance will be at the floor), and there will be a narrow range in the middle where there is a potential for variability based on specific syntactic structure. Fourth, a broad sampling of stimuli of various lengths and complexities should provide a reasonably good assessment of global proficiency. Fifth, if we are right about the optimal range of control levels for the task, imitation accuracy may often be relatively insensitive to high-level syntactic and semantic facts (binding relationships, quantifier scope, and the like), but relatively sensitive to phrase-level aspects of syntax. Remember, however, that the control level is variably set, so there may be fleeting sensitivity to facts at several levels.

Because of the lack of systematic research on the nature of EI per se, it is not possible to bring specific results to bear on whether each of these expectations is completely met. However, it does appear that the general picture in the available literature is consistent with the broad account outlined here.

Chaudron and Russell (1990) reviewed the general relationship between EI ability and global language proficiency. This relationship has been investigated in both L1 and L2 research on global language assessment (Call, 1985; Carrow, 1974; Clay, 1971; Connell & Myles-Zitzer, 1982; Dailey & Boxx, 1979; Gallimore & Tharp, 1981; Henning, 1983; Hood & Lightbown, 1978; Lee, 1974; Naiman, 1974; Newcomer & Hammill, 1977; Perkins, Brutten, & Angelis, 1986). These studies have found primarily general correlations between EI performance and various other measures of production in learners, with little precise relationship found between specific structural aspects and performance. When a large enough battery of sentence types and lengths are presented, subjects' performance can be scaled on a continuum of development. Thus, for example, Perkins et al. (1986) found an overall effect for complexity of sentences on L2 subjects' imitations, but low correlation with specific structures that were analyzed in terms of (transformational grammar-based) transformations.

If overall oral performance is partially predicted by EI batteries, it should follow that the individual items bear some relationship to language development as well. Although we think that this may be the case, the complexity of the language processing involved in EI makes such specific relationships difficult to detect. This is due in part to the characteristics of this task that involve memory constraints. We illustrate here how EI results tend to resemble the typical performance of subjects in serial recall tasks.

For comparison, we repeat here the findings of typical serial recall tasks, as illustrated in Lewandowsky and Murdock's (1989) review of the phenomenon. Figure 13.2 shows the performance of L1 subjects on a serial recall task, in which the accuracy of recall is plotted vertically on the y-axis against the number of items in the list to be recalled (4 to 11) on the x-axis. The list types that are plotted here represent series of digits, letters, or words, with letters and words specified as to whether or not they are limited to a known list. The ceiling effect is clear for the 4-item list, and the floor effect for lists of 10 or more items. More important is the result that in the middle range of list item numbers (5–9 items), the different types of items are recalled differently (this is the narrow band of sensitivity), with performance on digits (a well-known set) being superior, for instance, to performance on word lists of either limited or unlimited type. Presumably, lexical items, being from a much larger set that requires more encoding, are more difficult to retain in short-term memory than letters or digits.

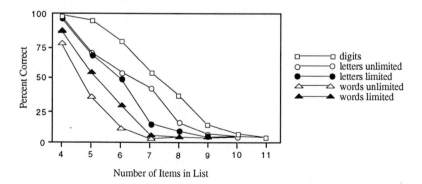

FIG. 13.2. Memory span functions for a variety of stimulus materials. Adapted from Lewandowsky and Murdock (1989).

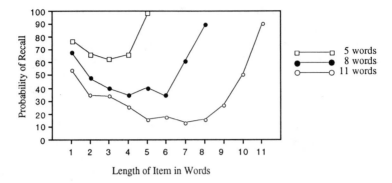

FIG. 13.3. Serial position curves for a partial report paradigm for different list lengths. Adapted from Lewandowsky and Murdock (1989).

Figure 13.3 (also from Lewandowsky & Murdock, 1989) shows a different aspect of serial recall that is important with regard to our concern about EI methodology, namely, the classic primacy and recency effects of recall of items by serial position in stimulus lists. Here it is seen that no matter how long a list, the last item is the best recalled, followed normally by the first item, unless the list is quite long. Intermediate items follow the curved plot, with the middle items being the worst recalled.

We suggest that, all other things being equal, this pattern will be evident in a word-by-word tally of accuracy of recall of EI stimuli. Only the particular processing competence of a subject at a given level of control will circumvent this pattern, and even in such cases, serial order effects should be controlled for. Such patterns are clearly seen in a study of L2 subjects' list recall by Spitze and Fischer (1981), in which lists of words organized randomly, by semantic relationships, and in scrambled and ordered sentence strings, were recalled by intermediate and advanced L2 subjects. We repeat these comparisons in Figs. 13.4 and 13.5 to show the similarity to the serial order effects.

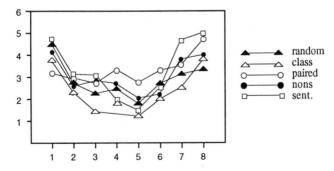

FIG. 13.4. Mean items recalled by serial position and list type, intermediate learners. Adapted from Spitze and Fischer (1987).

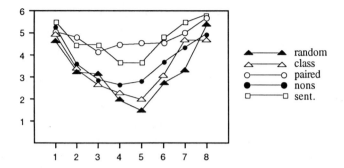

FIG. 13.5. Mean items recalled by serial position and list type, advanced learners. Adapted from Spitze and Fischer (1987).

The occurrence of ceiling and floor effects and the band of sensitivity to EI stimuli are, however, of greater concern in methodology. Flynn (1987) claimed that her finding of a difference between Japanese and Spanish ESL learners' imitation of sentences containing adverbial clauses and pronoun anaphors was a result of a differential in parameter setting. As we have noted elsewhere (see Figs. 1a–1b in Bley-Vroman & Chaudron, 1990), however, when Flynn's data are displayed fully, they reveal little beyond floor and ceiling effects. The effects are attributable to the differences in imitation ability between her two populations—differences that Flynn found to be fully independent of her target structures or (mis)matches between L1 and L2 parameters.

We see these effects in several other studies involving L1 and L2 subjects. Figure 13.6 reanalyzes the data reported in Clay (1971). When the different

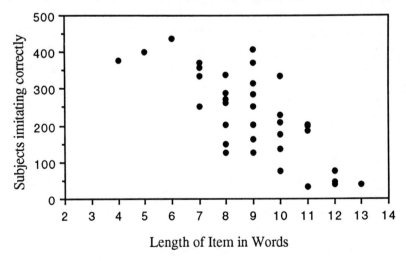

FIG. 13.6. Number of subjects repeating various sentence structures by length. Adapted from Clay (1971).

student proficiency groups (four age groups and three ethnic populations, which included one second-language ethnic group of Maori children) and different grammatical (sentence-level) structures Clay used are combined, we see the pattern of overall accuracy of recall of stimuli of differing lengths seen in Fig. 13.2. Here it is clear that below 7 words in length, and beyond 10 or 11 words, the stimuli fail to discriminate. A similar pattern of sharp decline with increasing length is seen in the plotting in Fig. 13.7 of Fouly and Cziko's (1985) discrimination indices for 14 dictation test items by the length of the items (our fitted curve is exponential).

What such results suggest is that researchers attempting to use EI to explore learners' grammars must control for length and complexity effects and their interaction. Comparisons among sentences in which structural distinctions involve serial order, length, and redundancy may interact with memory limitations and therefore will not be appropriate for investigation by means of EI.

The effects of serial position are especially important in studies of particular grammatical points, because serial position is easily confounded with grammatical function, as it was, for example, in the research of Munnich, Flynn, and Martohardjono (this volume, chapter 12). Munnich et al. were particularly interested in the contrast between relativization of subject and object and the (ungrammatical) use of resumptive pronouns, as in examples like the following:

(1) The man greeted the doctor who the actor reminded (*him).
(2) The lawyer questioned the student who (*he) answered the owner.

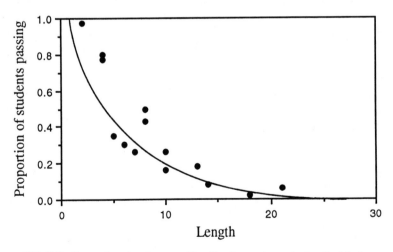

FIG. 13.7.   Proportion of students recalling dictation sentences by length. Adapted from Fouly and Cziko (1985).

In these examples, the contrast of interest (the difference between subject and object relativization) is confounded, in the ungrammatical examples, with a contrast in serial order that is likely to affect the ability to imitate such sentences.[4] The (ungrammatical) subject resumptive pronoun (*he*) in (2) is located in the middle of the sentence, whereas the (ungrammatical) object resumptive pronoun (*him*) in (1) is at the end of the sentence. Our model of EI would lead us to predict more accurate repetition of the ungrammatical resumptive pronoun in (1) than in (2). Indeed, this prediction is confirmed by the results of Munnich et al. Munnich et al., however, attribute the difference in repetition accuracy to a preference related to grammar, a preference for subject relativization.[5] However, no conclusion in terms of grammar is warranted when the same effect is predicted on serial-order grounds alone. In fact there is additional evidence from Munnich et al.'s research that their interpretation of the EI facts is in error: Strikingly divergent results were obtained in an orally administered grammaticality judgment task in which learners were actually less able to detect the error in (2) than in (1).[6]

We have thus conjectured that the optimal control level of the EI task is usually a relatively low level of syntactic analysis and that EI will often be rather insensitive to certain higher level aspects of syntax. Little can be derived from the existing literature with respect to this expectation, largely because it is so difficult to design an instrument that is sensitive to any particular

---

[4]A similar case of failure to disentangle grammatical effects from serial order effects is seen in Flynn's (1987) study of preposed and postposed adverbial clauses. There, the word *when* was more accurately repeated at the beginning of sentences than in the middle, in which case it was sometimes repeated as *and*. See Bley-Vroman and Chaudron (1990) for discussion.

[5]This is true at least in the cases in which the relative clause modifies the main clause object. Munnich et al. did not report results on relative clauses modifying main clause subjects. This obvious gap in the research should be filled. We expect that the results will not support Munnich et al.'s interpretation of the phenomenon.

[6]Munnich et al. actually claimed that the EI results and the oral grammaticality judgment results converged on a preference for subject relativization. But this so-called convergence depends on an equivocation on the word *prefer*. Munnich et al. used *prefer* in the case of EI to refer to the learners' ability to correct the error in (2), but they used *prefer* in the case of the oral judgment task to refer to the learners' inability to detect the error in (2). Although a discussion of the performance characteristics of orally presented grammaticality tasks is beyond the scope of this chapter, we note that the greater ability of the learners to notice the error in (1) than in (2) is probably related to the salience of final position. We omit here a number of other criticisms of this study and are only taking the results at face value as if they were valid. Many weaknesses make their results difficult to interpret: the small number of subjects (12), with consequently too few degrees of freedom for the comparisons they wish to make; the incomplete analysis of the $2 \times 2 \times 2 \times 2$ within-subject design (task by structure by grammaticality by modality, the modality factor being in fact at least three distinct ones nested within tasks), with individual F-tests conducted on only certain comparisons of factors and only 2-way interactions; the large standard deviations relative to means; the evidently unequal (sometimes zero) variances between cells, with consequent ceiling and floor effects. In many comparisons, only a few subjects could have contributed to the variability in the data.

grammatical point. The basic problem in interpreting all such studies is that the specific syntactic differences under investigation almost always implicate other differences that might affect imitation accuracy (raw length in words, serial order, number and interrelationship of chunks, etc.).

In the case of certain studies of pronouns and anaphora using EI (specifically those of Lust and her students; see Lust et al., 1987, for a review of representative work), the study of anaphora is related to syntactic branching direction in a way that greatly complicates interpretation of the results. In one study of reflexive binding, Merzenich (1989) did find that in an EI task learners often corrected reflexive pronouns that disagreed with their antecedents (*Jane wants Bill to scratch herself* might be repeated as *Jane wants Bill to scratch himself* or *Jane wants Bill to scratch her*). Native speakers, interestingly, only rarely made such corrections, instead repeating the deviant forms verbatim. Of course, in the case of the learners, it is unclear whether these substitutions are really corrections or merely inaccurate repetitions that happen to turn out correctly. (We also find substitutions like *Jane wants Bill to scratch him* for *Jane wants Bill to scratch himself.*) If some of these are true corrections, in our account we would propose that the learners were unable to perform the low-level analysis automatically and that they were therefore driven to a nonoptimal higher level and made these "errors."

SOME RECOMMENDATIONS

There are a number of methodological concerns that we believe are important in the investigation of EI but that have been generally neglected in research to date. We suggest more research on the processing stages of EI (perception, retention in echoic memory, parsing and analysis, and production) and more precise formulation of the theory of EI and also urge that alternative methods, such as reaction time, free production, and grammaticality judgments, be employed consistently to cross-validate EI performance on specific structures and sentence characteristics (see Masterson, Bley-Vroman, & Chaudron, 1992, for a report of a study comparing EI with reaction time and judgments).

With regard to the stimuli used in EI studies, we suggest better independent control over length and complexity factors and recommend that many samples of the target structure(s) be used, in order to avoid the "fixed effect fallacy" (cf. Clark, 1973) of eliciting too few instances of the structure, in which unknown factors such as word familiarity or even phonological features might facilitate or inhibit imitation. Within-subject variance is likely to be great in imitation, so that too few samples of each structure may be insufficient for statistical comparisons, especially given the elimination of many subjects by the limitations of floor and ceiling effects noted earlier. Finally, as is standard procedure in psychological experiments, in any large-scale administration of an EI battery of stimuli, the stimuli should be prerecorded but presented in systematically randomized order, in order to be certain that each subject's response is affected by the same factors in each stimulus, and that no other factors such as fatigue or interstimulus effects bias the results.

Although one can make certain specific recommendations even at our present state of understanding of EI, what is most urgently needed now is a systematic program of research into the process itself. Until that process is better understood, both empirically and theoretically, the specific findings of EI experiments, especially with foreign-language learners, must be interpreted with great caution.

REFERENCES

Abney, S. P. (1991). Parsing by chunks. In R. C. Berwick, S. P. Abney, & C. Tenny (Eds.), *Principle-based parsing: Computation and psycholinguistics*. Dordrecht: Kluwer Academic Publishers.

Berwick, R. C. (1991). Principles of principle-based parsing. In R. C. Berwick, S. P. Abney, & C. Tenny (Eds.), *Principle-based parsing: Computation and psycholinguistics* (pp. 1–39). Dordrecht: Kluwer Academic Publishers.

Berwick, R. C., & Weinberg, A. S. (1984). *The grammatical basis of linguistic performance: Language use and acquisition*. Cambridge, MA: MIT Press.

Birdsong, D. (1989). *Metalinguistic performance and interlinguistic competence*. Berlin: Springer-Verlag.

Bley-Vroman, R., & Chaudron, C. (1990). Second language processing of subordinate clauses and anaphora—first language and universal influences. *Language Learning, 40*, 245–285.

Bley-Vroman, R., & Masterson, D. (1989). Reaction time as a supplement to grammaticality judgments in the investigation of second language learners' competence. *University of Hawai'i Working Papers in ESL, 8*, 207–237. (To appear in *Second Language Research*)

Call, M. E. (1985). Auditory short-term memory, listening comprehension, and the input hypothesis. *TESOL Quarterly, 19*, 765–781.

Carrow, E. W. (1974). *Carrow Elicited Language Inventory*. Austin, TX: Learning Concepts.

Chaudron, C. (1983). Research on metalinguistic judgments: A review of theory, methods, and results. *Language Learning, 33*, 343–377.

Chaudron, C., & Russell, G. (1990, April). *The status of elicited imitation as a measure of second language competence*. Paper presented at the Ninth World Congress of Applied Linguistics, Thessaloniki, Greece.

Clark, H. H. (1973). The language-as-fixed-effect fallacy: A critique of language statistics in psychological research. *Journal of Verbal Learning and Verbal Behavior, 12*, 335–359.

Clay, M. M. (1971). *Sentence repetition: Elicited imitation of a controlled set of syntactic structures by four language groups*. Monographs of the Society for Research in Child Development, 36 (3, Serial No. 143).

Connel, P. J., & Myles-Zitzer, C. (1982). An analysis of elicited imitation as a language evaluation procedure. *Journal of Speech and Hearing Disorders, 47*, 390–396.

Dailey, K., & Boxx, J. R. (1979). A comparison of three imitative tests of expressive language and a spontaneous language sample. *Language, Speech and Hearing Services in Schools, 10*, 6–13.

Flynn, S. (1987). *A parameter-setting model of L2 acquisition: Experimental studies in anaphora*. Dordrecht: Reidel.

Fodor, J. A. (1983). *Modularity of mind: An essay on faculty psychology*. Cambridge, MA: MIT Press.

Forster, K. (1987). Binding, plausibility, and modularity. In J. L. Garfield (Ed.), *Modularity in knowledge representation and natural-language understanding* (pp. 63–82). Cambridge, MA: MIT Press.

Fouly, K. A., & Cziko, G. A. (1985). Determining the reliability, validity, and scalability of the graduated dictation test. *Language Learning, 35*, 555–566.

Frazier, L. (1987). Theories of sentence processing. In J. L. Garfield (Ed.), *Modularity in knowledge representation and natural-language understanding* (pp. 291–308). Cambridge, MA: MIT Press.

Freedman, S., & Forster, K. I. (1985). The psychological status of overgenerated sentences. *Cognition, 19*, 101–131.

Gallimore, R., & Tharp, R. G. (1981). The interpretation of elicited sentence imitation in a standardized context. *Language Learning, 31*, 269–392.

Garfield, J. L. (Ed.), (1987). *Modularity in knowledge representation and natural-language understanding*. Cambridge, MA: MIT Press.

Gee, J., & Grosjean, F. (1983). Performance structures: A psycholinguistic and linguistic appraisal. *Cognitive Psychology, 15*, 411–458.

Henning, G. (1983). Oral proficiency testing: Comparative validities of interview, imitation, and completion methods. *Language Learning, 33*, 315–332.

Hood, L., & Lightbown, P. M. (1978). What children do when asked "Say what I say": Does elicited imitation measure linguistic knowledge? *Allied Health and Behavioral Studies, 1*, 195–219.

Lee, L. (1974). *Developmental Sentence Analysis*. Evanston, IL: Northwestern University Press.

Levelt, W. J. M. (1989). *Speaking: From intention to articulation*. Cambridge, MA: MIT Press.

Lewandowsky, S., & Murdock, B. B., Jr. (1989). Memory for serial order. *Psychological Review, 96*, 25–57.

Lucas, M. M., Tannenhaus, M. K., & Carlson, G. N. (1990). Levels of representation in the interpretation of anaphoric reference and instrument inference. *Memory and Cognition, 18*, 611–631.

Lust, B., Chien, Y.-C., & Flynn, S. (1987). What children know: Methods for the study of first language acquisition. In B. Lust (Ed.), *Studies in the acquisition of anaphora* (Vol. II, pp. 271–356). Dordrecht: Reidel.

Masterson, D., Bley-Vroman, R., & Chaudron, C. (1992, July). *Instruments for measuring grammaticality and preference: The status of modified NPs in Korean and English*. Paper presented at the Pacific Second Language Research Forum (PACSLRF), Sydney, Australia.

Merzenich, A. (1989). *Relativity in research and the acquisition of reflexive binding*. Unpublished manuscript, University of Hawai'i, Department of ESL.

Miller, G. A. (1956). The magical number seven, plus or minus two: Some limits on our capacity for processing information. *Psychological Review, 63*, 81–97.

Munnich, E., Flynn, S., & Martahardjono, G. (1991). Elicited imitation and grammatical judgment tasks: What they measure and how they relate to each other. Paper presented at the Conference on Theory Construction and Methodology in Second Language Acquisition, Michigan State University, October 1991.

Naiman, N. (1974). The use of elicited imitation in second language acquisition research. *Working Papers in Bilingualism, 2*, 1–37.

Newcomer, P., & Hammill, D. (1977). *The Test of Language Development*. Austin, TX: Empiric Press.

Perkins, K., Brutten, S. R., & Angelis, P. J. (1986). Derivational complexity and item difficulty in a sentence repetition task. *Language Learning, 36*, 125–141.

Pritchett, B. L. (1988). Garden path phenomena and the grammatical basis of language processing. *Language, 64*, 539–576.

Slobin, D. I., & Welsh, C. A. (1973). Elicited imitation as a research tool in developmental psycholinguistics. In C. Ferguson and D. Slobin (Eds.). *Studies of Child Language Development* (pp. 485–497). New York: Holt, Rinehart, and Winston. (Reprinted from Working Paper 10, 1968, University of California, Berkeley, Language Behavior Research Laboratory)

Spitze, K., & Fischer, S. D. (1981). Short-term memory as a test of language proficiency. *TESL Talk, 12,* 32–41.

Tannenhaus, M. K., Carlson, G. N., & Seidenberg, M. S. (1985). Do listeners compute linguistic representations? In D. R. Dowty, L. Karttunen, & A. M. Zwicky (Eds.), *Natural language parsing: Psychological, computational, and theoretical perspectives* (pp. 359–408). Cambridge: Cambridge University Press.

Tannenhaus, M. K., Dell, G. S., & Carlson, G. (1987). Context effects in lexical processing: A connectionist approach to modularity. In J. L. Garfield (Ed.), *Modularity in knowledge representation and natural-language understanding* (pp. 83–108). Cambridge, MA: MIT Press.

Weinberg, A. (1987). Modularity in the syntactic processor. In J. L. Garfield (Ed.), *Modularity in knowledge representation and natural-language understanding* (pp. 259–276). Cambridge, MA: MIT Press.

CHAPTER

14

TWO HEADS MAY BE BETTER
THAN ONE: MENTAL ACTIVITY IN
SECOND-LANGUAGE
GRAMMATICALITY JUDGMENTS

Nancy Goss
Zhang Ying-Hua
University of Delaware

James P. Lantolf
Cornell University

As with theoretical linguistic research, a primary data source for Universal Grammar (UG)-based studies of second-language acquisition (SLA) is often found in learners' assessments of the grammaticality status of sentences in the target language.[1] Some researchers, however, have questioned whether judgmental evidence should be accorded the same ontological status in L2 research that it enjoys in theoretical research (e.g., Christie & Lantolf, 1992; Ellis, 1990, 1991; Sorace, 1988).[2] Fundamentally, the issue is to determine the basis on which L2 learners render judgments of test sentences. Do learners access abstract grammatical knowledge or do they rely on some other knowledge source, such as memory of what someone (e.g., a language teacher) has told them, memory of what they think someone has told them, their own folk knowledge, or L1 equivalents, when carrying out such tasks? Until the validity issue is resolved, it will be difficult to have confidence in the claims of L2 research predicated on judgment data. This chapter is intended as a contribution to the resolution of this problem.

---

[1]Although our focus in this chapter is on grammaticality judgments, we believe that alternatives such as preference judgments confront similar uncertainties.

[2]The debate on the status of grammaticality intuitions has a long and tumultuous history within linguistic and experimental psycholinguistic research. We suspect that the issue will never be settled to the satisfaction of all interested parties. See, for example, Garman (1990) for a brief but insightful history of the debate.

Several researchers have already addressed the question of the reliability of L2 grammaticality judgments. Beretta and Gass (1991), Ellis (1990), Gass (this volume, chapter 16), and Gass and Beretta (1991) have addressed the reliability issue using a test–retest procedure. These studies have produced somewhat conflicting results, with Ellis showing judgments to be inconsistent over time, and Gass and Beretta reporting a considerable degree of consistency in learner judgments.

Although it is important to determine the reliability of learner judgments, it is, perhaps, more important to answer the validity question. Even if learner judgments are consistent, we need to be certain that these judgments are predicated on abstract linguistic principles rather than on factors such as those mentioned earlier. Dreyfus and Dreyfus (1986), for example, found that novice, advanced beginning and even competent performers rely almost exclusively on learned rules and decision procedures imparted by someone else when carrying out such cognitive tasks as interpreting x-ray photographs of patients and airplane instrument panels. Experts, on the other hand, depend not on calculative and deliberative problem solving but on critical intuitive reflection:

> *When things are proceeding normally, experts don't solve problems and don't make decisions; they do what normally works.* Expert air traffic controllers don't experience themselves as seeing blips on a screen and deducing what must be going on in the sky. They 'see' planes in the sky when they look at their screens, and they respond to what they see, not by rules but as experience has taught them. (Dreyfus & Dreyfus, 1986, pp. 30–31)

It is precisely the intuitive knowledge exhibited by experts that grammaticality judgments are assumed to tap. Ellis (1991), using introspective techniques (to be discussed) provides some evidence that fairly advanced ESL speakers (his subjects had studied English for a minimum of 4 years and had been residing in England between 6 months and somewhat over 4 years) appear to render judgments on the grammatical status of sentences in their second language on the basis of genuine linguistic intuitions. Whether similar evidence can be uncovered for less advanced foreign-language learners with virtually no extraclassroom experience in the target language is the focus of the present study.

INTROSPECTION AND THE SOLIPSISTIC MIND

Psychologists, cognitive scientists, and, more recently, L2 researchers have attempted to access mental behavior through the use of introspection, or think-aloud techniques, in which subjects are instructed to verbalize their intramental activity as they complete specific cognitive tasks. Ellis (1990, 1991), as we have already pointed out, used introspection in his study of the grammaticality judgments of ESL speakers.

Some researchers have long been critical of introspective techniques. Although we cannot do justice here to the ongoing debate on the pros and cons of introspection, we would like to mention some of the more interesting objections that have been raised against it.[3] One problem, pointed out by Dreyfus and Dreyfus (1986), is that when experts are asked to introspect on their mental activity, they report not on the actual procedures they follow but on what they recall of their performance as novices or competent performers of the activity (i.e., following learned and sequentially arranged algorithms). Lyons (1986) claimed that when humans introspect, rather than providing privileged access to mental operations, they externalize a culturally stereotyped *folk psychological* account of cognitive life.

Vygotsky (1979, p. 27), in his criticism of the Wurzberg School of psychology and its reliance on introspection, argued that "consciousness cannot focus on itself." For Vygotsky, this meant that in the conduct of a mental task, it is difficult, if not impossible, for people to function at the metacognitive and cognitive levels simultaneously, without distorting one or the other process.[4] In other words, when humans are asked to attend to two psychological goals at the same time (that is, solve a mental problem and report on the solving of the problem), either the solving of the problem or the reporting of the solution is likely to break down.

In think-aloud tasks, subjects are asked to deploy language as a symbolic tool to solve a problem, a normal function of language, while at the same time using language to report on this normal function, not a typical use of language. To overcome this difficulty, researchers working within the introspective tradition are careful to train their subjects before a think-aloud task. Yet, even in these cases, breakdowns and gaps in reporting are not uncommon. In two think-aloud experiments reported on in Ericsson and Simon (1984), it was found that in a text recall task, subjects ceased to think aloud at precisely those points at which the task became difficult, thus obfuscating critical aspects of their problem-solving strategy.[5]

---

[3]For fuller discussion of introspection-based L2 research see, for example, Faerch and Kasper (1987). For a review of the general debate see, among others, Ericsson and Simon (1984) and Lyons (1986).

[4]It is interesting to note that Searle (1992), writing several decades after Vygotsky's original work, leveled similar criticisms against introspectionism.

[5]In her study of the translation process, Matrat (1991) reported that in think-aloud tasks, expert translators likewise failed to externalize their processing strategies and frequently produced only the target language translation rather than the route through which they arrived at the translation.

In what follows, we propose to address the validity of learner grammaticality judgments through use of a technique for accessing mental behavior that seeks to overcome the problem of bifurcated attention. The procedure that we want to explore here takes account of the fact that the human mind is not individually constituted but is socioculturally derived and therefore recognizes that the talk spontaneously generated by individuals in collaborative problem-solving situations offers a window into intramental processing.

SOCIOCULTURAL THEORY OF MIND AND JOINT ACTIVITY

Although we cannot present here, in full form, the theoretical underpinnings of the sociocultural (alternatively, sociohistorical) view of mind, we can, nevertheless, sketch out some of the relevant claims of this theory of human cognitive development and functioning. Wertsch (1991) remarked that American psychology (we include American psycholinguistics as well) insists on investigating "human mental functioning as if it exists in a cultural, institutional, and historical vacuum" and often bases its research "on the assumption that it is possible, even desirable, to study the individual, or specific areas of mental functioning in the individual in isolation" (p. 3). A sociocultural theory of mind, on the other hand, "emphasizes the productive intrusion of other people and cultural tools" (Newman, Griffin, & Cole, 1989, p. 68) in the formation of individual minds. For Vygotsky the social dimension of mind is "primary in time and in fact," whereas the individual dimension is "derivative and secondary" (1979, p. 4).

The individual dimension is constituted by and large through semiotic means, principally in the form of linguistic discourse.[6] Because certain aspects of human mental behavior are fundamentally linked to discursive processes, even mental action carried out by the individual in isolation is viewed as inherently social. Sheldon White stated in the forward to Newman et al. (1989) that attempts to differentiate individuals from groups, as was done in American experimental social psychology, for instance, create a false dichotomy. As Schrag (1986) eloquently put it, "no 'I' is an island, entire of itself: every subject is a piece of the continent of other subjects, a part of the main of intersubjectivity" (p. 125).

Thus, for sociocultural theory, mind is a phenomenon that "extends beyond the skin," in that it is often socially distributed and intimately linked

---

[6]Schrag (1986) argued that in addition to linguistic means, humans are also constituted by culturally sanctioned actions, such as schooling, play, and work.

to mediation. Thus mind "can appropriately be predicated of dyads and larger groups as well as individuals" (Wertsch, 1991, p. 14).[7] Because, in a sociocultural theory of mind, intramental and intermental functioning are mediationally linked, it can reasonably be argued that mediational devices, such as computers, number systems, and especially language, are "windows into the evolution and appearance of cognitive constructs" (Newman et al., 1989, p. 72).[8]

What we propose, then, is to take advantage of the distributed nature of mind (that is, mind as intermental activity) in order to explore the possibility of gaining fuller access to the cognitive processing that underlies L2 grammaticality judgments than has been possible from think-aloud research. Dyadic problem solving provides a potentially broader window into mental activity than think-aloud tasks, because the procedure generates more (collaborative) talk from subjects than is usually the case in introspective reports. In fact, from the sociocultural perspective, introspection loses its solipsistic quality and is paired with dyadic discourse as the other side of the same methodological coin.[9]

Furthermore, using the collaborative format minimizes the previously mentioned "simultaneous goal" problem that has frequently surfaced in the criticism of introspective techniques. In joint configurations, subjects use language analogously to the way they use it on an everyday basis in the real world. That is, they have a single goal, the solving of a problem, in this case one posed by a grammaticality judgment task, only they solve it through dialogic interaction with another person. We thus obviate the need for the special training required in the think-aloud technique.

THE PRESENT STUDY

The study reported on here represents the initial attempt to evaluate joint problem-solving methodology as a means of accessing the cognitive strategies deployed by L2 learners in responding to grammaticality questions involving UG effects.

---

[7]Any similarity between the notion of "mind as distributed" and the concept of "collective consciousness" discounted by social psychology is only superficial. For a full discussion of this issue, see Wertsch (1991) and Newman et al. (1989).

[8]Sociocultural theory does not discount the likelihood that certain aspects of mental functioning are constructed on the basis of innately specified principles, whether they be Piagetian or Chomskyan in nature. It does, however, maintain that mind cannot be understood solely on the basis of these principles, because, as Vygotsky showed, biological structures ultimately confront sociohistorical forces, under the impact of which they mature.

[9]For an extensive comparison of introspective and collaborative techniques in applied psycholinguistic research, see Howard (1991) and Matrat (1991).

Subjects

A total of 52 university students participated in the study. Of these, 34 were enrolled in a Spanish-as-a-foreign-language program—19 in a third-semester elementary course and 15 in a seventh-semester advanced conversation class. The remaining 18 students were undergraduate native speakers of English enrolled in either an introductory linguistics course or a freshman writing course. Of the total, 37 subjects responded to a grammaticality judgment instrument on an individual basis—10 from the advanced Spanish group, 15 from elementary Spanish, and 12 from the introductory linguistics course. The remaining 15 students responded to the survey in a dyadic or triadic format. Specifically, two dyads were drawn from elementary Spanish, one triad and one dyad were taken from advanced Spanish, and two dyads of native English speakers were drawn from the freshman composition course. Subjects participated in either the individual or the joint format (see Table 14.1).[10]

Given that sociocultural theory establishes a necessary link between individual and distributed mind, we would not expect to find substantial differences in the judgments rendered, between the individual and joint performance modes on the grammaticality task. Thus, it is essential to compare subject performance on the two formats in order to determine if there are any marked differences. If we were to find clear differences across formats within a given population, this would weaken the claim that joint activity can give us insight into the processes through which L2 learners arrive at grammaticality judgments for sentences in the second language. Of course, one might find some variation between individual and collaborative judgments, with the latter group scoring somewhat more accurately; after all, collaboration does often result in improved performance. The point we want to make clear, however, is that the discourse produced in the joint format not only informs us about how learners respond to judgment tasks collectively but also represents what is going on in the mind of individual learners from the same population when they respond to the same task in the individual format. Furthermore, in the joint format, the discourse generated by the dyad or triad taken as a whole is the proper unit of analysis and not the performance of any given individual participating in the format.

---

[10]Some might question why we did not use native speakers of Spanish rather than English-speaking natives as our comparison group. Because the native Spanish speakers available were, in fact, bilinguals who had either received instruction in English or were themselves teachers of Spanish, we felt it more appropriate to use linguistically naive monolinguals, even if this meant the languages compared were different. The study should be repeated with monolingual Spanish speakers.

TABLE 14.1
Distribution of Subjects

| | Format | | |
	Individual	Joint	Total
Elementary Spanish	15	2 × 2	19
Advanced Spanish	10	1 × 3	
		1 × 2	15
Native Speakers of English	12	2× 3	18
Totals	37	15	52

Task

All subjects were asked to respond to a grammaticality judgment survey in either a group or an individual format. The Spanish survey consisted of 43 sentences relating to properties assumed to cluster under the Null Subject Parameter (NSP). To our knowledge, although the status of the NSP continues to be debated in the theoretical literature, the null-subject feature itself and subject-verb inversion are still considered properties related to the parameter. Auxiliary (AUX) analysis, as proposed by Hyams (1986), and *that*-trace effects have a much more dubious link to the NSP. Be that as it may, the features on which we focus in the study represent properties relating to UG, "even though the precise analysis of some of the constructions is still a matter of considerable debate" (Felix & Weigl, 1991, p. 167). Furthermore, because our concern is with issues relating to research methodology rather than theory construction, the ultimate analysis of the NSP properties by linguistic theory will not radically alter the point of our study. This said, we concern ourselves here with the null subject and word order properties only.

In all, 17 items tested the *pro*-drop property; 9 assessed subject-verb word order (2 of these were responses to *wh*-questions, 4 contained ergative verbs, 2 contained nonergative verbs, and one was a *yes/no* question); 3 tested expletive constructions. For each item, three possible responses were provided—Grammatical, Ungrammatical, and Not Sure. In the case of ungrammatical responses, subjects were asked to indicate where they perceived the error to be and to correct it. The Spanish survey is given in Appendix A.

The English survey given to the native-speaking group comprised 15 sentences borrowed from the grammaticality judgment task developed by Bley-Vroman, Felix, and Ioup (1988). The sentences tested the Empty Category

Principle (ECP) and the Subjacency constraint.[11] 5 of these sentences were clearly grammatical, 5 were clearly ungrammatical, and 5 were questionable as to their grammatical status. We did not administer an English version of an NSP questionnaire, because the relevant NSP examples are clearly ungrammatical in English, and consequently, we felt that there would be little reason for the subjects responding in the joint format to talk to each other. As it turned out, neither the questionable ECP and Subjacency violations nor the long *wh*-movement items stimulated much talk from the NS triads. At the appropriate point in the data analysis, we present what we believe to be a reasonable explanation for such a response pattern. As with the Spanish survey, subjects were given three options for each item and were asked to correct sentences judged to be ungrammatical. The English survey is given in Appendix B.

Methodology

As we said earlier, the questionnaires were distributed to the subjects in either the individual or the joint format. In the individual format, the survey was administered in class by one of the researchers. The English questionnaire was given to the introductory linguistics students early in the semester. Thus we avoided instructional effects, because the class was studying phonology at the time and had not yet dealt with syntax. For the joint format, one copy of the appropriate questionnaire was given to each dyad. This was done to ensure that all participants would contribute to the response pattern and to lessen the possibility that any member of a particular dyad might choose to respond individually rather than as a dyad member.[12]

Despite this safeguard, not all participants contributed equally to each decision reached by the dyad. We hasten to point out, however, that we did not expect, nor was it necessary, for dyad members to be equal participants. What mattered in the joint format was that a collaborative response (that

---

[11]The ECP and the Subjacency constraint are related to movement of noun phrases and *wh*-elements. Specifically, the ECP requires that a trace (*t*) resulting from a moved NP or *wh*-word be properly governed (i.e., governed by a lexical category). If the *t* is not properly governed, an ungrammatical sentence results. The Subjacency constraint is a condition on distance of movement and stipulates that a moved element may not cross more than a single bounding node, or barrier, on any given movement cycle. Languages differ with respect to bounding nodes, which are thought to be parameterized. In English, NP and IP are the relevant nodes for movement, whereas in Spanish, NP and CP constitute the relevant nodes. For further discussion, see Haegeman (1991).

[12]We observed in earlier research on math problem-solving behaviors that distributing surveys to all members of a dyad occasionally resulted in subjects solving the problem individually and coming together to check and evaluate their answers. By giving only one set of problems to a dyad, this type of behavior was eliminated.

is, the response patterns and the processing strategies that led the dyad to its decision) were seen as representative of the behavioral patterns of the population from which the dyad was drawn. The contribution of a given individual member of the dyad was immaterial.

Each dyad received the same set of written instructions provided in the individual format. An audio tape recorder was then set in the record mode and the dyad was left alone. No time limit was enforced in either format. The average completion time for respondents in both the individual and the joint formats for the Spanish survey was approximately 25 minutes. In the case of the English questionnaire, the average completion time in both formats was about 10 minutes. We do not want to make too much of the time difference, because it was not the primary focus of our study. We believe, nevertheless, that the time differential was a consequence not only of the obvious difference in length between the questionnaires but also (as becomes clear in our analysis of the joint protocols) of the kind of cognitive processing exhibited by the L1 and L2 subjects.

Hypotheses

If we are to have any degree of confidence that the talk that emerges during joint problem solving provides evidence of underlying cognitive activity, it is necessary to ascertain whether the response patterns for individuals and dyads from each of the three populations are similar or different. Given the sociocultural perspective from which we are operating, we hypothesized that there would be no radical difference in response patterns between individuals and dyads within a given population. Moreover, we also expected that the error detection and correction patterns between the individual and the joint formats would not be markedly different.

If a correspondence is established between individual and joint response behaviors in terms of correction patterns, we can then proceed to analyze the discourse produced by the different groups in order to gain access to the strategies deployed by members of the corresponding population. Here, however, we need some criterion to differentiate between talk that reveals evidence of judgments based on genuine linguistic intuitions and talk that points to some other source, such as memorized rules or L1 translations, underlying the judgments. This is not an easy task. At the moment we believe that talk that cites rules, pedagogical or otherwise and accurate or not, the source of which may be an instructor or textbook, or that involves translations into the native language, is indicative of judgments based on something other than real linguistic intuitions. An idealized metarule for Spanish would be something like *Use the preterite tense when the sentence contains a temporal adverb.* On the other hand, talk characterized by the absence of rules, by remarks like *It sounds right*, or a difficulty on the part of respondents in putting what they know into words, we construe as evidence that abstract linguistic competence of some type underlies the judgments (see Dreyfus & Dreyfus, 1986 for discussion of the differences between rule following and expert performance).

For ease of discussion, we will refer to the format of nonindividual responses as either joint or dyadic, even though in some cases a triad was involved. As we anticipated, there were no differences in the response patterns between dyads and triads. Also, rather than referring to the relevant items according to the number scheme used in the original questionnaires, we number the relevant example sentences consecutively as our analysis proceeds.

Results

Descriptive Statistics

In Tables 14.2–4, we present the descriptive statistics for the individual and joint responses to the grammaticality survey for all groups participating in the study. Given the disparity between the numbers of individual subjects and groups, we did not carry out statistical analyses of the data. Neverthe-

TABLE 14.2
Response Patterns of Elementary Spanish Subjects

	NS	EX	WO	Total
Individuals (*n* = 15)				
Possible responses	255	45	135	435
CR	184	28	36	248
	72%	62%	27%	57%
IR	46	11	73	130
	18%	24%	54%	30%
Not Sure	25	6	26	57
	10%	13%	19%	13%
Joint (2 × 2)				
Possible responses	34	6	18	58
CR	26	5	5	36
	77%	83%	28%	62%
IR	7	1	11	19
	20%	17%	61%	33%
Not Sure	1	0	2	3
	3%	—	11%	5%

Note. NS = Null Subject, EX = Expletives, WO = Word Order, CR = Correct Response, IR = Incorrect Response.

TABLE 14.3
Response Patterns of Advanced Spanish Subjects

	EX	WO	NS	Total
Individuals (n = 10)				
Possible responses	30	90	170	290
CR	26	73	129	228
	87%	81%	76%	79%
IR	3	11	36	50
	10%	12%	21%	17%
Not Sure	1	6	5	12
	3%	7%	3%	4%
Joint (1 × 2, 1 × 3)				
Possible Responses	6	18	34	58
CR	6	16	26	48
	100%	90%	77%	83%
IR	0	2	6	8
	—	10%	18%	14%
Not Sure	0	0	2	2
	—	—	5%	3%

Note. EX = Expletives, WO = Word Order, NS = Null Subject.

TABLE 14.4
Response Patterns of English Language Subjects

	SUB	ECP	LM	Total
Individuals (n = 12)				
Possible responses	60	60	60	180
CR	58	39	30	127
	97%	65%	50%	71%
IR	1	16	15	32
	2%	27%	25%	18%
Not Sure	1	5	15	21
	2%	8%	25%	12%
Joint (2 × 3)				
Possible responses	10	10	10	30
CR	9	7	5	21
	90%	70%	50%	70%
IR	0	2	5	7
	—	20%	50%	23%
Not Sure	1	1	0	2
	10%	10%	—	7%

Note. SUB = Subjacency, ECP = Empty Category Principle, LM = Long Movement of *wh*-word, CR = Correct Response, IR = Incorrect Response.

less, the descriptive statistics reveal considerable similarity in responses between the individuals and the dyads at all three levels. In each case, the frequency and percentage of responses that correctly (CR) or incorrectly (IR) assess the status of a sentence are given. The frequency and percentage of Not Sure responses are also given. Tables 14.2 and 14.3 present results from the elementary and advanced Spanish subjects, respectively, and Table 14.4 presents the findings from the English-language subjects.

The descriptive statistics presented in Tables 14.2–4 display a considerable degree of similarity between the individual and joint responses. The accuracy of responses for the Spanish students in both the individual and the joint formats shows a similar pattern of improvement from the elementary to the advanced level. Except for a rather modest difference in the relative status of expletive and referential pronouns among the elementary subjects (Table 14.2), the response frequencies are quite similar across both formats. Particularly noteworthy here is the fact that the Spanish subjects in both formats showed remarkable improvement in their assessment of the grammatical status of the word order property from the elementary to the advanced level. At the elementary level, word order was correctly judged in approximately 28% of the cases in both formats, whereas at the advanced level, the subjects' accuracy increased in over 80% of the cases. Also of interest is the fact that the frequency of Not Sure responses declined considerably across levels for the Spanish respondents in both formats. As for the English-language students, we observe similar patterns across both formats. The only difference between the formats occurred in the case of long *wh*-movement. Here, the individuals divided their responses equally between CR and IR, and although the joint respondents concurred on the CR rating, they differed with respect to the IR and NS options.

Correction Profiles

Looking at the correction patterns manifested by the respondents, we observed a close parallel between the two formats in the erroneous assessment of grammatical sentences. Thus, for example, among the elementary Spanish students, the grammatical sentence (1) was ruled out on the basis of what was perceived to be incorrect word order by the two dyads and by 10 of the 15 individual respondents. Of the remaining 5 individuals, one ruled it out because of a perceived problem with the complementizer *que*, and 3 assessed it as ungrammatical for reasons that are not clear.

(1) Marta dice que vienen ellos en dos dias.
    "Martha says that they are coming in two days."

In only two instances across the three populations did we find disagreement between the individual and the dyadic correction patterns. To give one example, among the elementary Spanish subjects item (2) was judged by one of two dyads to be ungrammatical for morphological reasons, and not because it contains an overt pronoun in the position that in English requires the expletive *it*. No individual respondent ruled the sentence out for morphological reasons.

(2) *En Canadá, lo nieva mucho en invierno.
    "In Canada, it snows a lot in the winter."

Among the native English speakers, the joint and the individual respondents consistently concurred in their correction patterns. The grammatically correct sentence (3), for example, was assessed as ungrammatical by both dyads, who corrected the sentence by deleting *it*. Of the four individuals who judged the sentence as ungrammatical, all likewise eliminated the expletive pronoun.

(3) What kind of book is it necessary to read?
    Correction: *What kind of book is necessary to read?

Analysis of Dyadic Judgments

The evidence considered in the preceding sections gives us a fair degree of confidence that the dyadic response format did not radically alter the judgments of the subjects. Thus, we assume that our first hypothesis is tenable and move on to examine the evidence obtained from the joint protocols regarding the strategic processing deployed in reaching a grammaticality decision.

Native Protocols. We begin our analysis with a joint protocol of three subjects drawn from the English writing class. It is representative of all of the protocols generated by the English language dyads, and in the interest of space, we include only one protocol from this population. The sentence under consideration, (4), involves an ECP violation.

(4) *What did John say that would fall on the floor if we're not careful?

I. Joint protocol of three English composition students
   1. A: What did John say that would fall on the floor if we're not careful?
   2. B: Grammatical.
   3. C: Ungrammatical.
   4. A: Sounds ungrammatical.
   5. B: No, what did John say would, take out the that. What did John say would fall on the floor if we're not careful?
   6. A: Yeah, ungrammatical.

In Protocol I, A begins by reading the sentence aloud. B immediately assesses the sentence as grammatical. C contradicts B's judgment and A concurs with the contradiction, critically employing the word *sounds*, which we interpret as expressing an intuitive feel for the ungrammatical status of the sentence. B then amends his original judgment with a *No* that refers not to A's judgment but to B's own initial statement. He proceeds to demonstrate that by deleting the complementizer *that* the sentence can be rendered grammatical, thereby showing a degree of metalinguistic sophistication.

The relevant feature of the protocol is that the grammatical status of the sentence is assessed primarily on the basis of how the sentence sounds upon reading it aloud. The sentence is then corrected by means of a repetition-based strategy. Talk of deleting the complementizer in order to correct the sentence shows evidence of metalinguistic awareness, which could be interpreted as the externalization of a rule. Nevertheless, even in this case, it seems to us that in line (5) B is still assessing the sentence on the basis of how it sounds upon repetition.

The type of response pattern exhibited in Protocol I was consistent across all of the joint protocols produced by the native speakers, although not all protocols reflected an attempt to correct ungrammatical sentences. As we will observe in the L2 protocols, especially at the lower levels, a preferred strategy for dealing with the sentences is translation to the L1. A second strategy is to externalize some type of rule, which often has a pedagogical ring to it. In some cases, however, and especially with regard to the null-subject property, learners do appear to rely on how a given sentence sounds.

Elementary Spanish Protocols.   Consider Protocol II, produced by one of the two elementary Spanish dyads. The sentence under discussion is given in (5) and involves a grammatical verb-subject (VS) word order in an ergative construction.

(5) Llegan nuestros amigos a las ocho.
     Arrive our friends at the eight
     'Our friends arrive at eight o'clock.'

II. Joint protocol of two elementary Spanish subjects
    1. A: Llegan nuestros amigos a las ocho. That's definitely wrong.
       Wait.
    2. B: They arrive we and then.
    3. A: What's we? There's no we. Nuestros is . . .
    4. B: They arrive.
    5. A: Our friends, nuestros amigos.
    6. B: Our friends are arriving at eight.
    7. A: That would be in a question. That's a question. Like it has
       to be nuestros amigos llegan a las ocho. So, this is wrong.

    8. B: Yeah, cause it's a statement.
    9. A: Right.
    10. B: So, it's wrong.

In Protocol II the sentence is initially rejected out of hand. The learners then proceed to analyze it in terms of some English equivalent, which initially (line 2) is rendered incorrectly. Eventually they formulate an acceptable English equivalent of the sentence in line 6. At this point, however, they remember that the rule for *yes/no* question formation in Spanish requires inversion. This leads them to reject the sentence, because they accurately recognize it as a statement (line 8). Thus, the subjects reach their decision on the basis of the interplay of English and their metaknowledge of Spanish, rather than on the basis of how the sentence feels or sounds.

Next, we examine the response of the elementary Spanish students to the grammatical null-subject sentence given in (6).

(6) No hablo español con mis amigos.
    '(I) don't speak Spanish with my friends.'

III. Joint protocol of two elementary Spanish subjects
    1. A: No hablo español con mis amigos.
    2. B: Second one is right.
    3. A: Second one is right.

In III, the subjects repeat the sentence and immediately recognize it as grammatical. They do not translate the sentence, nor do they externalize a rule. Thus, it would appear that their judgment, in this case, is based on how the sentence sounds. From this kind of evidence, we conclude that for certain phenomena of the target language, in this case null subjects in simple sentences, even elementary students can behave as experts—native speakers—and respond on the basis of feel.

The situation is quite different, however, when we look at the final elementary protocol to be examined, in which the subjects assess the status of sentence (7), exhibiting a violation of proper government of a subject in an embedded tensed clause.

(7) *Pensamos que nosotros tenemos mucho dinero.
    '(We) think that we have a lot of money.'

IV. Joint protocol of two elementary Spanish subjects
    1. A: We think that we have much money.
    2. B: We think that . . . You don't need a que.
       Pensamos . . . oh . . . Wait . . . we think that we have enough. I'm glad somebody does. I don't understand that. I don't think that's wrong.

3. A: Pensamos que nosotros tenemos mucho dinero.
4. B: We think . . . We think that . . . We think . . .
5. A: There's no reason for the nosotros to be there.
6. B: Well, that doesn't matter. Tenemos que . . . tenemos que . . .
      Tenemos . . . That's wrong. I think it's wrong. You think it's right?
7. A: Yeah.
8. B: Okay, I think it's wrong.
9. Okay.

A begins protocol IV by translating the sentence into English, the principal, although not the only, strategy deployed in reaching a judgment on the sentence. Of course, as in most cases, the quality of the translation is, in itself, a problem. B first decides in line 2 that *que* is not needed in the Spanish sentence, but he appears to reach this decision on the basis of his partial repetition of the English translation of the sentence. Notice that in line 4 the same subject repeats the English segment with and without the complementizer. After trying it out in English, he deploys the same repetition strategy in Spanish (line 6), but with *tenemos que*, instead of the original *pensamos*. The construction is the Spanish equivalent of *have to*, as in an obligation, and most probably reflects interference from a pattern frequently practiced in Spanish language classrooms. Further on in line 2, B provides an alternative, though less adequate, equivalent (*enough*) for Spanish *mucho*. The alternative term permits a better sounding English translation (*We think that we have enough money*), and in fact, in the final utterance of line 2, B judges the sentence to be grammatical.

A repeats the sentence in Spanish (line 3) and actually hits upon the correct assessment of the sentence (line 5); yet in line 7 he states his belief that the sentence is correct. B, as a result of his repetitions focusing on the complementizer, arrives at the correct judgment, but for the wrong reasons. We believe this protocol, when taken together with Protocol III, is especially revealing. The almost cavalier rejection of the correct solution to the problem suggests that students, at this level at least, have a rule or heuristic procedure for optional subject deletion that makes no use of hierarchical structure.

Advanced Spanish Protocols.   The advanced Spanish dyads, much like their elementary counterparts, rely on metaknowledge, translation, and memory. We did observe a slight tendency for this population to rely somewhat more frequently on feel than did the elementary students.

We begin with an illustration of the feel strategy in Protocol V in which the subjects consider the grammatical null-subject sentence (6).

V. Joint protocol of two advanced Spanish students
1. A: No hablo español con mis amigos. Sounds good to me.
2. B: So it's grammatical.

The exchange in Protocol V is succinct. The sentence is not translated, nor do the subjects attempt to analyze its status. They make their decision solely on the basis of how the sentence sounds, just as did the elementary subjects for the same sentence.

Looking now at the complex sentence given in (7) and addressed in Protocol IV by the elementary students, we note that the advanced students rely to some degree on feel and on what could be construed as the reflection of a classroom-inspired rule, in incorrectly assessing its grammaticality status. Unlike the elementary students, however, the advanced students recognize precisely what is at issue in the sentence.

VI. Joint protocol of advanced Spanish students
1. A: Pensamos que nosotros tenemos mucho dinero.
2. B: We think that we have a lot of money.
3. A: That doesn't sound bad to me, does it? I mean . . .
4. B: I guess not.
5. A: Pensamos que nosotros tenemos mucho dinero. You don't really need the nosotros in there.
6. B: Yeah.
7. A: You might as well take it out of the sentence. Cause it's said with all the other mos's [*reference to first-person plural verb ending*], but other than that, it doesn't, don't you think?
8. B: I guess it's all right.

The subjects begin by translating the sentence into English (line 2). Interestingly, however, their translation of *mucho* as "a lot of" is more appropriate than that of the elementary students in Protocol IV.[13] They then make an assessment based on how the sentence sounds (line 3). However, in line 5 the sentence is also repeated in its Spanish version, at which point an apparent redundancy of the overt pronoun in the embedded clause is recognized. From the remarks in line 7, it seems that, much like the elementary students,

---

[13]The difference in quality of translation between the elementary and advanced students is in itself quite interesting. Although both groups are presumably equally proficient in their L1, the advanced students are able to formulate a more acceptable equivalent of an L2 sentence in their native language than are the beginning students. We cannot pursue the issue further here and we refer the reader to Lantolf, Labarca, and den Tuinder (1985), which examines the difference in greater detail.

the advanced subjects are considering a surface string rather than a hierarchically organized structure with respect to which the presence of *nosotros* entails a violation of proper government. That is, if they had felt the sentence to involve a proper government violation, they probably would not have said what they did in line 7. They seem to think that, given the co-occurring verbs, the embedded subject is *optionally* expressible, which would in most cases be a correct assessment. In this case, however, the option is not available. Consequently, they erroneously judge the sentence to be grammatical.

As for word order, illustrated in example (5) and already considered in Protocol II, the advanced students use a combination of translation, metaknowledge, and feel in arriving at the correct assessment.

VII. Joint protocol of two advanced Spanish Subjects
1. A: Llegan nuestros amigos a las ocho.
2. B: Inaudible whispering
3. A: Our friends arrive at eight.
4. B: That's the thing with the people in the middle of what's going on, isn't it? Nuestros amigos llegan a las ocho.
5. A: I think you can put it there because, cause it's . . . a las ocho is a preposition so you can just get rid of it. So nuestros amigos llegan, llegan nuestros amigos, it's all the same. I don't think it loses anything when you add on a las ocho.
6. B: Okay. So we put that one right?
7. A: Yeah, we think it's right.

In line 3, the subjects have no difficulty rendering an acceptable English equivalent of the Spanish sentence. The remarks in lines 4 and 5 are somewhat opaque. However, because of the discussion of an earlier sentence by the same dyad, we believe that initially the subjects consider the sentence to exhibit an adjacency violation. That is, at first, they erroneously construe *a las ocho* to be a direct object. If that were indeed the case, they could at least entertain the possibility that the sentence is ungrammatical by assuming that the strict adjacency property of English also holds in Spanish. This would explain the reordering observed in line 4. They quickly realize, however, that *a las ocho* is a prepositional phrase and reach their final decision on the sentence by repeating it with both word order options, presumably judging the sentence on how it feels.

Finally, we consider an advanced protocol relating to a sentence that was designed to test the null-subject property but instead gave rise to a particularly revealing discussion of mood. We present the protocol because it illustrates clearly the strategic effects of classroom learning on the grammaticality judgments of language learners. The sentence in question is (8).

(8) El cree que jugamos mucho.
    'He believes that (we) play a lot.'

VIII. Joint protocol of two advanced Spanish subjects
    1. A: El cree que jugamos mucho.
    2. B: He believes . . . are you sure? Cause all these have ques in
          them. Maybe it's . . . he believes that we play a lot. I don't
          see anything wrong with this.
    3. A: El cree que jugamos mucho. Jugamos . . . there's a change
          of subject, there's doubt and cree is a subjunctive.
    4. B: Yeah with creer.
    5. A: So, cause he believes. There's a doubt.
    6. B: My teacher always said, there's no doubt he believes. Third
          year.
    7. A: So shall we say not sure?
    8. B: Yeah.

The null subject in the embedded tensed clause is not even considered
at issue. The dyad immediately focuses attention on the possibility that the
embedded verb ought to be expressed not in the indicative mood, as it correctly is, but in the subjunctive. The apparent trigger for the ensuing discussion is the matrix verb *cree* and the change of subject (line 3). Students are
traditionally instructed that subjunctive is required in embedded tensed clauses
in Spanish if the matrix verb expresses doubt and if there is an accompany-
ing change of subject. The problem is that *creer* 'to believe' is not among
the verbs expressing doubt—a fact that most students have a difficult time
accepting (line 5). However, the teacher in A's third year of language study
(it isn't clear whether this is secondary school or university), apparently provided a mnemonic device for helping students remember that *creer* usually does
not co-occur with the subjunctive mood, at least not in declarative constructions (line 6). The final decision reached by the subjects, in this case Not Sure,
is not relevant to our discussion. What is relevant, however, is that the protocol presents convincing evidence that even advanced learners of a second
language rely on memory of their pedagogical experiences when making
grammaticality judgments.

CONCLUSIONS

The evidence considered here shows dyadic problem solving to be a promising methodology for uncovering the strategic processing accessed by second-
language learners in forming grammaticality judgments. To be sure, the
methodology requires additional exploration and fine-tuning. As we have

already suggested, for example, this particular study should be repeated with monolingual Spanish speakers as controls. It also needs to be carried out with second-language learners whose primary, or sole, exposure to the target language is in the natural, untutored setting. The joint format also calls for testing with linguistic structures that vary with respect to their level of abstractness. As we mentioned earlier, the fact that the native English respondents failed to integrate talk of rules in their joint discourse could be attributable to the abstract nature of the ECP and the Subjacency constraint. This group might behave differently with respect to discussion of rules if they were asked to judge sentences containing ungrammaticalities such as missing auxiliaries, incorrect word order in questions, or tense violations.

The preceding caveats notwithstanding, we can offer some tentative conclusions regarding the validity of learner grammaticality judgments. It is difficult to conclude that second-language learners, at least those whose primary exposure to the target language has been in a tutored setting, respond to grammaticality judgment tasks on the basis of abstract linguistic principles. Unlike native speakers, who rely on feel in assessing the grammatical status of sentences in their language, learners appear to deploy a variety of strategies when asked to render such judgments. This, in itself, presents a problem for research that relies on grammaticality judgments for making claims about the grammatical properties of some interlanguage.

Elementary learners use translation as an important strategy for assessing the grammaticality status of sentences in their L2. Although some might argue that learners translate in order to work out the meaning of test sentences rather than to determine their grammaticality status, it is difficult to imagine that accessing the native language in any way would not contaminate the judgment. As protocol IV demonstrates, once learners translate a sentence into their native language, they tend to work with the translation as they attempt to reach a grammaticality decision. Felix and Weigl (1991), in a study of English as a foreign language, similarly reported that their L1 German subjects often assessed the grammaticality status of English sentences on the basis of German equivalents (see also Lantolf, 1990). Elementary foreign-language learners also rely on recall of explicit metaknowledge derived in large part from pedagogical rules, which may or may not be accurate. Only for null subjects in simple sentences is there evidence that this group of learners uses linguistic intuitions when judging sentences in L2.

More advanced learners manifest response behaviors similar to those deployed by elementary students. Even though we observed some tendency to rely on feel among the advanced group, we uncovered no clear and consistent difference between the two populations in this regard. The major difference between the groups resides in the higher percentage of accurate judgments rendered by the advanced subjects. In itself, this is not a particularly interesting finding; after all, it is one of the things that makes advanced learners advanced. What is interesting, however, is that this group continues to rely on translation, explicit metaknowledge, and memory to make the more accurate judgments. The lesson of all this is that merely because some population of learners accurately assesses the grammaticality status of sentences in a second language, we cannot assume that these judgments reflect intuitive knowledge associated with an abstract linguistic competence.

Be that as it may, given the tendency, however slight, toward increased reliance on feel evidenced by the advanced learners studied here, we speculate that even more experienced second-language learners (whatever more experienced means) might indeed rely on feel or sound in making grammaticality decisions. Until we study the performance of such learners, however, we cannot be certain that this is so. We would not be surprised to discover, however, that on particularly complex structures, even very advanced speakers would fall back on those strategies favored by less experienced learners, that is, translation and pedagogical rules.

The point we want to make clear again in closing is that in analyzing joint problem-solving behavior, the group is seen as exhibiting the typical mental behavior of the population from which the members of the group are drawn. Thus, with regard to the elementary dyads, for example, our claim is that because the protocols show that subjects at this level rely on translation and pedagogical rules to determine the grammaticality of sentences in their L2, the same strategies are favored by individual learners when responding to the same type of task.

APPENDIX A: SPANISH GRAMMATICALITY SURVEY

1. Creo que tengo diez pesos.
2. No hablo español con mis amigos.
3. Quién va a llamar a las tres? Va a llamar Miguel.
4. Juan sabe que vivimos aquí.
5. El cree que jugamos mucho.
6. Maria sabe que hablamos español.
7. Quieren estudiar ahora.
8. *Ha Juan estudiado mucho para esta clase?
9. Ellos salen para Mardid mañana.
10. Pienso que ella va a la universidad todos los días.
11. Beben los niños la leche.
12. Marta come un sandwich y bebe una cerveza.
13. *Olga ha estudiado y Pedro ha también.
14. *En Canadá, lo nieva mucho en invierno.
15. *Quien cree usted vive con Ramon?
16. Juan escribe cartas cuando escucha la radio.

17. Llegan nuestros amigos a las ocho.
18. *Han cantado los muchachos en la fiesta?
19. *Pensamos que nosotros tenemos mucho dinero.
20. Parece que Gabriela es muy inteligente.
21. Viene Juan con su amigo.
22. Marta dice que vienen ellos en dos días.
23. El perro no quiere beber el agua.
24. Qué ciudad cree ella que es la más grande?
25. ?Jose vive en México ahora, pero el quiere estudiar en España.
26. Que está haciendo Luz? Luz está jugando.
27. Es muy dificil esta clase.
28. *Ricardo ha no terminado el libro.
29. Dice Jorge la verdad?
30. Hace mucho frío en Alaska.
31. *Pedro dice ella llega tarde.
32. *Juan no ha llegado, pero María ha.
33. Josefina cree que compran un coche nuevo.
34. *Qué cree usted que va a pasar ahora?
35. Yo debo estudiar mucho porque tengo un examen.
36. Roberto ha comprado un coche, no es verdad?
37. ?Yo hablo mucho cuando yo estoy en casa.
38. Miguel ha preparado la comida para su amiga.
39. Sale Carlos a las dos.
40. Mi amigo escribe muchas cartas.
41. *José puede no ir con muchas cartas.
42. Claudia ha trabajado much esta semana.
43. Sabemos muy bien que comen en este restaurante.

APPENDIX B: ENGLISH GRAMMATICALITY SURVEY

1. ?What does Mary want to know whether John has already sold?
2. What did John realize he could not sell?
3. *What did the police arrest the men who were carrying?
4. *She forgot what who said?
5. ?What did John say that would fall on the floor if we're not careful?
6. *What did Mary hear Bill's stories about?
7. Which bed does John like to sleep in?
8. Which information would it be possible for Mary to persuade Susan to tell the reporters?
9. *Where did Bill want to know who put the book?
10. *What did Sam believe the claim that Carol had bought?
11. *What did John find the Ball and?

12. *I can't remember who did what?
13. Who did Ellen say Max thought would pass the test?
14. What kind of book is it necessary to read?
15. ?What time will Mary arrive before?

REFERENCES

Beretta, A., & Gass, S. (1991). *Indeterminacy and the reliability of grammaticality judgments.* Paper presented at SLRF, Los Angeles.

Bley-Vroman, R., Felix, S., & Ioup, G. L. (1988). The accessibility of universal grammar in adult language learning. *Second Language Research, 4,* 1–32.

Christie, K., & Lantolf, J. P. (1992). The ontological status of learner grammaticality judgments in UG approaches to L2 acquisition. *Rassegna Italiana de Linguistica Applicata, 24*(3), 31–52.

Dreyfus, H. L., & Dreyfus, S. E. (1986). *Mind over machine: The power of human intuition and expertise in the era of the computer.* New York: The Free Press.

Ellis, R. (1990). Grammaticality judgements and learner variability. In H. Burmeister & P. L. Rounds (Eds.), *Variability in second language acquisition: Proceedings of the Tenth Meeting of the Second Language Research Forum* (pp. 25–60). Eugene, OR: University of Oregon, Department of Linguistics.

Ellis, R. (1991). Grammaticality judgments and second language acquisition. *Studies in Second Language Acquisition, 13,* 161–186.

Ericsson, K. A., & Simon, H. A. (1984). *Protocol analysis: Verbal reports as data.* Cambridge, MA: MIT Press.

Faerch, C., & Kasper, G. (Eds.). (1987). *Introspection in second language research.* Clevedon: Multilingual Matters.

Felix, S. W., & Weigl, W. (1991). Universal grammar in the classroom: The effects of formal instruction on second language acquisition. *Second Language Research, 7,* 160–180.

Garman, M. (1990). *Psycholinguistics.* Cambridge: Cambridge University Press.

Gass, S., & Beretta, A. (1991). *Syntactic constraints and the reliability of L2 grammaticality judgments.* Paper presented at AAAL, New York.

Haegeman, L. (1991). *Introduction to government and binding theory.* Oxford: Basil Blackwell.

Howard, D. (1991). *Test taking as problem solving: A developmental approach.* Unpublished doctoral dissertation, University of Delaware, Newark.

Hyams, N. M. (1986). *Language acquisition and the theory of parameters.* Dordrecht: Reidel.

Lantolf, J. P. (1990). Reassessing the null-subject parameter in second language acquisition. In H. Burmeister & P. L. Rounds (Eds.), *Variability in second language acquisition: Proceedings of the Tenth Meeting of the Second Language Research Forum* (pp. 429–452). Eugene, OR: University of Oregon, Department of Linguistics.

Lantolf, J. P., Labarca, A., & den Tuinder, J. (1985). Strategies for accessing bilingual dictionaries: A question of regulation. *Hispania, 68,* 858–864.

Lyons, W. (1986). *The disappearance of introspection.* Cambridge, MA: MIT Press.

Matrat, C. (1991). *Thinking aloud vs. joint translating: Comparative study of two research methodologies to investigate the translation process.* Unpublished doctoral dissertation, University of Delaware, Newark.

Newman, D., Griffin, P., & Cole, M. (1989). *The construction zone: Working for cognitive change in school.* Cambridge: Cambridge University Press.

Schrag, C. O. (1986). *Communicative praxis and the space of subjectivity.* Bloomington, IN: Indiana University Press.

Searle, J. (1992). *The rediscovery of the mind.* Cambridge, MA: MIT Press.

Sorace, A. (1988). Linguistic intuitions in interlanguage development: The problem of indeterminacy. In J. Pankhurst, M. Sharwood-Smith, & P. Van Buren (Eds.), *Learnability and second
languages: A book of readings* (pp. 166–207). Dordrecht: Foris.
Vygotsky, L. S. (1979). Consciousness as a problem of psychology of behavior. *Soviet Psychology, 17,* 3–35.
Wertsch, J. V. (1991). *Voices of the mind: A sociocultural approach to mediated action.* Cambridge: Harvard University Press.

15

INVESTIGATING THE VALIDITY AND RELIABILITY OF NATIVE SPEAKER AND SECOND-LANGUAGE LEARNER JUDGMENTS ABOUT SENTENCES

Ron Cowan
University of Illinois

Yukiko Abe Hatasa
Purdue University

A fundamental question for second-language (L2) research is whether certain techniques of investigation possess sufficient validity and reliability to ensure that the results of experimental studies where they continue to be used can be considered scientifically trustworthy. This concern is not shared or even acknowledged by all researchers. Sometimes a particular technique of investigation used in L1 child language acquisition research has been declared to be standard and then applied in studies with L2 adults, ignoring published reservations regarding the reliability and construct validity of the technique by other researchers who have used it extensively. Such was the case with Flynn's (1983, 1984, 1987) use of elicited imitation to investigate the effect of a parameter defined by Universal Grammar on the production of different groups of L2 learners. Fortunately, insightful critiques of this particular study by Eubank (1989) and Bley-Vroman and Chaudron (1990) have led to a reexamination of elicited imitation as an experimental instrument and recommendations for investigating its reliability with L2 learners (see Bley-Vroman & Chaudron, this volume, chapter 13).

Another widely employed technique of investigation that is being questioned is the elicitation of L2 learners' judgments about the target language. Although different kinds of judgments may be elicited, such as judgments of appropriateness, as in the speech act research exemplified by Cohen and Olshtain (this volume, chapter 8), the experimental task that has aroused the greatest debate among L2 researchers requires subjects to judge whether or not a sentence in the target language is grammatical. Both the validity (Goss, Ying-Hua, & Lantolf, this volume, chapter 14) and the reliability (Ellis, 1991; Gass, this volume, chapter 16; Gass & Baretta, 1991) of this technique have become subjects of increasing investigation. The first section of this chapter examines the validity of using judgment tasks to investigate L1 and L2 learner's perceptions of sentence complexity. Our approach will be the method of testing for concurrent validity—a comparison of a scalar judgment task with an established criterion measure. The results of the study we report are thus intended primarily to make a contribution to our general knowledge of a topic about which very little is known. However, in the course of studying how L1 and L2 subjects arrive at judgments about sentences that they believe to be grammatical, we discovered that structural features can interact with different word orders to affect the consistency of the judgments made by both groups. This led us to consider how other properties of sentences may affect the reliability of L2 learner grammaticality judgments, and the final section of this chapter contains a discussion of these effects and some recommendations for increasing reliability in experiments where this technique is used.

PREVIOUS RESEARCH

Sentence processing and sentence complexity are two linked concepts in the psychological literature. Regardless of the particular model one may favor, there is substantial agreement about two facts: Syntax plays a part in the processing (the derivation of semantic representations of sentences), and different syntactic configurations contribute to the complexity (reflected in the difficulty speakers have in deriving semantic representations of sentences). Sentence complexity/processing research typically uses *on-line* techniques in investigations where data consist of latency times. Psychologists prefer on-line techniques for sentence complexity/processing research because they assume the mental processes underlying comprehension of natural language to be highly automatized and obligatory. As Marslen-Wilson & Tyler (1980) noted, if one allows subjects "to reflect on the final products of the processes, then all sorts of 'off-line' variations can start to be introduced" (p. 260).

However, in much second-language acquisition research, off-line techniques such as the solicitation of L1 and L2 speakers' judgments have been used for verifying hypotheses about sentence complexity and processing. Three seminal studies using off-line procedures were carried out by Sheldon (1977) and Prideaux (1980, 1982). Sheldon's study was undertaken to seek empirical evidence for the universality of two principles governing complexity based on an earlier operating principle that Slobin (1973, 1979) had suggested guides L1 acquisition—*avoid interruption and rearrangement of linguistic units.* She had native speakers of Japanese and English rate the sentences in their respective languages containing the four relative clause configurations shown in Fig. 15.1 using a 4-point scale, where 1 indicated easiest (least complex) and 4 indicated hardest (most difficult to process). The first two capital letters designate the sentence types in Fig. 15.1. The first letter indicates the grammatical function of the noun phrase (NP) in the main clause that the relative clause is formed on; the second letter indicates the grammatical function of the identical NP in the relative clause which is converted to a relative pronoun in English. RP stands for relative pronoun, *wa*, *ga*, and *o* are postpositions in Japanese; S is subject; O is object. The relative clauses in both languages are bounded by square brackets.

Sheldon hypothesized a universal hierarchy of complexity for sentences containing relative clauses based on her interpretation of the two factors mentioned in Slobin's operating principle. Applied to the four types of English sentences containing relative clauses in Fig. 15.1, the hierarchy would make the following predictions. SO relatives should be judged by native speakers of English to be the most complex of all four types because they involve both interruption, that is, the main clause is interrupted by the relative clause, and rearrangement, that is, the relative pronoun is moved from its position as object at the end of the relative clause. SS and OO relatives in English should be seen as equally complex, because they each involve one factor, interruption and rearrangement respectively. Least complex should be English OS relatives, where neither factor plays a part. Sheldon's predicted hierarchy of complexity for English was thus OS > SS = OO > SO. (Elements to the left on this scale are always less complex than the elements that follow them; thus SS > OS means SS relative sentences are less complex than OS relative sentences.)

Because relativization in Japanese involves no rearrangement, interruption was the sole factor that could be considered a determinant of complexity. Hence, the hierarchy of complexity that Sheldon hypothesized for Japanese orders the two sentences that have relative clauses that interrupt the main clause—the OO and OS relative—as most complex. Her predictions for the same four sentence types in Japanese were thus SS = SO > OO = OS.

However, in her study's results the native speakers' complexity judgments indicated that at best the interruption principle held for English and could not be considered universal, due to the low ranking of the OS Japanese relative, which intervenes between the main clause subject and object. The complexity ratings Sheldon obtained for English were in fact OS > SS > OO = SO, and the results for Japanese were OS > SS = OO > SO.

To reconcile these almost identical rankings obtained for both languages, Sheldon suggested a solution provided by Keenan and Comrie's (1972, 1977) accessibility hierarchy—the results reflected the speakers' intuitions that object relatives are less accessible and hence more complex than subject rela-

Japanese

SS [Object o Verb] Subject wa/ga Object o Verb
onnanoko o   tataita gakusei wa/ga   otokonoko o   nagutta
girl   DO hit   student THM/SUB boy   DO hit
The student who hit the girl hit the boy.

SO [Subject ga Verb] Subject wa/ga Object o Verb
onnanoko ga   tataita gakusei wa/ga   otokonoko o   nagutta
girl   SUB hit   student THM/SUB boy   DO hit
The student whom the girl hit hit the boy.

OS Subject wa/ga [Object o Verb] Object o Verb
gakusei wa/ga   onnanoko o   tataita otokonoko o   nagutta
student THM/SUB girl   DO hit   boy   DO hit
The student hit the boy who hit the girl.

OO Subject wa/ga [Subject ga Verb] Object o Verb
gakusei wa/ga   onnanoko ga   tataita otokonoko o   nagutta
student THM/SUB girl   SUB hit   boy   DO hit
The student hit the boy whom the girl hit.

English

SS Subject [RP Verb Object] Verb Object
The student who hit the girl hit the boy.

SO Subject [RP Subject Verb] Verb Object
The student whom the girl hit hit the boy.

OS Subject Verb Object [RP Verb Object]
The student hit the boy who hit the girl.

OO Subject Verb Object [RP Subject Verb]
The student hit the boy whom the girl hit.

FIG. 15.1. Sentence types used in Sheldon's and Prideaux's experiments.

tives. Thus in both English and Japanese, sentences were judged less complex when the subject of the subordinate clause was relativized.

Suspecting that Haviland and Clark's (1974) *given–new contract* might provide a more adequate universal strategy for explaining differences in judgments of sentence complexity, Prideaux replicated Sheldon's study in two experiments, both of which used a 9-point self-anchored scale.[1] In the first of these, Prideaux (1980), 18 native speakers of English judged OO and OS relatives to be significantly easier than types SO and OO. This result appeared to confirm the interruption hypothesis. The second study, Prideaux (1982), involved 24 native speakers of Japanese and three exemplars of the same four sentence types. SS and OS relatives were judged significantly less complex than SO and OO relatives, and within the former pair, type SS was judged significantly easier than type OS ($p < .001$). To summarize, the following orders of complexity were obtained by Prideaux: for English, OS = OO > SS = SO; for Japanese, SS > OS > SO = OO.

Prideaux took the results for Japanese as support for an earlier hypothesis by Takahara (1978), which claimed that an OV sequence, where the subject NP of a clause is deleted, is seen as more natural than an SV sequence. Thus the application of the given–new contract to Japanese predicts the result Prideaux obtained, that is, that SS and OS sentences, which contain relative clauses with OV sequences, should be and are judged as less complex than SO and OO sentences. To reconcile the divergent English results he proposed a universal hierarchy of processing strategies in which the given–new contract was superordinate.

These three studies motivated the experiment reported in this chapter, which sought to address a potential problem that could arise as a result of a factor left uncontrolled by Sheldon and Prideaux—the choice of subject postposition in Japanese. The theme postposition *wa* can occur only in main clauses in Japanese, whereas the subject posposition *ga* can occur in both main and subordinate clauses. It seems reasonable to suppose that sentences that contain *wa* as an initial subject marker would be perceived as less complex and would be processed with greater ease, because they enable the speaker or reader to determine the clausal status of a preceding NP, whereas with *ga* the listener/reader would have to wait for some additional clue to determine whether the NP being processed is in the main clause or in a subordinate clause. Unfortunately, the stimulus sentences in Sheldon's study all used *wa* as a subject postposition, whereas those in Prideaux's study used only *ga*. To examine whether the presence of one or the other of these morphemes could affect speakers' judgments about sentence complexity, the subjects were exposed to sets of sentences containing both postpositions.

---

[1]This discourse-structuring principle states that old, rhematic, given information must precede thematic or new information in sentences.

It was mentioned earlier that SLA studies of sentence complexity have used only off-line judgment tasks. The validity of using off-line judgment tasks to investigate sentence complexity can be tested by the traditional approach of noting the degree to which judgment results agree with those obtained from an independent, reliable measure. The criterion measure in this case is an on-line task that collects reaction times. However, it is necessary to determine that the reaction times obtained from the criterion task reflect comprehension of the experimental stimuli by the L2 learners. For this reason, a comprehension task was also included in the experiment described in the next section.

THE STUDY

Subjects

Forty-eight native speakers of English who were studying Japanese and 48 native speakers of Japanese participated in the experiment. Thirty-four of the American subjects, the L2 learners, were completing a first-year course, Japanese 102, and 14 were just beginning the second-year continuation of it, Japanese 203. Thirty-four of the Japanese native speakers were students from Konan University and 14 were students at the University of Illinois.

Materials

The subjects viewed one of six sets of sentences involving the four different types of Japanese relative clauses shown in Fig. 15.1, which were used in Sheldon's and Prideaux's studies. All sentences were of the same length and were composed almost entirely of familiar words taken from the textbook the subjects had used; the few unfamiliar words that appeared were pretaught before the experiment was run. Each set of sentences was further divided into two subsets that differed only by the occurrence of the postposition, the subject marker *ga* or the theme marker *wa*. An example of one of the subsets created for the experiment, which illustrates how *wa* and *ga* were varied, is shown in Fig. 15.2.

Method

The first experimental task was administered on a PLATO computer to individual subjects. The subjects pressed the space bar to read 24 experimental sentences and 12 filler sentences, which appeared on a touch-sensitive screen. As soon as the subject had read and understood each sentence, they touched a box on the lower right-hand portion of the screen. This activated

SS　山田さんを　　ほめた人は／が　その　ともだちを　しっている。
　　Yamada-san o hometa hito wa/ga sono tomodachi o shitte-iru
　　Mr.Yamada DO praised man THM/SUB that friend DO know

　　"The man who praised Mr.Yamada knows that friend."

SO　山田さんがほめた人は／がそのともだちをしっている。
　　Yamada-san ga hometa hito wa/ga sono tomodachi o shitte-iru.
　　Mr.Yamada SUB praised man THM/SUB that friend DO know

　　"The man whom Mr.Yamada praised knows that friend."

OS　その人は／が山田さんをほめたともだちをしっている。
　　sono hito wa/ga yamada-san o hometa tomodachi o shitte-iru
　　that man THM/SUB Mr.Yamada DO praised friend DO know

　　"The man knows the friend who praised Mr.Yamada."

OO　その人は／が山田さんがほめたともだちをしっている。
　　sono hito wa/ga yamada-san ga hometa tomodachi o shitte-iru
　　that man THM/SUB Mr.Yamada SUB praised friend DO know

　　"The man knows the friend whom Mr.Yamada praised."

FIG 15.2.　Sample subset of experimental sentences.

an intervening task, which was introduced to guard against a ceiling effect that might have occurred due to the short length of the sentences.[2] The subjects were presented with four three-digit numbers; they had been instructed to touch the one that was divisible by four. Completing the intervening task activated a comprehension question that concerned the relationship of the head noun to the relative clause. The comprehension question for the SS and OS relatives in Fig. 15.2 and the three possible answers for this question are shown in Fig. 15.3. The computer stored the reading time (RT) of each sentence, the on-line processing measure, and the number of correct answers to the comprehension questions for subsequent analysis.[3]

Upon completing the first part of the experiment, the subjects carried out the off-line judgment task. The subjects were given a one-page questionnaire with six sets of four sentences with different relative clauses arranged in

---

[2]This was determined through pilot testing.

[3]The reliability of the computer-administered task was tested by analyzing the RTs and the errors to comprehension questions of the two sets and the RTs of answers to the intervening task. There was no significant difference between the two sets on both RTs and errors—$F(1, 92) = .037, p > .847$ for RT and $F(1, 92) = .028, p > .867$ for errors. The correlation between the reaction times for the intervening task and the errors was $r = .23$. Thus it is highly unlikely that the fluctuation in RTs for the intervening tasks affected the error rates.

だれが山田さんをほめましたか。
dare ga yamada-san o homemashita-ka
who SUB Mr.Yamada DO praised-Q

"Who praised Mr. Yamada?"

Possible Answers

1. その人　(that man)
2. そのともだち　(that friend)
3. 思い出せません。　(I don't remember.)

FIG 15.3. Sample comprehension question.

random order. The subjects had been previously assigned to four subgroups. Two subgroups with different native languages received the sentences with *ga* and the other groups received the sentences with *wa*. The order of the presentation differed for each group. The subjects were instructed to read the sentences and rank them in the order of perceived difficulty using the ranking scale employed in Sheldon's experiment, from 1 (easiest) to 4 (hardest). Both written and oral instructions were provided in the subject's native language.

Results and Discussion

A 2 (native vs. nonnative) × 2 (subject marker) × 4 (relative clause type) ANOVA was performed on logarithmic transformations of the RT data. An alpha level of .025 was employed to assure a level of .05 or below as a result of the multiple tests involved. Significant main effects were found for language background, $F(1, 94) = 294.67$, $p < .0001$; subject marker, $F(1, 94) = 10.31$, $p < .002$; and relative clause type, $F(3, 282) = 6.695$, $p < .002$, but there were no interaction effects. Comparison of the mean RTs revealed that native speakers processed the sentences faster than the L2 learners, and sentences with *wa* were processed faster than those with *ga* by both language groups. Post hoc comparisons revealed that OO relatives took significantly longer to process ($p < .001$) than the other three types, which did not differ significantly among themselves. The order for the RT data (from fastest to slowest) for both subject groups was SS = OS > SO > OO.

A 2 × 2 × 4 ANOVA run on correct answers to the comprehension questions revealed significant main effects for language background, $F(1, 94) = 12.268$, $p < .001$; and relative clause type, $F(3, 282) = 6.152$, $p < .001$. There was no effect for subject marker, nor were there any interaction effects.

Comparison of the two language groups revealed, not surprisingly, that native speakers answered more questions correctly than L2 learners. The relative ranking of the four sentence types in terms of correct scores was SS > SO > OS > OO. SS relatives received the highest number of correct answers to the comprehension questions posed about them, followed by SO and OS relatives. Type OO relatives received the fewest correct answers, with a mean of .90. Post hoc comparisons revealed significant differences for all pairs of sentence types except SS versus SO and SO versus OS.

The data from the judgment task were analyzed by a one-way ANOVA applied to the four sentence types with the four groups (native speaker *ga*, L2 speaker *ga*, native speaker *wa*, and L2 speaker *wa*). Significant differences were found for all groups except the L2 speakers' ratings of the sentences containing *wa* as a subject postposition ($p > .900$, n.s.). Further analyses of differences between sentence types in each of the three groups (native *ga*, native *wa*, and L2 *ga*) were carried out. The relative rankings for the four sentence types for each subject group and postposition are displayed in Table 15.1. The mean ranking for each sentence type is entered below it in parentheses.

Post hoc tests on the native speaker *wa* set revealed significant differences for all comparisons except SS versus SO and SS versus OO. Only the comparison SS versus OS was not significant for the native speaker *ga* set. In the L2 learner *ga* set, a significant difference was found for the comparison SS versus OO.

The fact that there were no interaction effects for the on-line processing measure and the comprehension scores is noteworthy because it means that in terms of these two indices of complexity the native speakers and the L2 learners patterned identically. The only difference between the two groups was that the former processed faster and answered more questions correctly. The processing hypothesis that postposition subject markers make a difference is clearly supported, because both groups processed sentences with *wa* faster.

TABLE 15.1
Native Speaker and L2 Learner Complexity Ratings

Group	Rankings			
Native Speaker *wa*:	OS >	OO >	SS >	SO
	(1.88)	(2.54)	(2.73)	(2.85)
Native Speaker *ga*:	SS =	OS >	SO >	OO
	(1.94)	(1.96)	(2.65)	(3.46)
L2 Learner *wa*:	OS >	SO >	OO >	SS
	(2.27)	(2.50)	(2.54)	(2.67)
L2 Learner *ga*:	SS >	OS >	SO >	OO
	(1.97)	(2.21)	(2.33)	(3.67)

Note. O = Object, S = Subject.

A comparison of the RT and the comprehension results ratings elicited in this experiment and those found by Sheldon and Prideaux reveals little congruence between the native and L2 speakers' judgments about complexity and what the on-line measurements indicate was actually complex for them. Notice that the ratings obtained by Sheldon agree with those obtained in this experiment when native speakers rated sentences with *wa* only at the ends of the continuum of complexity. The L2 learners' intuitions about complexity on sentences with *wa* suggest a completely different order from Sheldon's obtained order and from the order obtained for the native speakers in this experiment. The complexity judgments for sentences with *wa* obtained for native speakers and L2 learners show no correspondence at all with the RT measures or the comprehension data.

When we compare our native-speaker and L2-learner complexity judgments of the sentences containing *ga* postpositions with Prideaux's results, there appears to be agreement between these three groups in terms of a ranking of the sentence types. This is curious, given the presumable difference in sensitivity of the two scales used in these experiments. However, an examination of the rankings within each subject group reveals striking differences. Our native speakers ranked SS and OS relatives as virtually identical in complexity, whereas Prideaux's subjects and our L2 learners saw OS relatives as clearly more complex. Prideaux's subjects ranked SO and OO relatives equally as the most complex of all four types, an impression that does not accord with the intuitions of either our native speakers or our L2 learners. However, far more important is the fact that none of the rankings of the three subject groups accords with the on-line measure of complexity, the RTs. The RTs show the OO relatives to be significantly more complex than the other three types, which do not differ greatly among one another. Finally, the comprehension data show OS relatives differing significantly from the SS relatives though not from the SO relatives. This fact is reflected neither in our nor in Prideaux's rating results. The reason for this difference in comprehension scores seems to be that OS relatives with *ga* are classic garden path sentences in Japanese. The reader can process into the relative clause without realizing it, because basic word order in Japanese is SOV. Only when the second object is identified does the reader realize that he or she has been garden-pathed. The reason the pattern found for the comprehension data is not reflected perfectly in the RT data with regard to OS sentences is that longer sentences are required to register a reaction time effect with garden path sentences. This fact was determined in another experiment (Abe, Hatasa, & Cowan 1988), where these same sentences were lengthened by adding an indirect object. This produced consistently longer RTs for the OS, that is, garden-path, sentence over the two sentences that begin with relative clauses, that is, types SS and SO.

CONCLUSION

The moral of this story is: Don't trust anyone's judgments about sentence complexity. Our results indicate that no matter how delicate the scale, native-speaker and L2-learner judgment data will, at best, reflect sensitivity to only some structural characteristics that affect processing, and that they will always vary with on-line data, which are far more indicative of complexity. A clear implication of these results for L2 methodology is that processing research must employ some on-line task that elicits reaction or reading time plus some measure that provides an indication of the extent to which the stimuli used in the on-line task were comprehended. There is a great need to expand L2 processing research, which, to date, has enjoyed little rigorous development. In particular, it would be useful to plan experiments that compare on-line processing of oral and visual stimuli in the target language.[4] A number of programs that can be used with PCs to design processing experiments with single sentences or texts are available for studying visual processing. In addition to standard procedures for presenting recorded stimuli, shadowing might be tried for examining oral processing. However, we wish to stress that a key feature of such research should be the incorporation of some measure of subjects' comprehension.

The Reliability of Grammaticality Judgment Tasks

Even though judgments about sentence complexity and those about grammaticality cannot be said to tap the same set of competencies in speakers, it is quite likely that the data from experiments that use the latter are likely to produce data that display the same kind of variability we found in studies described in the previous section, where rating scales were used to assess complexity. Although we agree with Gass (this volume, chapter 16) that the reliability of judgment data is largely "a function of syntactic factors," we are not convinced that the kind of rating scale and elimination procedure she used in her study will isolate those sentences that are specious data. Our results indicate that the most delicate rating scales are at best capable of distinguishing very clear cases of grammatical and ungrammatical sentences, but they are not sufficiently reliable to determine whether the sentences that display high variability reflect subjects' lack of knowledge of the L2 grammar

---

[4]Recently, the use of "think-aloud" tasks has begun to enjoy some popularity with L2 researchers studying text processing (e.g., Block, 1985, 1986). However there are serious doubts that mental processes are really being tapped by this procedure. Indeed, as Afflerbach and Johnston (1984) pointed out, it is more likely that the characteristics of the task are influencing the data obtained by using it.

298 COWAN AND HATASA

or whether this variability is actually due to specific characteristics of the stimuli.

There are several potential sources of variability that may inadvertently be introduced through the investigator's selection of stimulus sentences: (a) choice of vocabulary that results in a syntactic pattern that is questionable but not totally excluded when a rule under investigation is activated; (b) experimental designs that interweave two or more factors, for example, anaphora resolution and branching direction, and in so doing create ambiguous sentences; and (c) the selection of syntactic structures that are comparable to those in the learners' L1 that are rarely used except when appropriate discourse conditions are present. Most of these sources of variability can be controlled by careful attention to the experimental design and adequate pilot testing (a practice that, sadly, appears to be neglected in a large number of published studies). However, variability may be introduced as a result of other factors that are more difficult to control, such as superficial similarity between syntactic patterns and sentence length.

A high degree of similarity between an ungrammatical and a grammatical pattern that results from the application of different rules may increase the likelihood of the former pattern being seen as borderline grammatical or grammatical in the speaker's dialect, but not grammatical in the dialect that is considered correct or the norm for the language (for a discussion of this latter phenomenon of *dialect separability* see Bley-Vroman & Masterson, 1989). A good example of this is the sentence *A doll was given the little girl*. Many native speakers will accept this sentence as grammatical; others are not absolutely sure that it can be rejected as ungrammatical, even though it violates a constraint that most linguists would maintain holds for American English; that is, after Dative Movement has applied in a sentence with a *to* dative verb that takes this rule, only the first NP can be moved into subject position by Passivization. The variation in judgment may arise because the speaker is aware that this sentence is acceptable for many dialects of British English, or it may be due to its close resemblance to the sentence *A doll was given to the little girl*, which is clearly grammatical in both dialects of English.

Sentence length also affects grammaticality judgments. Longer sentences with plausible vocabulary are often perceived as grammatical when they are in fact not, as the following example demonstrates.

(1) The mediator recommended to the strikers a tentative settlement that would have paved the way toward resolving many of the problems that they had, as yet, been unable to resolve.

Here the writer has shifted the long direct-object noun phrase, *a tentative settlement that would have paved the way toward resolving many of the problems that they had, as yet, been unable to resolve*, to the end of the sentence in order to avoid keeping it in sentence-medial position, thereby avoiding the awkward sentence shown in (2).

(2) The mediator recommended a tentative settlement that would have paved the way toward resolving many of the problems that they had, as yet, been unable to resolve to the workers.

This preference for keeping long noun phrases at either the beginning or the end of a clause has been recognized for some time, and it has even been codified as the stylistic rule of Heavy NP Shift. In English, this rule serves to make sentences easier to process by avoiding long separations of elements that are commonly adjacent to one another in shorter sentences. The activation of the rule actually produces ungrammatical sentences if the noun phrase that is moved is short, as (3) illustrates.

(3) *The mediator recommended to the workers a settlement.

Strictly speaking, (1) is as ungrammatical as (3). However, with long noun phrases, native speakers tolerate sentences like (1), preferring them over grammatical alternatives like (2).[5]

The fact that native speakers are more flexible in their grammaticality judgments for longer sentences may in fact account for the variability that has been found in the data from experiments that investigate whether principles of Universal Grammar are part of the latent knowledge of L2 learners. For example, Schachter (1989) discovered that even native speakers of English were frequently unable to recognize Subjacency violations in noun complements. Subjects often judged long sentences like *Which paper did the professor believe the claim that someone had stolen?* to be grammatical. This finding does not bode well for future experiments that must use long sentences, and it suggests that researchers who are committed to this technique must discuss individual sources of variation in their data, on a sentence-by-sentence basis, much more extensively than has been done in the past. As Bley-Vroman and Masterson (1989) have correctly noted, variability introduced by length remains a problem even if it is distributed across grammatical and ungrammatical sentences, because it will create larger standard deviations, making it difficult to achieve significant results with small sample sizes.

---

[5]Numerous examples of Heavy NP Shift can be found in writing. It also blocks the application of the rule of particle movement in phrasal verb (verb + particle) constructions and is applied to frozen expressions such as *kiss your chances (of doing something) goodbye*, as the following example from the *Daily Illini*, a campus newspaper, illustrates: "Whether you are Buddhist, atheist, liberal, feminist, agnostic Jewish or whatever, *you can kiss your chance goodbye of ever being acknowledged by some of the born-again Christians on this campus (except when they want to convert you)*."

Even though it may not be possible to control for all factors that introduce variability when creating stimulus sentences, the reliability of studies that use grammaticality judgment tasks can be increased by following a number of standard procedures. Not less than three exemplars of each sentence type should be included, and there should be an equal number of distractor items. Because reliability is increased with longer tests, a total of 60 to 72 sentences is recommended for this technique, although pilot testing with L2 learners will ultimately determine the total number of sentences that can be completed in a reasonable amount of time. These procedures must be preceded by careful pilot testing with native speakers. Our practice has been to discard any sentence on which at least 25 native speakers do not agree. Data should be analyzed by repeated measures ANOVAs, and individual stimuli that display high degrees of variability should be discussed. Finally, a crucial feature of experiments that use long sentences should be the inclusion of a native speaker control group.

A second source of variability in L2 data, one that must eventually be recognized, is the variance within subject-proficiency groupings. Many researchers seem to apply assumptions of homogeneity of variance to L2 subjects that are usually reserved for adult native speakers. The norm for many published L2 studies is a sample of 30 subjects or under, where little or no information regarding variance within proficiency groupings is reported. Having run several studies with four to eight times as many subjects, we are convinced that the results of small samples are totally unrepresentative of whatever L2 learner ability was investigated, simply because proficiency variability within the sample would preclude any generalizability. Of course, as L2 researchers we face a serious problem in finding a satisfactory proficiency measure, and the best we can do is use tests that have fairly high reliability coefficients and are readily obtainable. We can also markedly reduce variance within proficiency groupings, however, by increasing sample sizes. Our experience leads us to believe that samples of less than 50 subjects per proficiency grouping will display too much variability to be considered trustworthy.

Applying the foregoing recommendations will undoubtedly increase the reliability of the data obtained from experiments that employ the solicitation of grammatical judgments as an experimental technique, even though it is doubtful that they will effectively control for variability due to some characteristics of stimulus sentences. In a number of papers and articles (e.g., Bley-Vroman & Masterson, 1989; Eubank, 1991, 1992) it has been suggested that the very fast on-line sentence matching task used by Freedman and Forster (1985) in experiments with native speakers could be used as a supplement to grammaticality judgments. One potential problem with this technique is that the speed in detecting a difference between the two sentences presented is "greatly affected by the locus of the difference in an example. If, for example, the two sentences differ in their first words, the difference will always be detected very quickly, independent of grammatical status" (Bley-Vroman & Masterson, 1989, p. 214). As we stated earlier, we feel that it is necessary that on-line tasks used with L2 speakers demonstrate comprehension, and this requirement may be compromised with this particular task. Still, we applaud and support further research directed toward discovering very fast on-line tasks that can be used to check the reliability of grammaticality judgment tasks (which we believe will continue to be used in spite of the reservations we have raised about them here) and to provide dependable data on L2 processing.

Finally, we should note that, in our opinion, it would be a serious mistake to pursue techniques of investigation such as the one described by Goss, Ying-Hua, and Lantolf (this volume, chapter 14), where the investigator is allowed to decide which utterances manifest the appropriate "feel" to be considered true representations of target-language knowledge. This seems to be wandering into a dangerous area of subjective judgment. Only by developing objective research techniques that display a high degree of validity and reliability will we be able to test hypotheses about L2 acquisition with anything that approaches scientific rigor.

REFERENCES

Abe, Y., Hatasa, K., & Cowan, J. R. (1988). Investigating universals of sentence complexity. In M. Hammond, E. A. Moravcsik, & J. Wirth (Eds.), *Studies in syntactic typology* (pp. 77–92). Amsterdam: John Benjamins.

Afflerbach, P., & Johnston, P. (1984). The use of verbal reports in reading research. *Journal of Reading Behavior, 16*, 307–321.

Bley-Vroman, R., & Chaudron, C. (1990). Second language processing of subordinate clauses and anaphora—first language and universal influences: A review of Flynn's research. *Language Learning, 40*, 245–285.

Bley-Vroman, R., & Masterson, D. (1989). Reaction time as a supplement to grammatical judgments in the investigation of second language learner's competence. *University of Hawai'i Working Papers in ESL, 8*, 207–237.

Block, E. (1985). *The comprehension strategies of nonproficient native and non-native readers of English: A descriptive process in progress.* Unpublished doctoral dissertation, New York University.

Ellis, R. (1991). Grammaticality judgments and second language acquisition. *Studies in Second Language Acquisition, 13*, 161–186.

Eubank, L. (1989). Parameters in L2 learning: Flynn revisited. *Second Language Research, 5*, 43–73.

Eubank, L. (1991). *Is sentence matching sensitive to constraints?* Unpublished manuscript, Denton, TX.

Eubank, L. (1992). *Sentence matching and processing in L2 development.* Unpublished manuscript, Denton, TX.

Flynn, S. (1983). *A study of the effects of principal branching direction in second language acquisition: The generalization of a parameter of universal grammar from first to second language acquisition.* Unpublished doctoral dissertation, Cornell University, Ithaca, NY.

Flynn, S. (1984). A universal in L2 acquisition based on PBD typology. In F. Eckman, L. Bell, & D. Nelson (Eds.), (pp. 75–87), *Universals in second language acquisition.* Rowley, MA: Newbury House.

Flynn, S. (1987). Contrast and construction in a parameter-setting model of L2 acquisition. *Language Learning, 37,* 19–62.

Freedman, S., & Forster, K. I. (1985). The psychological status of over-generated sentences. *Cognition, 19,* 101–131.

Gass, S., & Baretta, A. (1991). *Syntactic constraints and the reliability of L2 grammaticality judgments.* Paper presented at AAAL, New York.

Haviland, S. E., & Clark, H. H. (1974). What's new? Acquiring new information as a process in comprehension. *Journal of Verbal Learning and Verbal Behavior, 13,* 512–521.

Keenan, E., & Comrie, B. (1972). *Noun phrase accessibility and universal grammar.* Paper presented at LSA annual meeting.

Keenan, E., & Comrie, B. (1977). Noun phrase accessibility and universal grammar. *Linguistic Inquiry, 8,* 63–99.

Marslen-Wilson, W., & Tyler, L. K. (1980). Towards a psychological basis for a theory of anaphora. In J. Kreiman & A. E. Ojeda (Eds.), *Papers from the Parasession on pronouns and anaphora* (pp. 258–287). Chicago: Chicago Linguistic Society.

Prideaux, G. D. (1980). The role of perceptual strategies in the processing of English relative clause structures. In *Proceedings of the Eighth International Conference on Computational Linguistics* (pp. 60–66), Tokyo.

Prideaux, G. D. (1982). The processing of Japanese relative clauses. *Canadian Journal of Linguistics, 27,* 23–30.

Schachter, J. (1989). Testing a proposed universal. In S. M. Gass & J. Schachter (Eds.), *Linguistic perspectives on second language acquisition* (pp. 73–88). Cambridge: Cambridge University Press.

Sheldon, A. (1977). Speakers' intuitions about relative complexity of relative clauses in Japanese and English. In S. S. Mufwene, C. A. Walkers, & S. B. Steven (Eds.), *Papers from the Twelfth Regional Meeting of the Chicago Linguistic Society* (pp. 358–367). Chicago: Chicago Linguistic Society.

Slobin, D. I. (1973). Cognitive prerequisites for the development of language. In C. A. Ferguson & D. I. Slobin (Eds.), *Studies in child language development* (pp. 175–208). New York: Holt, Rinehart, and Winston.

Slobin, D. I. (1979). *Psycholinguistics* (2nd ed.). Glenview, IL: Scott Foresman.

Takahara, P. O. (1978). Pragmatic functions of the given/new contract in child discourse. *Language Sciences, 1,* 244–272.

CHAPTER

16

THE RELIABILITY OF
SECOND-LANGUAGE
GRAMMATICALITY JUDGMENTS

Susan M. Gass
Michigan State University

A considerable amount of past and current second-language acquisition research is motivated by theoretical principles drawn from the field of linguistics. Along with this theoretical background have come methodologies typically used in linguistics. Chief among these methodologies for collecting linguistic data from primary languages involves what has come to be known as grammaticality judgments. As Birdsong (1989) pointed out, there is a theoretical distinction to be made between grammaticality judgments and acceptability judgments, despite the fact that the terms are often used interchangeably. The former, in strict linguistic terms, involve those sentences that are generated by the grammar, whereas the latter involve those sentences about which speakers have a feel of well-formedness. As a theoretical construct, the former are not directly accessible but are inferred through the latter. Throughout this chapter I will use the term grammaticality judgment, being cognizant of the theoretical distinction but also acknowledging the fact that grammaticality judgment is the term commonly in use.[1]

It is now commonplace for scholars to think about language not only in terms of language use in everyday communicative situations, but also "as an object of analysis and observation in its own right" (Cazden, 1976, p. 603). Grammaticality judgments are one (but certainly not the only) form of metalinguistic performance, or language objectification. One way of objectifying

---

[1]See Cowan and Hatasa (this volume, chapter 15) for further elaboration on this issue as well as that of sentence complexity.

language is to state whether a given sentence is acceptable or not. Responses to questions of acceptability are used to determine grammatical properties of language. That is, they are used to determine which sentences are possible and which are not in the grammar of a particular language.

Second-language researchers examining linguistic characteristics of learner-grammars have often used grammaticality judgments as data. However, the use of grammaticality judgments in second-language research has not been without difficulty or without controversy, as Birdsong (1989) and others have pointed out. As is evidenced by other chapters in this section, issues relating to reliability and validity are still debated.

More than two decades ago, Selinker (1972) argued that researchers should "focus . . . analytical attention upon *the only observable data to which we can relate theoretical predictions*: the utterances which are produced when the learner attempts to say sentences of a TL" (pp. 213–214). The exclusive focus on production data and the uncertainty regarding what is involved in providing judgments have led to a mistrust of this research instrument among some researchers (cf. Ellis, 1991) in the field of second-language acquisition. But, as Chaudron pointed out in his (1983) literature review, grammaticality judgments are complex behavioral activities that must be used with caution and with full understanding of their limitations. Nonetheless, despite such controversy, grammaticality judgments have been and continue to be used in second-language research. Interestingly, however, we often find that researchers who do use such data include a paragraph or a section in which they provide justification for their use.

Unlike most of the other chapters in this section (with the exception of Cowan & Hatasa's chapter 15, which is fundamentally concerned with issues of validity), the present chapter deals with reliability. Goss, Zhang, and Lantolf (chapter 14) claim that the more important question is the question of validity. Although I would acknowledge that validity is a crucial question, I would argue that it is not more or less important than reliability. If grammaticality judgments do not measure what they are purported to measure (validity), their use should be called into question. If one cannot access consistent judgments (reliability), this would also be reason to call their use into question. Given the centrality of grammaticality judgments to second-language acquisition research, both validity and reliability must be investigated.[2]

---

[2]J. P. Lantolf (personal communication, February 2, 1993) argued that there is a continuing problem in that one cannot always tease apart issues of comprehension and grammar. He pointed out that with regard to the present study, sentences on the lower end of the accessibility hierarchy are more difficult to understand than those on the higher end, asking, "How do we know people are making judgments of their grammatical status and not their comprehensibility?" It is for this reason that he and his co-authors argued that issues of validity must be settled before issues of reliability. Although I agree with his assessment regarding the difficulty of determining just what is being assessed, I still maintain that neither issue is more or less important

The main question this chapter addresses is: How reliable are grammaticality judgments as measures of a learner's grammatical knowledge? With regard to the task itself, there is clearly a difference between primary-language judgment data and second-language judgment data. In the former, one is asking native speakers to judge sentences of their own language system in order to gain information about that same system. That is to say, the two systems are isomorphic. In the case of second-language judgments, one is asking learners to make judgments about the language being learned at a stage in which their knowledge of that system is incomplete. Here, however, inferences are being made not about the system they are being asked about, but about some internalized system. In other words, there may be a mismatch between the two systems in question.

INDETERMINACY

The question of indeterminacy, which refers to the learner's incomplete knowledge or absence of knowledge of parts of the second-language grammar, is of central importance in any discussion of research methodology in second-language acquisition (see Sorace, 1988). Adjemian (1976) claimed that indeterminacy is a fundamental property of learner-languages: *The* salient characteristic of ILs is that they are linguistic systems which by nature are somehow incomplete and in a state of flux" (p. 308).

As Schachter, Tyson, and Diffley (1976) pointed out, there are many sentences about which second-language learners have indeterminate knowledge. This is not to say that native speakers of a language, either individually or collectively, do not have indeterminate knowledge, for surely they do. In fact, linguists recognize this on the printed page by placing question marks or question marks plus asterisks before certain sentences. For L2 learners, it is clear that indeterminacy exists, and it is conceivable that it embraces an even greater range of data than for native speakers of a language. Because there is a wide range of data that are potentially indeterminate, it is particularly important that we have a principled basis for determining what is truly representative of a learner's knowledge and what is not. How can we know which data are good data and which represent spurious exemplars of grammatical structures? This distinction is reminiscent of Corder's (1967) distinction between errors and mistakes. Clearly, we want grammatical descriptions to be based on actual knowledge rather than on guesswork or extraneous factors.

---

than the other. One could make a similar argument that we should not continue to discuss the issue of grammaticality judgments if we find that they are not reliable. Research investigating both of these issues in tandem is essential.

Tapping determinate knowledge is less problematic when using production data because, barring some sort of slip, the language produced is presumably generated by the learner's grammar. However, it is well accepted that unconstrained production data (free speech data) are inadequate for specific grammatical studies because the examples of a given grammatical structure are often lacking. As Corder (1973) aptly noted: "Elicitation procedures are used to find out something specific about the learner's language. . . . To do this, constraints must be placed on the learner so that he is forced to make choices within a severely restricted area of his phonological, lexical or syntactic competence" (p. 41).

But with grammaticality judgments what we are asking learners to do is evaluate sentences of a language that they do not have total control over; many of the sentences being asked about are beyond the domain of their current knowledge. Thus, responses to these represent little more than guesses. What we want to know is which sentences actually represent those sentences that are part of a learner's grammatical knowledge and which ones do not. Through the use of grammaticality judgments, we can establish whether learners' grammatical knowledge includes information about the impossibility of particular forms. This, of course, is of utmost importance when working within a theoretical framework such as Universal Grammar or within a typological universal framework, because in both instances one would want to know whether learners are able to violate universal principles. Thus, grammaticality judgment data provide a means to determine not only the possible utterances but also the impossible ones (see also Lakshmanan & Teranishi, this volume, chapter 10, for a discussion of this issue).

THE RELATIONSHIP TO COMPETENCE

As Birdsong (1989) noted, there is a danger of attributing to metalinguistic performance a "straightforward deterministic relationship to linguistic competence" (p. 60). There are numerous misconceptions in the literature of what grammaticality judgments represent. They are not a direct reflection of competence, for competence is an abstraction. There is no question that they provide performance data, but these performance data (because they provide information on allowable and disallowable sentences) do give us insight into competence.

White (1991), in her discussion of the misconceptions that abound regarding the nature of competence, provided quotations from the literature in illustration. I repeat them here because they reveal how misinterpretations have occurred and continue to occur.

> I am unable to accept that the preferred data of many UG-oriented researchers, grammaticality judgments, afford some kind of direct window on compe-

tence. A grammaticality judgment is just as much a performance as any other kind of language use. (Ellis, 1990, p. 388)

Researchers working in the UG paradigm assume that such results are a direct reflection of the learner's underlying competence and therefore evidence in support of UG. (Carroll & Meisel, 1990, p. 205)

Researchers in the UG/SL framework still face a fundamental question of what 'counts' as appropriate data. . . . Cook champions the use of grammaticality judgments as evidence for competence. (Birdsong, 1990, p. 337)

As White indicated, those working with grammaticality judgments as a research tool have not claimed a direct line to abstract representations. She cited the following as evidence:

In practice, we tend to operate on the assumption, or pretense, that these informant judgments give us 'direct evidence' as to the structure of the I-language, but, of course, this is only a tentative and inexact working hypothesis. . . . In general, informant judgments do not reflect the structure of the language directly. (Chomsky, 1986, p. 36)

A grammaticality judgment is no more central to UG than is any other experimental technique. It is tarred with the same brush of performance. (Carroll, Bever, & Pollack, 1981, cited in Cook, 1990, p. 592)

Linguistic competence is, of course, an abstraction. . . . There is no direct way to tap competence, but various aspects of linguistic performance can give insights into competence. Some aspects of performance are more revealing than others. (White, 1989, pp. 57–58)

More recently, G. Martohardjono (personal communication, January 15, 1993) stated, "Although based on competence, grammaticality judgments are not uniquely comprised of competence."

Thus, in any discussion of grammaticality judgments (or other elicitation techniques, for that matter), it is essential to keep in mind what they do and do not reflect. Grammaticality judgments do not give us direct access to learners' competence; they do, however, provide us with information about what are possible and impossible sentences in the learner-language.

ISSUES OF RELIABILITY

If we return to Corder's distinction between errors and mistakes, where the former refers to repeated use of a form and the latter to something more akin to a slip of the tongue, something easily correctable, and if we agree that we want our linguistic generalizations to be based on other than spurious data, we need a basis for eliminating just those data that are not representative of a learner's linguistic knowledge. One such means is through measures of reliability. Sentences about which there is no clear judgment are not sentences that should be included in our descriptions of second-language grammars.

With regard to reliability, questions abound and research presents conflicting results. I describe three representative studies that suggest the unreliability of grammaticality judgments.

Birdsong (1984) reported on a judgment task in a study of learners of French as an L2 in which 4 sentences were repeated within a task of 60 sentences. He found that for each of his 12 subjects, there was at least one pair of identical sentences for which judgments differed between the first and second appearance of the sentence.

Ellis (1990) presented the most recent attack on the reliability of grammaticality judgments. He attempted to discredit the reliability of a set of data in second-language acquisition research, pointing out that there had never been a test–retest reliability study carried out on the same group of learners. He studied the consistency in judgments of Japanese and Chinese speakers on English dative alternation, to rectify this shortcoming. He gave learners the same grammaticality judgment task twice, with a two-week interval between tests. On the basis of his results, he concluded that the variation in judgments from Time 1 to Time 2 suggested the lack of reliability of this instrument. However, a closer look at his instrument and the interpretation of results reveals problems. First, it is not clear how we can interpret his results, inasmuch as he did not cite a reliability coefficient despite the fact that the purpose of his study was an assessment of reliability. Second, there were slight differences in the methodology from Time 1 to Time 2. For example, in the Time 2 test for one of the groups, only a subset of the Time 1 sentences was presented.

Finally, to illustrate the uncontroversial nature of the controversy, consider a study by Christie and Lantolf (1991). They focused their research on aspects of UG, in particular on properties of the *Pro*-drop Parameter. Their subjects were English speakers learning Italian. There were two tasks, a grammaticality judgment task and an oral narrative task (depicting the events of a film). Fifteen months after the original data collection, the same grammaticality judgment task was administered to a subset of the original group. At this point, the subjects were more advanced in their Italian language studies (one of the subjects had spent time in Italy in the intervening period). In addition, oral protocols were administered at Time 2 to two of the subjects. We are not told whether or not it was the same elicitation measure as that used at Time 1. The results for the grammaticality judgment test for these two learners were quite similar from Time 1 to Time 2. Although no statistical comparisons were made, let's assume that in statistical terms there was no difference.

As far as the oral data are concerned, Christie and Lantolf focused on the use of grammatical subjects, in particular on whether there were full NP subjects, null subjects, or pronouns. Again, there were no statistical data presented, but it does appear that for one of the subjects there was a substantial difference from Time 1 to Time 2. That is, there was an increased use of null subjects (0 at Time 1 and 10 at Time 2) and a decrease in the use of full NPs (8 at Time 1 and 5 at Time 2). Thus, she appeared to move toward the standard target-language forms. To summarize, there was one subject with no difference on the grammaticality judgment task and a large difference on an oral task (possibly the same oral task). Christie and Lantolf's (1991) conclusion was the following:

> This finding is particularly interesting if one takes into account the results on the grammaticality judgment task, where neither of these two subjects made substantially different judgments from Time 1 to Time 2. It seems, then, that judgment data may not necessarily inform us of a learner's changing interlanguage grammar, since the results of the latter basically remained unchanged after 15 months, even though the oral narrative showed a major change for one subject but not the other. (p. 18)

However, we could just as easily discredit the oral data and say the following:

> This finding is particularly interesting if one takes into account the results on the oral data task, where one of these subjects made substantially different judgments from Time 1 to Time 2. It seems, then, that oral data may not necessarily inform us of a learner's stable interlanguage grammar, because the results of the latter changed after 15 months, even though the judgment data showed no change for either subject.

In other words, it is commonplace to discredit grammaticality judgment data unquestionably, and in this case with a paucity of evidence.[3]

I argue that all data elicitation measures must be examined to determine what they can and cannot inform us of. The present study attempts to pro-

---

[3]So as not to misrepresent Christie and Lantolf (1991), it is necessary to point out that what they were attempting to do was determine what grammaticality judgments were based on—grammatical knowledge or memory (reflected in memorized grammar rules). In J. P. Lantolf's words (personal communication, February 2, 1993), "I am convinced, for instance, that I can judge *pro*-drop sentences in a language like Russian as grammatical, but my judgment would be based on metaknowledge derived from having read a Russian grammar book. This is clearly not the kind of knowledge that could be usefully and systematically deployed in generating utterances in Russian. . . . Until we know the source of the judgment we cannot know anything about a learner's IL grammar on the basis of GJs [grammaticality judgments]. If the GJs had been based on the L2 linguistic competence of our subjects, we would have expected some evidence of this to show up in other tasks, like the narrative task."

vide evidence regarding one aspect of one elicitation measure: the reliability of grammaticality judgment data.

HOW JUDGMENT DATA ARE GATHERED AND USED

Before reporting the results of the present study, I briefly review some recent work that reflects a variety of ways in which grammaticality judgments have been used.

In looking at the literature, we find that there are three main dimensions in which grammaticality judgments vary. First, researchers differ in whether or not they ask learners to correct those sentences that are judged ungrammatical (see, e.g., Munnich, Flynn, & Martohardjono, this volume, chapter 12, who did not have subjects correct). Second, differences occur in what is being asked: In some cases learners are asked for judgments on single sentences; in others they are asked for preference judgments (see Lakshmanan & Teranishi, this volume, chapter 10). In other words, given two sentences, which is preferred? Within grammaticality judgment tasks, another difference arises: Some sentences are contextualized; some are not. A third dimension has to do with the number of possible responses that one can give. In some cases, responses are dichotomous; a sentence can be either grammatical or ungrammatical. In others, there is a range of possibilities that include the degree of confidence a learner has in making responses. Additionally, researchers vary widely in the number of sentences subjects are asked to give judgments about, ranging from 30 or 40 to more than 200.

ANALYZING RESULTS

To illustrate the range of data we deal with in second-language acquisition research and the range in interpretation of results, it is useful to take a look at a few recent studies.

Bley-Vroman, Felix, and Ioup (1988), in their investigation of Subjaceny and the Empty Category Principle, asked subjects to judge 32 sentences in one of three ways: the sentence is a possible English sentence, the sentence is an impossible English sentence, Not Sure. When analyzing the results, however, what to do with the Not Sure responses became problematic. Their solution was to count the Not Sure responses as if they were incorrect responses (i.e., marked as possible for ungrammatical sentences and impossible for grammatical sentences), a solution that they felt was justifiable, in large part, because there were so few responses in the Not Sure category (3.6% for the nonnative speakers). This post hoc arrangement was not principled because it is unclear what would have happened had there been a much larger percentage of Not Sure responses.

A second study is that of Coppetiers (1987), in which he counted the responses to the Not Sure option as if they were correct responses.

A third study is that of Schachter and Yip (1990). In their study, Schachter and Yip looked at the relationship between processing constraints and grammaticality judgments. They included 54 sentences, to be judged on a 4-point scale as clearly grammatical, probably grammatical, probably ungrammatical, or clearly ungrammatical. In this study they did not allow for a Not Sure option. Their display of the data and their descriptive statistics maintained the separateness of these categories. The question remains: How do we interpret the middle two categories (the "probably" ones)? Does this type of judgment reflect a learner's linguistic knowledge?

In a fourth study, Gass and Ard (1984) were looking at the acquisition of the progressive. As in the Schachter and Yip study, they used a four-way distinction, ranging from definitely correct to definitely incorrect. Their statistics incorporated these four distinctions, as they were looking at patterns of responses across language groups. However, the same question is raised as was raised with regard to the Schachter and Yip study: What does one do with the "possibly" answers?

Finally, we turn to another variation on the use of grammaticality judgments, a study by Schachter (1990) on Subjacency. Four possible responses were allowed in this study, as in the Schachter and Yip study, but here the responses were collapsed so that judgments of clearly correct and possibly correct were counted as correct responses. As with other studies, questions arise: Do we use a confidence scale, without some justification for that scale in our analysis of the results?

THE STUDY

The present study takes a slightly different perspective on ways in which grammaticality judgments are used, considering reliability as a function of syntactic constraints.

Subjects

The data base comprises judgments on relative clauses by 23 Chinese, Korean, and Japanese ESL learners at the English Language Center of Michigan State University. The subjects were all attending ESL classes to satisfy the language requirement specified by university policy for students wishing to pursue studies in substantive disciplines.

Materials

Test sentences reflected relative clause positions on the accessibility hierarchy (based on Keenan & Comrie, 1977, and Comrie & Keenan, 1979), a hierarchy that makes predictions about the frequency and occurrence of relative clause types in languages of the world. The accessibility hierarchy is given in (1):[4]

(1) SU > DO > IO > OPREP > GEN > OCOMP

The accessibility hierarchy is to be interpreted in such a way that if a language has, for example, OPREP relatives, it also has all relative clause types higher on the hierarchy (to the left), in this case SU, DO, and IO. Languages differ as to the lowest relative clause type they allow, and there is no way of predicting a priori the lowest position for any given language. In attempting to understand the extent to which learner-languages obey primary-language constraints, researchers have attempted to consider the accessibility hierarchy in the context of second-language learning. In general, it appears that the same constraints that govern primary languages do indeed hold for second languages (Gass, 1979).

Because this study deals with differences between determinate and indeterminate knowledge and because the accessibility hierarchy appears to represent some reality in terms of knowledge strength, it is hypothesized that the effects of reliability will be reflected in hierarchical orderings. That is, it is predicted that reliability will be greatest on SU relatives and least on OCOMP relatives.

---

[4]Examples of the various relative clause positions are given in (i)

SU	= subject
DO	= direct object
IO	= indirect object
OPREP	= object of preposition
GEN	= genitive
OCOMP	= object of comparative

(i) a. SU   The woman who saw the burglar called the police.
   b. DO   The woman who the burglar saw called the police.
   c. IO   The woman to whom the burglar gave the money called the police.
   d. OPREP   The woman about whom the children told a story called the police.
   e. GEN   The woman whose daughter was a burglar called the police.
   f. OCOMP   The woman whom the burglar is richer than called the police.

Method

Subjects were given 30 sentences about which they were asked to make judgments: 6 distractor sentences and 4 sentences (2 grammatical and 2 ungrammatical) of each of the 6 relative clause types (see Appendix). Subjects were first asked to judge categorically whether the sentence was grammatical or not by indicating (C)orrect or (I)ncorrect on their answer sheet; they were then asked to assess the degree of confidence they had in their judgment. The response sheet included a scale from +3 to −3, given in (2):

(2) −3   −2   −1   0   +1   +2   +3
     definitely   unsure   definitely
     incorrect   correct

A value of −3 meant that subjects were 100% certain that the sentence was incorrect and +3 meant that they were 100% certain that the sentence was correct. Other values indicated different degrees of certainty, with zero signifying Not Sure.

Subjects were told that there was no time limit, but that they were not to go back and change responses to earlier items. Two sample sentences were provided.

There were two administrations of this test with a one-week interval between the two. For each student the order of sentences was randomized in both the first and second version. Thus, 46 versions of the test were generated. After the first administration students were not told that there would be a second administration. In the intervening week, moreover, there was no instruction on relative clauses. Of course, despite the fact that there was no specific instruction in the intervening period, there remains the possibility that the first administration affected the subjects' knowledge base.

After the second administration, 4 subjects were interviewed to see if they could provide us with information on why they made changes.

RESULTS AND DISCUSSION

In displaying the results, two aspects of the data are considered: reliability and hierarchical orderings. For ease of comparison with other second-language studies, the IO and OPREP positions are combined (see Gass, 1979).

In Table 16.1 are the results from a Pearson Product-Moment Correlation. There are two correlations presented, one for dichotomous judgments and one for the judgments on the 7-point rating scale. As can be seen, correlations were significant in both instances (.5979, $p < .01$, in the case of dichotomous judgments, and .6443, $p < .01$, in the case of judgments on a 7-point scale).

TABLE 16.1
All Sentences Combined (552 Sentences)

Dichotomous Judgments		Seven-Point Scale	
r	p	r	p
.5979	< .01	.6443	< .01

TABLE 16.2
Changes in Judgments from Time 1 to Time 2

Number of Points Changed in 7-Point Scale	Number of Instances
0	317
1	105
2	22
3	20
4	22
5	30
6	36

In Table 16.2 are given the changes made on the 7-point scale. We see that in the majority of the sentences there was no change from Time 1 to Time 2 (317) and also that when there were changes, they were minimal (see Table 16.3 for changes made on the dichotomous scale by subject). Figure 16.1 graphically displays the results presented in Table 16.2.

If we look at the grammatical structures as separate entities, an interesting pattern emerges. This is seen in Table 16.4 and graphed in Fig. 16.2. Degree of consistency is dependent on sentence type.

In Fig. 16.3 a comparison of the reliability measures with a production measure is presented. In the production measure (from Gass, 1979), subjects were asked to combine two sentences to form a relative clause. The similarity of the patterns is clear. In the case of accuracy on a production task and reliability from Time 1 to Time 2, the pattern of the results is the same, including the oddity of the GEN position.[5]

---

[5]In Gass (1979) it was speculated that the GEN was seen as a constituent in the embedded sentence. For example, in the sentence *The man whose son just came home, whose son* may have been seen as the subject of *came*. On this view, GENs in this study and in Gass (1979) were either subjects or objects within the embedded clause. This would then account for the higher degree of accuracy in Gass (1979) and the higher degree of reliability in this study. That this may indeed be the correct interpretation is corroborated by data from a paper by Fuller (1983) in which she manipulated GEN relative clauses so that they fit the various positions on the hierarchy and found decreasing accuracy as would be expected given the hierarchical orderings.

TABLE 16.3
Changes by Subject

Subject Number	Changes on Dichotomous Scale (n = 24)
1	5
2	5
3	1
4	5
5	5
6	6
7	4
8	1
9	5
10	7
11	4
12	6
13	8
14	2
15	3
16	1
17	3
18	1
19	11
20	1
21	10
22	3
23	10

Note. $\bar{x}$ = 4.65.

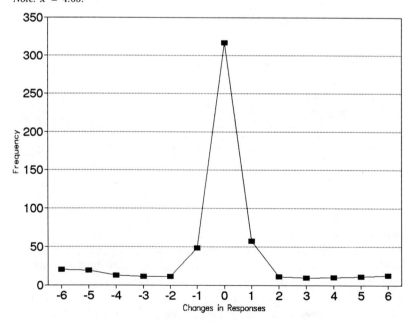

FIG. 16.1. Changes in responses Time 1 to Time 2.

TABLE 16.4
Reliability by Sentence Type (552 Sentences)

Sentence Type	Dichotomous Judgments		Seven-Point Scale	
	r	p <	r	p <
SU	.7620	.001	.8302	.001
DO	.5990	.01	.5861	.01
IO/OPREP	.6348	.01	.5832	.01
GEN	.6517	.01	.6806	.001
OCOMP	.4789	.05	.5442	.01

Note. SU = subject, DO = direct object, IO = indirect object, OPREP = object of preposition, GEN = genitive, OCOMP = object of comparative.

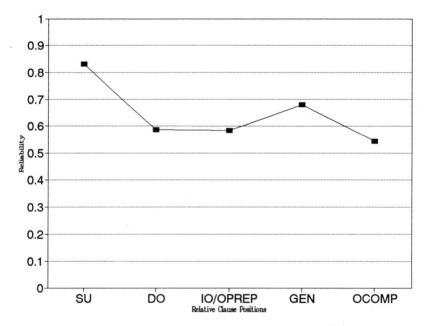

FIG. 16.2. Reliability as a function of relative clause positions.

It has been suggested (Ellis, 1990) that individual variation may be a major factor in inconsistent responses. Consistency may vary between subjects and, if so, this would mean that person-factors that contribute to inconsistency would have to be identified, and that sampling in future studies would have to take this into account. However, for the most part we see that there is not a wide range of variation from Time 1 to Time 2. This is seen in Table 16.3, in which the results are given for each subject on the dichotomous scale. Only three subjects (19, 21, and 23) seem to show considerable variability

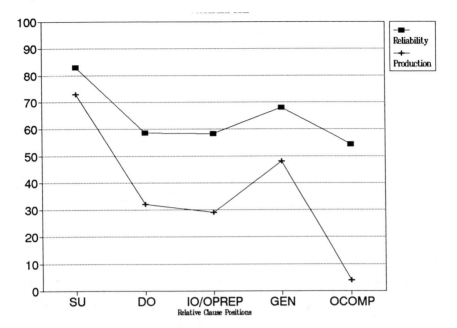

FIG. 16.3.   A comparison of reliability data and production data.

in their responses. If we further examine where those changes were made, we see that the greatest consistency is in those sentences that are high on the hierarchy and the least consistency is in those that are low (see Table 16.4). Thus, even when there is inconsistency, it is predictable on the basis of syntactic information.

What has been established thus far is that reliability is a function of syntactic factors. But what is of additional interest is the establishment of a means of extracting from the data those sentences that are determinate. It will be recalled that one of the major issues of this chapter is that of indeterminacy and the concern that some of the grammaticality judgments of learners represent little more than guesswork. What was of interest in this study was a methodology for eliminating just those sentences. Put differently, if we are to understand the nature of second-language acquisition, we must have some means of determining which sentences reflect a subject's knowledge base. To consider this question, those sentences on which there were major jumps from Time 1 to Time 2 were eliminated.

In Tables 16.5 and 16.6 and Fig. 16.4, we see what would happen if we eliminated from consideration just those sentences for which specific learners had demonstrated erratic responses. Specifically, all sentences in which there was a change of 6 points, that is, from +3 to −3 or vice versa (Table 16.5), or 5 and 6 points (Table 16.6), were eliminated. It was hypothesized

TABLE 16.5
Reliability by Sentence Type with the Extremes
of 6 Points Removed (516 Sentences)

Sentence Type	Dichotomous Judgments		Seven-Point Scale	
	r	p	r	p
SU	.8206	.001	.9025	.001
DO	.8034	.001	.8425	.001
IO/OPREP	.6348	.01	.7300	.001
GEN	.7385	.001	.7916	.001
OCOMP	.5933	.01	.7055	.001

Note. SU = subject, DO = direct object, IO = indirect object, OPREP = object of preposition, GEN = genitive, OCOMP = object of comparative.

TABLE 16.6
Reliability by Sentence Type with the Extremes of 5 and 6
Points Removed (486 Sentences)

Sentence Type	Dichotomous Judgments		Seven-Point Scale	
	r	p	r	p
SU	.8616	.001	.9374	.001
DO	.8154	.001	.9249	.001
IO/OPREP	.8676	.001	.8892	.001
GEN	.8244	.001	.8851	.001
OCOMP	.7306	.001	.8411	.001

Note. SU = subject, DO = direct object, IO = indirect object, OPREP = object of preposition, GEN = genitive, OCOMP = object of comparative.

that these indicated pure guesses and/or that factors other than linguistic knowledge were contributing to the results. There is justification for such a move. After the second administration, a small group of subjects was interviewed, in the hopes of obtaining information as to why they changed responses from Time 1 to Time 2. In most cases there was little if any change. That is, the results of Time 1 and Time 2 were identical. For one of the subjects, however, there were a large number of changes. He was unable to provide any reason for such changes until at one point he offered the following statement (R = Researcher; S = Subject):

(3) R: Do you know why you're not so sure here?
S: I think it's definitely correct.
R: O.K. Um.
S: I think that happens because I have three tests tomorrow and the next day so. . .
R: So you have a lot on your mind.

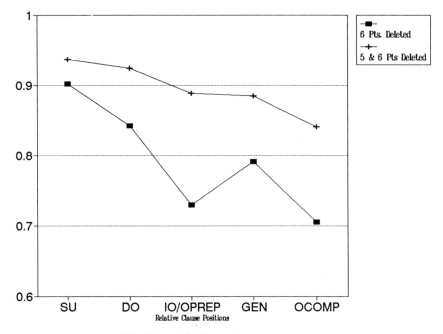

FIG. 16.4.   Reliability with extremes deleted.

S: Yea.
R: Yea.
S: So I'm so tired. . .
R: That it's hard to concentrate. . .
S: Yea.

In general, we see that without much loss in data, reliability coefficients are extremely high (Tables 16.5 and 16.6). This, of course, is not unlike what is done in scientific experiments when high and low scores are removed from the data pool. Thus, by removing what appear to be spurious data, most of the original data set remains, and we can feel more confident that these data represent a learner's linguistic knowledge.

CONCLUSION

It is clear from the results of this study that the issue of reliability cannot be separated from issues of indeterminacy. That is, from previous research it has become clear that the orderings of the Accessibility Hierarchy are reflected in acquisition orders and in acquisition difficulties. Interpreting these findings in terms of indeterminacy, the positions lowest on the hierarchy are those that are indeterminate. They are also the ones where, given our definitions of indeterminacy, we would expect less reliability.

The reliability coefficients, in general, indicate that although there is some variation from Time 1 to Time 2, the overall picture is one of consistency. The use of a 7-point scale permits sifting of the data to examine further the differences in judgments on two occasions by the same subjects.

The data do not provide evidence for the view that judgment data are unreliable. Nor do they provide support for the view that individuals behave in an inconsistent manner. On the other hand, there is evidence to suggest that low reliability occurs in just those areas where greater indeterminacy is predicted. Goss, Zhang, and Lantolf (this volume, chapter 14) claim that "we need to be certain that these judgments are predicated on linguistic principles rather than on some other factors." By comparing judgment data with data based more directly on linguistic principles, it has been shown that judgment data can, when used properly and appropriately, be useful in second-language acquisition research. In sum, we find that grammaticality judgments are indeed reflective of patterns of second-language use.

ACKNOWLEDGMENTS

Portions of this research were originally carried out with Alan Beretta. I am grateful to him for his contributions to the project. Thanks also to Gary Cook for his assistance on the statistical portion of this study and to Elaine Tarone for comments on an earlier draft. I alone am responsible for any errors that remain.

APPENDIX

I saw the man who crossed the street.
She watched the teacher who was giving the lecture.
He forgot the guest who he is in the kitchen.
He saw the boy who he is in the corner of the room.
He met the man whom you recommended.
She likes the same girl whom I like.
I saw the girl that the boy hit her.
She surprised the teacher whom the boy thanked her.
We washed the baby to whom you had given a doll.
He married the woman to whom you wrote the letter.
I heard the girl that the man gave a flower to her.
I saw the girl that the boy gave a book to her.
We respect the man with whom you danced with him.

John admires the woman for whom you wrote the letter.
Sam remembers the man about whom they told the story about him.
He kissed the woman with whom you were talking with her.
I saw the child whose sister ran away.
She kissed the child whose finger hurt.
He remembers the man who his brother is a doctor.
He likes the girl who her uncle is a baseball player.
He greeted the man whom I am smaller than.
That's the woman whom I am taller than.
He thanked the student whom he is smarter than her.
He laughed at the boy whom he is taller than him.

REFERENCES

Adjemian, C. (1976). On the nature of interlanguage systems. *Language Learning, 26*, 297–320.

Birdsong, D. (1984). *Variables in variation*. Paper presented to the Foreign Language Education Center Student Association, University of Texas, Austin.

Birdsong, D. (1989). *Metalinguistic performance and interlinguistic competence*. New York: Springer.

Birdsong, D. (1990). Universal grammar and second language acquisition theory: A review of a research framework and two exemplary books. *Studies in Second Language Acquisition, 12*, 331–340.

Bley-Vroman, R., Felix, S., & Ioup, G. (1988). The accessibility of universal grammar in adult language learning. *Second Language Research, 4*(1), 1–32.

Carroll, J., Bever, T., Pollack, C. (1981). The non-uniqueness of linguistic intuitions. *Language, 57*, 368–383.

Carroll, S., & Meisel, J. (1990). Universals and second language acquisition: Some comments on the state of current theory. *Studies in Second Language Acquisition, 12*(2), 201–208.

Cazden, C. (1976). Play with language and metalinguistic awareness: One dimension of language experience. In J. S. Bruner, A. Jolly, & K. Silva (Eds.), *Play—Its role in development and evolution* (pp. 603–618). New York: Basic Books.

Chaudron, C. (1983). Research in metalinguistic judgments: A review of theory, methods and results. *Language Learning, 33*, 343–377.

Chomsky, N. (1986). *Knowledge of language: Its nature, origin and use*. New York: Praeger.

Christie, K., & Lantolf, J. (1991). *The ontological status of learner grammaticality judgments in UG approaches to L2 acquisition*. Paper presented at Second Language Research Forum, Los Angeles.

Comrie, B., & Keenan, E. (1979). Noun phrase accessibility revisited. *Language, 55*, 649–664.

Cook, V. (1990). Timed comprehension of binding in advanced L2 learners of English. *Language Learning, 40*(4), 557–599.

Coppieters, R. (1987). Competence differences between native and non-native speakers. *Language, 63*(3), 544–573.

Corder, S. P. (1967). The significance of learner's errors. *International Review of Applied Linguistics, 5*, 161–170.

Corder, S. P. (1973). The elicitation of interlanguage. In J. Svartvik (Ed.), *Errata* (pp. 36–47). Stockholm: Rotobeckman.

Ellis, R. (1990). Grammaticality judgments and learner variability. In H. Burmeister & P. Rounds (Eds.), *Variability in second language acquisition: Proceedings of the Tenth Meeting of the Second Language Research Forum* (pp. 25–60). Eugene, OR: University of Oregon, Department of Linguistics.

Ellis, R. (1991). Grammaticality judgments and second language acquisition. *Studies in Second Language Acquisition, 13,* 161–186.

Fuller, J. (1983). *Relative clause comprehension and the noun phrase accessibility.* Paper presented at the TESOL Convention, Toronto.

Gass, S. (1979). Language transfer and universal grammatical relations. *Language Learning, 29*(2), 327–344.

Gass, S., & Ard, J. (1984). L2 acquisition and the ontology of language universals. In W. Rutherford (Ed.), *Second language acquisition and language universals* (pp. 33–68). Amsterdam: John Benjamins.

Keenan, E., & Comrie, B. (1977). Noun phrase accessibility and Universal Grammar. *Linguistic Inquiry, 8,* 63–99.

Martohardjono, G. (1993, January). *Commentary on the session on 'Movement'.* Paper presented at the Workshop on Recent Advances in Second Language Acquisition, MIT, Cambridge, MA.

Schachter, J. (1990). On the issue of completeness in second language acquisition. *Second Language Research, 6,* 93–124.

Schachter, J., & Yip, V. (1990). Why does anyone object to subject extraction? *Studies in Second Language Acquisition, 12*(4), 379–392.

Schachter, J., Tyson, A., & Diffley, F. (1976). Learner intuitions of grammaticality. *Language Learning, 26*(1), 67–76.

Selinker, L. (1972). Interlanguage. *IRAL, 10,* 209–231.

Sorace, A. (1988). Linguistic intuitions in interlanguage development: The problems of indeterminacy. In J. Pankhurst, M. Sharwood Smith, & P. Van Buren (Eds.), *Learnability and second languages: A book of readings* (pp. 167–190). Dordrecht: Foris.

White, L. (1989). *Universal grammar and second language acquisition.* Amsterdam: John Benjamins.

White, L. (1991). *Knowledge of interlanguage.* Paper presented at American Association for Applied Linguistics, New York.

17

A SUMMARY:
RESEARCH APPROACHES IN STUDYING
SECOND-LANGUAGE ACQUISITION OR
"IF THE SHOE FITS . . ."

Elaine E. Tarone
University of Minnesota

In this summary chapter, I examine several topics: (a) the existence of a range of research approaches to second-language acquisition (SLA), and the advantages of this situation to one in which a single research perspective dominates; (b) the role of Universal Grammar (UG) in second-language acquisition and the increasing debate over appropriate research methodology for exploring that role; (c) the study of interlanguage in context.

A RANGE OF RESEARCH APPROACHES TO SLA

Research approaches in SLA may be arranged in terms of one or more oppositions. One of these might be characterized as the opposition between two scientific traditions: a *nomothetic* tradition, which seeks to explain and predict how natural phenomena work, and a *hermeneutic* tradition, whose goal is to understand and interpret the way natural phenomena are organized (see Markee, this volume, chapter 5, for a discussion of these two traditions). It is useful to think of these two traditions not as polar opposites but rather as extreme end points of a continuum along which we might range the various research perspectives presented in this book.

A nomothetic approach generally seems to assert that there is a single, discoverable reality that obeys causal Laws of Nature and that can be best explained by means of a causal-process approach (Larsen-Freeman & Long, 1991). On the extreme end of the continuum, then, we have a nomothetic approach that relies upon an experimental, quantitative methodology to show causal relationships. In this view, qualitative research methodologies would serve only as exploratory, preliminary, or pilot studies, which can identify interesting questions but cannot provide evidence of causal relationships. This approach is one of several described by Larsen-Freeman and Long. Chapters in this book that seem to fall easily under a nomothetic, quantitative approach include Cowan and Hatasa, chapter 15, and Bley-Vroman and Chaudron, chapter 13.

At the opposite end of the continuum, we have a hermeneutic approach that assumes not one single Reality but multiple realities; a central assumption is that we can interpret human events only in terms of their contexts and their uses—that is, not in an idealized form. A second-language (L2) utterance may be perceived one way by the native speaker (NS) interlocutor, another way by the L2 learner, and yet another way by the researcher—and all perceptions are important, in this approach. The purpose of the research is what gives primacy to one or the other perception. There is thus a kind of pragmatic value assumed in this tradition, an assumption that the value of a phenomenon derives from its usefulness for some purpose rather than from some kind of approximation to abstract and ideal Truth. Chapters in this book that operate within a hermeneutic tradition include Markee, chapter 5, Douglas and Selinker, chapter 6, and Cohen and Olshtain, chapter 8. An extreme version of a hermeneutic approach uses a naturalistic, qualitative methodology.

There are of course many possible hermeneutic approaches to research, and not just the *ethnomethodological respecification* proposed by Markee. Ethnomethodology is an approach that discounts the use of ethnographic data, or data that specifically seek out the learner's point of view; thus, self-report data, interviews, and the like are clearly less preferable than direct observation of learner behavior. In ethnography, the investigator uses *triangulation* to check his or her interpretations against those of the participants by means of self-report procedures. It is clear that researchers such as Douglas and Selinker (chapter 6), Cohen and Olshtain (chapter 8), and others would certainly value research methodologies that seek out the learners' point of view, as yet another road to our goal of achieving a better understanding of the phenomenon of SLA. Hymes (1974) argues most persuasively for the need to add to one's observation of communicative conduct "the participants' own explanations and conceptualizations of their behavior" because "mere observation, however systematic and repeated, can obviously never suffice to meet . . . high standards of objectivity and validity" (p. 11). We simply need to recognize with this research methodology, as with all the others, the limitations of the research methodology itself—and the limitations of verbal-report methodologies are clearly laid out for us in Cohen and Olshtain's chapter in this volume.

There are other research perspectives in this book that fall not at the extreme ends of this continuum but somewhere in the middle. Here we have, for example, the range of studies examining the claims that Universal Grammar applies to SLA. Such studies tend to occur on the nomothetic end of the continuum, in that they clearly assume a single idealized Reality and value a causal-process model. However, they typically describe the behavior of a group of learners on a task, without using a control group, and so cannot be described as employing experimental research designs. In addition, UG studies may not put much emphasis on considerations normally considered important in quantitative methodology, such as having a large pool of randomly selected subjects (though some may). There are an increasing number of SLA studies that combine qualitative and quantitative methodologies in the service of both nomothetic and hermeneutic approaches and so might be said to fall in the middle of the nomothetic/hermeneutic continuum. As one example, Goss, Zhang, and Lantolf (chapter 14) use grammaticality judgment tasks in a quantitative, quasi-experimental design as well as verbal reports to address their research question.

What I suggest in this concluding chapter is that in *the field of SLA* there would appear to be multiple realities and multiple research methodologies for the study of SLA, *each of which is valid for certain uses and not for others.* The choice of one over the other is not guided by some abstract notion of Truth, but rather (as suggested in the Introduction to this volume) by the purpose of our research. In short, if we look at the combined behavior of all the SLA researchers represented in this book, we would have to say that there is no single best way to do SLA research, no single best road to the goal of explaining Truth, but rather many roads to the end goal of understanding the complex human event that we refer to as second-language acquisition. In this view, no research approach is inherently superior to any other in and of itself.

Crucially, however, although the various research approaches in this book are equally valid for their own purpose, they are typically *not interchangeable.* It should be clear that each research methodology and method of analysis has definite advantages and disadvantages; some are better for a given purpose than others. It is not a question of "letting a thousand flowers bloom"—we cannot randomly pick a methodology here and a methodology there and create a bouquet of research results that makes any sense.

In fact, much energy is devoted by the writers in this book to addressing and establishing what each research methodology is good for and what it is not good for. Consider, for example, Bley-Vroman and Chaudron (chapter 13), who argue that elicited imitation as a research methodology for exploring the role of Universal Grammar in SLA has strong floor and ceiling effects and a narrow band of extreme sensitivity to all kinds of interacting factors. The authors conclude that elicited imitation should be used not as the sole source of data on a learner's interlanguage competence but rather used together with a variety of other tasks in studying a given structure in order to gain a better understanding of the status of that structure in a learner's interlanguage at any given point in time.

Or, again, consider Cowan and Hatasa (chapter 15), who delineate some clear limitations on the validity of off-line learner judgments in providing an accurate picture of the learner's interlanguage. On-line tasks, it is argued, when used within clear limitations (e.g., with subject pools of a certain minimal size) provide a more accurate picture of the learner's implicit knowledge than off-line tasks, which tend to tap more explicit knowledge sources. Does this mean that we should never use off-line judgments? That on-line is good methodology and off-line is bad? No; rather, each provides a different kind of information about the learner's interlanguage. Gass (chapter 16), for example, lays out the way in which off-line grammaticality judgments become more unreliable for the more marked items on a hierarchy, the argument being that off-line tasks are not unpredictably unreliable but predictably (and informatively) so. Such guidelines are important in providing future researchers with information about the limitations inherent in the use of grammaticality judgment data.

What is absolutely crucial in this exchange of opinions about the strengths and weaknesses and the inevitable limitations of all of these research approaches is that we agree that all or most of the research approaches will, in the end, be useful to the field in helping us to understand *some* aspect of the phenomenon we are interested in: second-language acquisition. The goal of the debate is not to weed out the bad approaches and leave the single good one; the goal is to establish what each approach is good *for* (and, by default, what it is *not* good for).

Crucially, it is then the responsibility of the researcher who is using a particular research approach to restrict the claims that are made to the appropriate domain of that research approach. The researcher must not only *know* the strengths and weaknesses of the methodology being used but must also constrain the conclusions he or she draws at the end of the paper by framing those conclusions in light of those strengths and weaknesses. In general, the temptation is very great for a researcher to make grand claims regarding his or her findings, claims that far exceed what is permitted by their methodological underpinnings. Several of the chapters in this book make the point that researchers' claims should be constrained and limited by the sort of research methodology they are based on (see, e.g., Bley-Vroman & Chaudron, chapter 13; Markee, chapter 5).

It may be instructive to return to the Markee chapter for an example of this sort of constructive limitation imposed on one's claim by the sort of research methodology being used. Markee points out that some SLA researchers have proposed that negotiated comprehensible input is an important causal variable in SLA. These researchers, operating under a causal-process tradition, have operationalized the construct of negotiated input in arbitrary ways so that they could carry out experimental quantitative studies. However, this research tradition has been unable to provide empirical evidence as to "what successful input (i.e., input which results in demonstrable learning) actually looks like in context" (Markee, chapter 5, p. 97). This lack of evidence does not result from poor work on the part of the researchers, but follows naturally from the limitations of the research tradition within which these researchers have been operating.

A large-scale quantitative study at the nomothetic end of the continuum cannot, by its very nature, provide this sort of evidence. What is needed to show successful input resulting in learning is a study that can look at individuals in context over some period of time from several different points of view: in short, a qualitative naturalistic study conducted within a hermeneutic tradition. And, of course, as we have seen, Markee provides just such a bit of data, documenting the way in which a Chinese learner synthesizes information gleaned from several snatches of conversation during a course period to learn the meaning of the English term *coral*. Thus, in this example, an approach using conversational analysis can show what successful input looks like for a single learner in a very particular context. What it cannot show is that successful input always looks this way for all learners in all contexts. An approach that uses quantitative methodology to tabulate frequency of occurrence of categories like *confirmation check* or *clarification request* can show to what extent such categories can be identified in the speech of large numbers of learners in a variety of contexts. It cannot show what the mechanism is that might cause confirmation checks and clarification requests to have an impact in a particular context on second-language acquisition.

I began this section by pointing to one of several possible continua along which we might range research methodologies in second-language acquisition: the nomothetic/hermeneutic continuum. Another such continuum is that referred to in Yule and Tarone (in press), with regard to communication strategy research, as the Profligate/Conservative or external-focus/internal-focus continuum in SLA research methodologies. This continuum might be used to describe other types of SLA studies. At one end of this continuum are researchers (the "Pros") who tend to be *pro*fligate, or very open-ended, in the number of categories and constructs used in interpreting data, and who focus upon the external and contextualized interactive performance of L2 learners in order to infer something about their underlying abilities. At the other end are researchers (the "Cons") who tend to be *con*servative, or parsimonious, in setting up categories for use in data interpretation. Cons focus on the learner's internal cognitive processes in the abstract, outside of any particular context; the goal here is to characterize underlying learner competence in order to account for performance data. Some of the tensions between researchers who focus upon one or the other end of this continuum can be detected in the chapters of this book. For example, Eckman (chapter 1) describes the conflict between Gregg (a Con) and Tarone (a Pro) with regard to whether variation in learner performance should be considered in a theory of second-language acquisition. The essential difference between Gregg and Tarone is in their focus: Because Gregg focuses on internal mental processes and models an abstract (noncontextualized) competence, he discounts the importance of variation in learner performance. In fact, variation tends to wreak havoc with a parsimonious descriptive system. Tarone focuses upon external interactions and L2 learners' performance in a variety of social contexts and so finds variation to be closely related to change in learner performance over time. Variation is not a problem for a profligate, open-ended system of analysis.

Eckman (chapter 1) argues that this kind of difference in perspective can be resolved if variationists produce data that show how variation influences acquisition. However, the central difference between the opposite ends of the Pro/Con continuum seems to me to be one of focus and hence cannot be easily resolved by the discovery of data. Data can be interpreted in different ways depending on the focus of the interpreter.

For example, variationists might see in the example of the acquisition or learning of the word *coral* in Markee's chapter an important piece of data that shows the influence of variation on acquisition. The learner variably approximates the target language norm by gradually eliciting pieces of the definition of this term in a succession of interactions with several interlocutors. At any single point in the conversation, the learner has a tentative and variable notion of what coral is; she seeks and finds additional information about coral in her interactions, resolves her uncertainty about the meaning of the term, gradually adds more information about the term in additional interactions, and finally emerges with a pretty good definition of the term. Gregg might argue that what really matters in this case is the internal processing done by the learner in building up a definition of the term, and that the variable ways she uses the term in her interactions with others are irrelevant, or at best highly subsidiary, to those internal processes.

Thus, it would seem that a piece of data cannot cause researchers at opposite ends of this continuum to agree and share a focus. And why should they agree and take the same perspective? The process of second-language acquisition is surely both internal and external, a cognitive process and a socially mediated, highly contextualized phenomenon. It seems best, at this stage of the development of the field of SLA, to retain a tolerant attitude with regard to the selection of research approach and methodology and to continue to follow many roads in trying to understand the complex phenomenon of second-language acquisition (cf. Gass, 1988, for a similar position).

Here again, this position is taken with that important caveat: It is important not to confuse perspectives—it is important to keep in mind what an internal processing perspective is good for and what a social-interactive perspective is good for. One cannot make claims about internal processing if one applies only a social-interactive perspective, nor can one make claims about the importance (or unimportance) of social variables on acquisition if one applies only an internal-processing perspective.

PERSPECTIVES ON THE ROLE
OF UNIVERSAL GRAMMAR
IN SECOND-LANGUAGE ACQUISITION

The Theoretical Model Used

As we have seen, one research approach strongly emphasizes the importance of internal mental processes in second-language acquisition. The focus on the role of UG in second-language acquisition can be construed as a part of this approach. Basically, the central question here is the following: Do adult second languages abide by the same universal principles as native languages (cf. Bley-Vroman, 1989)? Adjémian (1976) asserted that interlanguages should be considered natural languages; because natural languages abide by principles of Universal Grammar, second languages should also abide by those principles. The principles of UG lay out the constraints on possible languages, and so the exploration of UG constraints is automatically also an exploration of at least some constraints on possible interlanguages.

Hagen (chapter 4) points out that almost without exception, research into the effects of Universal Grammar on the process of second-language acquisition has taken the Government-Binding (GB) framework for granted. In fact, there are other non-GB theories, in particular Generalized Phrase-Structure Grammar (GPSG) and Head-Driven Phrase-Structure Grammar (HPSG). A potential problem for research on Universal Grammar is that it has come to be almost exclusively dependent upon a GB framework, without systematically considering either GPSG or HPSG as possibly better theories for SLA. Berent (chapter 2), Lakshmanan and Teranishi (chapter 10), and Eckman (chapter 11) all assume a GB framework. Crucially, different theories make different claims about what sorts of constraints hold universally for natural languages. If it is found, as in Eckman (chapter 11), that interlanguages contain structures that violate the predictions of GB-formulated universals, it is crucial to ask whether those structures also violate the predictions of GPSG or HPSG before concluding that these ILs are in fact in violation of known universals.

Differing Standards for Interpretation
of Disconfirming Evidence

This point leads to a related problem: a problem of interpretation. When a UG study produces evidence that interlanguages do contain structures that violate the predictions of UG (whatever the syntactic theory on which these are based), how is that evidence to be explained? Researchers in this volume use differing and sometimes conflicting standards in interpreting such results. One obvious interpretation is illustrated by Hagen (chapter 4), who concludes that his results can be taken to support Bley-Vroman (1989) and Clahsen (1988): "UG principles available to L1 learners are not available to adults" (Clahsen, 1988, p. 69). The ensuing question would then become: Why do ILs differ from L1s in such an important way?

However, this is not the interpretation provided by other UG researchers in this volume. Eckman (chapter 11) suggests that possibly the unpredicted structures produced by the L2 learners in his study do occur in natural languages somewhere in the world—languages as yet undescribed by linguists. That is, the data base of natural languages upon which UG is based is incomplete; in this view, interlanguages can provide evidence of the possible structures of as-yet-undiscovered natural languages. This interpretation is considerably more liberal than Hagen's, and it seems hard to imagine how it could ever be disproved.

Another interpretation, one hinted at by Hagen and described below in more detail, is that the L2 data base is contaminated. In this view, it is argued that UG applies only to the output of a L2 learner's implicit knowledge source; however, in most UG studies, which rely on grammaticality judgment data, there is a strong possibility of contamination of the data by the learner's explicit knowledge base. Thus, SLA findings that show evidence of interlanguage structures that do not obey language universals cannot be taken to be accurate pictures of the L2 learners' implicit knowledge, or competence.

Under another interpretation (see Eckman, chapter 11, and others), a crucial characteristic of any adult L2-learner population is that there is a tremendous amount of intrasubject and intersubject variability. A great many sources of individual variation exist, among them native-language background, experience in the classroom, age of acquisition, socioeconomic background, motivation, and so on. Eckman (chapter 11) points out that UG studies have tended to report only aggregate, or group, data and have not examined the interlanguage grammars of individual learners. This approach is consistent with the idea of IL being among the set of natural languages, in the sense that the criteria for a natural language are never stated at the level of the individual user (G. Yule, personal communication, August 1993). However, Eckman here raises questions about this approach. Group IL data have often included data from those learners whose performance can be shown to be unsystematic with regard to the structure of interest. It is only the systematic grammars of individuals, Eckman claims, that ought to be studied, because only these can provide good evidence regarding language universals in interlanguage. Presumably, the failure of SLA studies in the past to shed light on this question has to do with their use of aggregate, or group, data as opposed to individual data.

Still another interpretation of IL data that violate UG predictions is advanced by Lakshmanan and Teranishi (chapter 10), who find that their learners apparently move from a larger (superset) grammar to a smaller (subset) grammar—a movement predicted to be impossible by the Subset Principle in the absence of explicit negative evidence. The possibility that the Subset Principle does not operate for these L2 learners is apparently not considered, and the possibility that explicit knowledge in the form of direct negative evidence in the input was available to the learners is considered briefly and discarded. Lakshmanan and Teranishi go on to suggest that L1 transfer in the form of interlingual identifications caused the learners to perceive English reflexives initially as simple forms, which will only later be reanalyzed in such a way that the Subset Principle could apply.

What are we to make of these disparate and apparently unprincipled attempts to account for research evidence that shows that L2 learners produce structures unpredicted by one or another theory of universal grammar? There seems to be a need for agreement among these researchers on a principle of interpretation that can be used in such situations (see Gass, 1993, for an argument similar to the one made here). When should disconfirming evidence in a UG study be taken to (a) invalidate the UG principle in question, (b) invalidate the syntactic theory within which the principle was framed, (c) invalidate the data base used in the SLA study, or (d) validate Clahsen's proposal: "UG principles available to L1 learners are not available to adults"?

Struggles With Research Methodology

Finally, UG-SLA researchers have been struggling with the issue of the data base upon which their studies are founded.

Hagen (chapter 4) outlines in clear and succinct terms the methodological problem entailed in investigating the role of Universal Grammar: The goal of this approach is to characterize the implicit L2 knowledge, or competence, of the learner. Gregg (1990) makes it clear that in doing this, it is crucial to exclude all learner data that derive from other sources, such as the explicit knowledge the learner has of the L2 grammar. The methodological problem, then, becomes the following: What sorts of elicitation tasks can include only information about the implicit L2 knowledge of the learner and exclude all other knowledge sources?

Several of the chapters in this volume address different sides of this thorny problem. For example, although grammaticality judgment tasks have been used a great deal as a source of information about L2-learner language, virtually all of the researchers in this volume express the strong concern that such data do not reliably tap the learner's implicit knowledge system. Gass (chapter 16) is perhaps the strongest proponent in this volume of grammaticality judgment data, arguing that such judgments become unreliable only when they involve areas of the grammar that are themselves indeterminate.

Goss et al. (chapter 14) use a joint problem-solving methodology that provides them with insight into the strategies L2 learners use to produce grammaticality judgments. The learners in their study do at times produce judgments on the basis of feel (or the implicit knowledge system), but they are as likely to produce judgments on the basis of explicit reference to classroom rules and memory (an explicit knowledge system). Because these learners produce the same judgments in pairs as they do individually, Goss et al. argue that the strategies described in the pair work are also used in individual work—and thus, the grammaticality judgment data are inevitably the product of explicit knowledge sources as well as implicit knowledge.

Hagen (chapter 4) attempts to gauge the differential effects of implicit and explicit knowledge bases by using a computer-driven format that permits a repeated-measures design and also permits him to measure response times; following Krashen's (1982) claims about the way in which acquisition and learning function, longer response times are taken to tap explicit knowledge bases, and shorter response times to rely on implicit knowledge bases. A difference in the accuracy of longer and shorter responses could be taken as evidence that (a) the UG principles unavailable to the implicit knowledge source are encoded in explicit knowledge, and (b) explicit knowledge is engaged in grammaticality judgment tasks when time permits. In Hagen's study, there is in fact no such difference in accuracy, so this study provides evidence for neither (a) nor (b).

Cowan and Hatasa's (chapter 15) strategy is related to Hagen's in that they use a technique specifically designed to prevent learners from resorting to explicit knowledge sources. Cowan and Hatasa argue that on-line judgments are preferred to off-line judgments by psychologists in sentence complexity/processing research precisely because the researcher wants to prevent subjects from reflecting on the task; with reflection, all kinds of off-line variations occur. In their chapter they compare the results of an off-line task with those of an on-line task and conclude that the on-line task provides a much better measure of actual sentence complexity. They conclude with a long and daunting list of variables that may contaminate grammaticality judgment tasks and prevent those tasks from accurately accessing the L2 learner's implicit knowledge base. These variables include choice of vocabulary, sentence length, and position of the target form in the sentence.

Interestingly, Munnich, Flynn, and Martohardjono (chapter 12) begin with the assumption that grammaticality judgment data are inherently unreliable sources of information about a learner's implicit knowledge; in their words, this is because a grammaticality judgment task measures L2 learners' "beliefs" or "prescriptive knowledge about their language" but cannot access the underlying competence that drives language production. They propose elicited imitation (EI) tasks as production tasks, which are preferable in this regard to judgment tasks in that EI tasks elicit spontaneous and unconscious processing. They describe a study that, in their view, shows that EI provides a more accurate picture of learners' implicit knowledge than does a grammaticality judgment task. Indeed, the technique of EI, with the rationale for its use proposed by Munnich et al., might be one of those notions identified by Shohamy (chapter 7) as potentially useful for language testers.

Bley-Vroman and Chaudron (chapter 13), however, point out numerous difficulties with elicited imitation tasks. In fact, their long list of variables that must be considered in constructing sentences used in EI tasks looks very similar to Cowan and Hatasa's list of variables to be considered in constructing sentences for judgment tasks (e.g., length of sentence and position in the sentence of the form being studied are important in both tasks). The crucial issue for Bley-Vroman and Chaudron seems to be that EI tasks provide accurate information for a given learner only when the sentences being imitated are not too short or long, when they are not too complex or simple, and when serial position of the target structure in the sentence does not confound the results (a factor that they claim is present in the Munnich et al. study in chapter 12). Even under the best of circumstances, they argue, EI results should be cross-validated by use of reaction time measures, free production data and grammaticality judgment tasks—though they do not specify how disparate results from these various tasks are to be interpreted.

In summary, it would seem that research on the role of UG in SLA is foundering at present on the twin issues of data elicitation and data interpretation. First, tasks are needed that can elicit information about the L2 learner's implicit knowledge of a structure without permitting influence from that learner's explicit knowledge; researchers need guidance in task design, possibly, as Shohamy (chapter 7) suggests, from work in language testing. The problems inherent in elicited imitation studies, for example, might be sorted out by testing experts through a careful piloting of all instruments and through checks for reliability and validity, as urged by Shohamy. Second, UG researchers need to agree on principles to be used in interpreting data that apparently do not conform with the predictions of UG.

THE STUDY OF SECOND-LANGUAGE ACQUISITION
IN CONTEXT

The researchers discussed in this section of the chapter tend to examine the effects of the external context on the language learner. In general, these researchers tend to take a more comprehensive view of L2-learner behavior. That is, they choose to study the behavior of L2 learners in social context, and the way in which both explicit and implicit knowledge sources may combine to result in systematic variation in learners' behavior in such contexts.

The study of language in context may draw from any point along the nomothetic/hermeneutic continuum. So, for example, Bardovi-Harlig (chapter 3) and Bayley (chapter 9) argue for the use of a highly quantitative design with very large learner samples, performing a multivariate analysis on interlanguage forms in teasing apart and assigning numerical weights to the influences of linguistic, social, and developmental factors. On the other hand, Douglas and Selinker (chapter 6) or Cohen and Olshtain (chapter 8) use ethnographic field techniques that lead to divergent interpretations of primary data. We have already seen that Markee (chapter 5) prefers an ethnolinguistic but not an ethnographic approach. Such researchers tend to use a variety of techniques and perspectives in a single study in which the L2 learner's performance in some larger context is the focus of study.

Bardovi-Harlig (chapter 3) attempts to evaluate two hypotheses on tense choice in discourse, asking whether verbal morphology in interlanguage is aspect-based or discourse-based at any proficiency level. In order to answer this question, she argues, multiple analyses must be performed on the same data base. Thus, Bayley's study (chapter 9), showing that past tense choice is conditioned by both the phonetic form of the past tense and grammatical aspect, is a model for Bardovi-Harlig. She argues that without such large-scale studies on complexly varied subject populations, executed with sophisticated tools for quantification, the field will be forced to rely only on anecdote. Indeed, Bayley argues convincingly for more consistent use of the VARBRUL statistical program in analyzing interlanguage data in studies carried out within this sort of nomothetic approach.

However, it seems clear that hermeneutic approaches are also needed in examining interlanguage in context. Clearly, Cohen and Olshtain (chapter 8), Douglas and Selinker (chapter 6), and Markee (chapter 5) provide excellent models for these sorts of studies. Indeed, some kinds of evidence can be obtained only by means of such studies. As we have already seen, Markee has argued that certain kinds of evidence crucial to the building of SLA theory can be provided only by means of research methods that examine individual learners in social context, gathering naturalistic data. Douglas and Selinker point to the possibility that their context-based approach could show, for example, that UG effects are context-bound; that is, for any given learner, an interlanguage can be shown to conform to UG in some social contexts but not in others.

SUMMARY

All of these concerns can be viewed as support for my original contention that the field of second-language acquisition needs a variety of research perspectives. It is hard to see how the field can progress without such a variety of approaches. The phenomenon of second-language acquisition is too complex to be studied in any other way.

A question frequently asked at the Michigan State University conference, which produced most of the chapters in this book, was: Is it time for a single, unifying theory of second-language acquisition? I believe that this book contains substantial evidence that this is the wrong question to ask, now or ever.

Research approaches in SLA are rather like footwear[1]: All serve basically the same purpose, but they vary according to the local needs of their users. In footwear, local needs might call for sandals or running shoes or ice skates. There is not a single shoe style and size into which all feet must fit. In SLA, local needs might call for approaches which are ethnographic or UG-based or variationist. Taking a single unifying approach to the study of second-language acquisition would seem to be analogous to binding our students' feet early in their development to ensure that they fit into the only shoe size available. (Or insisting that Hawaiians wear Minnesotan snowboots instead of thongs!)

Success in studying second-language acquisition depends on having as much information as possible about this complex piece of human behavior taking place in constantly changing local contexts. That information needs to be accurately collected from a variety of perspectives and interpreted consistently and honestly across studies, and a reasonable variety of possible courses of action must be open to SLA researchers—just as a reasonable variety of possible footwear must be available to humans in different local contexts.

REFERENCES

Adjémian, C. (1976). On the nature of interlanguage systems. *Language Learning, 26,* 297–320.
Bley-Vroman, R. (1989). What is the logical problem of foreign language learning? In S. Gass & J. Schachter (Eds.), *Linguistic perspectives on second language acquisition* (pp. 41–78). Cambridge: Cambridge University Press.

---

[1] I am grateful to George Yule (personal communication, August 1993) for the footwear analogy.

Clahsen, H. (1988). Parameterized grammatical theory and language acquisition: A study of the acquisition of verb placement and inflection by children and adults. In S. Flynn & W. O'Neill (Eds.), *Linguistic theory and second language acquisition* (pp. 47–75). Dordrecht: Kluwer Academic Publishers.

Gass, S. (1988). Integrating research areas: A framework for second-language studies. *Applied Linguistics, 9*, 198–217.

Gass, S. (1993). Second-language acquisition: Past, present and future. *Second Language Research, 9*, 99–117.

Gregg, K. (1990). The variable competence model of second language acquisition and why it isn't. *Applied Linguistics, 11*, 364–383.

Hymes, D. (1974). *Foundations in sociolinguistics: An ethnographic approach.* Philadelphia: University of Pennsylvania Press.

Krashen, S. (1982). *Principles and practice in second language acquisition.* Oxford: Pergamon Press.

Larsen-Freeman, D., & Long, M. (1991). *An introduction to second language acquisition research.* London: Longman.

Yule, G., & Tarone, E. (in press). Investigating communication strategies in L2 reference: Pros and cons. In G. Kasper & E. Kellerman (Eds.), *Advances in communication strategy research.* London: Longman.

AUTHOR INDEX

SUBJECT INDEX

definition, 92
discounts ethnographic data, 110n, 324
spoken definitions, 106, 107–108, 110–112
study, 99–112
evidence, convergent, 99
exemplification, 106
Exhaustive Constant Partial Ordering
property, 65–66
experimental approach, *see* nomothetic approach
explanation
in speech acts, 144
interpretive vs. predictive, 97, 98
expletives, 269, 272–273, 274
external-/internal-focus continuum, 327–328

F

factor-analytic studies, 72
factor value and weight, 166n
Faraday, Michael, 7–8
"feel" in grammaticality judgments,
271–272, 277, 278, 279, 280, 282,
301, 332
films, retelling of silent, 54
first language acquisition
Binding Theory studies, 30–31, 64
morpheme acquisition, 41n, 48, 138
relative clauses, 34–36
and saliency and aspect, 158
Subset Principle, 18–22, 189
UG and, 208
first language influence, *see* transfer
fixed effect fallacy, 258
focus, external-/internal-, 327–328
folk psychology, 265
Foot Feature Principle, 65n, 67
foreground and background
aspect and tense marking, 43, 46, 47,
48–49, 53, 54–56
task choice to elicit background
information, 51, 54
formal/informal language learning, 139
formality of utterance, 146
form–function model of SLA, 167
formulaic patterns, 119
formulas, semantic, 144
fossilization, 119, 129
free production, *see* spontaneous production
French
adjacency condition, 23–24

adverbs, 22–26, 66
aspect and tense, 43, 44, 45, 164
definite article, 63
pro/enclitic parameter, 69–70
r-binding, 68–74
telic verbs, 55n
vous/tu distinction, 146
frozen expressions, 299n
functional semantics, 42

G

ga (Japanese), 291, 292–296
garden path sentences, 296
GCP, *see* Governing Category Parameter
generalization
aspect/tense marking, 48–49
methodologies allowing, 62, 136
word order, 65
Generalized Phrase-Structure Grammar, 61,
64–65, 67, 83, 329
genres, intra-IL transfer between, 119, 124
German, 42, 45
given-new contract, 291
Governing Category Parameter, 18–22,
29–34, 208, 209
and Binding Principle A, 186–187
defined, 209–210
methodology to investigate, 185–206
/Proper Antecedent Parameter correlation, 210–211
previous studies, 190–194, 211–213
and pronouns, 18–22, 33–34
and reflexives, 29–34, 185–206, 207,
221–222
and Subset Principle, 29–34, 188–190,
194, 201–203
and transfer, 196–197, 199
violations, 218–223
government, structural, by verbs, 26, 27
Government and Binding Theory, 19,
29–30, 63–64, 65–66, 208–213
accessible subject and, 33
adjunct VPs, 68, 70, 75–80, 80–83, 84
and adverb placement, 23, 22–26, 63
alternatives to, 61, 64–66, 83, 329
Binding Principle A
and anaphors, 19, 64, 33–34, 64, 67,
186, 208–209
and Governing Category Parameter,
18–22, 186–187
and pronominals, 19, 64, 67, 208